Information Technology and Social Justice

Emma Rooksby
Charles Sturt University, Australia

John Weckert
Charles Sturt University, Australia

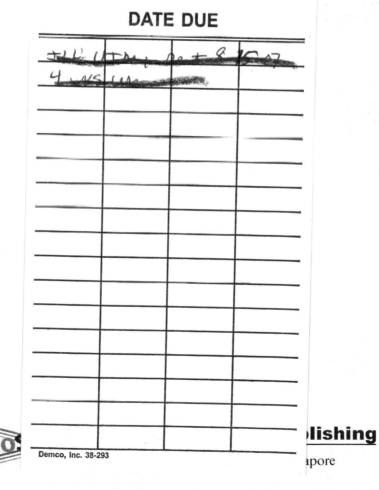

lishing

apore

71329783

12-18-06

Acquisitions Editor: Kristin Klinger
Development Editor: Kristin Roth
Senior Managing Editor: Jennifer Neidig
Managing Editor: Sara Reed
Assistant Managing Editor: Sharon Berger
Copy Editor: Dawne Brooks
Typesetter: Amanda Appicello
Cover Design: Lisa Tosheff
Printed at: Yurchak Printing Inc.

Published in the United States of America by
        Information Science Publishing (an imprint of Idea Group Inc.)
        701 E. Chocolate Avenue, Suite 200
        Hershey PA 17033-1240
        Tel: 717-533-8845
        Fax: 717-533-8661
        E-mail: cust@idea-group.com
        Web site: http://www.infosci-pub.com

and in the United Kingdom by
        Information Science Publishing (an imprint of Idea Group Inc.)
        3 Henrietta Street
        Covent Garden
        London WC2E 8LU
        Tel: 44 20 7240 0856
        Fax: 44 20 7379 0609
        Web site: http://www.eurospanonline.com

Library of Congress Cataloging-in-Publication Data

Information technology and social justice / Emma Rooksby and John Weckert, editors.
        p. cm.
    Summary: "This book presents conceptual frameworks for understanding and tackling digital divides. It in-
cludes information on access and skills, access and motivation, and other levels of access. It presents a detailed
analysis of the and value of access to information and communication technologies"--Provided by publisher.
    Includes bibliographical references and index.
    ISBN 1-59140-968-3 -- ISBN 1-59140-969-1 (softcover) -- ISBN 1-59140-970-5 (ebook)
    1. Information technology--Social aspects. 2. Social justice. I. Rooksby, Emma. II. Weckert, John.
    HM851.I5455 2007
    303.48'33--dc22
                        2006027710

British Cataloguing in Publication Data
A Cataloguing in Publication record for this book is available from the British Library.

Information Technology and Social Justice

Table of Contents

Section II: Interdisciplinary Perspectives

Section III: Regional and Country Perspectives

Preface

The sudden and immense rise of information and communication technologies (ICTs) to prominence in almost every aspect of life has prompted a great deal of thought and discussion about the moral significance of new ICTs. Books and articles, in what became known as computer ethics, have been written on topics ranging from computer fraud to the ethics of artificial life, and with every outlook from the optimistic to the apocalyptic (see Bynum, 1999, for a detailed discussion of the development of computer ethics).

This book treats what the editors believe may be one of the most serious moral problems associated with the new ICTS: the issue of justice in their distribution and in the distribution of the benefits of their use. This issue first rose to prominence in the nineteen nineties, and the phenomenon of brute inequalities in the distribution of ICTs—that some people have much greater access to ICTs than others—came then to be known as the "digital divide." The tag has stuck, despite significant conceptual developments in thinking about the relationship between inequalities in distribution of ICTs, and social justice more broadly, that make the term sound somewhat simplistic. Interestingly, in 1969 Joseph Weizenbaum, one of the founders of artificial intelligence, wrote of a potential "new cleavage in society" between those who could benefit from using computers and "that segment of the population that cannot use computing power for lack of training." It is worth noting that he did not talk of inequalities based simply on access to computers, but of inequalities based on *lack of training* to use the computers

In the last five years, with contributions from authors such as Norris (2001), Steyaert (2002) and van Dijk (2004), facts about the distribution of new ICTs are beginning to be analysed within a broader context of new and existing theories of equality and social justice. The term "digital divide" is still used regularly to characterize phenomena of injustice associated with inequalities in access to ICTs, but as the debate develops, contributors' understanding of this term is becoming more varied and nuanced. As things stand, many contributors to the debate about the digital divide share the awareness that the best way to articulate digital divide is to relate it to other aspects of social and distributive justice, using a mixture of pre-existing theories within moral and political philosophy, complemented with contributions from sociology, communication studies, information systems and a range of other disciplines.

Increasingly, as the debate continues and becomes more sophisticated, more and more aspects of the distribution of ICTs are singled out as relevant to characterizations of the digital divide, and of its moral status. These include:

1. Information relevant to various spheres of life (van den Hoven, 1995), such as:

   • health information, which may be more readily (and more affordably) available online than off-line;

   • information associated with opportunities for financial gain, including information about employment opportunities, information about economic trends, and investment information. This broad category has been addressed from many angles, including by government policy documents (such as the "Falling Through the Net" report produced by the U.S. Department for Commerce [1999]), which point to the strong potential for social exclusion resulting from a migration of these kinds of information to an online environment;

   • education of various kinds and at all levels; and

   • citizenship information (such as legislation and information about government services), which are increasingly delivered online by governments keen to cut the costs of printing and distribution.

2. The value of ICTs for participation in local and distributed communities, including:

   • political participation, such as contribution to political debates at all levels;

   • communication with friends, and establishing new relationships;

   • academic and knowledge-based conversations, such as are facilitated by online discussion groups dedicated to particular topics.

3. But there are also other aspects of digital divides that are rather less well explored. Two, highlighted in this volume, one by Bill Wresch's chapter on ICTs in Africa, is the value of being able to *provide* information; the other, in Kenneth Himma's chapter on intellectual property, is the value in restricting access for reasons of justice:

   • Sending/being able to distribute relevant knowledge to others. Closely related to participation, but not quite the same.

- In some cases, restricting access to intellectual property in order to protect the interests of its creators.

How Philosophy Might Help

It might seem at first glance that the most abstract of the social-scientific disciplines might be the one with the least to offer to a real-world debate about the use and distribution of information and communication technologies, a proposition entertained by Stahl in this volume. Even if we accept that philosophy *might* have something useful to say about how *best or most fairly* we should distribute information and communication technologies, we still face a further problem. This problem results from the open-endedness of philosophical debate itself: the internal wranglings among moral philosophers about how best to characterize ethics and justice suggest that there can be no easy way of applying ready-made philosophical concepts to the digital divide debate and coming up with neat and uncontroversial answers. Perhaps the best way to view this open-endedness is as a spiral. Philosophers continually return to old problems that have not been solved, but on each return they build on the previous arguments. Therefore, while the digital divide is still discussed, it is at a higher or deeper level, than it was previously.

The conceptual and analytical resources of philosophy are, the editors believe, useful for understanding and tackling digital divides in three primary ways. First, philosophy can provide conceptual clarification, that is, it can help us determine what exactly the subject we are concerned with is when we talk and write about the digital divide. Second, it can help to clarify what is at stake in debates about the digital divide; that is, it can help us determine what questions we need to ask about that subject. And third, it might even provide us with answers to those questions, or at least point us in the right direction for finding answers to those questions.

Conceptual Clarification

"Digital divide" is a notoriously muddy term. Hundreds of pages of discussion already, both for and against the moral significance of digital divide, have already appeared but so much of it not clearly argued or stated. For example, there is a tendency to *assume* that lack of computers is *the* problem, pure and simple (if there is a problem at all), and that everything will be all right once laptops are given to every primary school. Or the tendency to assume that everyone would benefit from access to new ICTs, whatever else they would like, which is patently untrue of the very poor (see al-Saggaf, this volume). Philosophical resources have the potential to contribute to conceptual analysis of the digital divide in a number of ways:

- Philosophy contains the analytical and conceptual tools to clarify the term, and to sort out the different ways in which technology and social justice are interrelated.
- There exists a substantial body of writing on social justice issues, relating to both national and international contexts, which can be adapted or extended to cover societies in which ICTs are used. Concepts such as equality, justice and fairness articulated and explained.
- Resources in epistemology are potentially very useful for understanding the nature and value of knowledge, a key aspect of digital divides.
- There is a substantial body of political theory relating to the nature of the state, democracy and other political forms, which can be (and have been) applied to the new electronic forms of political participation.

Hence, whatever other steps are taken to understand or to combat digital divides, philosophy is likely to be very important in the initial stages of clarifying the nature of the problem—is it a problem of justice or not? Is it a single problem or a range of related problems? And so on.

Question Clarification

Second, philosophy can help us to work out what sort of questions we should be asking about digital divides. The questions asked by policy-makers and the designers of computer hardware and software inevitably structure the answers that they give, and the policy responses that they provide. Hence, it is of vital importance that the right questions be asked. And philosophical theories of justice and equality can assist in this regard. Should we, for example, be concerned only with the distribution of ICTs in isolation, or also with the relationship between the distribution of ICTs and that of other social goods, such as education, money and well-being? Existing theories of justice, by illustrating how different aspects of social advantage and disadvantage are linked and interact, tell us that the distribution of ICTs is *not* an independent justice issue, to be tackled on its own. And should we be concerned at all? Perhaps this unequal distribution is just an inevitable part of life. Further, if it is a real concern, is it a matter of justice or rather one of pragmaticism related to the efficiency of the economy?

Answers

Only once these kinds of conceptual and analytical clarification have been performed can we be confident that policy development is taking place on a firm and at least relatively settled terrain, and is not mistaking the nature of the problem to which it is applied. The conceptual resources of philosophy are thus highly relevant to understanding the moral significance of digital divides, and potentially to articulating practical solutions to the moral problems associated with inequalities in access to new information and communication technologies. But it does not do to be too optimistic about the potential of a notoriously abstract discipline to gain traction on a practical problem, such as the digital divide. A number of challenges need to be met in bringing philosophical research and ideas to bear on discussions of digital divides, if the philosophical contribution is to be practicable and applicable:

- There is a need to integrate philosophical research with vast body of empirical research, much of it conducted with unarticulated presuppositions about the nature of digital divides.
- The inherently interdisciplinary nature of research in this area poses problems to the philosopher, as it does to any researcher. Contributions from a wide range of disciplinary perspectives, different conceptualizations of the problem/s, and the sheer volume of material all make for a daunting research task. Working on moral issues associated with the digital divide involves appreciating research from a wide range of fields including law, sociology, anthropology, psychology, cultural studies, and media studies, as well as philosophy.
- A related hurdle is the need to provide philosophical research that can be used easily and effectively by policy-makers. This is absolutely essential if philosophy is to be accepted as relevant and useful in tackling the digital divide, whether it is conceived of as a form of social inequality or injustice, or in some other terms.
- Finally, the diversity of philosophical research itself can also be considered a challenge to be addressed. As one author in this volume (Charles Ess) points out, different philosophical traditions in different countries mean different approaches to analyzing digital divides may be required, depending on the cultural-philosophical context. As another contributor, Bernd Stahl, points out, many of the deepest problems in moral and political philosophy remain, if not unsolved, at least deeply contested.

This book cannot hope to address all the above challenges at the depth and length that they deserve. But the contributions it contains do address all four of these issues. From the empirically informed work of al-Saggaf to the interdisciplinary reach of the chapter by Hacker, Mason, and Morgan and the efforts by Ess, Hongladarom, and Raghuramaraju to present some of the global diversity of philosophical research, the chapters in this volume develop philosophical positions and arguments in ways that relate to the broader social context in which digital divides unfold.

The editors believe that sophisticated conceptual frameworks are of vital importance for understanding and for tackling digital divides. Distinctions mapped to date include those between access and skills, access and motivation, various levels of access, and ever-more detailed analysis of what the benefits of access might be, and how these might be differentially valuable to different people. But there is much more work to be done. We offer this book as a contribution to the debate on what such frameworks should look like.

Organization of the Book

The book contains 13 chapters, organized into three separate sections. A brief description of the organization of the sections and chapters follows.

The organization of the chapters follows a trajectory from more general to more specific topics, beginning with chapters concerned primarily with philosophical and conceptual issues, and moving from there to more interdisciplinary, but still theoretical, approaches to the digital divide, approaches that utilize empirical research from a variety of disciplines beyond philosophy. The third and final section of the book contains chapters that focus on particular instances of digital divides, namely divides existing within particular countries, or the impact of the global digital divide on particular countries.

Section I: Philosophy and the Digital Divide

The first section of the book addresses specific conceptual and philosophical issues associated with the notion of the digital divide. This section contains the most abstract and conceptual contributions to the volume, grouped together to provide the reader with a sense of the conceptual and philosophical issues most closely associated with the digital divide today. While some chapters seek to further clarify the nature of the digital divide as it is popularly understood, or to articulate in more detail some aspects of the divide, others take a more critical approach.

In Chapter I, Sirkku Kristiina Hellsten develops an approach to the digital divide based on Amartya Sen's capability theory. Hellsten's argument is that capability theory can be more or less straightforwardly extended to include the capabilities associated with new information and communications technologies, and she takes some steps to extend the theory in this direction. Hellsten pays particular attention to the issue of knowledge, and its relationship to information. She observes that information is not valuable in itself, but rather as a means to knowledge and to wisdom, and argues that approaches to the digital divide that treat access to information as an end rather than a means are liable to make distributive errors.

In Chapter II, Don Fallis takes up the challenge of providing an answer to one of the questions that Hellsten deems so important to any adequate response to current levels of global social inequality in the context of the digital divide: what is a just distribution of knowledge? Like Hellsten, Fallis takes knowledge to be the key good, inequality of which is indicated by terms such as "digital divide," and in relation to which further theoretical work needs to be done. His chapter addresses the question of how to determine a just distribution of knowledge (whatever means are used to distribute the knowledge). As Fallis writes, "The *digital divide* refers to inequalities in access to information technology. Those people who do not have access to information technology are at a significant economic and social disadvantage. As with any other policy decision, in order to evaluate policies for dealing with the digital divide, we need to know exactly what our goal should be. Since the principal value of access to information technology is that it leads to *knowledge*, work in epistemology can help us to clarify our goal in the context of the digital divide." Fallis then goes on to argue that *epistemic value theory* can help to determine which distribution of knowledge to aim for, and he maps out how the determination might be made.

In Chapter III, Kenneth Einar Himma continues the theme of the just distribution of knowledge, but from the perspective of intellectual property protection. Intellectual property is not so commonly seen as a factor in the just distribution of goods but Drahos (2002) for one demonstrates that it does play an important role. Himma's argument is that creators of intellectual property deserve protection for their creations because they introduce things of value into the world and this involves both their time and effort. Creators then have an interest in their intellectual creations that ought to be protected. Others also have interests in these creations and on occasion these override the interests of the creators. In many cases however, the creators' interests ought to be protected and he presents general guidelines to show which cases there are. This protection limits distribution of the intellectual goods but not, Himma argues, in a manner that violates any principle of just distribution. There is no "intellectual commons" that is diminished by this protection.

Chapter IV, by Charles Ess, takes up a range of theoretical and practical issues associated with the discipline of information ethics, or computer ethics, as it has been called by some in the past. The issues that Ess includes under the rubric of "information ethics" are broad. They include the familiar issues of social justice associated with the distribution of ICTs, and the distributive impact of ICTs on societies more broadly. But they also include a range of interesting issues that are not often accorded a place in standard monographs and textbooks on information ethics, associated with the ethical status of the global spread of new ICTs, and of standardized (read: Western) discourses of information ethics. Ess addresses the question of "how may we develop information ethics and computer ethics that

a. address *both* local *and* global issues evoked by ICTs/CMC, etc.;

b. in ways that *both* sustain local traditions/values/preferences, and so on; *and*

c. provide (quasi-) universal responses to central ethical problems?"

Ess's chapter illustrates, by its example, how the conceptual and analytical tools of philosophy, coupled with careful empirical research, can help to shed new light on moral status of the digital divide.

Chapter V by Soraj Hongladarom provides grist to Ess's mill, indicating how the discourse of computer ethics is taken up in particular cultural contexts, namely in Thailand. Like the later chapter by Raghuramaraju (Section III), Hongladarom uses the existence of cultural differences and particularities to criticize the claim that there will be any wholly universal answers to moral questions associated with digital divides. He illustrates how the discourse of computer ethics had developed in Thailand, adapted to cultural norms and expectations associated with knowledge and technology. He starts from the observation that more is required, to bridge digital divides, than the mere provision of computers and Internet access. Of course, as he observes, this statements is in some ways a platitude, since many theorists of the digital divide agree that training, computer-literacy and other skills are required to make good use of computers and Internet access.

But in another sense, Hongladarom argues, this statement is anything but platitudinous. This is because the very characterization of the digital divide, like the ideals associated with the many possibilities that new ICTs open up is many, various, and deeply dependent on the cultures in which those ideals are articulated and pursued. That is, the "more" that is required is not in any sense determined, either by the nature of the technology or by any other single factor. ICTs are, in Hongladarom's terms, "second-order tools" that can be used for an indeterminate number of purposes. In this, they are unlike "first-order tools", such as toasters that can be used only for one or two specific purposes. The example of Thai culture is used to illustrate Hongladarom's position.

Section II: Interdisciplinary Perspectives

Chapter VI, by Kenneth L. Hacker, Shana M. Mason, and Eric L. Morgan provides a trenchant introduction to this section, taking a strongly critical line on the impact of structural inequalities in access to and usage of CMC/ICT on digital democracy. Drawing on both political theory and cultural studies research, the authors argue that the inequalities in access to and usage of CMC/ICT differentially affect the level of power that different individuals (and networks of individuals) can assert within the political process. As they write, "The inequities in power may become more severe as those who are able to obtain the most advantages from digital communication are those who can conduct politics both online and offline." Their chapter points to a vicious cycle between digital exclusion and other forms of social exclusion in current socio-political settings, while also setting out the case for the democratising potential of information and communication technologies.

In Chapter VII, Bernd Carsten Stahl takes a critical look at the potential of philosophical research to contribute to resolution of digital divides, either within countries or across countries. Stahl argues from the key premise that, despite centuries of debate, philosophy as a discipline has failed to reach agreed-upon answers to a range of key questions, including questions about justice and the nature of the just society. How, then, he asks, can philosophy hope to solve the problems of justice associated with new information and communication technologies? What is needed, Stahl argues, is political action rather than more theory. Despite his critical stance about the capacity of philosophy to resolve justice questions associated with new information and communication technologies, Stahl concludes by suggesting that philosophy may still have a useful role in relation to digital divides. That is, "philosophical and conceptual analysis are useful bases upon which to build political action."

The next two chapters, VIII and IX by Sheila French and Darryl Macer respectively, form a bridge between Sections II and II. Sheila French approaches the digital divide in the context of computer science in the UK using discourse analysis. Despite government initiatives to encourage greater female participation in ICT nothing has changed significantly and female participation is still substantially lower than that that of males. The basic reason, she argues, is that the initiatives assume that women "if the conditions are right, will want to be involved in the field of technology." This assumption is wrong, she contends, and demonstrates this through analyses of various discourses. This lack of female participation is not so much a result of lack of computing resources or opportunities to use them, but more a matter of perceptions of our identities and of our experiences with ICT. Her studies suggest that young males identify with the technology in a way that young females do not. The females see the technology as providing useful tools but not as part of their identities. The issue of gender segregation in ICT is just as much about "gendered attitudes and identities in relation to technology" as it is about equality. Darryl Macer, in Chapter IX, discusses the results of a number of surveys conducted in Japan and in Thailand, in the early 1990s and again about a decade later. He compares the attitudes to and perceptions of various new technologies in both countries and also looks at how these attitudes and perceptions changed over the period between the surveys. This kind of empirical he argues informs the ethical discussions of global social justice.

Section III: Regional and Country Perspectives

In Chapter X, William Wresch tackles similar issues to those addressed by Hellsten, but in his case from a more applied perspective, specifically that of the African experience of the global digital divide. As an emblem of the global digital divide, Wresch writes of the "million missing websites" in Africa: that is, the Web sites that would exist were Africa not already so disadvantaged relative to the rest of the world that its citizens have few resources to put into ICTs. One of Wresch's key points is distinctive, and makes rather different use of Sen's theory of capabilities than does Hellsten. He argues that Africa's lack of ICTs results, not only in Africans being unable to *receive* information of various kinds; importantly, it also means that many Africans are unable to *transmit* information of various kinds—for example, info relevant to other Africans (trade, culture, and so on) and relevant to people from non-African countries.

A. Raghuramaraju, in Chapter XI, looks at how the discipline of computer ethics has evolved in India. Like Hongladarom (Chapter V), Raghuramaraju relates Indian computer ethics to the Western philosophical tradition. But Raghuramaraju's approach is to critique the "standard" Western philosophical approach to computer ethics, and to argue for an alternative approach to computer ethics, more suitable for the Indian socio-cultural context. He holds that computer ethics can learn from the Indian philosophical tradition, as well as from the Western tradition that has proven so fruitful to date.

Chapter XII is another case study, this time set in Australia. Emma Rooksby, John Weckert, and Richard Lucas consider a digital divide that has captured public and media imagination in Australia, namely the divide between rural Australians and their urban counterparts. The authors argue that the rural digital divide in Australia is indeed of moral concern, and discuss a range of current funding initiatives that have been designed to overcome it.

Yeslam Al-Saggaf, in Chapter XIII, presents an unusual approach to the digital divide, looking at forms of informational exclusion that are not typically discussed in the literature on the digital divide. Al-Saggaf's empirical research base, online discussion groups in Saudi Arabia provide him with a window into the use of ICTs in a non-Western non-liberal country, and the kinds of informational exclusion he discovers are related to the nature of the Saudi polity. He finds that political censorship, threatened or actual persecution, and strict gender roles rather than social and economic inequalities, are key drivers of who has access to, and (perhaps more importantly) who can make use of ICTs to further their interests.

References

Bynum, T. W. (1999). The development of computer ethics as a philosophical field of study. *Australian Journal of Professional and Applied Ethics, 1*(1), 1-29.

Drahos, P., & Braithwaite, J. (2002). *Intellectual feudalism: Who owns the knowledge economy?* London: Earthscan.

Norris, P. (2001). *Digital divide: Civic engagement, information poverty, and the Internet worldwide.* Cambridge, NY: Cambridge University Press.

Steyaert, J. (2002). Much ado about unicorns and digital divides. Retrieved January 21, 2005, from http://www.steyaert.org/Jan/

van den Hoven, M. J. (1995). Equal access and social justice: Information as a primary good. *ETHICOMP95: An international conference on the ethical issues of using information technology* (pp. 1-17). Leicester: De Montfort University.

van Dijk, J. (2004). *The deepening divide: Inequality in the information society.* Thousand Oaks; London; New Delhi: Sage.

Weizenbaum, J. (1969). The two cultures of the computer age. *Technology Review, 71,* 54-57.

U.S. Department of Commerce. (1999). *Falling through the Net: Defining the digital divide.* Retrieved January 4, 2005, from http://www.ntia.doc.gov/ntia-home/fttn99/

Acknowledgments

The editors would like to acknowledge the help of all those involved in the collation and review process of this book, without whose support the project could not have been satisfactorily completed.

Many of the authors of chapters included in this volume also served as referees for articles written by other authors. Thanks go to all those who participated in this refereeing process, particularly to those who refereed more than one article and to those who provided comprehensive comments and constructive criticisms. Special thanks go to the publishing team at Idea Group Inc., particularly to Kristin Roth and Jan Travers, who offered a great deal of advice and assistance in pursuing the project and to meeting important deadlines in the publishing schedule, and to Mehdi Khosrow-Pour, who sent us the initial invitation to take on this project. Thanks to to Rachel Salmond, for her meticulous and intelligent copyediting of the entire volume.

Thanks are also due to the Centre for Applied Philosophy and Public Ethics (Charles Sturt University) for providing the Research Fellowship and Professorial Fellowship positions during which we edited this volume. The facilities, resources, and time made available by the Centre in 2004 and 2005 helped to make this book a reality.

In closing, we would like to thank all of the authors for their contributions to this book. This is really their book, rather than ours, and the majority of the credit for the success of the project should go to them.

Emma Rooksby
John Weckert

Section I:

Philosophy and the Digital Divide

Chapter I

From Information Society to Global Village of Wisdom?
The Role of ICT in Realizing Social Justice in the Developing World

Sirkku Kristiina Hellsten
University of Birmingham, UK, University of Helsinki, Finland, &
University of Dar es Salaam, Tanzania

Abstract

This chapter is about the role of ICT in global justice. It will analyze, firstly, the epistemological relationship between new information, knowledge and wisdom. Secondly, it examines the ethical relationship between information technology and the values and ideals that are attached to its use and applications. Thirdly, the chapter studies theoretical and practical obstacles that have prevented the developing countries, particularly in Africa, from fully benefiting from the enormous possibilities provided by the new ICT in relation to realizing human capabilities, well-being and better standards of living and social justice. The analysis applies Amartya Sen and Martha Nussbaum's capability approach to the distribution and use of the ICT in global context. Finally the chapter examines how global and the local inequality is maintained by the international information and technology markets, and how the distorted international markets as well as misguided local policies tend to create further division between "information rich" and "information poor."

Introduction

Globalization is the catchword of the day, and the worldwide requirement for more direct democracy, good governance and respect for human rights is at the core of the new millennium's development strategies. In order to fulfill these goals in global social, economic and political cooperation and development, access to information, knowledge and channels of reciprocal communication are of critical importance. Globalization of economy has been made possible and further expands through the business applications of the Internet and other information and communication technologies. The latest information and communication technology (ICT), which can be used for fast creation, acquisition, storage, dissemination, retrieval, manipulation and transmission of information, could greatly help the marginalized, less affluent countries to benefit from the positive side of globalization and to help them promote local and global democracy and participate more efficiently in the global economy. ICT could provide us powerful means for sharing our global prosperity. However, presently the trends of economic globalization have not led to either to more equal local and global access either to ICT or to the information it transfers. Instead, the Information Age has led to what has come to be called the digital divide between the affluent and the poor, the connected and disconnected, the developed and less developed (Sarrocco, 2002; Warschauer, 2003; Young, 2003).[1]

Despite the fact that new telecommunication technology undeniably has advanced rapidly and more and more people around the globe have today direct access to it and to the information it conveys, there are still vast regions in the world which have either no access or very limited access to these new means of communication and information exchange. The limited access is due to various structural, distributive, economic and political problems that have prevented the equal spread of modern technology, as well as its efficient implementation across the world. Some of these obstacles can be overcome through better and fairly planned distributive and implementation policies. Many of these places without access to the latest ICT may, in fact, have very restricted means for even local, let alone global, connections through more traditional information channels such as mail, newspapers and books, telephone, television, and radio. On the other hand, in many parts of the third world even those affluent and materially well developed countries, which now have access to the ICT, have not succeeded in using new technology internally and internationally to consistently promote national benefit, human well-being and the common good. Instead the technology available and the information it provides are still mostly shared by elites, the already influential, affluent and educated sections of the population. The poor and illiterate, and those in acute need, tend to remain beyond the information reach; local, and particularly rural, development and quality of life gain very little from the new technology.

This chapter focuses on two interrelated issues: firstly, it analyzes the relationship between new information technology and the values and ideals that are attached to its use and application. In this context, this chapter will study the relationship between information, knowledge and power in relation to the ideals of the "knowledge society" and what could be called the "global village of wisdom." It argues that in global ICT policies there is a need to pay more attention to the realization of human resources and well-being in the development, use and distribution of ICT. In the existing politico-philosophical frameworks, this would mean a shift from the neo-liberal market economy towards the promotion and realization of human capabilities as presented by the capability approach to human well-being constructed by Amartya Sen (1985, 1993, 2001) and Martha Nussbaum (1987, 1992, 1993).

Secondly, the chapter takes a look at the theoretical and practical obstacles that have prevented the developing countries, particularly in Africa, from fully benefiting from the enormous possibilities provided by the new ICT in relation to human capabilities and better standards of living. It will examine how the local and global digital divide between the information-rich and information-poor is created and maintained by international information and technology markets, as well as by political ambitions. Finally the chapter considers the role of culture and tradition in adoption, allocation and use of new technology.

Information vs. Knowledge Society: Ideals and Practice

The developments in new information and communication technology are in general taken to suggest not only efficiency, convenience and productivity but also utopian possibilities—new fortunes to be made, new careers and new lifestyles and, above all, progress that entails revolutionary democracy and increasing equality. This means that, particularly in the West, new information technology is usually seen to provide us with a fast, vast and environmentally friendly "information superhighway" that gives everybody across the world direct access to the sources of influence and the centers of power. In the most optimistic dreams, the possibilities brought to us by technological advancement are believed to mean the actualization of "a global village" which eventually leads us to a new age of wisdom which promotes democratic participation and social justice.

While this utopian ideal of information age may be shared by many ICT enthusiasts, there is no one agreed model of the information society that serves as the standard for sustainable and desirable development. Instead, the significance of the Information Age is that it is a global, diverse and multicultural reality. Thus, in order to realize the utopian visions and ideals, there is an urgent need to clarify further how the values we are striving for can be related to practice in various economic, political and cultural circumstances, as well as in globalization of ICT markets themselves. If we are to use the new information technology in order to strive for what we could consider as the ideal of the "knowledge society," we need to reflect on the values involved in the developmental realities in various global and local contexts.

Before that we need to clarify the values involved in the information utopias by making a clear distinction between what we have come to call "information society" and what we could call a "knowledge society," which, in an international context, could be also extended into a "global village of wisdom," based on the maximum use of not only physical, but also—and maybe particularly—intellectual and moral human capabilities.

Theoretically, I base this ideal of a "global village of wisdom" on the theoretical framework of the capability approach introduced by Amartya Sen (1990, 1992, 1999) and Martha Nussbaum (1987, 1992, 1993). The capability approach defends the moral appropriateness of the concept of well-being measured in terms of valuable human functioning and capability. More generally, it concentrates on our freedom to promote objectives we have reason to value, such as democracy, human rights and equality. According to Sen and Nussbaum, human capabilities that define human well-being, and should be the goal of development and distribution, are first—such basic capabilities as life and health. Second are capabilities relating to integrity, thought, emotions, practical reason, affiliation/participation, control over one's fate/environment. There are extensive studies on the capability approach in development. This chapter, however, does not try to analyze or criticize Sen's or Nussbaum's arguments in detail, but rather to search for ways of applying the capability approach as a criterion for a fair distribution of ICT in the global context. The reason for this choice of approach is that my main aim is to look for alternative approaches to global distribution and implementation of ICT. While problems in using a capability approach are important to take into account, the space available in this chapter does not allow me to go into these in detail, but leaves them to the critical reader's further assessment.

Using a capability approach as a normative ethical framework for distribution and implementation of ICT means that we need to reconsider the role of ICT in relation to what people can do with the new technology or what the technology can do for them in different cultural, political and economic settings, and geographic or environmental conditions, rather than assume that technological development has some intrinsic value, as the most eager proponents of information society appear to assume. Thus, if the distribution and implementation of global ICT policies would set the realization of human capabilities and the formulation of human capital at the core of ICT strategies, the presently digitally marginalized populations need not only to get access to necessary technology but also to gain the means to process the information available into knowledge that empowers them to participate actively and democratically in local, national and international development. Today, however, both the technology, and the data, information, intelligence, ideas, facts and figures it transfers, are often considered as commodities that are to be bought, sold and traded in expanding markets, rather than as basic goods in the Rawlsian sense (Castells & Himanen, 2002, pp. 2-3; Stovel, 1984).

Commercialization of information and knowledge is based on neo-liberal or libertarian market rationality that focuses on economic and technological development. It tends to pay less attention to the wider and more even realization of human capital and human capabilities in local and global contexts.[2] ICT and information trade is then, in many senses, the final result of the Information Age transition from an industrial economy to information economy, in which information itself is seen as raw material. The latest ICT, for its part, can provide not only the means of production, but also its own markets. Technological means, know-how and access to information will then shape the characterization of nations by digital divide as either (information-) rich or (information-) poor, and their categorization accordingly as developed or underdeveloped. This division, however, in most cases tends to be based on the physical access to ICT rather than on political, social and economic benefits of such technology (Jimba, 1999, pp. 79-83; Warschauer, 2003; Young, 2003).

If we want instead strive for the ideal of a "knowledge society" or "global village of wisdom," we need to see both technology and information as essential instruments in realizing the various human resources that they themselves can be used to develop each nation culturally, and in a locally sustainable manner. Information and communication technology could play a central role in realizing this ideal, but only if more attention is paid to the development of human capabilities and social, political and economic inclusion that can be realized with the help of the new technologies. At the moment the focus, however, tends to be on the advancement of technology itself and the markets of technology, rather than on the use of technology to improve the worldwide, reciprocal access to all markets.

IT: Means for Development or an End of Development

The millennium development goals emphasize good governance, human rights, democracy and social justice. In order for these goals to be convincing, they are to be striven for in both the local and the global context. While the gap between developed and developing countries has been gradually narrowing, the least developed countries (LDCs), still often marginalized in (local) technological development, are failing to catch up with ICT and, thus, are bypassed by its benefits. ICT, for its part, is directly related to both national and international development, because ICT brings the means to communicate beyond the interpersonal level and makes geographical distances between continents and states disappear. Since ICT today goes far beyond mass media communication and offers possibilities for change, knowledge and new perspectives on development, it permits rapid dissemination of ideas, values and processes, supplements education, science, health care, culture and, above all, economic interaction and markets. It provides the potential for two-way exchanges of information to learn what people really need, and to manage resources and data to facilitate the production and distribution of prosperity and wealth. Thus, while it is evident that ICT clearly cannot be used to solve all the problems of developing countries, it represents a potential that can be used to actualize human resources and human well-being in the form of capabilities within less affluent countries (Annan, 2003; Stover, 1984, p. 3).

If information age policies emphasized the realization of human capabilities, there would be a need to make a clear distinction between the concepts of information, knowledge and wisdom in our strategic plans and policies. The capability approach attempts to give human well-being a content that goes beyond rights and rational choice. Instead it focuses on the basic human condition by defining well-being in terms of valuable human "functionings" and capabilities that make our (ability to make) any choices possible (Nussbaum, 1992, pp. 202-246; Crocker, 1992, pp. 589-590; Sen, 1992, 2001).[3] This approach moves from mere technical protection of rights to the promotion of "human flourishing" by defending the moral appropriateness of the holistic concept of human well-being measured in terms of human capabilities. Thus, our rights, as well as our responsibilities, should be set in a context that increases our capabilities and promotes various human functionings—in a teleological sense, as the human beings that we (essentially) are. Thus, human capabilities provide fundamental moral categories for the evaluation of resource distribution that goes beyond protection of rights or satisfaction of needs and sets human beings in a wider social context. The capability approach then concentrates on our freedom to promote objectives we have reason to value, such as participation/democracy, human rights and the value of equality. According to Sen and Nussbaum human functionings and capabilities define human well-being and, thus, can be seen as the goal of distribution of social and material resources—in the end these resources include our moral and legal rights. By human functionings, they mean a person's physical and mental states or "beings" and activities or "doings."

There are many extensive studies on the capability approach in development, as well as critical analysis of some of its problems. In this chapter my purpose, however, is not to reintroduce or criticize Sen's or Nussbaum's arguments in detail or to point out theoretical differences and dispute between the two. Instead, I am searching for ways of applying the capability approach as a basis for a model for an ethical justification, where fewer of the needed resources and commodities can sometimes be better than their abundance, depending on their proper use for realizing human capabilities. In their search for a foundation for an ethic, Nussbaum and Sen both reject an "externalist" account that would depend on a metaphysical or scientific realism that purports to give, as Crocker has stated, a "God's eye view" of the way things, including humans, are in themselves. Sen and Nussbaum suggest that what we need instead is an "internalist" foundationalism. This, in part, means that we start digging from within human experience and discourse to find the things that we do and should count as intrinsically worthwhile in our human lives. We must ask what are the things that are so important that, without them, we would not count a life as a human life. This allows us to move from objective value statements on the value of human life to the value of human functionings and capabilities.

Thus, despite various criticisms presented against the capability approach, the value statements regarding human capabilities can still be considered fairly objective and universal in a sense that they are valid for all human beings, since basically all rational humans consider their capabilities and well-being valuable—no matter how they might otherwise react to cultural differences and/or difference in resources and to the various rights-based distributive frameworks for resources. In relation to the ICT, it then requires us to consider not only the distribution of resources but also the overall capabilities that can be realized with these resources.[4]

Democracy, Wisdom, and Information

In political philosophy, modern pluralistic democracy, particularly when described as a reciprocal social contract between morally autonomous, rational and reasonable individuals who rule themselves in their own interests and by their own considerations, values and decisions. This description leaves the individual participants in a context based on self-interest and promotion of one's own benefits. However, working democracy should be based on decision-making and self-government of enlightened citizens. This enlightenment is possible only if the decision-makers have a chance to realize all their human potential, that is, all their human capabilities.

This definition is not often an accurate picture of political reality, but it does give us the abstract ideal of modern democracy that we are hoping to realize in practice in our societies (Weinberger, 1995, p. 218). The formula of democracy can then be stated as follows: a functioning democracy presupposes a form of political liberty that realizes human capabilities in a manner that guarantees the participation of enlightened citizen in public matters. An enlightened citizen is not the same as a knowledgeable or well-learned citizen. A moral agent with full human capabilities differs from a mere self-interested and rational decision-maker who attempts to maximize his or her personal benefits (Clark, 2000, p. 84; Weinberger, 1995, pp. 218-222). Political liberty postulates freedom of individual will and the individual's own commitment to use this will to promote good—not merely the promotion of one's own good, but also the good of society in a form of sustainable and democratic development. Freedom of individual will, for its part, postulates a capacity for critical reasoning as well as knowledge of the options and alternatives available. This means that "knowledge search" has to go hand in hand with "knowledge use," which should, in turn, aim for wisdom.

One of the first steps towards solving some of the problems of the world's poorest countries is to find a way towards more democratic governance. ICT can play a central role in enhancing democracy if it is used to disseminate information freely, to provide open communication channels for mutual dialogue and unrestricted participation, and to enhance the responsiveness and accountability of those in public positions. However, in this context its use has to be tied to the realization of human capabilities at several levels. This means that in global ICT policies we need not merely focus on distribution of technology to those who have not previously had access to it, but we also need to pay attention to the use of technology—both in the form of training as well as in its content and goals.

This is a vicious circle. The democratic ideal does not work unless it gets the support of enlightened citizens. Ignorant, uneducated or merely self-interested leaders and citizens can use technology for counter-productive purposes and for their personal benefit rather than for the promotion of public good and public interest, all with are part of overall capabilities of human kind. Thus, ICT should be considered as the means to realize the essential human capabilities (from basic capabilities, to life and health in general, to more the complex combination of practical and theoretical reasoning, moral agency and social participation) needed to build and maintain any democratic process. It should not be seen as merely a means for participation. Participation without commitment to the democratic values of freedom, equality, moral autonomy and tolerance does not lead to social wisdom.

In order to understand the role of ICT in today's globalized world, we need to pay more attention to the complex relationship between knowledge, wisdom, democracy and power, as well as to the relationship between human capabilities and individual citizens' political (and moral) agency. A proper place to start is the relationship between the concepts of "information" and "knowledge." According to the classical Platonic definition, knowledge is a true, justified belief. By this very definition knowledge is given some intrinsic, positive value, that is, it is considered to be both justified and true. The same value judgment does not apply to what we call information. In fact, the value of information depends on what we do to change it into knowledge and wisdom. Information can be relevant or irrelevant; it can be honest or dishonest; it can be straightforward or misleading; it can be entertaining or educating. In other words, it can be justified or unjustified, true or false. Also information coming from different directions can feed our beliefs, but, in order to test or justify these beliefs, we usually need interactive, critical dialogue with others.

The relationship between information and knowledge can be summarized as follows: knowledge is information that is produced by our critical reasoning and tested by our communicative actions. Knowledge is then always more than pieces of information that are distributed in the media and computer networks. The idea of knowledge includes the human ability to produce and process information and judge its validity with the help of social dialogue. However, in the Information Age the very concept of knowledge has become more and more directly embodied in new technology. Thus, its usefulness appears to depend increasingly on the context of its application. This means that the production of knowledge is no longer centralized in the institutions of science and research or the media, but rather in the institutions with political and economical power. The focus on the acquisition, access and use of knowledge has become instrumental in economic and political activities. It is less often seen to be the intrinsic part of global human capital formulation that promotes well-being by helping to realize human capabilities in various circumstances (Clark, 2000, p. 84; Castells & Himanen, 2002).

Knowledge, Power, and Democracy

From the earlier-noted analysis of ICT in distribution of information and in production of knowledge, we can move to the relationship between knowledge and power. Because of its influence and usefulness for us, knowledge is also often equated with social power. In practice this is still the case in most parts of the world. With knowledge we can control not only our own but other people's lives; we can get authority over those who know less. This authority we can use either to dominate or to serve our communities. Thus, the obstacles—whether these are technological, economic, political, or cultural—in the way of the free flow of information are also obstacles in realizing human capital and human capabilities.

The main obstacle is related to the gain and use of power, which, for its part, is directly related to the concept of knowledge. Knowledge as power has traditionally held an intrinsically positive value. However, those who have access to and control of knowledge, and know how to apply it, can use the power knowledge gives them either in a positive and constructive way, or in a negative and destructive way, in regard to the ideals we have set for ourselves. We can use power to suppress and control others by keeping them in ignorance, or we can use it to pass on and share information and to promote individual freedom and democratic practices. If power and authority are used wisely, both developing and post-industrial countries can recognize the ideal of enlightened democracy that realizes the wide variety of human capabilities equally, locally and globally.

Thus, when and if information is turned into knowledge and knowledge into power, there is still no guarantee of equal and just political order. This is because democracy can work only if a nation's leaders and citizens use their personal social power with wisdom. Wisdom, however, is often difficult to come by in a modern market-led information age—regardless of whether we are talking about post-industrialized or developing countries. Wisdom, after all, does not follow directly from our access to information, from our capability to turn this information into knowledge, or from the power this knowledge gives us. Wisdom is a result of the development of the moral and social consciousness that integrates our intellectual capacities with our ethical outlooks and with our sense of justice, which is related to understanding the responsibility that comes with knowledge that is turned into power. Because the ideal of modern pluralist democracy is generally defined as the self-government of rational and reasonable autonomous moral and political agents, just as there is no knowledge without "knowers," there is no working democracy without wise and morally responsible citizens, whether at the grass-roots or the leadership level. Therefore, if we set full realization of human capabilities in all their forms as our goal, any discussion of development of a global knowledge society that is based on the more efficient and equal use of ICT cannot be detached from the civic, professional and ethics education.

Free Markets and Global Ethics

If human capabilities as the basis for increasing well-being were to be the goal of the ICT distribution, advancement, access and use, there would be a need to change the focus from business and economic benefits to education and civil participation. This does not apply merely to developing countries, but also to affluent information societies. Participation in global democracy does not follow directly from the number of Internet or mobile connections, though having them available naturally helps the process. As Warschauer (2003) has noted, access to technology does not guarantee its efficient or beneficial use. Thus, the practical problem is that the prevailing information society policies seldom follow the formula of democracy or pay enough attention to the human capabilities that are to be realized by and for democracy. They too often disregard the fact that the data that is disseminated and stored in information networks and in new media can be processed into knowledge and wisdom only by critical and autonomously developed human reasoning.

While access to relevant information has a central role in the globalized economy and profitable markets, free-market practice, civic education and democratic ideals do not always go hand in hand, particularly when technological advancement and information resources often do not reach those who need them most and would benefit from them most. Instead, free markets tend to enforce the development of information society and lead to the marginalization of groups of people in a manner that prevents all citizens from realizing their capabilities as rational, moral and political agents in the first place. If the distribution and use of ICT is left to the care of the invisible hand of market forces, the resulting society will tend to be fragmented by egoistic pursuits and self-interest. The division to the haves and the have nots, that is those who have access to technology and information and know how to use it for their benefit and those who are left to be socially and politically even more disconnected from the centers of power, knowledge and influence than they were before (Gauthier, 1986, pp. 11-30; Rawls, 1972, pp. 3-22, 54-81; NAME, 1993, pp. 11-39; Reiman, 1990, pp. 25-29; Weinberger, 1995, p. 218).

One main problem is that often technology is itself offered as a cure to the economic marginalization. Improved economy, for its part, is regularly needed in order to get into the technology markets. Thus, there appears to be no direct connection between globalized information economy and global justice. Instead, people, particularly in affluent countries, who have access to all the information channels possible are not using the information they receive, or the knowledge they process out of this information, to share their prosperity and abundant resources any more equally and in a way that will diminish global suffering. The fact that we can now, through satellite connection of television, radio, mobile phones and the Internet, get information more easily, more quickly and more accurately about any natural disasters, famines, victims of war and conflict, sufferers of diseases, or about any human agony that happens anywhere in the world, has not radically increased our solidarity or changed our habits in sharing our prosperity with those who are in urgent need and/or live in absolute poverty. The question then remains: if we cannot use the new ICT to take up our global responsibilities in affluent countries, how can we expect this technology to bring about local equality in the form of shared power and other essential resources in the underprivileged countries which have much fewer resources available, much poorer infrastructure, less efficient and inclusive educational systems, and limited civic participation? If we are not using ICT to enhance human capabilities at the local or global level, it can become a part of the problem rather than a solution for world inequality.

Global Obstacles: Prospects and Problems in Internet Use

Knowledge is still power in the hands of a few—globally as well as locally speaking. Knowledge and know-how guarantees power and influence also in international relations. International dialogue and the free flow of information both play a vital role in local and global social, political and economic development. Thus, new ICT could help us to increase efficiency and productivity, improve democracy and promote human rights. Access to new information and telecommunication technology could be used to empower the poorest and the weakest by helping them to connect with each other, share their problems and find solutions together and empower them economically and politically (Annan, 2003; Heldman, 1994, pp. 328-330; Hudson, 1997, pp. 179-205; Sarrocco, 2002; UNESCO, 2002; Williams, 1991, pp. 38-50; Wresch, 1996, pp. 23-91).[5] Since people no longer have to travel physically in order to communicate, exchange essential information, share knowledge or participate in different types of decision-making processes, we now have a realistic and unique chance to establish a global village of wisdom and social justice. At present, however, despite some positive development and the ambitious information society strategy papers with their global ethical guidelines and public rhetoric on social responsibility, the "information gap" and "digital divide" between industrialized and developing nations, and between the rich and poor in general is widening further (Annan, 2003; Gore, 1995; European Union, 1995 & 1997-2002; Sarrocco, 2002; UNDP, 2001; World Bank, 1999).[6] Instead of providing essential channels of interactive communication to those who need it most, new information technology is still for the most part connecting those who are better off and better connected to start with. Simultaneously in many parts of the world, the worst-offs have become even more disconnected from the centers of influence, power and resources (Heldman, 1994, pp. 264-265).[7]

Even in this information age, many of those who are living in isolated rural areas around the Third World have never read a book let alone a newspaper. About half of the world's population has never made a telephone call. Once again markets play an essential part in this inequality. For instance, in a poor nation local publication is minor, because production costs are high compared to those in industrialized countries. Paper prices are high, because most of the paper has to be imported; printing costs are high because all local presses are small and slow; editorial expenses are high because few people have editorial or design experience. While costs are high, sales are small and profits practically non-existent.[8] The problems are similar with telephone services. For instance, in Africa, still the poorest continent, the cost of getting a phone line and making telephone calls is, in absolute terms, higher and, in relative terms, extravagantly higher than in the United States or in Europe.[9] And even if one could get access to a telephone line and could afford to pay for the calls, it is not always possible to get an open line when wanted. Reasons for this are due to criminality (bugging of phone lines, looting of copper wire, cutting of cables, corruption with licenses and billing) and erroneous technology (Hudson, 1997, pp. 182-183).

Statistics also show that even if the know-how and technology are already there and there are some signs of change, the distribution of the latest telecommunication technology is globally and locally still very uneven. In 1996 about 700,000 people in Africa had access to the Internet, which meant that Tokyo had almost twice as many telephones lines than the whole African continent. The number of lines has rapidly grown; during 2000, sub-Saharan Africa passed the threshold of one telephone per 100 inhabitants. In the same year, all African countries achieved connection to the Internet. According to a report by the UN Information and Communication Technologies Task Force (UNICT) in September 2002, the proportion of Africans with Internet access rose by 20% between January 2001 and 2002. However, altogether only 0.2% of Africa's population has Internet access, and the lack of infrastructure and affordability has centralized these connections in the bigger cities and business centers.[10] In Tanzania, for instance, the best connectivity is essentially in Dar es Salaam, Arusha, Moshi, Mwanza and Zanzibar, all of which are centers of business, tourism and international events. Government institutions are still the most backward in connectivity. Many local government offices in smaller towns have no Internet, fax, mobile, or even fixed line connections.[11]

The increase in the Internet use in Africa does not match the proliferation of mobile phones on that continent, mainly because of the lack of fixed line technology. More Africans possess mobile phones than fixed line telephones, making the continent one of the very few regions in the world where this is the case. As a result of the mobile explosion, dilapidated fixed line infrastructure has suffered further as many governments and companies believe that the continent can skip the fixed line era and move straight into the mobile age. While mobile connections can help to expand access to the Internet in the long term, it makes access to the Internet more difficult in the short term. Mobile connections in third world countries are still unreliable, very slow for Internet use, and relatively very expensive (Ford, 2003, p. 52; Parker, 2001).[12]

Another option for wider Internet access and use would be to design computers that can be used away from electricity distribution grids. Such technology would enable potential users to bypass the inefficiencies of downstream power grids. Some initiatives are already beginning to put the concepts of non-grid dependent PCs into the Mtabila refugee camp in Tanzania, where people have been given access to the Internet as a result of a new source of electricity generation. The camp lies well away from the existing Tanzanian power distribution grid, so power is being generated using methane gas produced by fermented cow dung. However, there are no signs yet that computers powered by solar energy, for instance, are to be widely available in the near future (Ford, 2003, pp. 53-54; Sarrocco, 2002).

All in all, the mobile phones and other telecommunication devices available are still very unevenly distributed both globally and locally. In poor developing countries, it is mostly only the wealthy people who have access to new information technology and telecommunication services. The gaps are even greater between urban and rural areas. For instance, in Africa there are almost three times as many fixed telephone lines per 100 people in the largest city of the lower-middle-income countries than there are in their rural areas, and more than seven times as many lines per 100 people in the largest city of the low-income countries as there are in their rural areas. These gaps are even more significant given the fact that more than 50% of the population, and as much as 80% in the poorest countries of the world, lives in rural regions (Ford, 2003, pp. 52-54; Hudson, 1997, pp. 180-181; Kyaruzi, 2003, p. 8).

Thus, obstacles in access to information and knowledge, which are related to the global economic inequalities, are also connected to local conditions. In most parts of the developing world, the very same obstacles that we could overcome with the help of new information technology are the ones that prevent its widespread use in the poor parts of the world. Geographic isolation with no reliable means of transportation, lack of infrastructure, together with ignorance and poverty, mean that there are very few people who could use even the traditional communication channels, let alone the new technology. This means that providers must charge exorbitant fees to make up for their high investment costs. Because most private companies have to play according to the rules of market rationality, service providers are locked in charging higher prices in regions where there are fewer customers and where connections are more difficult to establish. Therefore, the use of new technology such as the Internet or cellular phones in much of Africa remains limited to a minuscule elite, often consisting mainly of foreigners or others who can afford the relatively high costs. This keeps demand low, which means lack of competition and little interest from private investors, which, in turn, keeps the prices unaffordable to the wider public at the grass-roots level.

What makes the situation even more difficult is the fact that not only is information technology and its allocation led by market forces, but information has itself turned into a commodity one has to pay for. The more valuable the information is the more people are willing to pay for it. This, once again, results in a market mechanism that makes it certain that the poor have even less chance of obtaining the most wanted and vital information.[13] In summary, the vicious circle is created by lack of infrastructure, unfavorable regulatory environment, high pricing, and an uncompetitive market structure, which cannot be broken without decisive intervention that focuses on the realization of human capabilities rather than the invisible hand of the globalized economy.

Good Fellows' Networks: Membership of the Global Village

One of the cruder ironies of the Information Age is that rich people get their information practically free, while poor people pay dearly for every morsel, be it a telephone call, a newspaper, a drive to the store, postal services or use of the Internet (Wresch, 1996, pp. 117-136; World Bank, 1999). Thus, the vast majority of information and communication channels are still today accessible only to those who live in the industrialized world, or in the prosperous urban centers of the developing countries. Access to information and communication all around the world remains elitist, since our virtual membership of the "global village" may make us close our eyes to the injustice just outside our own doors.

Thus, ironically enough, the new communication technology that was to be used to connect people with each other has created a digital divide, which actually often efficiently "disconnects" many from the problems of their own societies. A large part of the information people receive in developing countries through such international channels as the Internet, cable and satellite broadcast, fax and telephone lines, mobile The information they receive can be quite one-sided, and sometimes even biased. It presents the views and lifestyles of those who rule the commercial markets, entertainment industry, news media—that is, the views of the financial, political and industrial powers, mostly, those of the North and the West. Movies, television, international news agencies and publishers and the Internet all spread information that originates in the Western world, especially in the United States. This means that the information received in the developing world is often very limited in its scope. It is not an exaggeration to say that, for the better-off who live in urban centers of many developing countries, it is often easier to know what is happening on the other side of the world than to find out what is happening in the slums or villages just a few miles away from them.[14]

While the developed countries rhetorically demand that developing countries support the free flow of information, they evidently do not mean that information is going to be cost-free for them. Neither do they mean that information is free to flow in any direction (Wresch, 1996, pp. 117-136; Ford, 2003, pp. 52-53). After all, if we seem to live in a particularly productive time in the history of science, there is a wide division of those who are admitted in the global science community. Countries of the industrialized world do not pay much attention to scientific and research done in the developing world, unless they are involved in that research or are giving funding for particular research projects. Local scientists working in local universities without international financial support or connection networks have a much harder time in getting their results published internationally than do many of their Western colleagues. Consequently, when their work does not get international recognition, it easily loses its chance to be further developed. Information from developing countries that could be spread to the important research centers of the world and processed further into important knowledge that in the end could benefit everyone is often partially disregarded (Wresch, 1996, pp. 79-91). Only if it is regarded more fully could it consistently contribute to the realization of human capabilities and a holistic view of well-being. When information is used merely commercially or as technical means for information production, the goals of wisdom and full human development are set aside or ignored.

Thus, it appears that many Western countries have maintained their role not only as technological or economic advisers, but also as "intellectual advisers" and "the sources of proper knowledge." Instead of looking for equal partnership, the industrialized world tends to tell the third world how to do things, to put conditions on aid and give or take information it sees as suitable for its own purposes. As a result lots of important local knowledge is wasted and lost.

Local Obstacles:
Local Politics and Ambitions

In addition to the unequal distribution of information technology and information itself, there are other local cultural and political obstacles that prevent us from turning the information society into a global community of wisdom and that further widen the global gap between "the information privileged" and "the information beggars."

While new communication technology could provide citizens a channel to get involved in public matters and policy decisions, the ruling elite of many developing countries use this technology merely for their own purposes and for their own personal benefit. This is often due to authoritarian political orders in which the head of the state (or the ruling elite) declares a country a democracy. In reality, however, "politics of no choice" is practiced. Often there is only one serious political party and policy line and no real room for opposition. In this one-party "illiberal" democracy, the distinction between party and the state (or government or regime) is blurred and corruption, bribery and nepotism become common problems. The ruling elite lack the links to the problems of most of the society, particularly to those of rural populations. Nor do they encourage citizen involvement in public matters.

The only real citizen involvement in governance of a nation is often through taxes. The governments of many developing countries originally set high taxes on the new information and communication industry, basing these taxes on the attitude that the latest information technology is a luxury rather than a necessary and integral part of overall development. The tendency to prioritize basic services, such as building roads, educational facilities and health care units, sometimes disregards the possibilities that new communication technology could have in establishing these very services more quickly and more efficiently. However, it should be noted here that recently changes in this attitude have been evident and that taxing of ICT has become more customer friendly.

Nevertheless, earlier taxing policies have influenced the slow progress in nationwide adoption, distribution and use of ICT in the developing countries. For instance in Tanzania the rate of import duty on information technology accessories used to be the highest in East Africa, because computers were for a long time considered as luxury items rather than an integral part of setting up a working infrastructure in all fields of development. The heavy taxing made most Tanzanians unable to buy computers privately, and this led to a digital class divide in society. Even today many local educational institutions, including those that specialize in the use of new computer technology, have to wait until someone donates them the technology (often already out-dated or short-lived and unable to give students up-to-date know-how or access to the most advanced information/data/media resources). High taxes also prevented many computer centers from registering themselves officially. The result of this was usually inferior teaching and/or high fees. Import duty on a computer was, only a couple of years ago, 20% of its value, and a further 20% was charged for value-added tax. As well as these taxes, international shipping costs had to be paid. Thus, in the United States, one of the richest industrialized countries, a new computer can be sold at US$1000 or even less, while in poor countries like Tanzania the price of the same computer is almost double, unless you settle for an out-dated model or used computer (Heldman, 1994).[15] However, the heavy taxes on ICT do not prevent foreign residents and big businesses from obtaining the latest technology—usually tax exempt. In Tanzania the situation has recently changed with tax policy change and with the recognition that ICT is an essential element in the overall development of the country and not merely a luxury commodity (Mutula, 2001, 2002).

In many other developing countries with stricter authoritarian political order there are other coarser reasons for the heavy taxes and high prices on new technology. Some rulers simply prefer to keep most of the citizens ignorant and uneducated in order to secure their own position and power. History has shown that most of the totalitarian regimes take very tight measures to control information and citizen communication.[16] In many third world countries, for instance, there has been a tendency to protect existing power structures and hierarchies by limiting access to information and by suppressing the capabilities to process information into useful knowledge. As long as the citizens believe in their own "underdevelopment," social and political hierarchies can be maintained. Official documents are stamped confidential, secret, for limited distribution, depending on who we think deserves and has the right "to know" about particular issues. Information that is distributed widely is often trivial, misguided or unclear. For example, in various African countries the passing and distribution of information has turned out to be one of the biggest obstacles in developing "good governance" and participatory democracy.

People in positions of power and influence are protecting their authority by blocking, distorting and censoring information so that people's capabilities are not sufficiently realized so that they can efficiently and plausibly evaluate government actions, functions of state institutions and policies, monitor business management, and, in general, demand their rights, recognize their duties or complain about the misuse of power. Thus, the idea of an information "revolution" can be directly related to political revolution, which may not be appealing to many leaders. Instead, information and knowledge, with the help of the new technology, can be used to cover up corrupt activities that increase rather than decrease global and local inequality (Mutula,

2001, 2002). After all, when people do not know what is happening around them and when they are not informed about the abuses of political power, or if they do not understand how the political system works, they are much easier to control and keep satisfied. People who are disconnected from the outside world are less likely to stand up for their rights, fight against injustice and demand political change. One central question is then—while there were increasing technical possibilities for e-democracy, would the cultural and political context welcome wider participation and more open and transparent politics? Here again, in relation to the capability approach, new directions in national policies would help to find such a focus. When people participate and can more fully realize the capabilities they have, the leaders themselves learn to understand the benefits that democratic regime can bring to the whole society, and not feel threatened by giving power to people rather than hanging on to it as long as they can.

Culture and Tradition

All the previous text is at least partly related to the attempts of many countries to maintain their cultural independence and to avoid what they consider to be the negative effects of globalization. In some cases governments set restrictions and censorship on the Internet, since these are seen to import the culture of globalization, consumerism and Western individualism. In contemporary Iran, for example, while the use of Internet is encouraged up to a degree and its possibilities are seen as positive for the spread of the Islamic culture and ideology, the sites that are considered to pass on Western propaganda, moral deterioration or otherwise culturally or politically harmful materials and information are blocked and access to them is denied.

In relation to this, it is evident that in addition to economics and politics, culture plays an important role in development and in the adoption of new technology. Some cultures are more recipient to change and promote technical progress, while others are more oriented towards traditional wisdom. According to well-known philosopher from Ghana, Kwasi Wiredu, this is no accident. Instead, it is due to the cultural differences in worldviews and attitudes towards technology and mechanics. Wiredu (1980) notes that, for many African communities, development does not often mean merely the acquisition of sophisticated technology and material benefits; it also means searching for the intellectual and social conditions that will permit internal, positive freedom for human beings in the form of self-realization. In their search for self-development many African peoples simply do not care about new technology. When development is seen as self-development, learning about mechanical and technological details loses its importance. This is almost the opposite of the Northern view, which conceives development as external rather than internal progress. On the other hand, there has been some local resistance to modernization in a sense that it is seen to be a sign of further cultural colonization of developing countries.

These differences in attitudes are, at least in part, based on very distinctive intellectual traditions and value systems. If we make some very wide generalization, we could note that the Northern and Western countries have, at least ever since the Enlightenment, had a very individualist, atomistic and mechanistic world-view, which has traditionally equated a human being with a machine.[17] Many non-Western cultures, for their part, have more collectivist value systems which emphasize social harmony and communal interdependency, with understanding of the wholeness of the universe and our social interdependence. In the Western individualist culture the emphasis on reason and rationality requires that we constantly seek more specialized and specific information, which we can turn into scientific knowledge about the way world really is. In many more collectivist cultures with more holistic worldviews and value systems, knowledge about the world can better be achieved by understanding of the whole, with the help of mystical experience that computers and mobile phones cannot produce. In such cultures too much outside information can, in fact, be seen as taking attention away from our internal powers, personal moral development and wholesome wisdom. This is not always the way, however; some of the most technologically advanced countries are based on very holistic worldviews and have very collective social structures, for example, Japan and the technologically fast developing nations of southeast Asia. However, the personal or cultural experiences of the new technology might be very different. In the Eastern context, the idea of virtual reality may be seen as a sign of the holistic nature of the universe and the interconnectedness of (physical, intellectual and mental) human capacities with the immaterial dimensions of our world, while in the more atomistic Western worldview virtual reality may be seen merely as a device that provides us with the means to extend physical senses and capabilities further across our material world.

The Western emphasis on reason as the source of knowledge gives value to specialized data, that is, external information. In many other cultures the knowledge of the world is rather accomplished by inner awareness, that is, internal information. Achieving the understanding of the interdependence of all things requires us to empty our minds rather than fill them up with distracting piecemeal information. From an African point of view, for instance, the Western world may be seen to conceive knowledge as political and economic power, and thus it tries to monopolize, patent and commercialize all the knowledge it can produce. Since the Industrial Revolution, Westerners have used knowledge to control nature and to exploit it. In many parts of Africa knowledge is equated with moral and social wisdom and understanding the profound interdependence of people and nature and the universe as a whole.

Humans do not produce knowledge about nature. Instead they discover it with the help of the nature itself. While, in the Western worldview, wise men create or produce more knowledge, in Southern cultures it is often "the knowledge" that makes people wise. And wise men know that knowledge should not be used to technologically and commercially suppress and manipulate nature, but to live in harmony with it. After all, humans are merely partners or shareholders, with all other creatures, inanimate objects and invisible forces, in the resources of the earth, of which knowledge itself is one (Tangwa, 1999, p. 276).

Thus, different cultural traditions are often based on very different metaphysical outlooks and thus, may have very distinct views of knowledge and wisdom. People with different cultural backgrounds may therefore have very different ideas and ideals for how to form a global knowledge society. People coming from individualist cultures may see the holistic respect for universal harmony as inefficiency and primitive ignorance, while people from collectivist cultures may take the emphasis on individuals as arrogance and morally indifferent selfishness (Wiredu, 1980, pp. 53-59, 83, 105).

Understanding cultural differences is an integral part of global development. Part of this understanding requires that we accept that neither attitude towards technology is, in itself, superior to the other. Instead, both have their strong and weak sides and have a lot to learn from each other. While the Northern and Western mechanistic view is eager to develop new means to conquer nature, its emphasis on efficiency and profit often leads to environmental destruction, social inequality and moral indifference in an endless market rat race. While the Southern holism may not take full advantage of the technological progress and may sometimes disregard individuals' special practical abilities and rights, it can also encourage environmental harmony, social solidarity and personal peace.

Here discussion on human capabilities can also help us to overcome some cultural differences and different understandings of human well-being and good living. As noted in the beginning, people may have very different view of whether the aim of development is material, spiritual or social, but most human capabilities we are looking after in life are universal. We might have different cultural, political or economic contexts to realize them, but, nevertheless, our goals are shared. Thus, promoting human capabilities as the end that justifies the distribution and implementation of ICT should not mean that we have to adopt one global culture, but rather that, with the help of new technology, we have equal capacities to understand, promote and maintain our different cultural values and practices within a context of modern globalized world.

Primitive as an Ideal?

If we are to build a global society of knowledge and wisdom, different cultures have many important lessons to learn from each other. However, instead of seeing local in global, very often there are hasty polarizations made between modern and traditional. Instead of promoting the best parts of both, people (individuals or groups of people) are forced to make a dichotomized choice between modern and traditional ways of life.

These fallacious polarizations lead to cultural conflicts and to assumptions that local and global are incommensurate. When the fundamental differences in metaphysical, ethical or social outlooks of different cultures are not fully understood, there is a danger that we justify clear injustices as cultural diversity. Also, sometimes people from highly industrialized countries with materialistic values may be skeptical about the value of technological progress as such. Instead, they may romanticize traditional ways of life as resistance movements against technology and consider those who do not have modern technological access to outside world as noble savages.

In fact, those who defend traditionalism and set against modernization are not always residents of technologically and economically less developed countries. Quite the contrary, in many instances it is the information-rich rather than the information-poor who may envision the primitive way of life as an escape from the modern world and the information and consumption anxiety it creates. Some may even themselves sometimes join "the disconnected," on a desert, in a jungle or in the mountains for few days or even weeks.

The difference between the information-rich and the information-poor, however, is that the rich ones always know how and have enough resources to get back to civilization when the times get too rough. Anytime they want to, they can get back to their phones, faxes and communicators, drive their cars back to cities, and take an airplane back home. The idealized noble savage is usually isolated, poor, and in many other ways disabled. They have no hope for a better life, nor do they have any control over their fate, which is often decided for them by others living in the centers of power and influence. In most cases and most areas people have not chosen their own isolation. The poor simply lack the options to live in any other way (Wresch, 1996, p. 136). Helping these people to get connected with the outside world, and become involved in matters concerning their own lives, is not an attempt to rob cultural traditions; it may be the only way to maintain those traditions. It increases their chances to realize the full set of human capabilities and to see the plurality of human existence and well-being. Keeping people disconnected and ignorant may respect cultural difference, but shows moral indifference. It clearly blocks people from using their full potential, in whatever cultural, social, and material environment they live in.[18]

Conclusion

New ICT can play a central role in helping developing countries to improve their standard of living and quality of life in relation to realizing human capabilities. However, markets alone cannot bring the technology to those who would most benefit from it and technology alone cannot bring about positive changes. Instead, technology can be made to be a vehicle of positive or negative affects, depending on our personal values and goals, and our cultural beliefs and norms. Information technology can just as easily be used to gain one-sided market benefits or to impose a dominant political culture on different people as it can be used to build a just world order that promotes tolerance, equality and social justice. If we look for new ways to share our global prosperity, it is essential that we make a clear difference between means and ends in the advancement, application and distribution of ICT. An alternative normative framework that gives a promising start in finding new options for distribution and implementation of ICT is capability ethics that remind us that all material resources are a mere means—never the end in themselves—towards holistic well-being. Since ICT brings together in an intriguing manner both material resources as well as intellectual development, it is important to be clear about what are looking for in our attempts to create global connections. Are we realizing human capabilities and building a global village of wisdom? Or are we creating a superficial global information culture that focuses on market exchange of hardware, software, data, time and social relations?

While it is clear that world neo-liberal economic policies play a central role in global injustice, the Western neo-liberal market capitalism and cultural imperialism cannot alone be blamed for the existing inequalities within developing countries. In many developing countries governments abuse power and resources, as well as people's commitment to tradition. If we are serious about building a global knowledge society, we therefore need to consider first what the ideal of the knowledge society is and how it is related to the realization of human capabilities which are the basis of a working democracy and the moral development of any society. Second, we need to understand the fundamental differences between cultural traditions. Third, we have to conceive technology as a means to better quality of life as well as to more open cultural dialogue, instead of seeing it as an end in itself. If we want to build a global knowledge society, we have to acknowledge that technology *per se* is always value- neutral and, thus, all of us share the social responsibility to develop and use it for the common good and the realization of human capabilities, as is suggested by application of capability ethics to the global distribution and implementation of ICT. While this approach certainly needs to be further studied and its potential problems taken into account, it at least can give us a starting point for debates on global distribution, particularly in relation to technological advancement.

While there is no clear indication that any comprehensive change in our attitudes is to be expected immediately, keeping the dialogue going is important. Without any change the present trends of global development show that while Internet and other new telecommunication technologies reach more and more people rapidly, at least as many people are at the same time losing their connections to the sources of essential information, local knowledge and basic political participation and power to influence their own fate. This not only deepens material inequality, but also widens further the digital divide and communication gap between the information-rich and the information-poor.

References

AfricaOnline. (2003). *Facts and history*. Dar es Salaam.

Andinilike, M. (1999, October 4). Reflections: 25 percent private TV, radio coverage in Tanzania. *Daily News*, p. 7.

Annan, K. (2003). *IT industry must help bridge global digital divide*. Digital Divide Network. Retrieved November 5, from http://www.digitaldividenetwork.org/content/stories

APC (Association for Progressive Communications). (2003). *Women's survey, Part I*. Retrieved June 2003 from http://communty.web.net/apcwomen/part1.html#4

Castells, M., & Himanen, P. (2002). *The information society and the welfare state: The Finnish model*. New York: Oxford University Press.

Clark, N. (2000). Public policy and technological change in Africa: Aspects of institutions and management capacity. *Journal of Economic Studies, 27*(1/2), 75-93.

Cohen, G. A. (1993). Equality of what? On welfare, goods and capabilities. In M. Nussbaum & A. Sen (Eds.), *The quality of life*. Oxford, UK: Clarendon Press.

Crocker, D. (1992). Functioning and capability: The foundations of Sen's and Nussbaum's development ethic. *Political Theory, 20*(4), 584-612.

European Union. (1995). *Green paper on copyright and related rights in the information society*. Retrieved November 5, 2005, from http://europa.eu.int/scadplus/leg/en/lvb/l24152.htm

European Union. (1997-2002). *Towards knowledge based Europe: European Union and information society*. Retrieved June 12, 2002, from http://europe.eu.int/information_society/eeurope/index_en.htm

Ford, N. (2003, July). Africa joining the IT revolution. *New African*, 52-54.

Gauthier, D. (1986). *Morals by agreement*. Oxford, UK: Clarendon Press.

Gore, A. (1995). Information superhighway. *World Almanac and Book of Facts*. NJ: Funk and Wagnalls.

Grant Lewis, S. (1992). Microcomputers adoption in Tanzania and the rise of a professional elite. In S. Grant Lewis & J. Samoff (Eds.), *Microcomputers in African development: Critical perspectives*. Boulder, CO: Westview Press.

Heldman, R. (1992). *Global telecommunication: Layered networks, layered services*. New York: McGraw-Hill.

Heldman, R. (1994). *Information telecommunications: Networks, products and services*. New York: McGraw-Hill.

Hobbes, T. (1962). In M. Oakeshott (Ed.), *Leviathan*. New York: Collier MacMillan. (Originally published 1651)

Hudson, H. (1997). *Global connections: International telecommunications infrastructure and policy*. New York: Van Nostrand Reinhold/Thomason.

Jimba, S. (1999). Information technology and underdevelopment in the Third World. *Library Review*, *48*(2), 79-83.

Kyaruzi, I. (2003, June 13). Mobile telephony, bandwidth use doubles in Africa. *Business Times* (Tanzania), p. 8.

Miller, S. (1996). *Civilizing cyberspace*. New York: ACM Press.

Molosi, K. (1999, October/November). Making the Internet work for Africa. *Computers in Africa*, 37-38.

Mutula, S. (2001). Internet access in East Africa: A future outlook. *Library Review*, *50*(1), 28-34.

Mutula, S. (2002). The cellular phone economy in the SADC region: Implication for libraries. *Online Information Review*, *26*(2), 79-92.

Mwakaleba, L. (1999, July 5). Why many Tanzanian computer schools remain unregistered. *Business Times* (Tanzania), p. 8.

Ngonji, R. (2003, June 23). Mobile phone customers still await government word. *The Guardian*, p. 7.

Njau, A. (1999, October 30). Business people challenged to use Internet services. *Business Times* (Tanzania).

Nussbaum, M. (1987). *Nature, function, and capability: Aristotle on political distribution* (WIDER working paper 31). Helsinki, Poland: UNU/WIDER.

Nussbaum, M. (1992). Human functioning and social justice: In defense of Aristotelian essentialism. *Political Theory*, *20*(2), 202-246.

Nussbaum, M. (1993). Non-relative virtues: An Aristotelian approach. In M. Nussbaum & A. Sen (Eds.), *The quality of life*. Oxford, UK: Clarendon Press.

Parker, B. (2001). Puppet on a string—Africa's spineless Internet topology. *Nairobi, Africaonline holdings.* Retrieved June 4, 2003, from http://www.africaonline.co.tz

Perry, J. (1996). Introduction to *On the Internet,* Nov/Dec—Developing Countries. Retrieved May 3, 2002, from www.napanet.net/~janetp/articles

Rawls, J. (1972). *A theory of justice.* London: Oxford University Press.

Reiman, J. (1990). *Justice and modern moral philosophy.* New Haven, CT: Yale University Press.

Sakaguchi, T., & Dibrell, C. C. (1998). Measurement of the intensity of global information technology usage: Quantitizing the value of a firm's information technology. *Industrial Management & Data Systems, 98*(8), 380-394.

Sarrocco, C. (2002). *Improving IP connectivity in the least developed countries.* Retrieved November 5, 2003, from http://www.itu.int/osg/spu/ni/ipdc

Sen, A. (1985). *Commodities and capabilities.* Amsterdam: North-Holland.

Sen, A. (1990). Justice: Means versus freedoms. *Philosophy and Public Affairs, 19*(2), 11-121.

Sen, A. (1992). *Inequality reexamined.* Oxford, UK: Clarendon Press.

Sen, A. (1993). Capability and well-being. In M. Nussbaum & A. Sen (Eds.), *The quality of life.* Oxford, UK: Clarendon Press.

Sen, A. (2001). *Development as freedom.* Cambridge, UK: Cambridge University Press.

Stover, W. J. (1984). *Information technology in the third world. Can IT lead to humane national development.* Boulder, CO: Westview Press.

Tangwa, G. B. (1999). Genetic information: Questions and worries from an African background. In A. Thompson & R. Chadwick (Eds.), *Genetic information, acquisition, access, and control.* New York: Kluwer/Plenum.

UNCTAD. (2004). *UNCTAD E-Commerce and development report 2004.* Retrieved November 5, 2005, from http://www.unctad.org/en/docs/ecdr2004_en.pdf

UNDP. (2001). *The UNDP world development report 2001.* Retrieved January 10, 2005, from http://hdr.undp.org

UNESCO. (2002). *Medium-term strategy 2002-2007. Communication and information.* Retrieved November 5, 2004, from http://portal.unesco.org/ci/en/file_download.php/aab035d458fac5197544ca1ff10c5d5bCommunication+and+Information+Srategy.pdf

Vesely, M. (2003, July). New technology for an old continent. *African Business,* pp. 20-21.

Warschauer, M. (2003, August). Demystifying the digital divide. *Scientific American,* pp. 34-39.

Weinberger, O. (1995). Information and human liberty. *European Journal of Law, Philosophy and Computer Science, 2*(1).

Williams, F. (1991). *The new telecommunications: Infrastructure for the information age.* Ontario, Canada: Maxwell Macmillan.

Wiredu, K. (1980). *Philosophy and an African culture.* Cambridge, UK: Cambridge University Press.

World Bank. (1998/99). *The world development report: Knowledge and development.* Washington, DC.

Wresch, W. (1996). *Disconnected: Haves and have-nots in the information age.* New Brunswick, NJ: Rutgers University Press.

Young, J. R. (2001). Does "digital divide" rhetoric do more harm and good? *The Chronicle for Higher Education. Information Technology, 48*(11). Retrieved November 5, 2005, from http://chronicle.com/free/v48/i11/11a05101.htm

Endnotes

[1]   The term "digital divide" may be defined as the gap between individuals, households, businesses and geographic areas at different socio-economic levels, with regard both to their opportunities to access information and communication technologies (ICTs) and to their use of the Internet for a wide variety of activities. There are divisions between those individuals and businesses who can enjoy the advantages of the information age, and those who are still waiting to see these benefits. The concept of "digital divide," however, has been questioned as making a normative distinction between the technology savvy and technology ignorant.

[2]   When, for instance, we talk about knowledge workers, we mainly refer to those who can manipulate, control, transfer and store the growing amounts of data and information, and not to those who are working intellectually in order to process and distribute relevant knowledge out of all the information available. In the information society true knowledge is often the by-product of information markets rather than a valuable goal in itself.

[3]   According to Sen (1992, p. 42), functionings belong to the constitutive elements of well-being. Capability reflects freedom to pursue these constitutive elements and may even have a direct role in well-being itself, in so far as deciding and choosing are also parts of living.

[4]   See, for example, Sen (1985, pp. 6-11; 1990, pp. 113-114; 1993, pp. 30-50). There is no escape from the problem of evaluation in electing a class of functionings. This is particularly problematic in choosing the objects or commodities of distribution. Whose capabilities should have priority, and at what level? The focus has to be related to underlying concerns and values, in terms of which some deniable functioning may be important and others quite trivial and negligible. Many functionings are of no great interest to a person; for example, using a particular washing powder is much like using any other washing powder (Sen, 1993, pp. 31-32). For a criticism of Sen's capability approach, see Cohen (1993).

[5]   The new information and communication channels could promise poor countries a better life in the following ways: schools and hospitals could be assisted with online access to information resources all round the world. Computer conferencing and electronic mail could enable students

to participate in distance learning projects, seminars and tutorials in vocational schools or universities on the other side of the globe. Scientific researchers and doctors who lack the money to subscribe to leading journals and other publications could keep abreast of the latest work in their fields. Information on health issues could prevent and help to cure many illnesses. Health care workers in isolated areas could receive information on possible epidemics. They could also get distant specialists to diagnose rare conditions and recommend the proper treatments through telemedicine. The poor themselves could learn how better take care of their health and their children's health through access to professional health education and information, that, for instance, helps them to leave behind harmful practices based on ignorance, misinformation or coercion. Local journalists, news offices, development agencies and non-governmental organizations (NGOs) could use new technology to collect and disseminate essential information for rural areas. Information on local government policies and legal matters as well as access to national and international news could, for instance, help people to prevent abuse of power and educate them about their social and legal rights. Also businesses, large and small, would be able to market their goods widely, receive vital information about local and global market conditions, pricing and financial management or they could hunt for foreign partners cheaply. See also APC (2003) and Perry (1996).

6   Several international and regional organizations have undertaken new projects to bring the benefits of the information technology revolution to the developing world. These projects are often aimed at improving the access capacity of the least developed countries and providing their populations with equipment or multi-purpose telecenters and the knowledge necessary to use information resources. Among these are the ITU Multipurpose Community Telecenter pilot projects in Benin, Mali, Mozambique, Tanzania, Uganda and elsewhere sponsored by ITU, ICRC, UNESCO, UNDP and by national and private entities.

7   Multinational corporations have become more information-oriented, but they are also taking over the information markets. Now most of the exchange of information between countries is no longer controlled and regulated by governments, but by local individuals have become more tied to the information provided by the international corporations and local businesses have become more dependent on their multinational partners.

8   If people can read and can afford newspapers or books, they often have to buy imported ones, written by foreigners and published in a foreign language. For instance, in Tanzania, no history books were published at all by 1980. Thus, if Tanzanians wanted to learn about their own nation's history, they had to learn it from foreigners.

9   Miller (1996, p. 371) refers to how the prices spread piracy and vice versa, creating a vicious circle in technology and information markets in developing world.

10   The world distribution of online connections in 1999 was: World – 134 million (2.4% of the total population); Africa – 1.2 million (0.1% (excluding South Africa)); Asia – 22 million (0.6%); South America – 4.5 million (1.3%); North America – 70 million (14.9%); Europe – 34 million (4.7%) (In many Scandinavian countries, the percentage is considerably higher, now reaching close to 40% of the population) (Molosi, 1999). Since 2000, there were only about 580,000 regular Internet users in the LDCs, representing less than 1% of the population and 0.16% of global Internet users (Sarrocco, 2002).

11   Based on an interview with a Tanzanian *Business Times* ICT journalist, Samuelson Makilla in Dar es Salaam, 1 July 2003. His suggestion of a solution to poor connectivity was based on joint-ownership of a satellite link sponsored by donor and a local stakeholder conglomerate.

12   Internet connections are slow and commercially fragmented. For example, an e-mail to Somalia from Kenya may go by satellite to the U.S., under the Atlantic by fiber-optic cable to Europe and the Middle East and back up by another satellite from the United Arab Emirates and then to Somalia. Multiple strands of bandwidth connect individual Internet service providers to the

central thoroughfares of the Internet, mainly in the U.S. and in Europe. Each international ISP connection costs many thousand dollars to maintain. Most of sub-Saharan Africa in connected by satellite, which brings echoes and delays to Internet traffic.

[13]   Thus, at present the Information Age is not an age of equality and justice. The poor have enormous obstacles to overcome before they can even get to the global sources of useful information. Not only do they have to be able to read and write in their native language, but also they have to be educated enough to understand at least one foreign language (usually English). Then they have to have access to sources of information and they have to be able to pay for the information they are looking for. However, paying $US49 a year for the *Wall Street Journal* (US$29 to print subscribers) in a country where the average income is much less than $US50 a month is a rather irrational choice.

[14]   Even local television and radio stations and the local press often use the same stories because they are easier and cheaper to get than those gleaned by sending a local reporter abroad or to hard-to-reach parts of their own country. Stories about Third World countries are reported mostly by journalists and researchers from the industrialized world. Thus, they present a Western point of view and Western concerns about development aid, natural catastrophes, war, poverty, famines. Positive success stories are seldom reported and traditional wisdom from local sources is usually overlooked (Wresch, 1996, pp. 23-41).

[15]   Local development policies can affect poorer members of society adversely. As information education has taken hold in developing countries, priority has been given to the increase of food production and economic resources. Many of the poorer people have been forced to give up some of their land holdings to enable the growth of a more educated society.

[16]   Many conservative or fundamentalist religious nations have accepted the use of new technology itself, but mainly for their own propaganda purposes and they have blocked people's access to, for instance, what they consider to be sexually or politically sensitive data. Sometimes they may deny individuals' access to anything other than government information and may even spread misinformation about opposing views and possible enemies of the state.

[17]   See, for instance, Hobbes (1962), whose work presents the Western mechanical position on the norms of social and political order.

[18]   Within many traditional societies old social harmony is based on strict social hierarchy and suppression. The poorest and the weakest are often women living in patriarchal societies. They have the least chance to access external information and educate themselves in order to improve their lives. They are too exhausted from work, too sick from serious diseases, gender violence and continuous childbearing, and they are too suppressed and brain-washed by traditions to attempt to fight for their position in life. Everything these women know and learn comes from their physical environments and focuses on everyday survival. In a local village in the middle of Africa, for instance, the ideas of global village or virtual reality do not make much sense. Not only are these concepts obscure, but the reasoning behind them seems totally incomprehensible. People there see themselves as members of smaller and closer physical communities, hardly even as citizens of any particular state. They certainly do not relate to abstract cosmopolitanism and see themselves as citizens of the world, while, at the same time, they may hold a holistic worldview that acknowledges individuals as not only physical but also spiritual parts of the universe as represented in the world/nature around us. In such circumstances, direct spiritual connection, not technological devices, is needed to mediate needs, wants, hopes, desires, and despair.

Chapter II

Epistemic Value Theory and the Digital Divide

Don Fallis
University of Arizona, USA

Abstract

The digital divide refers to inequalities in access to information technology. Those people who do not have access to information technology are at a significant economic and social disadvantage. As with any other policy decision, in order to evaluate policies for dealing with the digital divide, we need to know exactly what our goal should be. Since the principal value of access to information technology is that it leads to knowledge, work in epistemology can help us to clarify our goal in the context of the digital divide. In this chapter, I argue that epistemic value theory can help us to determine which distribution of knowledge to aim for. Epistemic value theory cannot specify a particular distribution to aim for, but it can significantly narrow down the range of possibilities. Additionally, I indicate how the exercise of applying epistemic value theory to the case of the digital divide furthers work in epistemology.

Our Goal in the Context of the
Digital Divide

The *digital divide* refers to inequalities in access to information technology, such as personal computers, cell phones, PDAs, and the Internet.[1] Some people, the so-called *information have-nots*, have significantly less access than other people, the so-called *information haves*. This lack of access puts the information have-nots at a significant economic and social disadvantage (cf. Hacker & Mason, 2003, p. 101). As a result, there is a large literature on what should be done about the digital divide (for example, Doctor, 1992; Chabrán, 2001; Compaine, 2001; Mueller, 2001; De George, 2003, pp. 254-260; Hacker & Mason, 2003).[2]

Most of this literature focuses on what the likely consequences of adopting various policies for dealing with the digital divide. For example, some authors (for example, Compaine, 2001; Mueller, 2001) contend that the operation of the free market will eliminate the digital divide. Other authors (for example, Chabrán, 2001; De George, 2003) contend that eliminating the digital divide will require some intervention into the operation of the free market.[3] However, there is very little discussion of what consequences we would like to bring about (cf. Hacker & Mason, 2003).[4]

As with any other policy decision, we need to know which consequences count as *good* consequences in order to evaluate potential digital divide policies (cf. Kirkwood, 1997, p. 11).[5] In other words, we need to know exactly what our goal should be. For example, should the goal be to reduce inequalities in access to information technology or should the goal be to provide the information have-nots with more access? Clarifying our goal requires an analysis of the value of access to information technology.

In this chapter, I argue that the principal value of access to information technology is that it leads to *knowledge*.[6] As a result, work in epistemology can help us to clarify our goal in the context of the digital divide. In particular, I show how *epistemic value theory* can help us to determine which distribution of knowledge to aim for. Epistemic value theory cannot specify a particular distribution to aim for, but it can significantly narrow down the range of possibilities. Finally, I indicate how the exercise of applying epistemic value theory to the case of the digital divide can help us to develop epistemic value theory itself.

The Value of Access to
Information Technology

Some people have suggested that the digital divide is not a very important issue. For example, the former chairman of the Federal Communication Commission, Michael Powell, famously compared unequal access to information technology with unequal access to luxury automobiles.[7] There is, however, an important difference between the two.

Unlike access to luxury automobiles, access to information technology is a necessity of modern life. It is becoming very difficult for an individual without access to information technology to get all of the information that she needs to conduct her daily life. The Internet, in particular, is becoming a primary source of information about job opportunities, health care, travel, government services, paying taxes, political candidates, and so forth. Admittedly, most of this information is still available from other sources, such as books and newspapers. However, since it is quickly becoming prohibitively expensive and/or time-consuming to get this information from other sources, people without access to information technology are effectively denied access to this information. As a result, it has even been suggested that access to information technology is now a basic human right (cf. United Nations, 1948; Johnson, 1991, pp. 212-214; Chabrán, 2001, p. 138).

As Jeremy Moss (2002) points out, access to information technology opens up wider possibilities for action. For example, an individual can pay their taxes online, make travel arrangements, buy and sell products. The principal value of access to information technology, however, is that it leads to *knowledge* (cf. Tichenor et al., 1970; Lievrouw & Farb, 2003, p. 504).[8] Much of what we know about the world comes through our access to information technology, such as the Internet (cf. Fallis, 2006). In addition, access to information technology has many of the benefits that it does precisely because it allows people to acquire knowledge.[9] Knowledge of what jobs are available, for example, helps one to take advantage of economic opportunities.[10] Also, knowledge of the positions of political candidates helps one to participate effectively in the public sphere. As a result, when evaluating digital divide policies, it is useful to focus on knowledge rather than on the diverse benefits of having such knowledge (cf. Fallis, 2004b, pp. 102-103).[11]

Epistemic Value Theory

This analysis of the value of access to information technology, however, does not tell us enough to actually evaluate digital divide policies. Several different digital divide policies may all increase the amount of knowledge in society. But they will undoubtedly distribute this knowledge in different ways. Thus, in order to evaluate digital divide policies, we also have to be able to say which *distribution of knowledge* is best.[12]

The question of how to distribute knowledge is a question of distributive justice. However, since we are concerned specifically with how *knowledge* should be distributed, this is arguably also a question for epistemology. Epistemic goodness is an important part of overall goodness in the context of the digital divide. And, according to Alvin Goldman (1999), the job of social epistemology is to identify social policies (such as digital divide policies) that have good epistemic consequences.

Everybody having *all* knowledge is clearly the epistemically *ideal* distribution of knowledge. Epistemologists often discuss such ideal epistemic goals in the case of individuals. For example, Roderick Chisholm (1977, p. 14) claims that a person should try "his best to bring it about that, for every proposition h that he considers, he accepts h if and only if h is true." However, given the limits on our time and resources, it is just not possible for a person to have all and only true beliefs. Similarly, it is just not possible for *everybody* to have *all* knowledge. As a result, being able to say that *everybody* having *all* knowledge is the epistemically ideal distribution does not really help us to evaluate digital divide policies.

In order to evaluate digital divide policies, we need a more fine-grained *epistemic value theory* (cf. Goldman, 1999, p. 87; Fallis, 2004b).[13] In other words, we need to be able to say whether one distribution of knowledge is epistemically better than another. In particular, we need to be able to say which of the distributions of knowledge *that we can actually bring about* is epistemically best.

Several epistemologists (for example, Levi, 1967; Maher, 1993) have developed epistemic value theories that can be applied to the epistemic states of individuals (usually, scientists). However, there are many situations, such as the evaluation of digital divide policies, where we need to know how knowledge should be distributed among many different people (cf. Goldman, 1999, 93-94). Goldman (1999) has recently developed an epistemic value theory that can also be applied to the epistemic states of groups. He has used this theory to evaluate policies in several different areas, such the law, education, and science. But his theory is applicable to any area (including the digital divide) where epistemic consequences are at stake.

Fortunately, there are some clear-cut constraints on the *epistemic betterness* relation that are relevant to whether one distribution of knowledge is epistemically better than another.[14] For example, it is clearly epistemically better for a person to have more knowledge rather than less (cf. Goldman, 1987, p. 128).[15] In other words, it is epistemically better to have knowledge on a particular topic than to be ignorant (or in error) on the topic. In addition, it follows that it is epistemically better for more people to have knowledge rather than fewer (cf. Goldman, 1987, pp. 128-129).

These are the two most obvious constraints on the epistemic betterness relation. But it should be noted that there may very well be additional constraints that are relevant in the context of the digital divide. For example, the first constraint mentioned essentially says that it is epistemically better for there to be more *knowledge tokens* (my true belief that p, your true belief that p, etc.) rather than fewer. However, it is also clearly epistemically better for there to be more *knowledge types* (my true belief that p, your true belief that q, etc.) rather than fewer (cf. Fallis, 2004b, p. 109). This additional constraint is also relevant to whether one distribution of knowledge is epistemically better than another. In this chapter, however, I will set this complication aside.

Let us say that a distribution of knowledge D is *epistemically permissible* if no other distribution that we can actually bring about is epistemically better than D. Epistemic value theory clearly recommends that we always aim for an epistemically permissible distribution. In addition, let us say that a distribution of knowledge D is *epistemically required* if D is epistemically better than any other distributions that we can actually bring about. Epistemic value theory recommends that we aim for the epistemically required distribution if there is one.

A "Utilitarian" Distribution of Knowledge

It would be nice if there were a distribution of knowledge that was epistemically required. Goldman (1999, p. 93) seems to take the position that there is such a distribution. In particular, he suggests that a "utilitarian" distribution of knowledge that maximizes the average amount of knowledge possession in society is epistemically better than any alternative (cf. Goldman, 2002, p. 216, Fallis, 2004b, pp. 107-108).[16] But while this distribution may be epistemically permissible, it does not seem to be epistemically required.[17]

In fact, Goldman himself actually gives an example of an epistemically permissible distribution that does not maximize knowledge possession. When discussing how a ship's captain wants knowledge to be distributed among her crew, Goldman (1999, p. 96) notes that "information must be distributed to the people with a 'need to know'…even if that does not translate into a high average knowledge across the whole team." Even though she does not want to maximize the average amount of knowledge possessed by her crew, the captain still aims for knowledge rather than ignorance or error (that is, her preferences obey the two constraints on epistemic betterness given previously).

Furthermore, even though a "utilitarian" distribution may be epistemically permissible, it is probably not the distribution that we want to aim for in the context of the digital divide. The utilitarian distribution is consistent with a very wide digital divide *and* with the information have-nots actually being worse off. Maximizing the average amount of knowledge possession in society might require that some people (such as the information have-nots) know very little.[18]

An "Egalitarian" Distribution of Knowledge

Given the potential problems with aiming for a "utilitarian" distribution of knowledge, it might be suggested that we should try to distribute knowledge equally among the members of society. Such an "egalitarian" distribution would completely eliminate the digital divide. However, according to a strict egalitarian, "it is better, for the sake of equality, to take good from better-off people without giving any to the less well-off" (Broome, 1991, p. 184). Thus, in an "egalitarian" distribution, some people might have to have less knowledge than they could have had. In other words, an "egalitarian" distribution is not epistemically permissible.

Furthermore, it is also probably not the distribution that we want to aim for in the context of the digital divide. There are many cases where everybody does better if goods are not equally distributed. For example, train service can be provided to more people when there are several different levels of service (some of which some people may not be able to afford) rather than just one level (cf. Ekelund, 1970, pp. 275-276).[19] This suggests that we ought to be more concerned that knowledge be distributed *equitably* (or fairly) than that it be distributed equally (cf. Lievrouw & Farb, 2003, pp. 502-504).

A "Rawlsian" Distribution of Knowledge

Fortunately, there are epistemically permissible distributions of knowledge that seem to distribute knowledge equitably. One such distribution is suggested by the work of John Rawls (1971) on distributive justice. According to Rawls (1971, p. 75), "the social order is not to establish and secure the more attractive prospects of those better off unless doing so is to the advantage of those less fortunate." In other words, inequalities in the distribution of primary goods (such as knowledge) can be acceptable, but only if such inequalities are to the advantage of the least well off (such as the information have-nots).[20] Thus, we might want to aim for a "Rawlsian" distribution that maximizes the amount of knowledge possessed by the information have-nots.[21]

Such a distribution does not ensure an equal distribution of knowledge. For example, we probably need to have many highly knowledgeable experts in information technology in order to facilitate knowledge acquisition among the information have-nots. However, such a distribution does ensure that the information have-nots have as much knowledge as possible. In addition, taking this distribution as the goal of digital divide policy is in line with the view that access to information technology is a right that everyone has (cf. United Nations, 1948; Johnson, 1991, pp. 212-214; Lievrouw & Farb, 2003, p. 512).[22]

The Bad Consequences of Knowledge

The case of the "egalitarian" distribution establishes that not all distributions of knowledge are epistemically permissible. But, unless we can identify very tight constraints on the epistemic betterness relation, there are still going to be numerous epistemically permissible distributions of knowledge. The "Rawlsian" and "utilitarian" distributions are just two examples. And epistemology will not be able to tell us which of these epistemically permissible distributions we should aim for. Nevertheless, it seems clear that we should aim for the epistemically permissible distribution of knowledge that has the best consequences *all things considered*.

As noted earlier, of the epistemically permissible distributions, Goldman favors a "utilitarian" distribution of knowledge. However, Goldman (2002, pp. 218-220) has recently suggested that we should not necessarily aim for an epistemically permissible distribution of knowledge at all. After all, if we want to aim for the distribution of knowledge that has the best consequences all things considered, why should we limit ourselves to looking among the epistemically permissible distributions? Since epistemic goodness is only part of overall goodness, it could be that the distribution with the best overall consequences is not epistemically permissible. That this might actually be the case is suggested by the fact that having knowledge can sometimes have bad consequences (cf. Fallis, 2004b, p. 103).

Given this possibility, Goldman suggests that we should simply aim for the distribution of knowledge that has the best consequences *all things considered*. In other words, we should ignore the recommendations of epistemic value theory. The idea here is that epistemology should simply be concerned with what the epistemic consequences of various policies are likely to be. It need not take a position on which consequences count as *good* consequences, epistemically or otherwise.

However, Goldman's suggestion is not actually in conflict with the recommendations of epistemic value theory as long as the distribution of knowledge that has the best overall consequences is epistemically permissible. In the remainder of this section, I will address, in order of increasing relevance to the digital divide, the various ways in which having knowledge can have bad consequences. I will make the case that the good consequences are likely to outweigh the bad consequences.[23] In other words, I will argue that the distribution with the best overall consequences is likely to be epistemically permissible.

Knowledge that Harms Others

Having additional knowledge is sometimes harmful to other people (cf. Fallis, 2004b, p. 103). For example, when terrorists acquire more knowledge about reservoirs and dams, they are better able to harm the rest of us (cf. Lichtblau, 2001). This, however, seems to be a rather unlikely scenario in the context of the digital divide.[24] Only very specific pieces of knowledge (in the hands of very specific people) would be problematic.

Having additional knowledge is rarely harmful to other people. In fact, as Bruce Kingma (2001, p. 69) points out, people usually benefit from other people having knowledge. For example, we are better off if other people are better informed about traffic laws, disease prevention, and the democratic process as a result of access to information technology. Thus, it seems likely that the benefits of knowledge will outweigh these risks.

Knowledge that Harms the Knower

In addition to sometimes being harmful to others, having additional knowledge is sometimes harmful to the people who have it (cf. Nozick, 1993, pp. 69-70). The knower is certainly *epistemically* better off, but she might be worse off *all things considered*. For example, a person who is trying to quit smoking is better off not knowing where her roommate keeps his cigarettes.[25] This worry about harm coming to the knower has actually been raised in the context of the digital divide. For example, Soraj Hongladarom (2002, pp. 4-7) describes how a culture can be destabilized by access to information that comes from other cultures (cf. De George, 2003, p. 258).

In fact, a culture can be destabilized by access to information that comes from that very culture. For example, Michael Brown (2003, p. 34) describes a case where ethnographic (in this case, religious) knowledge had been collected about an Aboriginal tribe in Australia. The tribe had reason to believe that the dissemination of this knowledge within their community would have bad consequences.[26] In particular, they were worried that it would "undermine the social and religious stability of their hard-pressed community" if this knowledge got into the hands of "children, women, and uninitiated Aboriginal men."

Even so, it is again only very specific pieces of knowledge that would be problematic. In general, having additional knowledge is beneficial to the knower.[27] Knowledge allows people to figure out how to get what they want (cf. Goldman, 1999, pp. 73-74). Knowledge about job opportunities and about political candidates are just two examples. In fact, there is evolutionary pressure for people to be successful at acquiring knowledge (cf. Papineau, 2000). Our ancestors were only able to pass on their genes because they knew things like whether a predator was nearby and where food could be found.

This suggests that information policies that facilitate knowledge acquisition will typically have good consequences for the people who acquire the knowledge. Thus, in evaluating information policies, it makes sense for us to focus on practices that lead to epistemically permissible distributions. This is so despite the fact that such policies will, in rare circumstances, have some bad consequences. Consider an analogy. Public health policies that facilitate hygiene will typically have good consequences. Thus, it makes sense for public health officials to focus on hygienic practices, even though there is a small chance that such practices will have some bad consequences. For example, it was actually better hygiene that led to the outbreak of polio at the beginning of the twentieth century (cf. Rogers, 1992).

Finally, there is one particular way in which having additional knowledge can harm the knower that should be explicitly addressed. Namely, more knowledge can actually sometimes lead people to acquire false beliefs that can have bad consequences (cf. Nozick, 1993, p. 69).[28] For example, it is frequently better not to perform a diagnostic test, even if that test accurately reports the presence of indicators of disease (cf. van den Hoven, 1995, p. 10; Kolata, 2001). On learning the results of such tests, patients often overestimate the likelihood of disease and undertake unnecessary (and sometimes harmful) courses of treatment. For similar reasons, evidence is sometimes excluded from a court of law, even though it is accurate, because the jury is likely to misestimate its probative value (cf. Goldman, 1999, p. 294). With their limited experience with information technology, it seems legitimate to worry that the information have-nots might make such errors (for example, be misled by inaccurate information on the Internet).

However, the appropriate solution (in the general case as well as in the specific context of the digital divide) is not to provide people with less knowledge, but to provide them with even more knowledge. For example, it is better to educate juries so that they will not be misled by evidence (cf. Goldman, 1999, p. 295). Similarly, it is better to teach people how to evaluate the accuracy of information on the Internet rather than simply keeping them from accessing this information (cf. Fallis, 2000, pp. 313-314).

Inequalities in Knowledge Possession

There is another way in which having additional knowledge can have bad consequences that are especially relevant in the context of the digital divide. It is possible to increase the amount of knowledge that everybody possesses and, at the same time, to increase the digital divide. In other words, it is possible that an epistemically permissible distribution will involve huge inequalities between the amount of knowledge possessed by the information haves and the amount of knowledge possessed by the information have-nots.

Here is an example of how this can happen: One way in which people have tried to reduce inequalities in access to information technology is by providing free Internet access at public libraries. This policy certainly has the benefit of increasing the amount of knowledge that information have-nots are able to acquire. However, it turns out that the people that make the most use of such access tend to be those that already have Internet access at home (cf. Hull, 2003, p. 135). Thus, providing such access would actually seem to increase, rather than reduce, the knowledge gap between the information haves and the information have-nots.[29]

Such inequalities can harm the information have-nots, even if they have more knowledge than they would have had otherwise (cf. van den Hoven, 1995, p. 16). For example, people often prefer to have a lesser amount of some good (for example, income, beauty, knowledge) and do better relative to others than to have a greater amount of that good and do worse relative to others (see Solnick & Hemenway, 1998). But it is not necessarily just a matter of preferences not being satisfied. Huge inequalities in the distribution of knowledge might allow the information haves to impose their will on the information have-nots (cf. Moss, 2002).[30] For example, investment advisers, automobile repairmen, and totalitarian governments have all been known to take advantage of people's ignorance. Thus, the overall costs of distributing knowledge in a way that involves huge inequalities might very well exceed the epistemic benefits.[31]

However, the epistemically *impermissible* "egalitarian" distribution is not the only way to avoid such inequalities. It is also clearly possible to bring about epistemically *permissible* distributions that do not involve huge inequalities. We can increase knowledge possession and minimize inequalities by engaging in activities that are specifically designed to make the information have-nots better off. For example, instead of providing free Internet access equally in all public libraries, we might put more of our resources toward providing free Internet access in public libraries in poorer neighborhoods. In addition, we might put more of our resources toward giving information have-nots the online skills that will allow them to take advantage of this access.

Furthermore, epistemically permissible distributions that do not involve huge inequalities will arguably have very good consequences.[32] As noted earlier, for example, we are typically better off if other people are well informed about all sorts of things. Thus, while many epistemically permissible distributions may involve huge inequalities and have bad consequences, there also seem to be many epistemically permissible distributions that do not. In other words, by focusing on epistemically permissible distributions, we are not limiting ourselves to suboptimal outcomes.

The High Cost of Acquiring Knowledge

There is yet another way in which having additional knowledge can have bad consequences. Even where the knowledge itself is a good thing, the cost of acquiring the knowledge can sometimes exceed the benefits of having the knowledge (cf. Rescher, 1989, pp. 9-10).[33] For example, certain scientific experiments are too expensive (or even unethical) to perform, even though they would allow us to acquire more knowledge. In the context of the digital divide, it might be that money spent improving access to information technology could be better spent on other things, such as food or housing.

In fact, it seems quite likely that we could reach a point of diminishing returns when it comes to improving access to information technology. The marginal value of an additional unit of almost any good decreases (cf. Kingma, 2001, pp. 30-31). For example, the more barrels of oil that you own, the less an additional barrel is worth to you. The same undoubtedly applies to knowledge.[34] As a result, there will probably be a point where using any more of our limited resources to facilitate knowledge acquisition will make us worse off overall. Thus, it might be that the distribution with the best overall consequences is such that someone could have had more knowledge (without anybody else having less). In other words, it might be that the distribution with the best overall consequences is not epistemically permissible.

However, this does not mean that we should ignore the recommendations of epistemic value theory as Goldman suggests. This only means that we need to slightly modify our definitions of "epistemically permissible" and "epistemically required." In particular, we should say that a distribution of knowledge D is *epistemically permissible* if no other distribution that we can actually bring about *using the very same resources* is epistemically better than D.[35] In other words, epistemic permissibility should be relativized to the amount of resources that will be used to bring about a new distribution of knowledge. In that case, even if knowledge has declining marginal utility, we should still follow the recommendations of epistemic value theory and aim for a distribution of knowledge that is epistemically permissible.

Of course, if epistemic permissibility is relativized in this way, then we cannot use epistemic value theory to identify a distribution to aim for until we know how much of our resources should be allocated toward facilitating the acquisition of knowledge. In other words, we need to know how the benefits of knowledge compare with the benefits of other goods that we might pursue. But, unsurprisingly, this is not a question that epistemology can answer by itself.

The Value of Epistemic Value Theory

Even if the distribution with the best overall consequences is among the epistemically permissible distributions, we still have to identify this distribution. In order to do this, we have to do an all-things-considered evaluation of the epistemically permissible distributions. But since we are going to have to do all-things-considered evaluations anyway, someone might object that epistemic value theory is not doing any work. It might seem simpler to just follow Goldman's suggestion and do an all-things-considered evaluation of all the distributions of knowledge that we might bring about.

There is a practical advantage, however, to focusing on epistemically permissible distributions of knowledge. By doing so, we speed up our search for a specific distribution of knowledge to aim for. We *only* have to do an all-things-considered evaluation of the epistemically permissible distributions (that is, the distributions that we have determined to have good epistemic consequences).

Also, from the perspective of the epistemologist at least, there is a beneficial side effect to following the recommendations of epistemic value theory. By focusing on epistemically permissible distributions, we retain the normative role that has always been central to work in epistemology. If we followed Goldman's suggestion, the normativity of epistemology would be completely captured by the normativity of means-ends rationality. We could criticize people for choosing bad means to their epistemic ends. But we could not criticize people for choosing bad epistemic ends (such as ignorance or error).[36]

Conclusion

In order to evaluate policies for dealing with the digital divide, we need to identify the distribution of knowledge that has the best consequences. Since the principal value of access to information technology is that it leads to *knowledge*, work in epistemology can arguably help us to identify this distribution. Unfortunately, epistemic value theory cannot provide all of the answers that we will need. In particular, there may not be a single distribution of knowledge that is epistemically required. As a result, we will still have to determine which of the epistemically permissible distributions of knowledge to aim for.

Even so, there is further work to be done to sharpen and supplement the answers that epistemic value theory can give. First, I have focused on just a few of the constraints on the epistemic betterness relation that are relevant to evaluating information policies. However, in order to evaluate policies for dealing with the digital divide, it would be useful to have a complete list of constraints that are relevant to whether one distribution of knowledge is epistemically better than another. The exercise of using epistemic value theory to evaluate information policies can help us to compile such a list. Second, I have argued that the distribution with the best overall consequences is likely to be an epistemically permissible distribution. It would be useful to empirically confirm this. Finally, I have claimed that epistemology can only tell us, for a fixed amount of resources, which distributions of knowledge are epistemically permissible. Thus, in order to determine how much of our limited resources should be allocated toward dealing with inequalities in access to information technology, it would be useful to know how the benefits of knowledge compare with the benefits of other goods that we might pursue.

References

Broome, J. (1991). *Weighing goods*. Cambridge, MA: Basil Blackwell.

Brown, M. F. (2003). *Who owns native culture?* Cambridge, MA: Harvard.

Camp, L. J., & Tsang, R. P. (2000). Universal service in a ubiquitous digital network. *Ethics and Information Technology, 2*, 211-221.

Chabrán, R. (2001). Immigrants, global digital economies, cyber segmentation, and emergent information services. In S. Luévano Molina (ed.), *Immigrant politics and the public library* (pp. 131-140). Westport, CT: Greenwood.

Chisholm, R. (1977). *Theory of knowledge*. Englewood Cliffs, NJ: Prentice-Hall.

Compaine, B. M. (2001). Declare the war won. In B. M. Compaine (Ed.), *The digital divide: Facing a crisis or creating a myth?* (pp. 315-335). Cambridge, MA: MIT.

De George, R. T. (2003). *The ethics of information technology and business*. Malden, MA: Blackwell.

Doctor, R. D. (1992). Social equity and information technologies: Moving toward information democracy. *Annual Review of Information Science and Technology, 27*, 43-96.

Egan, M., & Shera, J. (1952). Foundations of a theory of bibliography. *Library Quarterly, 44*, 125-137.

Ekelund, R. B. (1970). Price discrimination and product differentiation in economic theory: An early analysis. *Quarterly Journal of Economics, 84*, 268-278.

Erdelez, S., & Houston, R. D. (2004). The digital divide: Who really benefits from the proposed solutions for closing the gap? *Journal of Information Ethics, 13*, 19-33.

Fallis, D. (2000). Veritistic social epistemology and information science. *Social Epistemology, 14*, 305-316.

Fallis, D. (2002). Goldman on probabilistic inference. *Philosophical Studies, 109*, 223-240.

Fallis, D. (2004a). Social epistemology and the digital divide. In J. Weckert & Y. Al-Saggaf (Eds.), *Conferences in research and practice in information technology* (Vol. 37, pp. 79-84). Sydney, Australia: Australian Computer Society. Available at http://www.crpit.com/confpapers/CRPITV37Fallis.pdf

Fallis, D. (2004b). Epistemic value theory and information ethics. *Minds and Machines, 14*, 101-117.

Fallis, D. (2006). Social epistemology and information science. *Annual Review of Information Science and Technology, 40*.

Garnham, N. (1999). Amartya Sen's "capabilities" approach to the evaluation of welfare: Its application to communications. In A. Calabrese & J. C. Burgelman (Eds.), *Communication, citizenship and social policy* (pp. 113-124). Lanham, MD: Rowman and Littlefield.

Goldman, A. I. (1987). Foundations of social epistemics. *Synthese, 73*, 109-144.

Goldman, A. I. (1999). *Knowledge in a social world*. New York: Oxford.

Goldman, A. I. (2002). Reply to commentators. *Philosophy and Phenomenological Research, 64*, 215-227.

Hacker, K. L., & Mason, S. M. (2003). Ethical gaps in studies of the digital divide. *Ethics and Information Technology, 5*, 99-115.

Hamburg, M., Ramist, L. E., & Bommer, M. R. W. (1972). Library objectives and performance measures and their use in decision making. *Library Quarterly, 42*, 107-128.

Harman, G. (1986). *Change in view*. Cambridge, MA: MIT.

Hongladarom, S. (2002). *Hope in the information society*. Available at http://pioneer. netserv.chula.ac.th/~hsoraj/web/Hope.pdf

Hull, B. (2003). ICT and social exclusion: The role of libraries. *Telematics and Informatics, 20*, 131-142.

James, F. (2001, February 7). FCC's Powell makes clear contrast with predecessor. *Chicago Tribune*.

Johnson, D. G. (1991). Equal access to computing, computing expertise, and decision making about computers. In R. Dejoie, G. Fowler, & D. Paradice (Eds.), *Ethical issues in information systems* (pp. 210-218). Boston: Boyd & Fraser.

Kingma, B. R. (2001). *The economics of information* (2nd ed.). Englewood, CO: Libraries Unlimited.

Kirkwood, C. W. (1997). *Strategic decision making.* Belmont, CA: Duxbury Press.

Kolata, G. (2001, December 30). Questions grow over usefulness of some routine cancer tests. *New York Times.*

Levi, I. (1967). *Gambling with truth.* Cambridge, MA: MIT.

Lievrouw, L. A., & Farb, S. E. (2003). Information and equity. *Annual Review of Information Science and Technology, 37,* 499-540.

Lichtblau, E. (2001, November 18). Rising fears that what we do know can hurt us. *Los Angeles Times.*

Maher, P. (1993). *Betting on theories.* New York: Cambridge University Press.

Moss, J. (2002). Power and the digital divide. *Ethics and Information Technology, 4,* 159-165.

Mueller, M. L. (2001). Universal service policies as wealth redistribution. In B. M. Compaine (Ed.), *The digital divide: Facing a crisis or creating a myth?* (pp. 179-187). Cambridge, MA: MIT.

Nozick, R. (1993). *The nature of rationality.* Princeton, NJ: Princeton University.

Papineau, D. (2000). The evolution of knowledge. In P. Carruthers & A. Chamberlain (Eds.), *Evolution and the human mind* (pp. 170-206). Cambridge, UK: Cambridge University Press.

Quine, W. V. O. (1969). Epistemology naturalized. In *Ontological relativity and other essays* (pp. 69-90). New York: Columbia University.

Rawls, J. (1971). *A theory of justice.* Cambridge, MA: Harvard University.

Rescher, N. (1989). *Cognitive economy.* Pittsburgh, PA: University of Pittsburgh.

Rogers, N. (1992). *Dirt and disease.* New Brunswick, NJ: Rutgers University.

Sartwell, C. (1992). Why knowledge is merely true belief. *Journal of Philosophy, 89,* 167-180.

Shapiro, C., & Varian, H. R. (1999). *Information rules.* Boston: Harvard Business School.

Solnick, S. J., & Hemenway, D. (1998). Is more always better?: A survey on positional concerns. *Journal of Economic Behavior and Organization, 37,* 373-383.

Tichenor, P. J., Donohue, G. A., & Olien, C. N. (1970). Mass media flow and differential growth in knowledge. *Public Opinion Quarterly, 34,* 159-170.

United Nations. (1948). *Universal declaration of human rights.* Available at http://www.un.org/Overview/rights.html

van den Hoven, M. J. (1995). Equal access and social justice: Information as a primary good. In *ETHICOMP95: An International Conference on the Ethi-*

cal Issues of Using Information Technology (pp. 1-17). Leicester, UK: De Montfort University.

Endnotes

1 There is certainly a sense in which printed materials, and even clay tablets, count as information technology. In this chapter, however, information technology will refer exclusively to digital or electronic devices.

2 As Hacker and Mason (2003, p. 102) point out, there are actually many different digital divides (for example, between ethnicities, between genders, between urban communities and rural communities, between rich and poor nations). In this chapter, however, I will focus on the digital divide that cuts along socioeconomic lines within a single society.

3 See Fallis (2004a, pp. 79-80) for a more detailed discussion of these arguments.

4 Johnson (1991), Doctor (1992), and van den Hoven (1995) are a few authors that do address this issue.

5 This chapter will be concerned with which policies have the best consequences. Of course, there may also be non-consequentialist reasons for adopting particular policies. However, many (if not all) such reasons can be incorporated into a consequentialist framework with a sufficiently broad notion of *consequence* (cf. Broome, 1991, pp. 3-4).

6 This chapter is a substantially revised version of Fallis (2004a).

7 At a press conference, he once quipped that "there's a Mercedes divide. I'd like to have one; I can't afford one" (quoted in James, 2001).

8 In a similar vein, it has frequently been suggested that knowledge acquisition is the main consideration when evaluating library policies (cf. Egan & Shera, 1952, p. 132; Hamburg et al., 1972, p. 111).

9 Access to information technology is not intrinsically valuable (cf. Chabrán, 2001, p. 138; Hacker & Mason, 2003, pp. 103-104). It is only valuable if it is a means to other things that we care about. For example, unless content that is relevant to one's interests is available and one has certain online skills (for example, the ability to find, read, and evaluate such content), there is little benefit to having access to the Internet.

10 Knowledge can also be intrinsically valuable (cf. Goldman, 1999, p. 75). However, in the context of the digital divide, we are primarily concerned with its instrumental value.

11 In his work on distributive justice, John Rawls (1971, p. 92) adopts this same sort of strategy when evaluating social policies in general. He focuses on *primary goods* rather than on the diverse benefits of having such goods (cf. Kirkwood, 1997, pp. 24-25). Primary goods, such as liberty and income, are "things that every rational man [sic] is presumed to want. These goods normally have a use whatever a person's rational plan of life" (Rawls, 1971, p. 62).

12 It might be suggested that we ought to be concerned with the distribution of the *capability* of acquiring knowledge rather than with the distribution of knowledge itself (cf. Garnham, 1999). The intuition here is that people should be allowed to choose for themselves how they make use of their capabilities. (In addition, we cannot actually distribute knowledge itself; we can only distribute the means to acquiring knowledge.) However, the capacity to acquire knowledge is only valuable because knowledge itself is valuable (cf. Goldman, 1999, p. 351). As a result, in

this chapter, I will focus on the distribution of knowledge. In any event, what I have to say about distributing knowledge should also apply to distributing the capacity to acquire knowledge.

[13]   In his work on social epistemology, Goldman (1999, p. 24) defines knowledge as true belief (cf. Sartwell, 1992). Thus, he actually refers to his epistemic value theory as a theory of "veritistic value." However, nothing in this chapter will turn on the precise definition of knowledge that we adopt.

[14]   Value theory in general places certain minimal constraints (for example, transitivity) on any *betterness* relation (cf. Broome, 1991). Epistemic value theory simply adds additional constraints.

[15]   This is a *ceteris paribus* constraint. For example, when there is a conflict, it does not say whether it is better for person X to have more knowledge or for person Y to have more knowledge.

[16]   This distribution is only "utilitarian" in the sense that it maximizes the average amount of some particular good. In this case, the good in question is *knowledge* rather than *happiness*.

[17]   Even if there are additional constraints on the epistemic betterness relation, the "utilitarian" distribution does not seem to be epistemically required. A similar critique can be made with respect to other parts of his epistemic value theory. For example, Goldman (1999, p. 89) claims that the epistemic benefit of a true belief has the same magnitude as the epistemic cost of a false belief. However, while this may be an epistemically permissible value assignment, it does not seem to be epistemically required (cf. Fallis, 2002).

[18]   This is analogous to a standard criticism of utilitarianism in general (cf. Rawls, 1971, p. 26).

[19]   The same sort of scenario arises with access to information technology (cf. Shapiro & Varian, 1999, pp. 56-57).

[20]   Although Rawls himself does not explicitly discuss *knowledge*, it clearly counts as a primary good (cf. Nozick, 1993, p. 68; van den Hoven, 1995).

[21]   The justification for this theory of distributive justice is that it is what people would adopt in a *fair* deliberation (see Rawls, 1971, pp. 17-22). In other words, it is what people would agree to if they did not already know what their position in society would be. Appealing to such a hypothetical agreement is especially appropriate in the context of the digital divide. Erdelez and Houston (2002) provide evidence that what people think should be done about the digital divide depends a lot on their position in society.

[22]   Article 19 of the "Universal Declaration of Human Rights' states that "everyone has the right … to seek, receive and impart information and ideas through any media and regardless of frontiers." Also, aiming for the Rawlsian distribution supports the adoption of universal service policies (cf. Camp & Tsang, 2000).

[23]   It will require empirical study to conclusively establish that the good consequences (which include the diverse benefits of having knowledge as well as the intrinsic value of knowledge) will outweigh the bad consequences.

[24]   For example, it is doubtful that information have-nots are more likely to be terrorists.

[25]   Also, as an anonymous referee pointed out, we are probably all better off not knowing the time and manner of our own deaths.

[26]   This is in contrast to the more standard worry about indigenous knowledge getting into the hands of outsiders (cf. Brown, 2003, pp. 11-42). In response to this example, it might be objected that the tribe was simply wrong about the dissemination of this knowledge having bad consequences. In particular, we might think that things will typically be better if the uninitiated are not kept in the dark. But I will not press this objection.

[27]   There are many diverse benefits of having knowledge. As suggested previously, knowledge is what Rawls would refer to as a primary good.

[28]   This can happen even if the knower only has epistemic interests. For example, if a scientist knows which subjects are in the experimental group and which subjects are in the control group, it can potentially bias the results of the experiment. Also, more knowledge can sometimes lead people to acquire fewer true beliefs. For example, if I did know the time and manner of my own death, I might lack the motivation to go out and learn new things.

[29]   Under the "Rawlsian" distribution of knowledge, any inequalities in knowledge possession must be to the advantage of the information have-nots, but such inequalities might still end up being very large. In other words, the "Rawlsian" distribution is consistent with a very wide digital divide.

[30]   Such large inequalities might also have bad consequences if the information have-nots were to violently overthrow their oppressors.

[31]   In this case, the bad consequences flow from the *distribution* of the knowledge rather than from the *content* of the knowledge.

[32]   In a similar vein, utilitarians often argue that, as a matter of fact, overall happiness tends to be greater when happiness is more equally distributed (cf. Broome, 1991, pp. 175-177).

[33]   Even if there were no financial costs associated with acquiring the knowledge, there would typically be *opportunity costs*, such as time spent in the classroom (cf. Kingma, 2001, p. 127).

[34]   In fact, beyond a certain point, additional knowledge may even be counterproductive (cf. Harman, 1986, p. 12).

[35]   In a similar vein, in discussions of the value of evidence in science, authors (for example, Maher, 1993, p. 173) typically make the assumption that gathering evidence has a fixed (usually, zero) cost. In addition, the necessity of this sort of amendment is not unique to *epistemic* value theory. It is going to be necessary for any specialized theory of value (for example, nutritionally better, aesthetically better, hygienically better, etc.).

[36]   There are a few philosophers (for example, Quine, 1969) who have suggested that epistemology should be such a purely descriptive enterprise.

Chapter III

Justifying Intellectual Property Protection:
Why the Interests of Content Creators Usually Win Over Everyone Else's

Kenneth Einar Himma
Seattle Pacific University, USA

Abstract

I argue that the law should provide limited protection of intellectual property interests. To this end, I argue that whether the law ought to coercively restrict liberty depends on an assessment of all competing interests. Further, I argue that the interests of content creators in controlling the disposition of the content they create outweigh the interests of other persons in using that content in most, but not all, cases. I conclude that, in these cases, morality protects the interests of content creators, but not the interests of other persons and hence would justify limited legal protection of the content creators' interests.

Introduction

Whether or not intellectual property rights ought, as a matter of political morality, to be protected by the law surely depends on what kinds of interests the various parties have in intellectual content. Although theorists disagree on the limits of morally legitimate lawmaking authority, this much seems obvious: the coercive power of the law should be employed only to protect interests that rise to a certain level of moral importance; indeed, it would be wrong for the law to coercively restrict behaviors in which no one has any morally significant interests (i.e., interests that are important enough from the standpoint of morality that they receive some protection from moral principles) whatsoever.

In this essay, I argue that the interests that content creators have in the content they create (or discover) outweigh the interests of other persons in all cases not involving content that is necessary for human beings to survive, thrive or flourish in certain important ways. While this might not imply the existence of moral rights to intellectual property, it surely provides a strong reason for affording some stringent legal protection to the interests of content creators in the contents of their creations. And one eminently sensible way of protecting their interests is for the law to allow them limited control over the disposition of their creations.

Nevertheless, this should not be taken to imply any sort of endorsement of copyright law as it is currently formulated in the U.S. or in any other nation. For what it is worth, I think it quite reasonable to believe that various elements of these laws are morally problematic and hence should be rethought and reformulated. For example, though I cannot argue the point here, I think it fair to say that the existing length of copyright protection in the U.S. lacks an adequate justifying rationale. My point in this essay is not to offer a sympathetic analysis of any body of existing copyright law, but is rather to show that the interests of content creators deserve some reasonably stringent legal protection. How much protection, however, is not something I will address here.[1]

Learning from Locke

The Lockean Approach to Justifying Property Rights in Material Objects

It is instructive to begin with a brief look at the classical Lockean argument for original acquisition of property (i.e., conversion of an object that no one owns into an object that someone owns). Locke realized that the existence of a moral right to property depends critically on the idea that persons can acquire a property right in objects to which no one else has a prior moral claim or entitlement (i.e., objects that are not the property of anyone else). Here it is helpful to note that the idea that one can acquire a property right in something that *is* antecedently owned by someone else is comparatively unproblematic: if I own X and am hence morally entitled to dispose of it as I see fit, then it seems clear that I may transfer my property right in X to you by giving X to you, selling X to you, or otherwise abandoning my claim in X. Although it might not be entirely clear exactly why it is that I can do this, there are no obvious problems, from the standpoint of ordinary intuition, with the idea that one person can transfer a property right to another person.

Original acquisition of property, however, is another story because our appropriating something that does not belong to us bears some resemblance to theft. While theft is, strictly speaking, the intentional appropriation of *someone else's* property without permission or legitimate authorization, the idea that one can take some object out of the commons—an object that does not belong to anyone—and make it one's own without the consent of any other person requires some justification. If, as Locke expressed the concern, God gave the world to all humanity in common, there is a puzzle about how it is that any one person can acquire an exclusive property right in some worldly object.

Locke's solution is, of course, justifiably famous and remains the foundation for much classically liberal theorizing about property rights. According to Locke:

Though the earth and all inferior creatures be common to all men, yet every man has a property in his own person; this nobody has any right to but himself. The labor of his body and the work of his hands we may say are properly his. Whatsoever, then, he removes out of the state that nature hath provided and left it in, he hath mixed his labor with, and joined to it something that is his own and thereby makes it his property. It being by him removed from the common state nature placed it in, it hath by this labor something annexed to it that excludes the common right of other men. (Locke, 1690, Chapter V)

There are at least two different constructions of this argument grounded in Locke's claim that we have a moral property right in our bodies and hence in our labor. On one interpretation, we acquire a property right in antecedently unowned objects in which we labor because we literally *mix* our labor and hence our property into those objects; since our property is inextricably mixed into such objects, we attain a moral right to them that is parasitic on our moral right to our labor. On the other interpretation, we acquire a property right in antecedently unowned objects that we improve by our labor because our labor creates value that did not exist in the world; since we created that new value with our labor and hence with our property, it follows that we have a right to the objects we improve with our labor provided that no one else has an antecedent claim to them.

Either way, the problems with the Lockean argument are as well-known as the argument itself. First, it is simply not clear that it makes sense to think of our relationships to our bodies as a property relation. While we naturally use the term "my" to refer to our bodies, we do not intend this pronoun in the same way that we use it in talking about other objects. I am not my house, but I am, in part, my body. To characterize the relationship between me and my body as one of ownership seems misleading at best and confused at worst.[2]

Second, and more importantly, it simply does not follow from Locke's premises that we have a property right in those unowned objects we improve with our labor. It might very well be that we forfeit the expenditure of our labor or the value we create when we labor on some object that does not belong to us. If I swim out to the middle of the Atlantic Ocean and somehow fence off a portion and improve it by cleaning it of all pollution, most people will agree that I do not thereby acquire a property right in that portion of the ocean. The claim that I own my labor, even if true, does not imply that I own whatever material entities I mix it with or use my labor to improve.[3]

Not surprisingly, the consensus among property theorists is that the argument as Locke specifically formulates it is unsuccessful in justifying property rights—though many theorists, including myself, believe that Locke is on the right track and continue to tinker with the Lockean argument to produce a viable justification for property rights.

Applying the Lockean Approach to Intellectual Objects

It is important to note that both interpretations of Locke's argument for original acquisition of material property depend critically on the assumption that we causally interact with pre-existing material objects. To "mix" one's labor with some pre-existing object is, at the very least, to causally interact with that object. I can put my labor into a piece of wood only because I can causally interact with the wood in the following sense: my labor changes the form taken by the piece of wood. Likewise, we can improve some material object only by changing it in a way that is more easily appropriated for the satisfaction of human wants or needs. It should be clear that we can *change* a material object only by causally interacting with it.

Even if Locke's argument were successful in justifying original acquisition of material property, it does not have any direct or obvious application to intellectual property because this assumption does not apply to intellectual content. If it makes sense to think of intellectual content as constituting objects that exist independently of us, they are *abstract* objects with radically different properties from material or mental objects (i.e., ideas, thought, perceptions, etc.). In contrast to material objects, abstract objects, if such there be, lack extension, solidity, and spatio-temporal location; it should be clear, for example, that the object denoted by the symbol "2" is an entity of a very special kind: it is intangible and neither here nor there. In contrast to mental objects, abstract objects exist without being present to anyone's consciousness; it seems reasonable to think that the number denoted by "2" and the proposition expressed by "2 + 2 = 4" exist in a world where there are no minds to think about those objects.

Of course, there are some difficult issues regarding the nature of certain artistic content.[4] It seems clear, for example, that a sculptor mixes her labor (and hence causally interacts) with pre-existing materials when she creates a sculpture; sculptures are, after all, physical objects. Here it is helpful to note that the sculptor has potentially two interests here. One is in the physical object that is the sculpture, but this is not the relevant interest from the standpoint of intellectual property debates; there is no issue, after all, about whether the sculptor can exclude people from appropriating the physical object that is that particular sculpture. The relevant interest is the sculptor's interest in the "content" of that sculpture; her interest is in protecting the content of that sculpture so that it cannot be reproduced in some other material object. (At this point, no claim is being made about the legitimacy of this interest.) Although the ontological nature of this content is not entirely clear, I am inclined to think that it is an abstract object—perhaps something like the "form" (though not necessarily Platonic form) that the sculpture has.

However, if the ontological character of sculptural content is not entirely clear, it should be clear that much intellectual content has the form of an abstract object. A set of propositions, such as is expressed by a novel, constitutes an abstract object that contains as its members abstract objects, since both sets and propositions are abstract objects if anything is an abstract object. Likewise, a string of linguistic symbols (as opposed to their representations on a page) is an abstract object containing abstract objects as members if, again, anything is an abstract object. Accordingly, novels, plays, and other forms of intellectual content that are linguistic in character are abstract objects.

What this means, it seems, is that we cannot causally interact with such objects—assuming they exist in a genuine way and are not merely theoretical posits. I can think about the abstract object denoted by "2," but I cannot causally interact with that object in any way. I can express some idea about "2" by means of the appropriate linguistic representation and communicate that idea to you, but I do not seem to have any direct causal access to that object; I cannot perceive "2" by any of the five senses, nor is it plausible to think that I have a sixth sense made for "perceiving" abstract objects. An abstract object might be important enough to warrant the expenditure of a great deal of human energy, but that energy will not be appropriately spent trying to causally interact with it. Reasoning about an abstract object is the way in which we come to understand it and does not involve causal interaction with such objects.[5]

It is not clear what Locke thought, if anything, about intellectual property, but the foregoing analysis suggests that neither version of the classical Lockean argument can be directly deployed to justify property rights in, at the very least, intellectual objects that are linguistic in character, such as novels, poems, and so forth. If I cannot causally interact with abstract objects, then I can neither mix my labor with an abstract object nor use my labor to create new value by improving some existing abstract intellectual object. The Lockean argument—as he formulated it—would have to be modified in some significant way to apply to these intellectual objects. Further, if all intellectual content is abstract in character, as seems eminently reasonable to me, the Lockean argument would have to be modified to apply to any intellectual content whatsoever. As Locke formulates the argument, it has no bearing on the issues of intellectual property that currently divide us.

The Deeper Insight in the Lockean Arguments

Despite these problems, however, I think that the Lockean argument points in the direction of a more promising approach to justifying legal protection of both material and intellectual property. While it is undoubtedly true that the mere fact that I expend my labor in some unowned object does not imply that I have a property right to that object, the fact that I labored on the object is of obvious moral significance in deciding whether I have any moral claim to the object. After all, it seems clear that I have a morally significant interest in my body and its activities. If this interest is not sufficient to immediately confer some sort of right in me to things on which I labor, it is a consideration that surely weighs in favor of my having a property right (of some strength) in those things. It might not entail such a right and might be outweighed by other considerations, but it is surely one consideration that must figure into determining whether I have such a right.

Similarly, it seems reasonable to think that the interests of other people in such objects will also figure into determining whether one has something resembling a property right in some object. One of the most plausible reasons for thinking that I cannot acquire a property right in some portion of the Atlantic Ocean by laboring on it is the importance of other persons' interests in the ocean. My acquiring a property right in some significant portion of the ocean can cause tremendous damage to the interests of others. If I also had a right to the airspace above it, for example, this could make it much harder to ship necessities from one part of the world to the other.

This is not to deny that the fact that I expended labor on that portion of the ocean is a consideration that operates in favor of my having some sort of claim to that portion of the ocean (or perhaps instead to some compensation). It seems reasonable to think that I fail to acquire a property right in that portion of the ocean, not because the fact that I labored on it counts for nothing, but rather because the interest I have in the labor I spent on that portion is greatly outweighed by the interests that other people have in that portion of the ocean.

If the two interpretations of the Lockean justification of material property rights fail to show that the expenditure of labor is sufficient to create property rights in intellectual or material objects, they are suggestive of a plausible approach for determining whether someone should be afforded a limited legal right to exclude others from appropriation of an object. To determine whether the law should allow someone to exclude others from appropriating some material or intellectual object, we must weigh all the competing interests. If my interests in X outweigh the interests of all other parties, then that fact is a pretty good reason (though not necessarily a conclusive one) to think that my interests in X are justifiably protected by the law.

Of course, I do not pretend to have some sort of algorithm for assessing the various interests.[6] Weighing competing interests is a messy, imprecise business that relies much more heavily on gut reactions and feels than other ethical arguments—though it is fair to say that all ethical theorizing—applied, general, and meta-ethical—is, at the end of the day, grounded in such gut-level intuitions. The imprecise character of such reasoning surely diminishes the level of confidence we can have in any conclusions it supports. Even so, there are easy cases. One reason that most people agree that it would be wrong for me to shoot someone in the back as he flees with my stolen property is that our interests in life are much more weighty than our interests in property; in just about every case, a thief's interest in his life is much more important than my interest in the property he steals from me.[7] Life, after all, is sacred and property is not. For this reason (or something like it), most people, and the criminal law in every Western nation, agree that property may not be defended with deadly force.

I think there are some fairly easy assessments in the case of intellectual objects. As I will argue next, content creators have a stronger interest in the time and effort they expend in creating content not needed to survive or thrive than the interests that other persons have in that content. Since I lack an algorithm for assessing these interests, my argument will rely on certain gut-level intuitive reactions to certain cases. But although I do not have an argument for thinking that my reactions to these cases are the correct ones, I think most readers will share my reactions to these cases and are hence committed to the conclusions I defend in this chapter.

Assessing the Interests of Content Creators and Other Parties

Content Creators: The Value of Time and Labor

This much should be clear at the outset: content creators have a *prudential* interest (i.e., an interest from the standpoint of objective or perceived self-interest) in controlling use and dissemination of their creations. To devote time and energy to creating intellectual content, time and energy must be diverted from other activities. This means that any particular deployment of time and energy involves costs that are significant from the standpoint of prudential rationality (i.e., those standards governing rational self-regarding or self-interested behavior), including opportunity costs involved when one foregoes other opportunities to devote resources to a particular activity.

It also seems clear that we have a strong prudential interest in not wasting or squandering time and energy. Even if I do not feel like working, my time could be spent doing something that has value to me. Though we tend (incorrectly, on my view) to think of play and rest as counterproductive, I think it is clear that sometimes time invested in rest and recreation is well spent. As paradoxical as this may sound, I would rather not waste time that can be spent watching or playing basketball when I have that time available for those purposes.

It is important not to underestimate the significance of this prudential interest. My time and energy matter a great deal to me because I know that I have a limited supply of both. Like everyone else, I am a finite being with an all-too-limited life span. Every moment I devote to a particular task spends one of a limited supply of moments I have in life to do all the things that make life worth living. Squandering these moments is nothing less important than squandering precious bits of my life.

The importance of this prudential interest seems to grow with time; the older I get, the more precious my time and energy seem to me. There are three reasons for this—one biological and the others psychological. First, and most obviously, our supply of time and energy is diminished over time as we get nearer to the end of our lives. Second, we tend to become more sensitive to the fact of our own mortality as we grow older. It is well-known that older people have a far more acute sense of their own mortality than younger people and that this sense becomes more acute over time. Third, a person's experience of time tends to change as she grows older; the passage of a year is experienced as much quicker by an older person than by a younger person. As a general matter, these elements lead people to assign more value to expenditures of time and energy as they grow older because all draw attention to the unhappy fact that one's supply of moments is limited; sooner or later, we all die.

It seems clear, then, that, as a purely *descriptive* empirical matter, people generally regard their time and their energy as prudentially valuable.

It is true, of course, that the mere fact that people generally have a prudential interest in something tells us little about whether they have a morally-protected interest in it. By itself, the claim that X wants something does not imply that X has a morally-protected interest in it. People commonly want things, like prestige and power over others, to which morality affords no significant protection. But the point here is not just the descriptive point that people generally value their time and energy: it should also be clear that, as a normative matter of practical rationality, people *should* regard their time and energy as prudentially valuable. Someone who cares nothing about how she spends her time and energy is fairly characterized as doing a disservice to herself—if not to the community in general.

Indeed, I would be tempted to regard such an attitude as signaling some fairly serious psychological disease. Other things being equal, it is reasonable to hypothesize that someone who cares nothing about how her time and energy are spent is severely depressed, and possibly suicidal. It is clearly irrational from the standpoint of prudential interest to care so little about what is, in essence, the central resource for pursuing the goods that make life worth living. Someone who does not value her time and energy at all is, it is reasonable to hypothesize, probably in need of medical or psychological treatment. From the standpoint of prudential rationality, we *should* care about how our time and energy is spent.

Of course, morality and prudence sometimes depart. It might be that not everything that is reasonably in my interest is of moral value or receives moral protection. Perhaps it is rational from the narrow standpoint of self-interest to prefer having power over other people to not having power over other people. I am not entirely sure about even this, but it seems clear to me that such an interest has no value from the standpoint of morality and hence does not receive any moral protection—at least none specific to this particular interest.

But the idea that morality assigns no value to what is absolutely necessary to pursue any of the things that human beings ought, as a moral matter, to have seems paradoxical. We cannot pursue anything of moral value without having time and energy. If we have any interests at all that receive significant moral protection (as is true if we have any moral standing at all and especially true if we have the special status of "moral personhood") because they are morally valuable, then the limited supply of time and energy available to each of us must be valuable from the standpoint of morality, because these are the resources that must be spent to pursue any other interests at all. Having time and energy is a precondition for achieving any other interests—and this makes our time and energy very important.

At the very least, this means that, as a moral matter, we should care enough about the expenditure of our time and energy not to waste them. I think it also means that we should care enough about the time and energy of other people not to waste them. A person's time and energy are precious not only from a purely prudential point of view, but also from a morally normative point of view. We should care about our and other people's time and energy because they are so central to ensuring that human beings flourish in all the ways that human beings should flourish. This distinguishes our interests in such matters from interests that are more trivial from a moral point of view—such as our interests in even more affluent standards of living that allow us, say, to buy bigger and more expensive cars.

A stronger argument is available with respect to the moral significance of our interests in our expenditures of time (as opposed to energy or labor). It is reasonable to think that we do, and should, value *our* time (as opposed to time itself) as an end in itself—and not merely as a means. While it might be true that energy is only instrumentally valuable (i.e., valuable as a means) because it enables us to achieve other ends by doing things, time is both instrumentally and intrinsically valuable.[8] Our time is, of course, of considerable instrumental value because having some time is a necessary condition to being able to achieve *any* end; we can be and do nothing if we do not have an available supply of time. But if continued sentient life is, as seems reasonable, of considerable intrinsic value (i.e., valuable as an end in itself), then it follows that having a supply of time is also of considerable intrinsic value to a sentient being: someone who has no available time is no longer alive and hence no longer sentient. To have time to do X (for beings like us) is to be conscious for that period and have the ability to devote some of that consciousness towards performing X.

Again, there are two points here—one descriptive and one normative. The descriptive point is that people generally regard the moments of their lives as ends-in-themselves and, hence, as valuable for their own sakes. The normative point is that we *ought to* regard the moments of our lives as ends-in-themselves and hence as valuable for their own sakes. If practical rationality requires that we regard our continuing lives as intrinsically valuable, then it would seem to require that we regard the moments of our lives as intrinsically valuable—since, again, a continuing sentient life consists of the moments that a being remains sentient.

Moreover, it seems clear from the standpoint of ordinary moral intuitions that people should also regard *other people's* time as intrinsically valuable as ends-in-themselves—precisely because every other person's time is, and should be, so intrinsically valuable to her. If, as seems reasonable, we should value the *lives* of others as intrinsically valuable, then it seems to follow that we should value the moments that constitute those lives as intrinsically valuable.

This suggests that our prudential interests in time are afforded significant protection by morality. While the claim that some resource *r* is, or ought to be, regarded as *instrumentally* valuable does not imply that morality protects persons' interest in r,[9] the claim that r is—and *ought to be*—regarded as *intrinsically valuable* does seem to imply that morality protects the interest in r. As a matter of substantive moral theory, what is, and ought to be, regarded as intrinsically valuable to beings like us with the special moral status of personhood is deserving of moral respect because these values constitute our ultimate ends; and it is very difficult to make sense of the idea that we deserve respect *qua* persons if what we ought to regard as our ultimate ends do not deserve respect from others.

One plausible way of respecting this intrinsically valuable resource is to respect the interest of content creators in controlling the use and dissemination of what they have expended their time to create. To respect another person's time requires refraining from doing something that would ultimately convert a worthwhile expenditure of time into a waste of a valuable resource. And it should be clear that legal protection of the interest in controlling the use and dissemination of one's creation is a value-preserving form of respect. Paying you, for example, a negotiated price for limited use of your creation, and respecting those limits, clearly preserves the value of your expenditure of time.[10] Allowing a content creator limited legal authority to exclude others from using or disseminating the content she creates might not be the only way to respect this interest, but it is clearly one way to do so.

These meta-ethical considerations regarding the sense in which moral protection is grounded in attributions of intrinsic value suggest, then, that we have a morally protected interest in the time and energy we spend on creating intellectual content. While our interest in the energy spent might be only instrumentally valuable, it is sufficiently central to our flourishing that it is reasonable to think it receives some protection from morality. Moreover, our interest in the time we spend is intrinsically valuable and hence deserving of respect. And one way of protecting these interests is to allow an author some control over the content she makes available to the world—though, of course, this might not be the only way.

Content Creation and Considerations of Justice

Normative principles of justice also suggest that the interest in controlling the disposition of one's creations is afforded some moral protection. In this connection, it is crucial to realize that intellectual objects are not naturally occurring in a form that can readily be appropriated by any person. While it might be true that all possible intellectual objects exist in logical space (whatever that is), not every intellectual object is immediately available for appropriation. Intellectual objects are made available through the creative work of content creators who discover or invent that content and thereby render it in a form that can be consumed by others. If, for example, Charles Dickens does not write *A Tale of Two Cities*, it will never be available for consumption.

This has an important implication for one very common criticism of intellectual property rights. It is commonly argued that legal protection of intellectual property rights is illegitimate because such protection has the effect of "depleting the information commons."[11] The idea is that intellectual property laws, then, deprive people of something to which all have legitimate claims—namely, the objects in the information commons.

But there is no intellectual commons that is stocked independently of the efforts of people who create (or discover) content. Unlike the material world, there is no stock of ready-made objects with which people mix their labor to produce something valuable. Whereas a house is constructed out of naturally occurring materials (or materials that ultimately owe their existence to naturally occurring materials) with which we can causally interact, content must be, so to speak, conjured up by someone out of nothing. While all possible content might, as noted previously, exist in logical space as abstract objects, human beings do not produce content by causally interacting with abstract objects; as far as I can tell, it is metaphysically impossible for us to causally interact with abstract objects—though we can surely think about them just as we think about material objects.

This is important for the following reason. If there were an intellectual commons consisting of intellectual objects to which human beings have such causal access that producing content is akin to picking an apple, then that fact would be a pretty good reason (though one that is far short of being conclusive) for thinking that intellectual property protection is illegitimate. But that is simply not the case: *A Tale of Two Cities*, a poem, a song, or a proof of Fermat's Last Theorem cannot be picked from some commons the way an apple is picked from a material commons. For all practical purposes, people invent such content, and no one has access to a particular piece of content unless someone, perhaps the user, invents it; if Dickens does not write *A Tale of Two Cities*, it will never be written. The argument that intellectual property protection is problematic because it depletes the information commons rests on a fundamental misconception about our access to content.

The fact that intellectual content is not available unless invented by someone is important for another reason: it implies that the efforts of content creators introduce *value* into the world when they make available previously inaccessible intellectual content. When Dickens completes *A Tale of Two Cities* and makes it available to others, he has thereby produced something of value and introduced new value into the world. Content creators create value that did not exist in the world by investing their own valuable resources (time, energy, and labor) into producing that value.

Ordinary considerations of justice suggest that what people deserve is determined by the value and disvalue they introduce into the world by their free acts and that people should, other things being equal, get what they deserve and hence have some sort of morally protected interest in what they deserve. Such a view underlies, most conspicuously, most theories of punishment,[12] but it also underlies positive views about how to distribute the material benefits and burdens of a society—which, of course, entail views about the extent to which property rights are legitimate.

This should not be taken to mean that the claim that someone created new value logically implies that they have a moral right to that value that deserves legal protection; as we saw earlier in discussing the original Lockean arguments, the claim that someone created new value does not have such strong implications. And, by itself, this should not be taken to say much of anything about exactly how far those interests range. The analysis previously-mentioned, for example, would not imply that Dickens has a legitimate interest in excluding people from using variations on the title *A Tale of Two Cities*; in particular, it would not imply that Dickens has a legitimate interest in stopping people from using the title *A Tale of Seven Cities*. But it is to assert that, according to ordinary intuitions about justice, people have some sort of morally legitimate interest, other things being equal, in the value they bring into the world via their intellectual efforts. It might not rise to the level of a right, and it might be defeasible by other considerations; however, our ordinary intuitions seem to imply that they have an interest in the value they bring into the world that receives theoretically significant protection from morality.

Interests of Other Parties in Intellectual Content

The reason there is such a contentious dispute over intellectual property rights is that content creators are not the only persons with a morally significant interest in intellectual content. Other persons have significant interests in intellectual content that has been created or discovered by others. Because people generally assign significant value to different types of intellectual content, it is quite natural that they might resist theories attempting to justify intellectual property rights that make it more difficult for them to obtain and use such content.

As before, many of these valuations are at least partly prudential in character. I value intellectual content for both instrumental and intrinsic reasons, but all these reasons are largely prudential. This is particularly clear in the case of content I value instrumentally (again, as a means to some other end). I might value the content provided by an education because it enables me to earn a better living and achieve a better quality of material living than I could otherwise achieve. I might value a piece of music because it gives me great pleasure when I listen to it. I might value a film because it entertains me for a couple of hours and fills up the time.

This also seems to be true of some intellectual content we value intrinsically. I value information about the existence and nature of God for its own sake (as well, of course, as for instrumental reasons) but the interests that I am looking to satisfy by my pursuit of such information *as an end* are largely my own. I might want value knowledge as an end-in-itself and hence pursue intellectual content for its value, but my pursuits are still being motivated by my interests and priorities, which presumably reflect some sort of view about my well-being. The value is an end-in-itself, but the motivation for pursuing it is at least partly because I have an interest in it and that content fulfills the interest *and me*.

If this sounds a little odd, it might help to note that the claim that my interest in some content is prudential does not imply that my interest is selfish or self-centered. The notions of selfishness and self-centeredness seem to connote the violation of some moral obligation to consider the interests of others. I do not mean to suggest either of those things by characterizing these interests as "prudential." I merely mean to suggest that these interests are motivated by desires that are explicitly self-regarding: I want this content because I find it valuable and hence have an interest in obtaining this content.

The strength of the prudential interest varies from one piece of content to the next. It is reasonable to think that there is some intellectual content that one needs to survive independently (i.e., without direct assistance from others) in a particular cultural context. For example, while it is possible to survive in a society like ours without being able to read or add, one will require considerable assistance from other people in order to feed, clothe, and shelter oneself. In most situations in a society like that of the U.S. with an inadequate safety net, a person will not be able to take care of basic needs by herself without knowing how to read and do simple arithmetic. Obviously, a person will have the strongest prudential interest in such content.

I think it is fair to say that people have the strongest prudential interest in intellectual content having to do with the existence and nature of God. Regardless of whether one believes or does not believe that a personal God exists, it should be clear that the various issues are of tremendous prudential significance. Not surprisingly, people care a great deal about being able to access intellectual content that will help them to reach an informed opinion about whether god exists and, if so, what God requires of us.

Not all intellectual content, however, has such importance from the standpoint of self-interest. Some intellectual content is fairly characterized as needed for individuals to thrive in all the ways that human beings ought to thrive. Artistic and philosophical (of course!) content might very well be necessary for a person to lead a meaningful human life. Without such content, our lives would be very different—and probably would not be much different from that of some non-human animals. Although theorists disagree on what sorts of goods are needed to live a genuinely human life (and hence to "thrive"), I would be surprised if anyone denied the claim that some access to certain kinds of content is needed for people to thrive in the appropriate ways.

But the vast majority of the intellectual content desired by people is essential neither to survive nor to thrive. We seek much intellectual content in order to entertain or amuse ourselves. Most of the time I spend watching films, for example, is intended to achieve nothing more noble than to make me laugh or entertain me in some other way. Most of the time I spend listening to music is intended to create a mood (perhaps one that is appropriately intense during a workout) or to produce aesthetic pleasure. The same is true of a fair bit of the time I spend reading; while much of it is intended to enlighten me, much of it is done for amusement.

Again, the claim here is not purely descriptive. It is not just that people tend to care about surviving, knowing about God, thriving, or being entertained; rather, it is that, from the standpoint of prudential rationality, people ought to care about these things (though not to the same degree). Someone who cares nothing about her own survival is, other things being equal, probably in need of immediate inpatient psychiatric care, as is probably true of someone who does not care at all about whether or not a personal God exists who punishes wrongdoing with everlasting suffering (imagine, for example, someone who says—and means— "I really do not care whether or not I suffer eternal torment in hell"). Likewise someone who does not care at all about her own amusement or entertainment is, at the very least, mildly depressed.

As before, these prudential interests seem to have some moral significance; but how much significance they have from the standpoint of morality depends on how strong these interests are. It is always a morally relevant fact about some piece of content that somebody wants it, but this does not tell us much about how much protection it might receive from morality. It seems reasonable to think that morality would afford much more protection to a person's interest in information necessary to survive in a self-sufficient way than to her interest in information necessary to thrive; food, water, shelter, and the truth about God are much more important than art and philosophy. Likewise, it seems reasonable to think that morality would afford more protection to a person's interest in information necessary to thrive than to a person's interest in being entertained or amused—though, again, it is always a morally relevant fact that some piece of content would amuse a person.

None of this should be taken, of course, to deny that intellectual content might be protected by morality for some other reason than just that it has prudential value. For example, intellectual content that people need to compete in a society like ours might be protected by something like a principle of equal opportunity. Other things being equal, it is better from the standpoint of morality that all persons have free access to such content, because a society that does not make it equally available to all will afford some persons an unfair advantage in the marketplace. Here the motivation is not to protect the interests of persons, but to ensure that the distribution of opportunities is fair to all; although we might have a prudential interest in things being fair, fairness is about something other than prudential interests. There is nothing in the analysis of this chapter that should be construed as inconsistent with the fact that prudential considerations might form one part of the explanation as to why some content gets protection from morality, but need not exhaust the explanation.

Weighing the Competing Interests

As is evident from the foregoing discussion, content creators and other persons have conflicting interests that must be weighed. Content creators must expend valuable resources in the form of their time, energy, and labor in order to bring new value into the world in the form of intellectual content to which people did not previously have access. Content creators, as we have seen, have a morally protected interest in their time, energy, and labor, in part, because our supply of those resources is limited. Ordinary considerations of justice suggest that they have some claim to the value they bring into the world in virtue of the expenditure of such resources. Other things being equal, this suggests that content creators have a limited morally protected interest in controlling (at least for some reasonable period of time) the disposition and distribution of the value they bring into the world in the form of new intellectual content.

Of course, other things are not always equal. It is quite reasonable to think, as noted previously, that third parties have a special interest in intellectual content needed for survival that outweighs whatever interest its author might have in the value she brings into the world—though this should not be taken to mean that the author is owed no compensation. It is also reasonable to think that we owe it to individuals and nations to ensure that they have sufficient information to compete in a global economy; this seems to be required by the principle of equal opportunity.[13]

The distinction between factual intellectual objects and non-factual objects is relevant here. It is not unreasonable to think that third parties have a special interest in important factual information that outweighs such interests on the part of the author. Facts, after all, are not likely to stay undiscovered forever; if one person does not discover some fact, someone else probably will—something that is just not true of non-factual intellectual objects like novels and songs. If Dickens does not write *A Tale of Two Cities*, then it will never be written; in contrast, if Andrew Wiles does not prove Fermat's Last Theorem, someone eventually will, though it might take many additional years.

Two considerations converge here to support the idea that people have some sort of special interest in factual content discovered or created by others. First, it is not unreasonable to think that we have some sort of special interest in knowledge of our world.[14] Second, it is not true that if one content creator does not produce a particular piece of factual content, then that piece of content is not likely to be produced; factual content, again, is different from non-factual content in that respect. Accordingly, if it is true that people have some special interest in factual information, say, because we have some special interest in knowledge about our world, this would support the altogether plausible claim that, for example, it is wrong to assign property rights in genetic sequences.

Still, it is not clear that the interests of other persons always outweigh the interests of a content creator in factual content she creates such as to preclude any legal protection of the creator's interest in controlling disposition of that information. At an intuitive level, there is a world of difference between factual information needed for survival and factual information not needed for survival, as well as between factual information that is readily discovered and factual information that requires some special talent and effort to discover. While this should not be taken to imply that factual content should ever be afforded intellectual property protection, it is to assert that the issues are different with respect to non-essential factual content and factual content not easily discovered.

It also seems reasonable to think that the interests of other persons in content needed to thrive sometimes outweigh the interests of the creator of that content, but the issues here are just not very clear because the nature of our interest is just not clear. The fact that we need access to some artistic content to thrive does not imply that we need access to *all* artistic content to thrive.

Indeed, the idea that we need access to *all* artistic content to thrive is simply too strong to be plausible. It seems ridiculous, for example, to assert that I need access to the latest 50 Cent tracks in order to thrive. While it might (or might not) be fun to listen to the latest offering from 50 Cent, it is simply implausible to think that any person cannot thrive without free access to it. What this means is that the interests of other persons in thriving will defeat the interests of content creators in some, but not all, cases of artistic content.

Exactly which cases is a difficult issue that would require a much more detailed analysis than I can pretend to give here, but I would like to hazard the following observation. It seems plausible to me that what is currently in the public domain by way of artistic expression is sufficient to ensure that people thrive in all the ways they ought to thrive. We do not need immediately to provide free access to new artistic content to ensure that all have an adequate opportunity to thrive in the ways that artistic content enables one to thrive. If this is correct, then the interests of content creators outweigh the interests of other persons in such content—at least in cases of content that is of comparatively recent vintage.

But with respect to content that is merely *desired*, it is not even a close call. While it is, as I noted earlier, always a morally relevant fact that some agent A wants some thing p, the mere fact that A wants p is not strong enough to give rise to any significant protection of that interest. Other things being equal, if A wants p and I can satisfy A's desire for p, it would be a good thing from the standpoint of morality for me to provide A with p. But the claim that A wants p, by itself, does not imply that it would be wrong for me not to provide A with p if I can do so. Indeed, failure to provide someone with something they want is not even a wrong-making property of an act; while it would be good, other things being equal, to provide A with p, the claim that A wants p does not provide any reason whatsoever for thinking that not providing *A* with *p* is even *prima facie* wrong. Our desires just cannot do that kind of heavy moral lifting.

In cases where content is merely wanted, then, it seems clear that the interests of the content creators in limited control over the content they create outweigh the interests of other persons. On the one hand, the content creator expends precious resources in the form of a limited supply of life and energy in order to bring value into the world. On the other hand, other persons want merely to pass the time or enjoy themselves with such content.

Of course, there might be many people who want the content and just one content creator whose interests are at stake, but this is not enough to defeat the content creator's interest. The content creator's interest is significant enough to receive moral protection: insofar as my behavior wastes another person's life or energy, it is morally problematic. In contrast, the fact that someone wants content is not significant enough, by itself, to warrant any moral protection: while it might be good for me to give someone something she wants, my failure to do so is not even presumptively problematic. An interest that receives moral protection, like the content creator's, cannot be defeated by aggregating interests that do not; the difference between the two interests, from a moral point of view, is *qualitative* and not *quantitative.*

Ironically, most of the content that critics of intellectual property want for free is non-informative content that is merely desired. It is reasonable to think that the vast majority of contemporary music, film, and novels (which are not, strictly speaking, information because they do not purport to express true propositional content[15]) are wanted primarily for entertainment and amusement. Those people who are illegally sharing music files online are violating the law for no better reason than they want to be entertained and to experience the pleasure of listening to the newest music—as though this desire is so much more important than the time and effort of the content creators.

Here it is worth noting that, at least with respect to artistic content, content creators create not only a piece of content, *but also the demand for it.* There would be no demand, for example, for *A Tale of Two Cities* had Dickens never written that novel. There can be no demand for a song that has never been written.[16] Although it is true that people want artistic content and might want content from a particular artist, this desire has no particular focus until a content creator sharpens it by making available a suitable piece of content. Artists satisfy wants that they bring into existence. Yet many people believe that these desires, which they would not have if not for people who create, take precedence over any interests that an artist has to control the distribution of her creations. As far as content that is merely wanted is concerned, this should seem implausible to put it mildly.

Summary and Conclusion

In this essay, I have argued that the issue of whether legal protection of intellectual property is morally legitimate depends on how strong the interests of content creators in the content they create are relative to the interests of other parties. I have also argued that, in most cases, the interests that content creators have in the content they create (or discover) outweigh—and hence receive greater moral protection—than the interests of other persons in at least those cases not involving content human beings *need* in order to either survive or thrive. This, of course, does not obviously imply the existence of a moral *right* to intellectual property. But, as far as I can see, it provides a justification for laws that provide some protection of the interests of content creators in the contents of their creations.

Again, this should not be taken as a justification for copyright law in the U.S., or even for the idea that the proper protection for the interests of content creators in the form of a legal *right*. I think existing copyright law is deeply flawed in a number of particulars, including the duration of copyright protection and the ease with which copyright can be renewed and perpetually transferred from one entity to another. I am also not sure that the most appropriate means for protecting the interest of content creators is by affording something fairly characterized as a "right" (though I am not sure what the alternatives might be).

What I am asserting, however, is that there are strong reasons for protecting intellectual property that are not consequentialist in character. The idea is that the primary reason for protecting intellectual property is not that protecting intellectual property maximally conduces to community utility, however defined, or the common good, assuming this is true. Rather, it is that, from the standpoint of morality, the interests of the content creator are more important than the interests of other persons in most cases and hence are the ones that receive the benefit of some fairly stringent moral protection; indeed, in many instances, the interests of other persons, though prudentially significant, are not significant enough from the standpoint of morality to receive protection.

It is worth reiterating in closing that, though related to and in some sense derived from Locke's argument, this reasoning does not presuppose a Lockean framework for justifying property. The idea is not that such interests are morally significant because the author has mixed her labor with some sort of intellectual raw material in a way that cannot be extracted and thereby created value. Rather, the idea is that such interests are morally significant because they implicate uncontroversial principles of fairness that are widely accepted among persons in our culture. From the standpoint of fairness, I have some minimal claim to the value I bring into the world through expenditures of my time, energy, and intellectual labor—regardless of how minimal those expenditures might be.[17]

References

Floridi, L. (2004). Information. *Blackwell Guide to the Philosophy of Computing and Information*. Oxford, UK: Blackwell.

Hettinger, E. (1989). Justifying intellectual property. *Philosophy and Public Affairs, 18*, 31-52.

Himma, K. E. (2004a). There's something about Mary: The moral value of things *qua* information objects. *Ethics and Information Technology, 6*, 145-59.

Himma, K. E. (2004b). The moral significance of the interest in information: Reflections on a fundamental right to information. *Journal of Information, Communication, and Ethics in Society, 2*, 191-202.

Himma, K. E. (2004c). The question at the foundation of information ethics: Does information have intrinsic value? In T. Bynum et al. (Eds.), *Challenges for the Citizen of the Information Society: Proceedings of the Seventh International Conference on the Social and Ethical Impacts of Information and Communications Technologies (ETHICOMP 2004)*.

Himma, K. E. (2005). Information and intellectual property protection: Evaluating the claim that information should be free. *APA Newsletter in Philosophy and Law, 4*, 2-8. Available at http://ssrn.com/author=328842

Locke, J. (1690). *Second treatise of government*. Available at http://www.constitution.org/jl/2ndtreat.htm

McFarland, M. C. (1999). *Intellectual property, information, and the common good*. Presented at the Proceedings of the Fourth Annual Ethics and Technology Conference.

Moore, A. (2001). *Intellectual property and information control: Philosophic foundations and contemporary issues*. Newark, NJ: Transaction Publishing/Rutgers University.

Nozick, R. (1974). *Anarchy, state, and utopia*. New York: Basic Books.

Rosen, G. (2001) Abstract objects. In *Stanford encyclopedia of philosophy*. Available at http://plato.stanford.edu/entries/abstract-objects/

Tavani, H. (2005). Balancing intellectual property rights and the intellectual commons: A Lockean analysis. *Journal of Information, Communication, and Ethics in Society, 2*, supplement.

Endnotes

[1]   I am indebted to a number of people for their very helpful comments on an earlier draft of this chapter: Herman Tavani, Richard Spinello, Steve Layman, Philip Goggans, and Patrick McDonald. Their comments significantly improved this chapter.

[2]   Indeed, Locke's position is in tension with the Christian doctrine he frequently seems to presuppose. In one common view, we are holding our bodies in trust for God, who is the sole owner of those bodies. I find it somewhat odd to think of human beings as being divine *property*, but this seems a plausible view to many Christians.

[3]   As Robert Nozick puts the point: "But why isn't mixing what I own with what I don't own a way of losing what I own rather than a way of gaining what I don't? If I own a can of tomato juice and spill it in the sea so that its molecules (made radioactive, so I can check this) mingle evenly throughout the sea, do I thereby come to own the sea, or have I foolishly dissipated my tomato juice?" (Nozick, 1974, pp. 174-175).

[4]   I am indebted to Steve Layman for pointing this out to me.

[5]   This is a standard view of abstract objects. See Rosen (2001).

[6]   For a very plausible (non-algorithmic) device for balancing competing claims, see Moore (2001), Chapter 5 and 7. Moore argues for something he calls the Weak Pareto Proviso: If the acquisition of an intangible object makes no one else worse off in terms of level of well-being (including opportunity costs) compared to how they were immediately before the acquisition, then the taking is permitted. As is readily evident, the Weak Pareto Proviso attempts to balance all the competing interests.

[7]   In a case where the thief steals something from me that is necessary for my survival, the calculus seems different to me.

[8]   For a discussion of the significance of the distinction between intrinsic and instrumental value in ethical theorizing, see Himma (2004a, b, c).

[9]   This is not to deny that morality protects much that we value instrumentally; it is only to assert that the fact that we value something instrumentally is not sufficient to imply that morality protects it.

[10]   One could argue, of course, that authors who do not wish to give away their creations should refrain from expending time in creating content, but one needs an argument in support of this counterintuitive claim that goes beyond pointing out that other people want those creations. As I will argue next, the mere fact that someone wants something does not entail that she has a morally protected interest in it.

[11]   For an outstanding discussion of this view, see Tavani (2004). Himma (2005) gives a criticism of this view.

[12]   Indeed, even utilitarian theories frequently attempt to justify a principle that punishment is justified only insofar as deserved. What distinguishes pure retributivist views from such views is that the retributivist thinks that considerations of desert are both necessary and sufficient to justify punishment, while the utilitarian believes that such considerations are necessary but not sufficient. In addition, it must be the case that punishment maximally promotes community utility.

[13]   I am indebted to Herman Tavani for this point.

[14]   It would be incorrect, however, to think that knowledge is necessarily valuable as an end-in-itself. See Himma (2004b).

[15]   See Himma (2005) for a detailed defense of this point; see also Floridi (2004).

16   While I am not prepared to argue the point here, I am inclined to think this interest rises to the level of a right. The interest we have in the ideas, time, energy, and intellectual labor we invest in creating new content (and hence bringing new value into the world) are sufficiently important, it seems to me, to give rise, irrespective of effects on utility, to a right that binds any third parties who lack any greater interest in the products of those expenditures than a *desire* for those products. Of course, the suggestion that content creators have a right over their products is not to say anything about the content of that right. In particular, it is not to endorse the conception of that right that is incorporated into, or expressed by, copyright law in the U.S.

17   It is worth noting that such considerations provide stronger support for intellectual property rights than for material property rights in one important respect. One can always plausibly argue that one's investment of labor in a material object is lost because it is invested in an external material object in which one has no antecedent claim; after all, if I carve a sculpture out of an unowned tree, I am putting my labor into something in which I have no antecedent claim. In contrast, one's investment of labor in creating content does not involve working on something to which one has no antecedent claim; I do not carve a novel out of some previously existing object that is external to me.

Chapter IV

Universal Information Ethics?
Ethical Pluralism and Social Justice

Charles Ess
Drury University, USA

Abstract

The explosive, global diffusion of information and communication technologies (ICTs) and computer-mediated communication (CMC) confronts us with the need for an information ethics that can resolve ethical problems evoked by ICTs and CMC in ways that provide shared, perhaps (quasi-)universal responses. At the same time, however, in the name of a transcultural social justice that preserves diverse cultural identities, such an ethics must also reflect and sustain local values, approaches, and traditions. Important ethical claims from both within Western and between Eastern and Western cultures exemplify an ethical pluralism that is able to meet these requirements as this pluralism represents important ethical differences as issuing from diverse judgments and applications of shared ethical norms.

Introduction: We've Got the Technology, so What's the Problem?

One of the central consequences of the exponential, if not explosive, growth of the Internet and the World Wide Web is the facilitation of cross-cultural encounters of a speed and scope that would have been unimaginable in the era of print and post. The emergence of these technologies and the cross-cultural encounters they make possible have inspired a number of responses, ranging from the rosy-eyed optimism of Marshall McLuhan's (in)famous "electronic global village" to darker views that suggest our choices are rather between a global homogenization (aptly called "McWorld" by Benjamin Barber [1995] and described as "Disneyfication" by Cees Hamelink [2000]) or "the clash of civilizations" famously predicted by Samuel Huntington (1993), as diverse cultures and peoples understandably enough insist on preserving their cultural identity and integrity—even if such preservation requires the use of violence. These diverse scenarios force upon us a central question: are there ways in which we might avoid the Manichean polarities of sheer homogenization versus fragmentation and violence—ways that, I suggest, would allow for global cross-cultural engagements that simultaneously respect and protect cultural integrity and diversity?

These larger issues and concerns are taken up in a more specific way in the relatively nascent fields of computer ethics and information ethics. In the West,[1] computer ethics traces its origins to the work of Norbert Wiener (1948, 1950) and tends to focus on the specific ethical problems encountered by professionals in computer science and related disciplines, along with central social and political issues such as privacy, copyright, and intellectual property (see Tavani [2004] for an excellent introduction and overview). The still younger but broader domain of information ethics expands the scope of computer ethics in a number of ways, so as to include, for example, classic philosophical questions of ontology and epistemology (for example, Floridi [2003]). Moreover, information ethics recognizes that in developed and developing countries "information" and its ethical dimensions directly concern other professional disciplines such as library science, and, indeed, all professionals and citizens whose lives are increasingly defined by and dependent upon information and communication technologies (ICTs).

As information ethics and computer ethics thus analyze and attempt to resolve the ethical issues entailed in the design and deployment of ICTs, they inevitably do so by taking up specific values and ethical decision-making approaches—which, of course, vary from culture to culture. At the same time, however, especially because ICTs are central engines and media for global cross-cultural encounters, information ethics and computer ethics thus face in specific ways the larger problem of how to bring together radically diverse cultures and peoples across the globe—but in ways that, ideally, will avoid the Manichean polarities of sheer homogenization versus radical, if not violent fragmentation. That is, can we develop an information ethics that will help us (a) analyze and resolve both local and global ethical issues evoked in the design and deployment of ICTs, in ways that (b) will provide, where needed, at least quasi-universal responses, that is, responses that enjoy ethical legitimacy and power across a range of global cultures, while at the same time (c) recognizing and sustaining the particular values and traditions of specific cultures, so as to thereby respect and preserve cultural integrity and identity?

While these questions are central for an information and computer ethics that seeks to "work" on a global scale, such questions, clearly, are not simply of concern to information and computer science professionals. On the contrary, these questions should be of interest to anyone concerned with the larger problems of a transcultural social justice—one that intends to respect and preserve cultural diversity in the face of a range of forces that push rather in the direction of homogenization, and thereby various forms of colonization and imperialism. This is to say, that the problem of sustaining globally-linked ICTs while sustaining local cultural identity and diversity may be seen as a microcosm of the larger problem of finding a middle way between global homogenization and cultural identities preserved at the cost of fragmentation and violence. As the larger problem is one of avoiding colonization and imperialism that results from allowing a homogenous global culture to trample down distinctive cultural identities, while at the same time allowing for global communication and its real and potential benefits, so the problem in information and computer ethics is one of avoiding an ethical imperialism that, in the name of establishing global or "universal" ethical norms, would nonetheless impose the ethical approaches and norms specific to a given set of traditions and cultures, that is, those of the West. It may be, then, that resolutions to this central problem in information and computer ethics will prove fruitful for resolutions to the broader, macrocosmic problem of preserving cultural identity in the face of homogenizing forces. Moreover, as our lives in the developed and developing nations become increasingly defined by and dependent upon ICTs, resolutions to this central problem in information and computer ethics will be required precisely as part of a larger effort to find ways to preserve cultural identity and integrity in a "global city" that is increasingly interconnected through ICTs.

In the following, I hope to show that we may discern and articulate middle grounds between homogenization and fragmentation by way of *ethical pluralisms*. Such pluralisms hold together shared ethical norms alongside the irreducible differences that define diverse cultures. They do so by recognizing that these defining differences may be result of applying shared norms by way of *judgments* as shaped precisely by the specific traditions, histories, worldviews, and practices of a given culture: this means that a shared ("universal") norm may be interpreted, understood, and/or applied in sometimes radically different ways within diverse cultural frameworks, resulting in a structure of agreement (on a shared norm) alongside the irreducible differences that define culture identity and integrity (as the result of diverse judgments rooted precisely in the defining values and frameworks of those cultures). I seek to show this, moreover, not simply in a theoretical way, but in a way that depends first of all upon demonstrating such ethical pluralism in *praxis*. So I begin with real-world examples in information ethics and computer ethics that show how ethical pluralism across significantly different cultures is at work with regard to specific ethical issues. While these initial pluralisms remain clearly within "the West," I then turn to examples drawn from information and computer ethics in Asia. On the one hand, of course, we find here even greater cultural and ethical differences between Western and Eastern approaches. At the same time, however—and with regard precisely to the most central issues of privacy and data privacy protection—an ethical pluralism emerges here that appears to be capable of holding together important ethical norms alongside the distinctive ethical traditions and approaches that define diverse cultural identities.

Ethical Pluralism in International/Interdisciplinary Contexts

Association of Internet Researchers Ethical Guidelines

The Association of Internet Researchers (AoIR) has developed what is, to our knowledge, the first set of ethical guidelines for online research that seeks to incorporate the research ethics of both the wide range of disciplines (including both the social sciences and the humanities) *and* diverse national traditions that intersect in research on various online environments (AoIR 2002). Such research realized early on precisely the ability of the Internet and the Web to bring together researchers from both a variety of disciplines and diverse national traditions—and thereby immediately confronted the central problem: how to develop a *shared* research ethics that respects distinctive cultural differences?

Central in developing the AoIR guidelines was our strategy of determining whether or not we could discern *pluralistic* middle grounds between the familiar poles of *ethical relativism* and *ethical dogmatism*. Ethical dogmatism may be briefly defined as the view that there is only one set of values, universally valid for all peoples in all times in all contexts, and so differences in ethical values and practices can only mean that one set is right and the others are wrong. By contrast, ethical relativism claims that there are no universal values whatsoever, and so any set of values and practices are as good as any other—all values are legitimate only relative to a given individual and/or culture. Ethical pluralism seeks to articulate a middle ground between dogmatism and relativism. Such pluralism points to an agreed-upon value or norm (as we are about to see here, for example, the *expectations* concerning privacy, as these establish requirements for informed consent). Such a norm or value, however, avoids ethical dogmatism, as pluralism instead emphasizes that different cultures may interpret, apply, and/or understand these norms in different ways that reflect—and thereby preserve—each culture's distinctive history, traditions, values, and so forth.[2]

The AoIR ethics working group encountered early on a striking difference between the United States and Norway regarding whether or not informed consent was thought to be necessary for recording (e.g., audio and/or video) in public spaces. In Norway, for example, informed consent for such recordings is in fact required; this requirement is justified, first of all, on the basis of people's *expectations*—people do *not* expect such recordings without consent (Elgesem, 2002). By contrast, in the U.S. no informed consent for such recordings is required. Again, this appears to be a matter of *expectations*; in the U.S. context, people have no *expectations* of privacy in public spaces—in contrast, for example, with conversations in a psychologist's office, and so forth (Walther, 2002). Hence, we find *different expectations* regarding privacy in the U.S. and Norway. At the same time, however, the ethical approaches defining informed consent in both countries agree that *expectations* are a primary starting point for *judging* whether or not informed consent is required.

There emerges here, then, an ethical pluralism that conjoins a critical *agreement* on the normative importance of expectations with the recognition that *diverse* expectations, as reflecting irreducibly different cultural values, justify (otherwise apparently opposite) norms regarding informed consent. Such a pluralism points to the (quasi)-universal standard of *expectations*; but it simultaneously preserves irreducible differences between the cultures of the United States and Norway. Such a pluralism thereby articulates a shared norm critical to an information and computer ethics that seeks legitimacy beyond the boundaries of a single culture. But at the same time, such a pluralism avoids an ethical ethnocentrism that would imperialistically impose the ethical norms of a specific culture upon all others—an ethnocentrism that ethical dogmatism is especially prone to, as it takes a specific set of ethical norms as "universal". Such pluralism thus meets a central demand of transcultural social justice—namely, of preserving differences in values that define distinctive cultural identities, rather than allowing these to be steamrolled by a homogenous and homogenizing ethical dogmatism that insists on a single "universal" value that must be applied in the same way at all times and in all places.

Others have identified similar sorts of pluralisms operating across significant cultural differences. For example, Joel Reidenberg (2000) has highlighted the striking differences between data privacy protection in the European Union and the United States. Very briefly, the policies of the European Union recognize the state's role of protecting individual rights—including privacy and data privacy rights as rooted in fundamental human rights—through legislation (Reidenberg, 2000, p. 1331f). The United States, by contrast, hopes to protect privacy primarily through self-regulation rather than by way of governmental regulation, that is, "through practices developed by industry norms, codes of conduct, and contracts rather than statutory legal rights. Data privacy becomes a market issue rather than a basic political question, and the rhetoric casts the debate in terms of 'consumers' and users rather than 'citizens'" (p. 1332).

In different terms, the U.S. may be characterized as taking up a *consequentialist* position, one emphasizing economic benefit for the many, even at the cost of possible risks to the privacy of the individual. By contrast, the European Union approach may be understood as a more strongly *deontological* approach, that is, one that emphasizes the rights of the individual as primary, even if protecting those rights first may interfere with "market efficiencies" (cf. Burkhardt, Thompson, & Peterson, 2000, p. 329). But Reidenberg argues that these strikingly—indeed, apparently opposite—approaches to data privacy protection are in fact different ways of attempting to implement *shared* "first principles" of data protection. That is, both approaches *agree* on centrally important norms and values—specifically those Reidenberg finds articulated in the recommendations of the Younger Committee (Reidenberg, 2000, p. 1327). The differences at work here are then differences of *implementation* of these shared norms and values in the diverse cultural contexts of the U.S. and the EU. Simply put, the primary values and norms of individual privacy and data privacy protection are brought into play in *praxis* in ways directly and clearly shaped by the distinctive cultural values, traditions, and approaches that define the U.S. vis-à-vis the European Union. Hence, there emerges here again a *pluralistic* structure in which *agreement* on first principles stands alongside distinctive cultural/national *differences* regarding how to implement and apply these first principles.[3] Again, such pluralism seeks to thereby avoid an ethical imperialism or colonization, precisely as it holds and preserves distinctive cultural differences alongside shared norms.

Other examples within the fields of Western information ethics and computer ethics *per se* can be noted as well. As I have documented elsewhere, Terrell Ward Bynum has argued that in these fields there is a convergence in the work of Norbert Wiener and Luciano Floridi—one oriented towards the central values of contributing to human flourishing, advancing and defending human values (life, health, freedom, knowledge, happiness), and fulfilling "the great principles of justice" drawn from Western philosophical and religious traditions. Bynum further sees agreement on these central values in the work of such computer ethics pioneers as Deborah Johnson, Philip Brey, James Moor and Helen Nissenbaum, and in my own emphasis on using computer-mediated communication (CMC) technologies in ways that preserve "thick" or local cultures. In these ways, Bynum thus argues for a broad ethical pluralism in computer and information ethics that conjoins centrally important values with their diverse interpretations and applications among both U.S. and European ethicists (Ess, 2005c).

NESH (National Committee for Research Ethics in the Social Sciences and the Humanities, Norway)

As a last example of ethical pluralism already at work in the *praxis* of information and computer ethics, we can contrast the United States and Norway with regard to requirements for informed consent—now in conjunction with the basic ethical issues of protecting research subjects' confidentiality and anonymity.

The Norwegian guidelines for research ethics (NESH, 2001) are noteworthy as they first provide another instance of the contrast we saw earlier with regard to privacy protection—namely, between more *utilitarian* approaches and more *deontological* approaches. As in the earlier example, the U.S. (and the UK) tend to emphasize in utilitarian fashion the potential *benefits* of knowledge, arguing that these possible greater goods for the greater number (a classic expression of the utilitarian "calculus") may justify at least minimal risks to subjects' rights and well-being (for example, the U.S. Code of Federal Regulations). By contrast, the NESH document, echoing the EU *deontological* emphasis on protecting the basic rights of individuals first and foremost, begins by emphasizing the *intrinsic* value of knowledge as the primary reason for its pursuit. In addition, the NESH guidelines insist that researchers are ethically obliged to respect and protect the basic rights of the individual as a human subject (i.e., rights to confidentiality, anonymity, informed consent, etc.) —*and* these rights as enjoyed by those persons in close relationship with the primary subject (NESH, 2001, para. 40). That is to say, for example, researchers must prevent the publication of information of a sensitive and/or potentially damaging sort (e.g., health information such as testing positive for HIV/AIDS), not only with regard to the primary subject, but also with regard to those in his/her close web of relationships. This understanding of human beings as not simply atomistic rights-holders, but as members of communities that likewise enjoy basic rights, contrasts sharply with U.S. and UK emphases on the individual as the sole rights-holder to be considered in ethical codes and protections.

Again, however, these strong differences can be resolved into an ethical pluralism that conjoins shared norms and values with irreducibly different cultural and ethical beliefs and approaches. Both U.S. and Norwegian codes agree precisely that human beings as research subjects must enjoy basic rights to privacy, confidentiality, anonymity, and informed consent. But the two countries clearly differ in their understanding and implementation of these rights; these differences reflect, and thus preserve, important national/cultural differences between U.S. and its traditional emphasis on the individual, and Norway and its more communitarian traditions focusing on persons as not simply individuals, but as embedded in webs of human relationships.

In sum, I suggest that these examples of ethical pluralism—drawn not simply from philosophical theory, but from the real-world *praxis* of research ethics as well as from computer and information ethics—demonstrate that the facts of cultural differences and diversity do not require us to choose between ethical relativism or ethical dogmatism, and thereby, between political fragmentation, on the one hand, or global homogenization, on the other. On the contrary, ethical pluralism manifests itself in these examples as articulating a middle ground between these extremes—one that, as it holds shared norms alongside diverse interpretations and applications of those norms, thereby respects and protects the irreducible differences that define diverse cultures.

To be clear: I by no means intend to suggest that every example of ethical difference between nations and cultures will be successfully resolved in such structures of ethical pluralism. To be sure, while these examples demonstrate that such pluralisms are already at work, important differences remain in other areas, leading to perhaps intractable legal and ethical conflicts.[4] But that said, ethical pluralism nonetheless stands as one strategy for meeting a central requirement for a global information ethics—namely, to discern and articulate ethical norms that will enjoy validity beyond the boundaries of specific cultural/national traditions, while simultaneously preserving the irreducible differences that define distinctive cultural identities. Thereby, ethical pluralism may further work at the larger political level, that is, as establishing the shared agreements necessary for communication and cooperation in our "global city," but in ways that preserve the differences central to distinctive cultural identities. In this way, ethical pluralism would thus meet the requirement of a transcultural social justice—that basic rights to individual and cultural identity be protected against various forms of colonization and imperialism—including an "ethical imperialism" that would threaten to override local cultural norms in the name of sheerly homogenous "universals."

Such pluralisms, as crossing the considerable cultural differences between the U.S., Europe, and Scandinavia, are thus no small accomplishment and contribution; but obviously, these examples of pluralism nonetheless remain restricted to Western cultures. A genuinely *global* computer and information ethics, however, must be capable of crossing the even greater cultural divides between East and West—not simply as a theoretical matter, but precisely for the directly practical reason that Internet and Web use in Asia now exceeds that of North America. While ethical pluralism may "work" within Western frameworks, especially given its roots in ancient Western philosophy, what reason do we have to believe that we might find, as such pluralism would demand, that the even greater cultural differences between Western and Asian cultures may be resolved as different interpretations and applications of shared norms and values?

East-West Approaches to Information Ethics

We can in fact discern several examples of ethical pluralism in information and computer ethics that resolve even the greater cultural differences between East and West—starting with some possible philosophical foundations for a global information and computer ethics that relies on ethical pluralism in these ways.

Confucius, Aristotle, and East-West Information Ethics?

In point of fact, comparative philosophers have extensively explored a number of such pluralisms that emerge between Eastern and Western ethical traditions, especially with regard to Aristotelian and Confucian thought. These pluralisms can be initially seen in terms of similar conceptions of *human nature*, and extend from there to similar understandings of the primary aims of *ethics* and *politics* (see Ess, 2004a, 2004b, 2005b, 2005d, 2006b for more complete discussion).

First of all, Confucius and Aristotle understand human beings as inextricably bound up with one another in *community*. So Aristotle famously says that "man is by nature a political animal," so that "he who is unable to live in society, or who has no need because he is sufficient for himself, must be either a beast or a god: he is no part of a state" (Aristotle, 1943, pp. 54f./1253a). From here, Aristotle develops what becomes a foundational tradition in ethics and politics—one that is at work both in classic moderns such as Kant and contemporary Habermasian discourse ethics, as well as in contemporary feminist communitarian approaches (cf. Ess, 2005a). Aristotle's emphasis on our inextricable interconnection with one another has its counterpart in Confucius' "processional" or "relational" ontology, characterized by Ames and Rosemont as "not a concern to describe how things are in themselves, but how they stand in relation to something else at particular times" (Ames & Rosemont, 1998, p. 23). Given this ontology, Ames and Rosemont go on to point out, "Persons are not perceived as superordinated individuals—as agents who stand independent of their actions—but are rather ongoing 'events' defined functionally by constitutive roles and relationships as they are performed within the context of their specific families and communities" (1998, p. 29). Hence, Confucius anticipates Aristotle's understanding of human beings; for Confucius, as for Aristotle, "one cannot become a person by oneself—we are, from our inchoate beginnings, irreducibly social" (1998, p. 48).

Given these closely similar starting points, it is perhaps not surprising that core components of Confucian ethics and politics anticipate Aristotle in other ways as well—first of all, as Confucian ethics and politics emphasize *harmony* in a community, beginning with the family:

*Ancestor reverence as the defining religious sensibility, family as the primary hu-
man unit, authoritative humanity (perhaps more literally, "co-humanity", 人 ren,
"human" or "humankind") and filiality (孝 xiao) as primary human values, ritual-
ized roles, relationships, and practices (力 li, "power" or "energy") as a communal
discourse, are all strategies for achieving and sustaining communal harmony (和,
he "harmony").* (Ames & Rosemont, 1998, p. 30)[5]

Harvard University comparative philosopher, Tu Wei-Ming, argues that, given this
emphasis on harmony, Confucian ethics further resonates with both Aristotle's virtue
ethics, as well as with contemporary feminist and environmental ethics. Similar to
Western ethics of care for both the human and ecological communities, a Confucian *ethos* stresses fidelity and fiduciary responsibility to a community that begins
in family and finally encompasses the world (Tu, 1999, p. 35).

As we would expect of a genuine pluralism, however, these basic similarities, run
alongside irreducible differences between Confucius and Aristotle. To begin with,
Aristotle considers ethics and politics as expressions of what he designates as the
practical dimensions of human reason and experience; but these must be coherent
with a theoretical knowledge that will eventually approach a God-like understanding
of the world in terms of what we might think of as the scientific laws of nature. By
contrast, for Confucius, such interests are comparatively less significant. Indeed,
Ames and Rosemont argue that such scientific interests, as framed in terms of a
dualistic metaphysics that would separate the surfaces of ordinary experience from
ostensibly more rational and causal mechanisms and laws as underlying such surfaces, are literally inconceivable within the framework of classical Chinese (1998,
p. 20ff). To be sure, Confucian thought in particular and Chinese philosophy more
generally certainly assume an orderly nature, our ability (up to a point, at least) to
understand that order, and the importance of our working in harmony with that nature; and over the centuries, China has developed important scientific insights and
technological discoveries. Nonetheless, in these ways, Aristotle and Confucius take
up irreducibly different understandings of nature, especially the role of a scientific
knowledge of nature in developing their ethical and political teachings.

These irreducible differences thus distinguish these traditions from one another
in important ways; but these differences do not exclude the possibility of ethical
pluralisms that might conjoin such differences alongside important coherencies and
convergences in Aristotelian and Confucian thought with regard to basic conceptions
of human nature, ethics, and politics.

Indeed, both traditions allow for pluralism *per se*. To begin with, for Aristotle such
pluralism is "built in" to human ethical judgment as *phronesis*. As *practical* judgment, *phronesis* must determine which general principles and values first apply to
a specific situation, and then seek to interpret those principles and values as they
suggest a specific course of action within a specific context. Such application by

definition allows for a range of possible interpretations—a point made especially clear by Aquinas:

Practical reason... is concerned with contingent matters, about which human actions are concerned, and consequently, although there is necessity in the general principles, the more we descend to matters of detail, the more frequently we encounter deviations. (Summa Theologiae, 1-2, q.94, a.4 Responsio, cited in Haldane, 2003, p. 91)

Such a pluralism of judgments that nonetheless refer to a shared set of principles and norms, moreover, is also recognized as a feature of Confucian ethics. So Confucian scholar Joseph Chan points out that "Insofar as the framework of *ren* [authoritative humanity or co-humanity] and rites remains unchallenged, Confucians are often ready to accept a plurality of diverse or contradicting ethical judgments" (Chan, 2003, p. 136). Indeed, Chan's description of how this can occur closely resembles just the ethical pluralism we have seen in Aristotle and Aquinas—that is, one holding that the same ethical standard (in this case, *ren*) can be interpreted, applied, or understood in more than one way. In particular, for the Confucian, "If after careful and conscientious deliberation, two persons equipped with *ren* come up with two different or contradictory judgments and courses of action, Confucians would tell us to respect both of the judgments" (2003, p. 137).

Indeed, both West and East embed such pluralisms in their traditions as they use *harmony* and *resonance* as examples and metaphors of precisely the pluralistic structure of irreducible differences held alongside shared agreements and unities. As comparative philosopher Rolf Elberfeld points out, such notions of *harmony* and *resonance* appear within Western traditions, beginning with the Pythagoreans and including Socrates' comments about music and education in *The Republic*, 401d (cf. 443d). Similar notions, according to Elberfeld, further emerge in East Asian traditions, including just the notion of harmony [和 = *he*] that we have seen to be central to Confucian thought (Elberfeld, 2002).

These notions of harmony and resonance explicitly entail the structures of connection and difference we have seen at work in ethical pluralism. That is, for example, a musical chord—as a harmony—is thereby a unity that is nonetheless made up of irreducibly different but resonant notes. Harmony and resonance, then, as notions of unities that hold together irreducible differences, thus stand as canny metaphors and analogues to the notions of ethical pluralism, that is, precisely as structures of unitary foci that include diverse, even contradictory, interpretation. Indeed, Elberfeld suggests that we might see here a "Resonance Ethics" [*Resonanz-ethik*] that works both *within* Western and Eastern philosophers such as Plato and Confucius, and thereby may serve as a resonance *between* these two very different traditions (Elberfeld, 2002, pp. 132-137).

More broadly, I have argued that as these Aristotelian-Confucian resonances thus bridge important Western and Eastern traditions, they may serve as an important component of a *global* information ethics—one that takes up ethical pluralisms that conjoin shared agreements with the irreducible differences that define distinctive historical and cultural traditions (Ess, 2004b, 2006b).

From Theory to *Praxis*: Contemporary Examples of Pluralism East-West

These theoretical reflections, moreover, are consistent with real-world examples of such ethical pluralism that are now emerging between Eastern and Western approaches to information ethics. To see how this is so, I will review examples of such pluralism from Japan and China, and conclude with a discussion of what appears to be a strong example of ethical pluralism concerning Western and Eastern conceptions of privacy and data privacy protection laws.

Japanese Internet Research Ethics?[6]

Information ethics is a comparatively recent development in Japan. It has been fostered, for example, by the work of the Foundations of Information Ethics (FINE) project (http://www.fine.bun.kyoto-u.ac.jp/index_en.html). The work of Masahiko Mizutani and his colleagues represents this emerging information ethics in English-language literature (Mizutani et al., 2004). Perhaps not surprisingly, however, an Internet research ethics (IRE) *per se* has yet to emerge in Japan—but it can be noted that important components drawn from the larger fields of research and information ethics in the Western development of IRE function are also in place in Japan, such as human subjects research protections, including rights to privacy, as well as copyright law.

Not surprisingly, however, Japanese approaches to Internet research ethics show manifest differences from their Western counterparts (as expressed, for example, in the AoIR guidelines). As one example: a recent study of an online therapy group included direct quotes from group participants—*without*, however, having received informed consent to do so. The researchers apparently believed that by using pseudonyms, participants' identity was sufficiently protected (Yasukawa & Ando, 2002, cited in Tamura, 2004). The AoIR guidelines, by contrast, explicitly counsel against using direct quotes in this way: a simple search of quoted text-strings through Google and other search engines will, in many cases at least, lead directly to their authors.

By contrast, however, another Japanese researcher, Mr. Tamura Takanori, more closely followed what the AoIR guidelines recommend in his study of messages exchanged in a public forum. Mr. Tamura requested consent for use, not of direct quotes, but of paraphrases (which, to be clear, would be much harder to track down using simple string searches). Moreover, he invented pseudonyms for the authors (Tamura, 2004). Such an approach is striking, first of all in light of the radical differences between Western expectations of privacy, as these undergird the AoIR guidelines, and those at work in Japan. That is, until recently at least, notions of individual privacy as *positive* goods that must be protected (so Western research ethics traditions and the AoIR guidelines) are more or less absent in Japan: on the contrary, in part because of the influence of Buddhism and an emphasis on "no-self" (*musi*), there is rather the view that "privacy" is something to be done away with, especially if one seeks the Buddhist enlightenment of extinguishing the ego altogether (see Nakada & Tamura, 2005). In this light, Yasukawa and Ando's "failure" to protect the privacy of their subjects can be seen as a practice more in keeping with a more traditional Japanese sense of privacy as a more negative rather than a positive value, while Mr. Tamura's effort to protect the privacy of his research subjects reflects the increasing presence of a more Western-style emphasis on individual privacy as a positive good.

While the situation in Japan is clearly changing, it appears that currently at least there remain remarkable contrasts—indeed, an apparent opposition—between Western and Japanese conceptions of privacy; this opposition, moreover, is reflected in the research practice of Yasukawa and Ando. At the same time, however, Mr. Tamura's research practice comes closer to a Western-style IRE that would protect individual privacy—but in a Japanese context that retains many of the traditional values and attitudes of Japanese culture and tradition. We may see here, then, an ethical pluralism that balances *agreements* (between AoIR, on the one hand, and Mr. Tamura, on the other) concerning the importance of protecting privacy online, alongside irreducible *differences* between Western and Japanese culture regarding conceptions of the individual and privacy. This ethical pluralism thus works to preserve the differences that define radically diverse cultural identities, and thereby fulfills the requirements of a transnational social justice that insists we recognize and protect diverse cultural identities, especially as these rest on distinctive ethical norms and traditions.

Information Ethics in China

Professor Lü Yaohuai has written the first book in Chinese information ethics (Lü, 2002).[7] Lü focuses especially on issues that arise as China and the Chinese are increasingly communicating via ICTs with the larger world. Much along the lines I have outlined earlier, Lü argues, on the one hand, for a universal ethics suited to the global reach of the Internet and the World Wide Web. At the same time, however, he carefully articulates the often deep differences between information ethics as developed in the West and what he sees as an indigenous Chinese information ethics rooted specifically in Confucian and Buddhist traditions (Lü, 2005).

Lü's own resolution to the problem of a global information ethics—that is, one that enjoys both global scope and legitimacy, on the one hand, while preserving, on the other hand, precisely the distinctive values and traditions that define specific cultures and societies—further stands as a remarkable example of East-West ethical pluralism. To begin with, recognizing that especially on a global scale, neither law nor ethical imperatives alone can prevent people from acting unethically online, Lü turns to the neo-Confucian notion of *shen-du* (self-regulation, or self-control) [8] as a potential resolution to this problem.

In fact, such a notion of self-regulation is strikingly similar (indeed, we can say, resonates with) approaches to research ethics in several Western countries, including Germany, Denmark, and Sweden. While in response to (in)famous examples of human rights abuses in medical and social science research, the United States, Canada, the UK and Australia have developed Institutional Review Boards (U.S.), Research Ethics Boards (National Research Council, Canada), external Learning and Teaching Support Networks' subject centres and internal Academic Standards and Policy committees (UK), the National Health and Medical Research Council (Australia) and the Australian Research Council—Germany, Denmark, and Sweden have no such "institutional watch-dogs" in place. So far as I have been able to gather, there operates in these countries instead an institutional culture that assumes that researchers, especially as trained through the pertinent disciplines and university systems, will do the right thing. In those—apparently rare—instances when they do not, it is possible to complain to national boards or committees, such as the Danish Research Council for the Humanities, who may issue comment or reprimands (cf. Lundh, 2004).

Whether or not the neo-Confucian notion of *shen-du* will gain the needed ethical legitimacy it needs to function meaningfully in China very much remains to be seen. But at least, as a proposed component of a distinctively *Chinese* information ethics, it further constitutes one side of a potentially strong ethical pluralism that would hold together both Chinese and Western notions of self-regulation alongside the distinctive and irreducible differences between these two great traditions.

Ethical Pluralism in East-West Notions of Privacy

Computer ethics pioneer Deborah Johnson develops an extensive account of the range of justifications for privacy, especially in the U.S. context (Johnson, 2001). These justifications begin with privacy as an *intrinsic* good—that is, something that is considered to be good in itself that needs no further justification. In addition, privacy serves as a means—an *instrumental* good—to several other goods, including our efforts and rights to develop a sense of self and personal autonomy, intimate relationships, and so forth. Finally, privacy is central to the conditions required for participating in a democratic society, beginning with our sustaining and developing personal autonomy and freedom, our capacities for dialogue and debate, and so forth.

Not surprisingly, we find similar justifications for privacy in the German context. To begin with, privacy is understood as a basic right of the autonomous person *qua* citizen in a democratic society. Moreover, similar to Johnson's description of privacy as an instrumental good, in Germany, privacy is seen as instrumental to the protection of private autonomy, the freedom to express one's opinion, the "right to personality" (*Persönlichkeitsrecht*), and the freedom to express one's will. Finally—and here emerges a distinctive difference from the U.S. view—privacy protection, specifically data privacy protection, is seen as necessary for the development of business online (Bizer, 2003).

In fact, this last justification is at work in recent efforts to justify data privacy protections in Hong Kong and China. In Hong Kong, for example, rights to data privacy are justified as necessary for developing and expanding e-commerce (Tang, 2002). Similarly, emerging data privacy protection in China is justified primarily as a means to developing e-commerce. So we see a sharp contrast between Western (especially U.S.) and Asian justifications—a contrast, moreover, consistent with the contrasts between the two in terms of cultural traditions and understandings of privacy. That is, in contrast with Western emphases on individual privacy as a positive good (emphases, to be fair, that did not develop until the Enlightenment and industrialization), *individual* privacy was not a concern in China, in large measure because of long traditions of emphasizing (especially in Confucian thought) the good of the larger society first of all—a philosophical and cultural view that justified traditional Chinese practice of strong governmental control (cf. Lü, 2005).

As Professor Lü points out, we can see this historically *negative* understanding of individual privacy more sharply as it contrasts with the emergence of a new, more Western-style concept and term for privacy in China:

In 1985, the Chinese law dictionary only explained the concept of Yinsi. At that time, Yinsi (阴私) meant "privacy". But now people usually distinguish the difference between a "shameful secret" (Yinsi, 阴私) and "privacy" (Yinsi, 隐私). The term Yinsi (阴私) is defined as a hidden, bad thing, while the term Yinsi (隐私) is defined as a personal thing people do not wish to tell others or to disclose in public. (Lü, 2005)

This suggests that in 1985, Yinsi (阴私) was the closest equivalent to "privacy" in Chinese— but clearly one that, like its counterparts in other Asian countries such as Japan and Thailand, was strongly associated with things kept hidden because they were bad or shameful. It is only recently—and apparently, as an artifact of increased engagement with Western countries in recent decades—that we find in China (as well as in Japan and Thailand) a relatively new, more positive, concept of privacy that is in the Chinese example, 隐私, *yinsi*.[9]

Along with this more recent, more positive conception of privacy, Chinese citizens are guaranteed at least modest rights to data privacy protection, though these remain limited as compared with Western countries, in part precisely in order to preserve traditional Chinese emphases on the role of the state in establishing needed social order and harmony. As is the case in Hong Kong, data privacy protection is justified first of all instrumentally—precisely as it is needed for commerce and business efficiency (Chen, 2005).

We can see, then, that alongside the sharp contrasts between Eastern and Western countries, especially with regard to basic notions of *individual* privacy, there emerges here nonetheless a central and shared value of rights to privacy and data privacy protection. Indeed, there emerges here precisely an ethical pluralism that bridges not simply in theory, but in the *praxis* of information ethics, the considerable cultural divides between East and West. As with the other examples of pluralism we have seen, a set of shared values and expectations emerge—in this case, of privacy and data privacy protection. But these norms and expectations are clearly refracted through the "lenses" of specific cultural traditions and practices, and thereby interpreted and implemented in ways that both reflect and, even more importantly, preserve distinctive cultural values and traditions. So, from a Western perspective, rights to privacy and data privacy protection in China and Hong Kong are comparatively limited, and they are justified primarily by appeals to economic interests rather than to notions of the individual and citizen required for democratic governance. But these differences make perfect sense as they reflect precisely the deep differences between Asian and Western notions of the individual vis-à-vis the larger collective and the proper role of the state. And despite these clear differences—better, alongside these clear differences—the two understandings and implementations of privacy and data privacy protection are recognizably similar to one another: that is, there is here, if not commonality, sufficiently close similarity or resonance between the two to function in the ways needed for a *global* information ethics. In particular, Asian appeals to economic interests are closely similar, if not simply identical, to the economic rationale for privacy we see in German law; but at the same time, of course, both the U.S. and Germany endorse notions of privacy as critical to the individual and democracy, in clear contrast with their Asian counterparts.

In sum, I argue here that current understandings of privacy and data privacy protection in the West and Asia can be seen to constitute in *praxis* an ethical pluralism, one that holds together recognizably similar notions of privacy and data privacy protection alongside their distinctively different interpretations and implementations—where these differences in interpretation and implementation reflect and thus work to sustain the distinctive values and traditions that define each culture. In this way, we can see at both the levels of theory (i.e., the comparative philosophical reflections on the important resonances between, in our case, Aristotelian and Confucian thought) and in *praxis* an ethical pluralism that preserves distinctive cultural values and identities in a global information ethics intended for an interconnected and interdependent global society, and thereby meets the basic requirement of transcultural social justice of respecting and sustaining cultural diversity while further facilitating intercultural engagements on a global scale.

Concluding Remarks: Pluralism and Social Justice

To draw from Aristotle's famous comment about being, we can say that privacy, like being, is said in many ways.[10] On the one hand, we have seen—and not surprisingly—clearly distinctive understandings of "privacy" in U.S., the EU, Japan, China, Hong Kong, and Thailand; but these distinctive and important differences are held together by a shared focus on recognizably similar notions of privacy and data privacy protection. This pluralism thus parallels the first examples of pluralism we examined within Western traditions, starting with the example of a shared focus on *expectations* regarding informed consent for recording in Norway and the U.S., a focus nonetheless refracting into two very different (indeed, apparently opposite) requirements for informed consent in public spaces. We further saw a similar pluralism at work with regard to the "first principles" of data protection, as these were again implemented in distinctively different ways between the United States and the European Union.

It seems fair to say, then, that there is likewise a pluralism and resonance *between* Western and Eastern cultures in their approach to privacy and data privacy protection   that is, one that holds together the crucial differences defining each cultural tradition in terms of understandings and implementations of privacy and data privacy protection, alongside a clear resonance or harmony as both traditions point toward the shared value of privacy and data privacy protection as basic elements and practices of information ethics.

I by no means intend to argue here that ethical pluralism will thus resolve all crucial differences that will emerge as globalization continues to foster—apparently at an exponential pace—cross-cultural engagements that will make us increasingly aware of our differences as well as our similarities. But the theoretical strengths of ethical pluralism, both within the Western tradition and between especially Aristotelian and Confucian traditions, including its allied notions of resonance and harmony, coupled with what I take to be significant, real-world examples drawn from the *praxis* of information ethics, including the central concern with privacy and data privacy protection—these taken together suggest first of all that within the microcosm of information ethics we are not condemned to the Manichean choice of either dogmatism, ethnocentrism, and imperialism, on the one hand, or ethical relativism and its dangers of fascism on the other hand. Moreover, insofar as information ethics may serve as a microcosm for the larger macrocosm of the political dimensions of the cross-cultural encounters fostered by globalization and the spread of ICTs, I would suggest that ethical pluralism may serve as a potentially fruitful middle ground that might inspire similar approaches in the larger macrocosm that could help us avoid the otherwise lose-lose choices between global connectivity (but at the cost of homogenization that eliminates cultural diversity and identity), and a fragmentation that preserves cultural identity (but at the cost of isolation and sometimes horrific violence).

How far ethical pluralism might succeed in these ways on either the microcosm or macrocosm level remains very much to be seen. Such matters, in my view, can only be determined by making the effort to discern and articulate such pluralisms where they might exist. However, all of this will turn out in *praxis*. It seems fair to say that ethical pluralisms of the sort described here in both theoretical and practical terms are important devices and strategies for an information ethics that seeks to be genuinely *global* ethics—that is, an ethics that intends to discern and articulate (quasi-) universal norms that at the same time reflect and preserve the distinctive ethical norms and approaches that define cultural identities. In doing so, such ethical pluralisms are to be recommended as they thereby meet the demand of justice to recognize and respect the basic integrity of diverse cultures.

References

Ames, R., & Rosemont, H. (1998). *The analects of Confucius: A philosophical translation*. New York: Ballantine Books.

Association of Internet Researchers (AoIR). (2002). *Decision-making and ethical Internet research*. Retrieved January 10, 2006, from http://www.aoir.org/reports/ethics.pdf

Aristotle. (1943). *Aristotle's politics* (B. Jowett, trans.). New York: Modern Library.

Aristotle. (1968). *Metaphysics I-IX*, with an English translation by Hugh Tredennick. Cambridge, MA: Harvard University Press.

Barber, B. (1995). *Jihad versus McWorld*. New York: Times Books.

Bizer, J. (2003). Grundrechte im netz: Von der freien meinungsäußerung bis zum recht auf eigentum. In C. Schulzki-Haddouti (Ed.), *Bürgerrechte im netz* (pp.

21-29). Bonn, Germany: Bundeszentrale für politische Bildung. Available at http://www.bpb.de/publikationen/UZX6DW,,0,B%fcrgerrechte_im_Net.html

Burkhardt, J., Thompson, P., & Peterson, T. R. (2000). The first European congress on agricultural and food ethics and follow-up workshop on ethics and food biotechnology: A U.S. perspective. *Agriculture and Human Values, 17*(4), 327-332.

Chan, J. (2003). Confucian attitudes towards ethical pluralism. In R. Madsen & T. B. Strong (Eds.), *The many and the one: Religious and secular perspectives on ethical pluralism in the modern world* (pp. 129-153). Princeton, NJ: Princeton University Press.

Chen, Y. (2005). *Privacy in China.* Unpublished master's thesis. Nanyang Technological University, Singapore.

Eickelman, D. F. (2003). Islam and ethical pluralism. In R. Madsen & T. B. Strong (Eds.), *The many and the one: Religious and secular perspectives on ethical pluralism in the modern world* (pp. 161-180). Princeton, NJ: Princeton University Press.

Elberfeld, R. (2002). Resonanz als grundmotiv ostasiatischer ethik [Resonance as a fundamental motif of East Asian ethics]. In R. Elberfeld & G. Wohlfart (Eds.), *Komparative ethik: Das gute leben zwischen den kulturen* [Comparative ethics: The good life between cultures] (pp.131-141). Cologne, Germany: Edition Chora.

Elgesem, D. (2002). What is special about the ethical issues in online research? *Ethics and Information Technology, 4*(3), 195-203. Available at http://www.nyu.edu/projects/nissenbaum/ethics_elgesem.html

Ess, C. (2004a). Beyond *contemptus mundi* and cartesian dualism: Western resurrection of the bodysubject and (re)new(ed) coherencies with eastern approaches to life/death. In G. Wohlfart & H-G. Moeller (Eds.), *Philosophie des todes: Death philosophy East and West* (pp. 15-36). Munich, Germany: Chora.

Ess, C. (2004b). Moral imperatives for life in an intercultural global village. In R. Cavalier (Ed.), *The Internet and our moral lives* (pp. 161-193). Albany: State University of New York Press.

Ess, C. (2005a). Discourse ethics. In C. Mitcham et al. (Ed.), *Encyclopedia of science, technology and ethics.* New York: MacMillan Reference.

Ess, C. (2005b). Can the local reshape the global? Ethical imperatives for humane intercultural communication online. In J. Frühbauer, R. Capurro & T. Hausmanninger (Eds.), *Localizing the Internet: Ethical aspects in an intercultural perspective.* Schriftenreihe des ICIE, Bd 4. Munich, Germany: International Center for Information Ethics.

Ess, C. (2005c). *What is information ethics?* Retrieved January 10, 2006, from http://www.drury.edu/ess/CAP04/cap04infoethics.html

Ess, C. (2005d). "Lost in translation"?: Intercultural dialogues on privacy and information ethics (Introduction to special issue on privacy and data privacy protection in Asia). *Ethics and Information Technology, 7*(1), 1-6.

Ess, C. (2006a, forthcoming). Culture and communication on global networks: Cultural diversity, moral relativism, and hope for a global ethic? Or: Can Plato's *cybernetes* / Confucius' *junzi* navigate an interconnected world? In J. Weckert & J. van den Hoven (Eds.), *Moral philosophy and information technology.* Cambridge, UK: Cambridge University Press.

Ess, C. (2006b, forthcoming). Ethical pluralism and global information ethics. In L. Floridi (Ed.), Information ethics: Agents, artifacts and new cultural perspectives. Special issue of *Ethics and Information Technology.*

Floridi, L. (2003). What is the philosophy of information? In L. Floridi (Ed.), *The Blackwell guide to the philosophy of computing and information.* Oxford, UK: Blackwell. Available at http://www.blackwellpublishing.com/pci/downloads/introduction.pdf

Hamelink, C. (2000). *The ethics of cyberspace.* London: Sage.

Huntington, S. P. (1993). The clash of civilizations? *Foreign Affairs, 72*(3), 22-49.

Johnson, D. (2001). Privacy (ch. 5). In *Computer ethics* (3rd ed., pp. 109-136). Upper Saddle River, NJ: Prentice-Hall.

Kitiyadisai, K. (2005). Privacy rights and protection: foreign values in modern Thai context. *Ethics and Information Technology, 7*(1), 17-26.

Lü, Y. (2002). *Xin xi lun li xue* [Chinese information ethics]. Hunan, China: Middle South University Publication.

Lü, Y. (2005). Personal e-mail to the author.

Lundh, L. G. (2004). *En fornemmelse for forskning. En empirisk undersøgelse af forskningsetik i Dansk Internetforskning [A feeling for research: An empirical investigation of Internet research ethics within the humanities in Denmark].* Unpublished master's thesis, University of Copenhagen, Denmark.

Madsen, R., & Strong, T. (2003). *The many and the one: Religious and secular perspectives on ethical pluralism in the modern world.* Princeton, NJ: Princeton University Press.

Mizutani, M., Dorsey, J., & Moor, J. (2004). The Internet and Japanese conceptions of privacy. *Ethics and Information Technology, 6,* 121-128.

Nakada, M. (2005). Personal e-mail to the author.

Nakada, M., & Tamura, T. (2005). Japanese conceptions of privacy: An intercultural perspective. *Ethics and Information Technology, 7*(1), 27-36.

National Institutes of Health, Office of Human Subjects Research. (2005). *Code of Federal Regulations Title 45, Department of Health and Human Services, Part 46, Protection of Human Subjects.* Retrieved January 10, 2006, from http://ohsr.od.nih.gov/guidelines/45cfr46.html

National Committee for Research Ethics in the Social Sciences and the Humanities (NESH). (2001). *Guidelines for research ethics in the social sciences, law and the humanities.* Retrieved January 10, 2006, from http://www.etikkom. no/Engelsk/NESH/Publications/NESHguide

NESH. (2003). *Research ethics guidelines for Internet research.* Retrieved January 10, 2006, from http://www.etikkom.no/Engelsk/NESH/Publications/internet03

Persondataloven [Personal Data Law, Denmark]. (2001, April). *Lov. Nr. 429 af 31. Maj 2000 som ændret ved lov. Nr. 280 af 25.* Retrieved December 2, 2003, from http://147.29.40.90/_GETDOC_/ACCN/A20000042930-REGL. English version available at http://www.datatilsynet.dk/eng/index.html

Ramasoota, P. (2001). Privacy: A philosophical sketch and a search for a Thai perception. *Manusya: Journal of Humanities, 4*(2), 89-107.

Reidenberg, J. R. (2000). Resolving conflicting international data privacy rules in cyberspace. *Stanford Law Review, 52,* 1315-1376.

Stahl, B. C. (2004). *Responsible management of information systems.* Hershey, PA: Idea Group Inc.

Tamura, T. (2004). Unpublished manuscript.

Tang, R. (2002). *Approaches to privacy—the Hong Kong experience.* Retrieved January 11, 2006, from http://www.pco.org.hk/english/infocentre/speech 20020222.html

Tavani, H. (2004). *Ethics and technology: Ethical issues in an age of information and communication technology.* New York: Wiley.

Taylor, C. (2002). Democracy, inclusive and exclusive. In R. Madsen, W. M. Sullivan, A. Swiderl, & S. M. Tipton (Eds.), *Meaning and modernity: Religion, polity, and self* (pp. 181-194). Berkeley: University of California Press.

Thomson, J. J. (1971). A defense of abortion. *Philosophy and Public Affairs, 1*(1), 47-66.

Tu, W.-M. (1999). Humanity as embodied love: Exploring filial piety as a global ethical perspective. In M. Zlomislic & D. Goicoechea (Eds.), *Jen Agape Tao with Tu Wei-Ming* (pp. 28-37). Binghamton, NY: Institute of Global Cultural Studies.

Walther, J. (2002). Research ethics in Internet-enabled research: Human subjects issues and methodological myopia. *Ethics and Information Technology, 4*(3), 205-216. Available at http://www.nyu.edu/projects/nissenbaum/ethics_walther.html

Warren, K. J. (1990). The power and the promise of ecological feminism. *Environmental Ethics, 12*(2), 123-146.

Wiener, N. (1948). *Cybernetics: Or control and communication in the animal and the machine.* New York: Wiley.

Wiener, N. (1950). *The human use of human beings.* New York: Houghton Mifflin.

Yasukawa, J., & Ando, T. (2002). *Online therapy— characteristics and problems for media mediated social service activities.* Retrieved January 11, 2006, from http://ofc-hjm.misc.hit-u.ac.jp/hjm/MyDesk/Bib/2002a_1.pdf

Zhang, N. (2005). Personal e-mail to the author.

Endnotes

1. Of course, post-colonial scholarship has effectively demonstrated that the terms "East" and "West" are the artifacts of colonialism and imperialism, and as such, their meaning and use are problematic for a range of reasons. Nonetheless, I use the terms, in full recognition of their history and limitations, simply as useful shorthand.

2. *Ethical pluralism* is itself a term that has a number of meanings in contemporary philosophy. In this context, I first of all follow the usage of Richard Madsen and Tracy B. Strong, who suggest that we use the term to refer to attempts to discern and establish connections in the face of irreducible *cultural* differences (2003, p. 4).

3. As I have argued more fully elsewhere (Ess, 2006a, b, forthcoming), this project of attempting to discern how diverse ethical norms and approaches may be reconciled (in part, at least) through structures of ethical pluralism that conjoin irreducible cultural differences alongside connections (including resonances and harmonies) that thus form a complementarity is rooted in the *pros hen* equivocals of Aristotle—and before that, in what I call the interpretive pluralism of Plato. This interpretive pluralism argues that at least some ethical differences may reflect *agreement* upon basic norms, values, and so forth, but these are interpreted, applied and/or understood in diverse ways by diverse communities. Such interpretive pluralism, as thereby marking out a middle ground between ethical relativism (no universal values exist) and ethical dogmatism (only a single value may hold universal validity, applied homogenously in all times and places), in fact can be seen in contemporary feminists such as Karen Warren (1990), and in discourse ethics, especially as applied in information ethics by Bernd Carsten Stahl (2004). Finally, such pluralism is not simply a central element of Western ethical thought; on the contrary, it can be found at work in the ethical traditions of Islam (Eickelman, 2003) and Confucian thought (Chan, 2003) as well.

4. We will see one example of such conflicts next, in the contrast between the research ethics at work in the Yasukawa and Ando study from 2002 and the AoIR ethical guidelines. An even

more striking contrast is at work in an example I have documented elsewhere. Briefly, a sharp contrast emerges between the ethical assumptions underlying an online game, designed in an Asian country for the sake of determining customer preferences for next-generation network services, and research ethics and privacy law in Western countries, specifically Denmark. For the Asian designer, the game is morally unproblematic because it collects no personal information—defined to include IP addresses, personal names and addresses, and so forth. From the standpoint of Danish data privacy law, however, the demographic information collected in the game (age, gender, income) is included *within* the definition of personal information, and thus requires the basic protections of informed consent and guarantees of privacy and confidentiality (Persondataloven, 2000, 2001). Moreover, the game design is morally problematic from a Western standpoint because it fails to inform participants of the purpose of the game; nor does it ask for informed consent for using the demographic data provided by users, and the design has no procedure for protecting this data. Beyond considerable differences between Western and Asian countries and traditions regarding privacy (explored more fully later in the text), the contrasts here may further reflect the contrast between Western conceptions of rights as focusing on the *individual* as rights-holder, and Asian traditions (especially as influenced by Confucian thought), as these emphasize group consensus and harmony as primary (Ess, 2005d). In any event, this example makes clear that whatever pluralisms may emerge between elements of Asian and Western information ethics and computer ethics—again, such pluralisms will not eliminate all conflict and disagreement.

[5]   My thanks here to professors Zhang Ning and Nakada Makoto for their help with determining the Chinese characters at work here and elsewhere in this chapter.

[6]   I owe virtually all of the material here regarding information ethics in Japan to the work of Mr. Tamura Takanori, primarily, his unpublished report (2004), along with subsequent discussions with Mr. Tamura and his colleagues, including Professor Nakada Makoto, Mr. Takenouchi Tadeshi, and Ms. Leslie-Tkach Kawasaki.

[7]   My access to this volume is thanks to the translation efforts of my students at the University of Trier during winter semester, 2004—Na Yang, Wen Li, and Chenchen Song. I am very pleased to be able to express my gratitude to them for their hard work and assistance in making portions of professor Lü's volume accessible to me.

[8]   According to Professor Zhang, this term has "no equivalent in Japanese but this term means something shameful or something wrong in a private and hidden area of life" (Zhang, 2005).

[9]   Somewhat more carefully: this initially negative sense of individual privacy thus parallels the Buddhist emphasis on *musi* (no-self) we have seen in Japan. By the same token, "privacy" appears primarily as a loan-word in Japanese (Mizutani et al., 2004, p. 121; cf. Nakada & Tamura, 2005). Similarly, Priongrong Ramasoota notes that, "The Thai language does not have a word for privacy but refers to it by descriptively translating from English as *khwam pen suan tua* or *khwam pen yu suan tua*, meaning "the state of being private" (Ramasoota, 2001, p. 97). Ramasoota goes on to argue that "the traditional Thai conception of privacy is fundamentally *collectivistic*," shared in the first instance "by *intimate members of the same household*." By this token, individualistic privacy is said to have no place in traditional Thai culture" (2001, p. 98). And as we saw in the Japanese example, Western-style notions of the individual and privacy directly *conflict* with largely negative attitudes in Buddhism towards notions of the individual or self; Buddhist thinking sees the obsession with one's individual self and one's possessions, material or not, as the root source of suffering. Emancipation…means disillusionment with and relinquishing of selfdom and worldly desires. Therefore, individuality can be seen as both the beginning and the end to human emancipation in Buddhism (Ramasoota, 2001, p. 100f.). I am indebted to Professor Soraj Hongladarom for making me aware of this chapter. For additional discussion of notions of traditional and contemporary notions of privacy in Thailand, see Kitiyadisai (2005).

[10]   Most famously, *Metaphysics* IV, II / 1003a33-35: "The term 'being' is used in various senses, but with reference [*pros hen*] to one central idea and one definite characteristic, and not as merely a common epithet" (Aristotle, 1968, p. 147).

Chapter V

Global Digital Divide, Global Justice, Cultures and Epistemology

Soraj Hongladarom
Chulalongkorn University, Thailand

Abstract

The problem of global digital divide, namely disparity in Internet access and use among the various regions of the world, is a growing concern. Even though, according to some reports, the gap is getting narrower, this does not mean that the problem is disappearing, because the problem does not just consist in getting more people to become "wired," so to speak. This chapter investigates the various relationships among the global digital divide, global justice, cultures and epistemology. Very briefly stated, not getting access to the Internet constitutes an injustice because the access is a social good that can lead to various other goods. Furthermore, as information technology is a second-order technology, one that operates on meaning bearing symbols, access to the technology is very much an issue of social epistemology, an attempt to find out the optimal way to distribute knowledge across the social and cultural domains.

Introduction

The digital divide has been one of most talked about phenomena in recent years. Trying to bridge the gap has been on the agenda of virtually all public policy makers since the products of information and communication technologies started to become more common not too long ago. It is recognized almost universally that the digital divide, basically a gap in access to and use of information technology and the global network that access makes possible, and especially the *global* digital divide, represent a significant policy problem that governments at various levels in all countries feel the need to address. The amount of attention and, more importantly, of physical and intellectual resources devoted to the issue has been really staggering. It has been so intensive in recent years that the World Bank announced a little while ago that the global digital divide is indeed disappearing (*Digital divide closing fast*, 2005).

Hence it might seem that the topic of this chapter is beginning to be outmoded. After all, if the digital divide is really closing, then why should we be concerned with its ethical or social implications? The exercise may cease to be relevant for current public policy formulation and may indeed become one of history—what kind of social and ethical implications arose when the digital divide prevailed? However, I do not believe that discussing the ethical dimensions of the digital divide would become irrelevant; nor do I believe that we would cease talking about the phenomenon, even if it really is the case that it is indeed disappearing. For reasons that will be made clear in this chapter, the sheer fact that more and more households in the world are equipped with computer technology and are getting wired to the Internet does not automatically translate to the realization of all the goals and visions that characterized attempts to close the digital divide. Simply having a tool does not always mean that one uses it in the way that was originally intended. We are now just beginning to see how the tools of information and communication technologies are going to be used in the various localities around the world.

What I would like to do in this chapter is to begin to explore the relations between the global digital divide, global justice, cultures and epistemology. This is pertinent to the discussion earlier because attempts to bridge the global digital divide, I would like to argue, are a species of attempts to bring about global justice and that the attempts need first to start from an appreciation of local cultures and how these cultures view their own epistemic practices, which are invariably part and parcel of their own cultures. Nevertheless, I can do no more than present a brief sketch of the relations here, because to do justice to each of the aspects of the relations would take us further afield than the space of this chapter allows. The sketch is also intended as an invitation to further research. The World Bank report that the digital divide is disappearing everywhere may be convincing, but it does not lessen the urgency of making an effort to understand how these factors are related to one another. This is so because simply providing the population with hardware and software and access to the Internet seldom suffices to realize the kind of "utopian" information society that the earlier pioneers and evangelists of information technology had in their visionary eyes.

Narrowing of the Global Digital Divide and the Persistence of Old Problems

It was just only slightly more than two decades ago that personal computers started to make their way into our lives; and the Internet started to appear on the scene little more than a decade ago. Yet these seem to most of us like ages ago. This points to the extreme speed at which the technology is evolving and spreading throughout the world. When it was in its infancy, proponents of information technology usually hailed it as a harbinger of a time when time itself and distance were eliminated. A result of this would be, in their view, a complete merging of ideas and information in such a way that every piece of information would be at everybody's fingertips. Ideas such as democracy and freedom would float around the world and enter the consciousness of the people who would presumably take these ideas as a basis for changes in their own communities and societies. Knowledge would be readily available and the whole world will be blessed with better-informed and knowledgeable global citizens.

However, it seems that even as the digital divide is closing, these visions have not been fulfilled in many parts of the world. Universal knowledge, for example, is still a dream, as the near universal attempts at promoting the use of ICTs in schools can attest. Entz and Hongladarom (2004) argue that simply providing hardware and software to people seldom suffices in bringing about any kind of desired change in their worlds and communities. In the late 1990s the Thai government tried to bridge the digital divide problem in the country through a direct injection of hardware and software to villages. Computers were provided to village schools free of charge. What happened, however, was that many of the computers were not used to their full potential, and not in a way that would bring about any kind of universal knowledge or flow of information; many were not used at all. In many areas there was no electricity; in others there was a lack of qualified personnel who could operate computers reasonably well. Giving away computers in this case became a symbolic act of the powerful and centralized government, acting on its own without consultation with the village schools (Entz & Hongladarom, 2004).

The problems remain because there is no simple equation between possession of hardware and software on the one hand, and being able to use that software and hardware to their full potential on the other. Furthermore, it is difficult to say precisely what actually constitutes "using the computers to their full potential." This alone requires much more conceptual and empirical study. Thus, one should not take the World Bank Report that the global digital divide is closing as evidence that the problems are disappearing. It may be the case that the World Bank Report does not specifically refer to the Thai case or similar ones, because they may already have factored in the conditions that would make computer access and use a real possibility before they announced that the gap is indeed closing. Thus, they might not have counted the Thai case as an example of the divide closing. Nonetheless, even if the scenario they are reporting is true, even if a proportionally large number of people, say in Africa and Asia, are actually using computers that are wired to the Internet, that by itself does not mean that the utopian dream is automatically realized. The old problems, of poverty, inequality and so on, seem to persist even in the face of the virtually total diffusion of ICTs.

To see how this is the case let us look at the utopian dream in more detail. Early proponents of diffusion of information technology have pointed out that ICTs could facilitate and engender rapid development in various areas, such as education, health care, finance and taxation, and many more. It was envisaged that the diffusion, in integrating data and information scattered in many places, would result in eradicating poverty in rural areas through providing needed information to the rural poor so that they could build up their capabilities and rise above the poverty line. The Ministry of Information and Communication Technology of Thailand (www.mict. go.th/), established in 2003, also subscribed to the idea, and has as one of its prime missions to facilitate development through bridging the digital divide within the country. In 2003 the Ministry had a plan of selling low-cost computers to the Thai population, and it contracted a number of hardware manufacturers to produce machines according to its own specifications in huge numbers so that the economy of scale would drive the price down to make the machines become more affordable. The operating system was originally set to be a version of localized Linux developed by a research arm of the Ministry. However, the buyer could also choose to have Microsoft Windows XP installed in these systems after Microsoft offered to sell their products at a much reduced price (Entz & Hongladarom, 2004). In early March 2005, the Ministry of Information and Communication Technology again declared a policy of providing 250,000 computers, together with broadband Internet connection, to schools nationwide. The stated target is one computer for 20 students and funds from the national budget are to be used. (*Lofty plans for schools*, 2005).

Despite these efforts, however, the promise of the information society has not been fulfilled. Of course empirical research on the local Thai context here is necessary to substantiate the claim, but as the Thai examples alluded to earlier show, providing hardware and software alone does not seem adequate. To date there have been no systematic studies to measure the effectiveness of these measures, and we can see the same line of thinking behind these policies, viz. centralized government acting as if the entire country were a pliant mold that they can shape whatever way they want. In any case, many researchers have pointed out that attempts to bridge the digital divide require much more than hardware and software. In a background report to the InfoDev Symposium in Switzerland, Kerry McNamara says:

The presence or absence of ICTs (the "digital divide") is a symptom, not a cause. And the underlying causes of persistent poverty often have little to do, except indirectly, with the supply or absence of ICTs. By focusing on the "digital divide" (another in a long series of gaps that international development agencies have identified and sought to bridge over the past several decades) the proponents of ICT-for-development often misdirected their energies and weakened their own cause. (McNamara, 2003, p. 4)

Lisa Servon argues that one needs to change one's thinking about the digital divide and broaden the concept to more than the simple provision of hardware and software because when "we provide people with computers, we find that not much changes. IT on its own does not function as a ladder out of poverty" (Servon, 2002, p. 6). She indicates dimensions of the digital divide problem other than access, which have to do with training and content (Servon, 2002, pp. 7-8). Her findings indicate that access is an "incomplete solution" and that "tech-fix is a myth" (Servon, 2002, pp. 222-223). Even though the gap is narrowing, this does not necessarily show that the problem is disappearing, for she found that many who are using the computer a lot are actually performing low-level tasks such as data input or other secretarial tasks (Servon, 2002, p. 222). In addition, it seems that the technology provides resources, freedom, flexibility and opportunities for the already powerful group in society (Servon, 2002, p. 223). It seems, then, that the old problems of social inequality still persist, even in a supposedly "information-intensive" society where the global digital divide and the divide within countries are fast disappearing.

Much more, then, is needed to close the digital gap. It is, however, surprising that many policy initiatives still aim at doing nothing more than providing hardware and software infrastructure and hoping that they alone can do the trick. In an attempt to reformulate how the digital divide problem should be conceptualized, Mark Warschauer sees the issue as a problem of social inclusion rather than a divide, which he regards as too restrictive and as presupposing a binary opposition between the "haves" and "have-nots" which is not supported by the facts (Warschauer, 2003). According to Warschauer, the main aim of is not to narrow or to close the digital divide, but to find ways for marginalized groups to be included in sharing the benefits that information and communication technologies can bring about (Warschauer, 2003, p. 211). He spells out the need for thorough analyses of the social structures, problems, organizations and relations involved, which naturally are different from one context to another, as an important factor in any attempt to formulate policies in that context. Moreover, the capabilities of individuals need to be promoted (Warschauer, 2003, p. 211). It is clear that Warschauer, too, does not see sheer provision of hardware and software as sufficient.

Global Digital Divide and Global Justice

The disparity between the amount of access to and usage of information technology among the nations of the world, to the extent that it exists in a form that constitutes inequality, is thus an issue of global justice. Many discussions of global justice by social and political philosophers have typically tended to focus on the more abstract aspects of the issue centered around the justification of global justice. Onora O'Neill focuses on the more theoretical aspect of global justice, arguing that Rawls's conception of justice is too restrictive and calling for the international organizations to play their part, even though these organizations do not, as a rule, have the kind of power needed to ensure justice in a "bounded" society (O'Neill, 2000). Andrew Hurrell argues that international organizations have a moral role to play in ensuring global economic justice and that they are "dense" enough to do the job. However, they "constitute a deformed political order," namely in distribution of advantages and disadvantages, in who sets the rules, in the capacity of states themselves to adjust to the economy, and in the "limited capacity of international laws and institutions to constrain effectively the unilateral and often illegal acts of the strong" (Hurrell, 2001, p. 43). Furthermore, Thomas Pogge argues that the Western nations have often put their priorities regarding global justice in the wrong place. He deeply criticizes the new global economic order led by the United States, which he sees to be responsible for mass poverty in the developing world. In her Olof Palme lecture, Martha Nussbaum calls for a new alternative theory of global justice to the dominant contractarian and Rawlsian one, or the one favored by Pogge, which attempts to broaden Rawls's conception across national borders (Nussbaum, 2004). She would like to base consideration of global justice on certain fixibility of outcomes, rather than on fair procedure as is prominent in the contractarian theories. Following Amartya Sen, Nussbaum argues for a "human capabilities approach" of global justice that focuses more on facilitating the realization of certain human capabilities rather than on sheer provision of economic goods. Hence, narrowing the digital gap might presumably be included in the list of Nussbaum's list of capabilities also. Fred Dallmayr seems to be one of the rather limited number of philosophers who take up the gap in knowledge as a factor contributing to global injustice. Dallmayr (2002) issues a "plea for global justice," an action that is needed as a result of globalization and its consequent social and economic inequality across the globe. He indicates three areas of global inequality, viz. power, wealth and knowledge (Dallmayr, 2002). It is especially inequality in knowledge that is of particular concern in Dallmayr's paper and the next section of this chapter will be devoted to this.

What these philosophers share in common here is that they look at global justice from a wider perspective, emphasizing not only the actual contents of justice, but also the theoretical foundation—how a particular version of global justice is to be justified. Pogge, for example, argues that Western nations are morally bound to re-think their priorities in ensuring global justice. He does not spend much time in his paper detailing what a particular developing nation, such as Thailand or Cambodia, might need in order to achieve a kind of parity in terms of information and com-munication technologies that presumably would alleviate the problem. Nussbaum offers an alternative theory of global justice, but her paper does not focus specifically on how information technology itself should figure in an attempt to delineate the list of capabilities that should be fulfilled. Consequently, the time has come for an investigation of how the discussions on the global digital divide should have any bearing on those on global justice.

Taking the digital divide as an issue of global justice would mean that access to the benefits of information and communication technologies is a good—something, like health and opportunities, that should be equally shared among the population in the community. However, as it is by no means clear what actually constitutes the benefits of access to the information and communication technologies, more work still needs to be done to clarify this point. On the one hand, access to ICTs and the Internet should in itself be considered as a good, because, presumably, having it enables one to realize one's own goals and desires, just as being in possession of good health enables one to enjoy one's life and to perform activities that one could not do had one not been healthy. On the other hand, there are many people nowadays who choose not to get connected and not to use the computers at all, but these people are not considered unequal to others because they have other social and economic goods, such as an adequate level of income, education, welfare and so on. But there are not very many who would deny having good health. Hence it seems that having access to ICTs alone is not the answer. Moreover, we have seen in the last section that hardware and software alone are not enough to achieve the kind of parity that would qualify for there to be justice. Someone might counter that those who chose not to get connected did not get connected out of their own choice. They are not unequal to their peers, as mentioned, since they could easily get con-nected as soon as they wanted to, whereas those who are denied access, such as the rural poor in Thailand, would not get access to ICTs, even if they really wanted to. But this only shows that access to ICTs may not be a primary good, but a secondary good. A primary good is one that satisfies some basic need of those in possession of the good. Thus health is a primary good because just about everybody desires it for its own sake, as Aristotle said. Access to ICTs, on the other hand, appears to be more secondary, since having it enables one to enjoy other kinds of goods, such as information (in an age where information itself is considered a *good*) or income (through e-commerce). This points to the extreme importance of the content of the flow of data facilitated by the network. In some way the content being transmitted through the network is itself a primary good, and the network is then a secondary good because it enables the former to be distributed to where it is needed. Thus, if one wants to tie this up with the global justice issue, one would then need to elaborate upon what it is that the possession of would reduce global inequality. Here knowledge, or epistemic practices, and culture have a very important role to play, and attempts to bridge the global digital divide effectively would not be successful if these are not taken into consideration.

Talking about the global digital divide as an instance of global justice is a step down toward the more specific from the often highly abstract papers on theories that the literature offers. It seems that taking the digital divide as an issue of justice would need a special set of vocabulary, because of the technical nature of the phenomenon. Most policy analysts and researchers on diffusion of ICTs in Thailand are bureaucrats working for the government. Most of them have a technical background and usually regard their jobs to be technical tasks of studying and conceiving policies in a rather formulaic manner. In Thailand it is usually the case that policy researchers on a technical issue consist of technicians in that area. Thus, it is mostly medical doctors who formulate the country's health care policy and it is usually engineers and computer scientists who propose policies to the government in the areas of information technology and the digital divide. This may stem from the Thais' belief that in technical matters, including policy studies on those matters, things are better left to the technicians or experts in question, since they know best about their own field. Hence, discourse on these topics is often couched in technical language and jargon, which further deepens the public's attitude toward such matters as being purely technical requiring technical solutions. Talks about the digital divide, in Thailand at least and presumably in other developing countries as well, are often couched in the technical jargon of computer scientists and network specialists. Thus a knowledge gap that is already in existence between the educated urban elites and the less educated majority in the countryside is exacerbated. The digital divide then becomes a symptom of a wider divide between the elites who seem to have everything and the poor who do not seem to have anything. And the use of specialist jargons by the authorities has become a symbol of power for them against the local villagers. If there is to be a solution to the digital divide problem, then language has to be considered too; and, as we shall see in this chapter, language is but one of the aspects of culture that needs to be taken into consideration in any attempt to solve the problem.

At any rate, the issue of the use of computer and specialist jargon in policy formation and deliberation is related to another, more theory-oriented, issue of which set of vocabulary is most suitable for discussion of the philosophical and ethical components of the digital divide problem. In fact, one might make the case that talking about the digital divide in this context does not require a special set of vocabulary, that is specific to the technology in question and that makes its discussion different from talking about other goods, such as income and education. In this sense, taking the global digital divide as an issue of global justice is no different in principle from taking the global divide in health care as an issue in global justice. Since what is being emphasized here is the provision of health care to the world's population in a just and equitable manner, so too the provision of access to information and communication technologies should be in the same vein. No special vocabulary needs to be involved. However, the issue of which set of vocabulary is suitable is a very complicated one and cannot be treated in full detail in this chapter.

While this position is plausible, it is nonetheless the case that there are different levels of abstraction when one discusses global justice and its content, and these different levels make it necessary for there to be at least two sets of vocabulary to work with. This difference is not the same as that of the policy formulators mentioned in the previous paragraph. On the one hand, there is the general vocabulary that discusses global justice; this is often found in the literature on the topic among social and political philosophers. On the other, there is the special set of vocabulary that pertains to information and computer technologies in particular. This set is not the exactly the same as that of the technicians discussed earlier, for it focuses not on the technical nature of the technology, but on the more conceptual problem of how the diffusion of information technology is related to the goals and values of a community and the life-world of a people. Thus this latter set is more in tune with the conceptual resources found in philosophy of technology. In this sense, a case could perhaps be made that discussion of the global digital divide as an issue of global justice requires some set of vocabulary that is specific to the issue.

This set of vocabulary can be found, for example, in the works of philosophers of technology when they analyze the role technology plays in human life. One of the chief problems in philosophy of technology concerns technological determinism—the view that infusion of technology in society invariably brings about certain changes in the attitudes and structures of that society. It is well-known that this view is subscribed to by such philosophers as Martin Heidegger and Jacques Ellul. In the context of the global digital divide, the issue is whether the infusion of the technology, which is the aim of proponents of attempts to narrow the divide, would bring in certain changes which are inevitable. The early proponents alluded earlier in the chapter argued that the infusion would certainly bring about desirable changes, and it is clear that the belief is based on technological determinism. However, technological determinism is being challenged from many angles. Charles Ess and Fay Sudweeks (1998, 2000, 2001, 2002, 2004) have shown that the belief that computer-mediated communication will bring about certain inevitable changes in any culture where it is practised is unfounded empirically. This is mainly because cultures usually have within their resources the capability of "co-opting" these influences to make them their own. Thus, it has not been shown to be the case that all cultures will change in the same way as a result of their participating in the Internet and in the global communication network (Hongladarom, 2000, 2001a).

If this is indeed the case, then it is ultimately up to the cultures themselves to determine their course of action regarding the Internet. The implication for the global digital divide issue is that, at the very least, a special set of vocabulary, that of philosophy of technology and analyses of computer-mediated communication and culture, pioneered by Ess and Sudweeks, should be of value in aiding us to understand the complexities surrounding the global digital divide and global justice better.

Information Technology, Epistemology and Culture

Ess and Sudweeks have done a lot to show that information technology, computer-mediated communication and cultures are interrelated to a great extent. We have already seen that information and communication technologies can indeed be considered a good, albeit in a secondary manner, and that social inequality can indeed happen when one section of a population has more of their products and benefits than another section. In addition to these aspects, information and communication technologies do have their own special quality, which merits a separate type of discussion apart from the usual one in political and social philosophy when social inequality is discussed. Another reason for this is that information and communication technologies, including the Internet, are pliable and can be used in daily life in very diverse ways, and it is here that the technologies have an intimate relation with culture. While older technological products, such as the tractor or the plough, can only be used in a limited number of ways, computers can be programmed to do many tasks, as many are, no doubt, familiar. Operating a tractor or a plough does not seem to require as much knowledge and skill as one needs to work a computer efficiently.

In this sense, the computer can be seen as a *second-order* technology, as opposed to the *first-order* technologies exemplified by the tractor or the toaster oven. First-order technology, like the toaster, operates on a chunk of concrete reality. But computers do not directly do so, as they operate on binary digits acting as symbols capable of referring to anything, including non-existent things in future plans. It is true that computers do actually operate on chunks of reality, namely the electronic signals representing ones or zeroes, but these do not mean anything and the binary digits always refer to something other than themselves. An older tool such as an abacus can actually do the same kind of work that a computer can do, though much more slowly. In this case the abacus can be considered a second-order technology also. But the immense speed and power of computers to operate on these electronic signals seems to make them a breed apart from the older tools, even from the electronic calculator. Computers can be used in many ways, from playing video games to speculating on the stock market. The toaster or the automobile, as first-order technologies, can do only limited things.

The epistemological implication of this is that, as a second-order technology, the computer's capability in manipulating symbols makes it, in a real sense, an extension of the cognitive power of human beings. Traditionally, epistemologists are concerned with the normative problems of knowledge—what counts as knowledge, how a piece of information should be justified so that it becomes a piece of knowledge, and so on. However, with the influx of the information technology, these problems have expanded quite significantly in range. Goldman, for example, is calling for a revamp in how epistemology is done in that he calls for a "social epistemology" that takes into account the societal aspects of knowledge (Goldman, 1999). He writes:

In what respects is social epistemology social? First, it focuses on social paths or routes to knowledge. That is, considering believers taken one at a time, it looks at the many routes to belief that feature interactions with other agents, as contrasted with private or asocial routes to belief acquisition. This "social path" dimension is the principal dimension of sociality that concerns me here. Second, social epistemology does not restrict itself to believers taken singly. It often focuses on some sort of group entity—a team of co-workers, a set of voters in a political jurisdiction, or an entire society—and examines the spread of information or misinformation across that group's membership. Rather than concentrate on a single knower, as did Cartesian epistemology, it address the distribution of knowledge or error within the larger social cluster. Even in this second perspective, however, the knowing agents are still individuals. Third, instead of restricting knowers to individuals, social epistemology may consider collective or corporate entities, such as juries or legislatures, as potential knowing agents. This third approach will occasionally be taken in this volume, but only rarely. (1999, pp. 4-5)

It is these aspects of social epistemology mentioned by Goldman, especially the one on distribution of knowledge across a group of population and societies, that most concern us here. Basically what Goldman has done is to relocate the focus of epistemology from the exclusive attention toward the individual knower to the wider array of individuals in groups and societies. Nonetheless, the normative interest of epistemology still remains. It is relocated in new problems concerning how the best approach in knowledge distribution across groups of individuals is to be effected, for example. Goldman's rough answer to this problem is that the distribution should be such that the amount of knowledge across the array of groups is maximized, where he defines knowledge roughly as "true belief" (Goldman, 1999, pp. 3-7). I have no quarrel with Goldman's proposal in this chapter (that was an occasion for another of my papers (Hongladarom, 2002), but I agree with his social epistemology project, especially on the normative problem of knowledge distribution, and it is this that is most relevant to the topic of this chapter.

The digital divide exacerbates the knowledge distribution problem in many ways. First of all, the divide clearly shows that knowledge distribution is skewed. As in individualistic epistemology, where the concern is on how to find the best route toward knowledge for an individual. Here the concern is also on how to find such a route for a society. The computer's role as the symbol manipulation tool for the modern age—its role as a second-order technology—makes it the key player in knowledge distribution. Secondly, when the discussion turns toward the global digital divide, the focus then is on knowledge distribution across nations; hence the issue becomes intertwined with those in political philosophy. Thirdly, discussions of culture further complicate the issue because, as I will elaborate further in this chapter, culture could be regarded as the sum total of the beliefs and practices of a group of people who have stayed together for a long time sharing a system of symbols, meanings and traditions together. Thus epistemic practice, which is the practice of a culture regarding production, dissemination and evaluating knowledge, plays an obvious role in knowledge distribution and digital divide problems. A social epistemology that seeks to illuminate the digital divide problem needs to pay serious attention to cultures and their epistemic practices.

The computer's capacity to operate on anything that human beings can think of or talk about make it a very powerful tool. In this case computers can even operate on non-existent things like future plans and fictional works. As the works of Ess and Sudweeks show, culture permeates the use and design of information technology, and the second-order nature of information technology means that it functions as more of a transparent medium through which *content* is transmitted, stored and processed. Since content depends largely on the goals and agenda of all who are communicating through the medium, it is a perfect means by which the cultural traits of the people communicating with one another emerge.

The capacity of computers to operate on symbols makes it a very powerful cultural tool. "Culture" is taken here in the anthropological sense that refers to the sum total of a group of humans' symbolic and meaning-giving activities. Thus language is definitely part of human culture, as well as all activities that have symbolic meaning attached to them, such as religions and ways of greeting. In this sense the computer can be regarded as a tool that facilitates and extends human symbol production and manipulation, in much the same way as pencil and paper, or charcoal and cave wall in the past. So there is a strong connection between computers and cultures. On the one hand, computers are a symbol manipulation tool *par excellence,* and human culture is nothing if not production and interpretation of symbolic representations. What Ess and Sudweeks have found is that computers and computer-mediated communication have largely been co-opted into the worlds of local cultures. Instead of computer use dictating how a particular local culture produces its own content and in what manner the computer itself is being used, computers and information technology have become integrated to local cultures in such a way that the technology itself, the symbols being produced, and their meanings, are all included within the horizon of that culture.

Technological determinists may object to this, saying that it may be too simplistic to say that information technology is a transparent medium. After all, so the argument goes, operating a computer requires one to change many of one's habits. Firstly a stable source of electricity has to be installed; then the user has to have learned the skills needed to work on the computer; and then the computer requires one to work on it in a certain way which, in a way, limits the freedom of the user, because one has to follow the prescribed rules and choices of the operating system which means that the user seems to have no choice other than what is dictated them by the software. However, this does not necessarily mean that the user is constrained to the extent that her creative talents or her distinctive cultural traits are not possible at all. Nowadays members of all cultures in the world do use pencil and paper as a matter of course, and this older technology is so pervasive that one hardly pauses to think about it. Yet it does not seem that the identity of a particular culture does change as a result of the culture's adoption of pencil and paper. Furthermore, there is no denial that the culture itself also changes as a result of their adoption of the technology. The determinists do, in fact, have a point—only that technology and culture seem to determine each other, since one is part and parcel of the other, rather than one determining the other externally, so to speak (Warschauer, 2003, pp. 199-216).

This distinctiveness on the part of computers makes it the case that running it effectively requires much more knowledge and skill than is required for running the first-order technologies. Much more is needed before those who have not found a place for computers and the network in their lives can be fully "computer literate" and function in a way that alleviates the inequality exemplified by the divide. Education is, of course, important. The second-order characteristic of computer technology makes it the case that one needs to factor in epistemological considerations in a kind of philosophical endeavor to make sense of the whole phenomenon, and in any attempt to lay a foundation for a workable and effective policy for solving the digital divide problem. This is so because, in addition to the fact that one needs to possess a certain amount of knowledge and skill in order to operate a computer relatively well, the second-order characteristic, the one that enables computers to work on symbols capable to referring to anything whatsoever, makes them prime epistemic tools which could prove instrumental in bridging the knowledge and information gap that undoubtedly exists in the world. And, in this sense, looking for ways to solve the digital divide should go hand in hand with solving the knowledge and information divide too. Furthermore, as the problem takes on a global dimension, the epistemological considerations become global, too, and in the same manner, the digital/knowledge/information gap becomes global, which adds another dimension to the whole discussion. It is here that discussions on global/local epistemic practices have a role (Hongladarom, 2002).

The Digital Divide and the Knowledge Gap

Fred Dallmayr (2002) points out that there are three main areas of global inequality, namely power, wealth and knowledge. Thus he raised the knowledge distribution issue mentioned earlier as a serious problem facing the world today. The discussion on knowledge is the more interesting, since disparities in power and wealth are rather commonplace. According to Dallmayr, the global knowledge gap is exemplified by the fact that more than four-fifths of the world's output in science and technology comes from the West, that the vast majority of scientific and technological experts reside in the West, and that there exists in the West a policy guarding knowledge and information as a highly precious commodity (Dallmayr, 2002, pp. 148-149). This gap is a result of the "expertocracy" and "Europeanization of the earth" (Dallmayr, 2002, p. 148). Dallmayr argues that the rise of globalization and ICTs has made it possible for the few who possess the technical know-how to rule over the majority of the world's cultures and population. These few who hold the power are the ones who manipulate the images and content of the mass media that is distributed via the global network, including satellite television, the print media and the Internet. The power exists through a manipulation of symbols and images through these media in such a way that the ordinary citizens of the world have become "image consumers and pliant tools of telegenic politicians and pundits ruling over a televisual or phantom democracy" (Dallmayr, 2002, pp. 149-150).

The technological determinist bent in Dallmayr's paper here is unmistakable. Taking a rather pessimistic stance, Dallmayr views the contemporary infusion of information and communication technologies as a system of control by which the world's population is mesmerized and virtually enslaved by the few manipulators of images and symbols who hold the real power. If the hold on the consciousness of the people through the "information revolution" is a strict causal relation, then there are only two ways out—either abandon all information revolution altogether and build a protective shield around the people so as to prevent the effects of the technology from harming them, or stage another revolution and take the power of manipulating symbols and images to the people themselves. Following the first course sounds like one is trying to turn back the clock. Even today there are people who choose not to get connected to the outside world; but I think this is no longer a viable option for most people. The second alternative is a radical one. Looking at the mass media regime as a seat of political and psychological power and trying to destroy that power would mean that the people take the power of producing and distributing media images themselves. In fact this is already happening in the case of the Internet. The problem is only that the images and stories being produced and disseminated are so huge in volume that the effects tend to cancel one another out. When there are billions of Web sites to turn to, the power that one particular Web site can hold on to someone's imagination is minimal indeed. More importantly, the technological determinist thesis is that it is the technology itself that is to blame; thus sharing the technology with a large number of population would just spread the blame to all over the place, and this does not seem to be a good solution.

The implication of Dallmayr's idea here on the global digital divide problem is that he reiterates the need for a critical stance on the media regime of today. He reminds us that there still exists a huge knowledge gap between the West and the rest of the world in terms of production of scientific and technological output and other related measures, and that attempts to bridge the divide should proceed in an equitable and democratic manner. Bridging the divide, wiring the remote villages so that they have access to the Internet, should not be tantamount to ensnaring these people with centrally produced media images so that they are forever addicted to them. Instead providing access to the Internet to the remote villagers should proceed in such a way that the technology needs to become integrated into the lives of the villagers themselves. According to Dallmayr, this does not seem possible because the premise of his argument is that the Internet is a kind of symbolic manipulation on a grand scale by a few "expertocrats." But it is very important that the villagers, those on the receiving end of the divide, be helped so that they can stand on their own feet and take the Internet as yet another of the long list of tools that they rely on to make their living.

Another point is that Dallmayr seems to think that most knowledge comes from the West. The knowledge gap in modern science and technology may be the case, but this does not preclude there being systems of knowledge and technology that are indigenous to the local cultures. As I also pointed out in another paper, the digital divide problem can be solved partly through recognizing the knowledge potential in local communities and seeking ways to make such knowledge and information "transparent"—meaning making it easier for local knowledge and information to become a productive force (Hongladarom, 2001b). It is possible that such systems now lie dormant without their potential being tapped fully. As philosophers and scholars in science studies, such as Sandra Harding (1998) and Susantha Goonatilake (1998), have pointed out, there is a vast store of indigenous knowledge systems in the world's cultures, to which modern science itself owes its origins. Furthermore, locals have relied on these systems for centuries in their lives. It is only because of the mindset, influenced by Western colonialism that regards modern, Western science and technology as the only possible knowledge and technological system, that the potential of these systems have not been tapped. Moreover, Harding has also argued that Western science as it is currently practised contributes to global inequality (Harding, 2002). Hence, an account of how to bridge the knowledge gap should also include a recognition of the important role of indigenous systems, and, as Goonatilake has argued, such systems can indeed be "mined" so that their treasures are revealed to the local people and the world at large (Goonatilake, 1998). In this sense, bridging the digital divide effectively also includes improving local knowledge systems and the means by which the content of these systems can be effectively retrieved.

Conclusion

Some conclusions can be made from the previous discussion. Firstly, it is clear that the global digital divide is an issue of global justice. This is clearly a truism, but an implication is that deliberations on global justice need also to pay attention to how the global digital divide problem is to be addressed. More specifically, one needs to find out exactly how the fruits of information and communication technologies are to contribute to global justice. If provision of hardware and software is not enough, then what could be adequate? Are training and content sufficient? What kind of content? How should the training be developed? And what aim should the training be geared to achieve? These questions are all important, and obviously they cannot be answered satisfactorily in this chapter. Much more work needs to be done.

Secondly, discussion of the normative aspects of the digital divide should also pay attention to the fact that computer technology is a second-order device, which makes it distinct from other first-order social goods. The second-order nature of computer technology makes it the case that cultural epistemological considerations do have an important and necessary role to play; hence, policy deliberations on the global digital divide need to pay attention to the role played by the epistemological considerations.

That is, the deliberation needs to consider the specificities of the culture and their epistemic practices. Hence, I agree with Anthony Wilhelm's idea of the Digital Nation, especially when he says, "a Digital Nation is much more than industrial policy; it drives the social agenda as information, skills and knowledge become building blocks of a learning culture" (2004, p. 131). What this means is that a policy aiming at solving the digital divide problem first of all should start from the ground up. The locals themselves should be the ones who decide which kind of technology they will be using and according to what agenda. For example, in a rural village in Thailand, which is experiencing a host of changes and has become ever more tightly integrated with the world economy, attempts should be made toward computer literacy as well as installing the necessary infrastructure. But, more importantly, it is the emphasis on their own agenda, beliefs and values, that should take precedence. The villagers have their goals and their aspirations, as does everyone else. The problem is how to find a way, through the attempt to solve the digital divide problem, for their goals and aspirations to be realized. A necessary condition for that to happen is, I believe, that computers should be integral to their lives and not something foreign to them.

References

Dallmayr, F. (2002). Globalization and inequality: A plea for global justice. *International Studies Review, 4,* 137-156.

Digital divide closing fast—World Bank. (2005). Retrieved March 24, 2005, from http://xtramsn.co.nz/news/0,,11965-4145138,00.html

Entz, A., & Hongladarom, S. (2004). Turning digital divide into digital dividend: Anticipating Thailand's demographic dividend. In K. Wongbunsin (Ed.), *Six last golden years of economic competitiveness: Results of demographic change* (pp. 135-146). Bangkok: Thailand Research Fund [in Thai].

Ess, C., & Sudweeks, F. (Eds.). (1998). *Proceedings of the International Conference on Cultural Attitudes Toward Technology and Communication.* Sydney, Australia: Key Centre for Design and Computing, University of Sydney.

Ess, C., & Sudweeks, F. (Eds.). (2000). *Proceedings of the International Conference on Cultural Attitudes Toward Technology and Communication 2000.* Perth, Australia: School of Information Technology, Murdoch University.

Ess, C., & Sudweeks, F. (Eds.). (2001). *Culture, technology, communication: Towards an intercultural global village.* Albany, NY: SUNY Press.

Ess, C., & Sudweeks, F. (Eds.). (2002). *Proceedings of the International Conference on Cultural Attitudes Toward Technology and Communication 2002.* Perth, Australia: School of Information Technology, Murdoch University.

Ess, C., & Sudweeks, F. (Eds.). (2004). *Proceedings of the International Conference on Cultural Attitudes Toward Technology and Communication 2004.* Perth, Australia: School of Information Technology, Murdoch University.

Goldman, A. J. (1999). *Knowledge in a social world.* Oxford: Oxford University Press.

Goonatilake, S. (1998). *Toward a global science.* Bloomington: Indiana University Press.

Harding, S. (1998). *Is science multicultural?* Bloomington: Indiana University Press.

Harding, S. (2002). Must the advance of science advance global inequality? *International Studies Review, 4*(2), 87-105.

Hongladarom, S. (2000). Negotiating the global and the local: How Thai culture co-opts the Internet. *First Monday, 5*(8). Retrieved July 26, 2005, from http://www.firstmonday.dk/issues/issue5_8/hongladarom/

Hongladarom, S. (2001a). Global culture, local cultures and the Internet: The Thai example. In C. Ess & F. Sudweeks (Eds.), *Culture, technology, communication: Towards an intercultural global village* (pp. 305-324). Albany, NY: SUNY Press.

Hongladarom, S. (2001b). Making information transparent as a means to close the global digital divide. *Minds and Machines, 14*(1), 85-99.

Hongladarom, S. (2002). Cross-cultural epistemic practices. *Social Epistemology, 16*(1), 83-92.

Hurrell, A. (2001). Global inequality and international institutions. *Metaphilosophy, 32*(1/2), 34-57.

Lofty plans for schools. (2005, March 6). *Bangkok Post.*

McNamara, K. S. (2003, December 9-10). Information and Communication Technologies, Poverty and Development: Learning from Experience: A Background Paper for the infoDev Annual Symposium, Geneva, Switzerland. Washington, DC: World Bank.

Nussbaum, M. C. (2004). Beyond the social contract: Capabilities and global justice. Olof Palme lecture, delivered in Oxford, UK, on June 19, 2003. *Oxford Development Studies, 32*(1), 3-18.

O'Neill, O. (2000). *Bounds of justice.* Cambridge, UK: Cambridge University Press.

Pogge, T. (2001). Priorities of global justice. *Metaphilosophy, 32*(1/2), 6-24.

Servon, L. (2002). *Bridging the digital divide: Technology, community, and public policy.* Oxford, UK: Blackwell.

Warschauer, M. (2003). *Technology and social inclusion: Rethinking the digital divide.* Cambridge, MA: MIT Press.

Wilhelm, A. G. (2004). *Digital nation: Toward an inclusive information society.* Cambridge, MA: MIT Press.

Section II:

Interdisciplinary Perspectives

Chapter VI

Digital Disempowerment

Kenneth L. Hacker
New Mexico State University, USA

Shana M. Mason
New Mexico State University, USA

Eric L. Morgan
New Mexico State University, USA

Abstract

The digital divide involves fundamental ethics issues concerning how democracy and democratization are related to computer-mediated communication (CMC) and its role in political communication. As the roles of CMC/ICT systems expand in political communication, existing digital divide gaps are likely to contribute to structural inequalities in political participation. These inequalities work against democracy and political empowerment and produce social injustices at the same time as they produce expanded opportunities of political participation. Our guiding premise is that CMC/ICT policies that minimize inequalities of access, usage, and participation are more ethical than policies that neglect the democratization of new communication technologies and networks.

The objective of this chapter is to argue that the ethics concerns regarding the digital divide entail fundamental issues about how democracy and democratization are related to computer-mediated communication (CMC) and its role in political communication.[1] As the roles of information and communication technologies (ICT) and CMC systems expand in political communication, existing digital divide gaps are likely to contribute to structural inequalities in political participation. These inequalities work against democracy and political empowerment and produce social injustices at the same time as they produce expanded opportunities of political participation. Our guiding premise is that CMC/ICT policies that minimize inequalities of access, usage, and participation are more ethical than policies that neglect the democratization of the new communication technologies and networks.

There are three basic assumptions that guide the development of this chapter. First, we assume that the rapid and accelerating adoption of Internet, World Wide Web, and CMC/ICT technologies is changing how social and political structures are formed and changed. The societal formation we know today as network society is produced by patterns of social interaction that are increasingly tied to the emergence and expansion of communication networks. The era of single and unrelated communication technologies is over. Even TV and radio are integrating more into Internet-based systems of communication. Our second assumption is that the perpetuation of political inequalities that appears to accompany the embedding of CMC and Internet communication into everyday life raises moral (ethical) issues concerning participation in a democratic political system.[2] This is because online technologies are becoming more common for political communication (Bimber & Davis, 2003). Our third assumption is that CMC and Internet communication, notwithstanding past hyperbole, are capable of enabling citizens to extend their scope of political influence.

We begin our analysis with a review of existing trends that produce the social formation known as network society and the expanding role of CMC in political communication. We then move into an examination of political theory and how it affects the development of American democracy, including digital democracy. From there we discuss the linkages between political theory and communication theory. Next, we argue that there are numerous and strong ethics issues related to indications that CMC may be facilitating structural inequalities in democratic systems such as the United States. We view the formation of these inequalities as digital disempowerment. Finally, we proffer some recommendations for research and policy considerations including an ethic of CMC-based deliberation.

The Dynamic Nature of CMC

Network Society

Human communication is changing with the accelerating adoption of CMC/ICT systems of communication. For instance, there are new forms of communication such as virtual communities and hybrid types of communication that function between both interpersonal and mass communication (van Dijk, 1999). Jan van Dijk (1999) defines network society in terms of communication networks that shape the most important forms of organization in a society. Mass society, with isolated members being informed and entertained by mass media, appears to be giving way to a newer form of society, called network society, in which social structures involve interconnected individuals using computer networks to seek out information, relationships, and networks of influence. In network society, power and politics are more about relationships among people than characteristics of individuals (van Dijk, 1999). Dimensions of geographical space are accompanied by a kind of technological space. A concept that is related to this is known as social geography, wherein social networks become the basis for closeness or distance instead of physical space, as in land geography. Even political systems, which traditionally have been modeled as top-down organizational charts, may be changing into polycentric systems of power in which political power is based more on network position than traditional roles (van Dijk, 1999).

Political movements have been employing the Internet to organize their struggles, and some of these users are developing a practice known as "self-directed networking" (Castells, 2000, p. 55). Self-directed networking involves people inventing personal ways of organizing and disseminating information. As more formal political structures such as civic organizations have less public membership today, Castells (2001) argues that political movements which employ CMC can effectively mobilize political action. Those who are involved with online politics have an advantage over those with less involvement since online politics are becoming more common and influential.

As we proceed with a discussion about the digital divide, it is important to remain aware of the fact that there are many areas of divide gaps that involve much more than the commonly referenced ones of physical access (computer and net access). Kotamraju (2004), for example, notes that women tend to be employed in Web site design more than in Web site programming, even if they have both sets of skills. While schools are more connected to the Net, studies show that few teachers know how to use the technology to augment their classroom instruction. The students attending Internet-wired schools may not be developing the skills they need to function well in an Internet-based economy. The gaps in ethnic and social class levels of learning may be worsened by this pattern of poor teaching proficiency.

While there is expanding diversity, there are also gaps in usage and skills as well as in abilities to pay for what is becoming less free in new media and moving toward pay-per-view models of network access (van Dijk, 2004).

The Embedded Infrastructure

As Wellman and Haythornthwaite (2002) indicate, the Internet is increasingly becoming embedded in the everyday lives of its users. Rather than functioning as a special medium that exists separate from users' lives, the Internet is incorporated into daily routines and provides a platform for numerous personal, social, economic, and political forms of communication and action. Its convenience facilitates all of the activities that were done offline prior to its implementation. Thus, those who use the Internet are afforded an additional avenue of communication to facilitate their daily activities, such as finishing work or doing research for school, contacting friends, and conducting commercial transactions, such as shopping or banking. Howard, Rainie and Jones (2002) show that levels of usage experience characterize the most significant differences between access and use of the Internet among groups. Those who have been using the Internet the longest are most likely to have access to it and to use it more heavily (Wellman & Haythornthwaite, 2002). Longer-term users tend to find ways to incorporate the Internet into all aspects of their lives, including personal and work environments.

The critical realization regarding CMC embeddedness is that a means of communication that was once necessary for a minority of citizens in a given population is now important for many, if not most, people in both developed and developing societies. The speculation that CMC usage is a luxury is becoming more false each day. This can be seen in the historical changes of new communication technologies.

Technology Changes

In addition to the emergence of more network societies, there are many technical changes complicating the divide issues. CMC, for example, is mainly constituted of text-based email messaging. More recent forms of CMC, such as instant text messaging, also entail typing and reading as the main modalities of interaction. Today, however, email is increasingly capable of becoming video mail with text messages added. Additionally, wireless networks are making personal communication networks, as well as links to larger social, economic, and political networks, increasingly possible.

In 1952, the most common communication technologies in the American home were land-line telephone and radio. Today, Americans have land-line telephones, radio, cell phones, TV, and Internet communication. The technologies tend to be additive and increasingly interoperable. Communication system engineers predict patterns of increasing mixes of wired and wireless networks, higher demands for services that require broadband connectivity, and uses of communication technologies that are important for being members of modern societies (Institute of Electrical and Electronics Engineers, 2002). There is a steady transformation of analog communication media to digital media and with digitalization comes convergence (Meadows, 2002). Technologies like TV, radio and telephone that were previously independent of the Internet are now part of it (Meadows, 2002). There is also increasing progress toward personal and home communication networks (Grant, 2002).

With the adoption of each new Internet-related communication technology, there are new ethics issues to consider. For example, some municipalities in the United States are considering the provision of low-cost or free Internet access to citizens via wireless networks ("muni Wi-Fi"). Those leaders who seek to do this consider Net access to be an essential city service (Levy, 2005). Some of these officials believe that cities can provide Internet access at a fraction of the cost charged by other Internet service providers. However, as Levy (2005) notes, telecommunications and cable TV companies are opposed to this. Companies like Verizon and Comcast are lobbying actively against such efforts and argue that taxpayer-sponsored competition makes the marketplace unfair. Part of their lobbying efforts consists in funding think tanks that churn out white papers that support their view of marketplace freedom. A bipartisan bill called the Community Broadband Act will stop states from banning muni Wi-Fi projects if passed (Levy, 2005).

Municipal Wi-Fi projects represent a new battleground for the types of ethics issues we address in this chapter. Is it ethical for these corporate giants to get laws passed to constrain muni Wi-Fi projects? While the major communications corporations were granted virtual monopolies by the federal government with older forms of telecommunications technologies, the question now becomes whether it is ethical for these giants to argue about unfair government intervention in the marketplace. Furthermore, how will political action (or inaction) be facilitated following an ethical assessment of such battles?

Another ethical issue accompanying technological evolution is the issue of emerging broadband gaps. While general computer and Internet access have improved for most ethnic groups over recent years, new gaps have appeared for broadband usage. Discussions about ethics issues can be stifled by governments that do not accurately report CMC usage and adoption statistics. In the United States, for example, the Federal Communications Commission (FCC) reports broadband access in areas that have a slow-speed rate of connectivity measured at 200 Kbps (Turner, 2005). This speed is four times faster than typical dial-up rates of transmission but far below what is generally considered broadband and high-speed transmission (Turner, 2005).[3] It is too low to enable good-quality streaming video which requires a transmission rate of 1 Mbps or greater (Turner, 2005).

There are dangers in the acceleration of a broadband divide that follows the existing digital divide gaps among people with the same forms of Internet access. Broadband is projected to become more important as Web sites will increasingly be designed for broadband, and services like Internet telephony may become more commonly used (Vanston, Hodges, & Savage, 2004). Along with increasing bandwidth capability and speed (referred to as broadband), CMC users need to have personal computers with increased amounts of processing speed and memory (Vanston, Hodges, & Savage, 2004). As computing and CMC become more ubiquitous, devices will continue to become more sophisticated, interconnected, and operable as nodes in personal communication networks. There are certainly ethics concerns about access differentials to computers and the Internet. Stronger ethics issues, however, concern network communication usage and skills.

In summary, we see that society is shifting toward a network society as new communication technologies are increasingly embedded within infrastructures. As these technologies emerge and become important to the functioning of society, there are a number of ethics issues that become relevant. Paramount among these issues are the new and different manifestations of the digital divide. In the following two sections, the digital divide is explained as it is manifested in the United States and on a global scale.

The Digital Divide in the United States

The digital divide generally consists of demographic gaps in computer and Internet access and usage that have been observed by scholars and analysts over approximately the last ten years. There is a well-documented history of the gaps and their progression in the United States. Since 1995, the National Telecommunication and Information Administration (NTIA) and U.S. Department of Commerce have collected data and issued reports documenting the digital divide in the United States.

Ethnicity

The latest National Telecommunications and Information Administration (NTIA) data indicate the presence of digital divide gaps for ethnic groups in the United States. This NTIA report represents data gathered in 2003. Sixty-five percent of European Americans (EA) are Internet users, in contrast to 45% of African Americans (AA), 63% of Asian and Pacific Islander Americans (APIA) and 37% of Hispanic Americans (HA) (NTIA, 2004). These percentages reflect net usage from any location. Broadband gaps among ethnic groups also appear in this latest report. Households with broadband Internet access are found in 26% of EA, 14% of AA, 35% of APIA, and 13% of HA homes (NTIA, 2004).

There are about two million tribal Americans (Native Americans) and many of them have poor Internet access in addition to poor supplies of water and telephone service (Wilhelm, 2003). In the last year of the Clinton administration and in the NTIA reports of the Bush administration this ethnic category was dropped.[4] Native American leaders have argued that this exclusion removes Native Americans from public discourse about the digital divide, which further disadvantages them in our changing society (Twist, 2002).

It is important to note that the ethnic gaps in the digital divide persist even when controlling for income and education (Hacker & Steiner, 2001; van Dijk, 2004). This means that while income and education differences are areas of gaps in their own right, ethnicity retains a unique contribution to the digital divide gaps.

Gender

There is a slight reversal of the early gender bias in the United States. In the 1990s, males had more Internet access from any location than females. Today, 59% of females have access and 58% of males have access (NTIA, 2004). For broadband access, however, males have a 24% to 22% advantage. A study conducted by Ono and Zavodny (2003) shows that while women were significantly less likely to use the Internet in the mid-1990s. This difference had completely disappeared by the year 2000. Indeed, their data indicate that women may be more likely than men to use the Internet outside the home. However, Ono and Zavodny (2003) report that women still have fewer uses for the Internet, although they argue that this difference may be decreasing.

Disabilities

The highest categories of Internet access from any location for disabled Americans is for those under 60 years of age and in the workforce who have multiple disabilities (59%), blindness or severe visual impairment (64%), deafness or severe hearing impairment (72%), walking difficulties (64%), typing difficulties (64%), and trouble leaving home (68%) (NTIA, 2004). The categories of Internet access from any location with the lower percentages are for those 60 years of age or older with multiple disabilities (8%), blindness or severe visual impairment (23%), deafness or severe hearing impairment (24%), walking difficulties (21%), typing difficulties (26%), and trouble leaving home (11%). In 2002, 65% of disabled Americans stated that they did not intend to go online in the future (van Dijk, 2004). Additionally, the number of disabled Americans going online did not change substantially between 1999 and 2002 (van Dijk, 2004).

Social Class

Current NTIA data indicate that 31% of the lowest income earners use the Internet from any location while 86% of the highest income earners do (NTIA, 2004). While 16% of those with the lowest level of education use the Internet from any location, 88% of those with the highest levels of education do. For home broadband access, those with the highest incomes lead those with the lowest by 58% to 8%. For home broadband access, those with the highest education lead those with the lowest by 38% to 6%. Of those with broadband access in the workplace, 54% have college degrees (Horrigan, 2004).

Designers

An alternative way of considering the digital divide is to look at the designers of new computer and communication system technologies. There, some of the data are even worse than the data for CMC users. A contemporary study by the Information Technology Association of America (ITAA) shows that women and most ethnic minorities are underrepresented in the high technology industries of the United States (ITAA, 2005). The percentage of women in the IT workforce diminished by 21% from 1996 to 2004. Hispanic Americans are underrepresented by 50% and African Americans by 22%, while Asian Americans are overrepresented by nearly 200%. Representation of African Americans is diminishing while representation of Hispanic Americans is increasing.

While there is increasing gender equity in the United States for basic Internet access, there are still inequalities among designers. West (2001) notes, for example, that there are large gender gaps in technical positions in companies like Microsoft and Intel, that women make less money in communication technology careers than men, and that small percentages of university computer science professors are women.

It is clear that the digital divide in the United States can be defined in a number of different ways by using different demographic categories. One interesting category concerns which users produce content, such as Web sites, with their Internet usage. A Pew Internet and American Life Project survey found that content is produced by 77% of whites in contrast to 9% of blacks and 9% of Hispanics, and by 51% of men and 49% of women (Lenhart, Horrigan, & Fallows, 2004). While such differences are interesting and appear to confirm the argument that gaps persist with various aspects of CMC, they must be explained in terms of what effects they have on social, work and political life. Also, the manner in which the digital divide gaps are framed becomes important for interpreting the differences.

Alternative Frames

The digital divide can be framed in numerous ways. Two opposite frames are one that says there is not a problem and one that says there is a problem. In 1997, the Department of Commerce NTIA division released reports on the Divide with titles such as *Falling through the Net*. By 2001, the title changed to names referring to "digital inclusion" and "a nation online" (Klotz, 2004). Benjamin Compaine (2001) argues that the digital divide gaps are comparable to those that occurred with the introduction of other technological innovations, such as the radio, VCR, and television set, and notes that near universal adoption quickly occurred without government intervention. Compaine (2000) argues that the gaps are "less a crisis than a temporary and normal process" (p. 19) that will eventually close as early (wealthier) adopters subsidize the computer and Internet markets for later (usually less economically advantaged) adopters. In a 2002 interview, Compaine maintained that "the digital divide is a non-issue at this point" (Talerico, 2002, para. 4), citing research indicating that the rate of adoption among ethnic minorities was on the rise. Grant (2002) argues that "the most recent research indicates a disappearance of the 'digital divide'" (p. 242). He says that this is true because low-income households are catching up with computer and Internet access as well as gaining benefits from CMC. In opposition to the argument that the divide is not a significant problem is the argument by van Dijk (2004), who maintains that the divide is not only getting worse, but that the consequences are becoming more severe.[5]

According to van Dijk (2004), the arguments about a closed divide are based on a trickle-down assumption of communication technologies. This assumption says that CMC technologies are always becoming more affordable and, therefore, all groups will eventually have them. van Dijk (2004) challenges this assumption by arguing that CMC technologies quickly become obsolete and need replacement and that they still cost more than old media like TV and radio sets. He also argues that services that accompany CMC such as computer software and Web site access have conditional access, meaning that usage is dependent on the user's ability to pay for online content (van Dijk, 2004). He also notes that broadband access clearly provides users with more control and better content, yet remains expensive for most people.

Van Dijk (2004, p. 20) argues a "Matthew Effect" for CMC adoption. This effect (based on the Bible passage "unto every one who hath shall be given") indicates that those who already have good Internet and CMC access and usage patterns are gaining more and more network power while those who do not are losing their ability to catch up (van Dijk, 2004). As information becomes more important in jobs and everyday routines, the Matthew Effect becomes more deleterious for those with less CMC usage experience. Digital skills and usage are becoming more important for increasing numbers of professions and jobs. Thus, those with access and enhanced usage tend to become more valuable to their employers in the workplace (van Dijk, 2004). As distance education and online learning become more common and accepted, those with online usage and skills have easier access to educational courses and degrees (van Dijk, 2004). Research shows that those who combine online communication with offline social interaction expand their social networks and increase their social capital (van Dijk, 2004; Wellman & Haythornthwaite, 2002).

CMC users are able to extend their communication networks in terms of both strong and weak ties in ways that non-users cannot (van Dijk, 2004). People with more material resources have always had the ability to build more social capital and larger communication networks with weak and strong ties, as well as geographically disperse ties, than people with fewer resources. That difference is heightened with current patterns of CMC usage and skills gaps (van Dijk, 2004). This is the kind of divide that we refer to as structural inequality. There is little indication that CMC is drawing new people into democratic political processes, but there is substantial evidence that people who already participate are becoming enabled in participating more (Bimber & Davis, 2003; van Dijk & Hacker, 2000). It is easier to find issue positions for political candidates online than in traditional media like television (Bimber & Davis, 2003). It is also easier for CMC users to contact government officials, obtain government documents, and join political discussions with people they do not know (van Dijk, 2004). Bimber and Davis (2003) argue that CMC is providing effective tools for political activities and mobilization, but that "the divide between those who are political activists interested in electoral campaigns and those who are not will expand" (168).

McSorley (2003) argues that debates about the digital divide turn around competing definitions, and, over time, there has been less reliance on static views which tend to focus on dichotomies such as those who are "falling through the net" (NTIA, 1995, 1998, 1999, 2000) and those who are safe. Rather than depending so much on demographic differences in access, newer research shows more about differences among groups in what kinds of political and cultural capital they build through their Internet usage (McSorley, 2003). Some scholars argue that the divide should be reframed in terms of what kinds of participation users are able to create and sustain (McSorley, 2003). Van Dijk (2004) also takes part of this position. He argues that too much extant digital divide research focuses on individual differences and treats categorical variables (nominal) as causes of differential access and usage.

Van Dijk (2004) proposes a relational view as an alternative. This view is presented in opposition to the view that tends to assume that the digital divide is a technical problem. It also opposes the view that the technologies at issue in the divide are likely solutions to the social, cultural, and political problems of social inequalities, oppression, and lack of political participation (van Dijk, 2004). Of course, while van Dijk is correct in arguing that giving someone a computer and Internet does not fix sociopolitical problems, we need to remember that what they do and create with CMC may contribute to some remedies for those problems. The relational view rejects the individualist approach that is most common in digital divide analysis. The latter assumes that attributes of individuals explain gaps in Internet access and usage (van Dijk, 2004). According to van Dijk (2004), structural inequalities in network society are instantiated in gaps between high and low users (including no usage) in the areas of education, employment, social life, family communication, cultural participation, and political communication. Computer networks are increasingly important to the accomplishment of organizational tasks (van Dijk, 2004). For education, those with digital skills and opportunities are able to obtain distance education and vast supplies of educational resources (van Dijk, 2004). While CMC does not diminish face-to-face contacts, it does expand distance communication and contacts. This means that CMC usage can increase the scope of one's social network (van Dijk, 2004). CMC usage for politics can mean easier and faster access and distribution of political documents, more access to political discussion groups, and more channels with which to reach political leaders (van Dijk, 2004).

The digital divide in the United States is a prominent issue made more understandable by examining the phenomenon through different frames. The digital divide, however, is certainly not limited to the U.S. Indeed, within the context of an increasingly globalized economy, the digital divide on a global scale is, in many ways, more pronounced.

The Global Digital Divide

Norris (2001) argues that access to the information and communication opportunities offered by the Internet may be most influential in the poorest nations. The lack of distance barriers and relatively cheap implementation of the Internet (once access is possible) allow business owners in countries such as Mexico the opportunity to participate in the global marketplace. Health information and education are available via the Internet in areas like Calcutta as they are to doctors in New York. Physicians in developing nations would be able to network and share information and resources with those in more developed nations through the Internet. Distance education would allow increased access to sophisticated educational tools, enabling universities in disenfranchised nations to offer educational tools and training comparable to those in industrialized nations (Norris, 2001). According to the Organization for Economic Cooperation and Development (OECD), the harmful results of natural disasters, such as the earthquake and accompanying tsunami that struck nations around the Indian Ocean in 2004, are also lessened by new communication technologies. These are thought to provide important tools to warn of the impending catastrophe, mitigate its impact by speeding information and relief efforts, and provide a place for victims and family members to post messages and pictures regarding the missing (OECD, 2004).

Additionally, Norris maintains that the Internet may increase the mobilization of grassroots campaigns and their visibility, enabling groups to network and share resources in order to impact policy makers at a higher level. "Foreign policymakers…can no longer assume that the usual diplomatic and political elites can govern political affairs with a passive 'permissive consensus' without taking account of the new ability for public information, mobilization, and engagement engendered by the new technology" (Norris, 2001, p. 2). In the Soviet Union, for example, the Internet network Relcom is credited with playing a significant role in the dissemination of information during the coup attempt of 1991 (Press, 1993).

Marginalized societies can become increasingly marginalized as societies become more globalized and information is increasingly the most valuable commodity (Norris, 2001). The differences in economic growth between those nations that have reliable, high-speed access to the Internet and those who do not may be exacerbated as the affluent nations are able to profit from increased visibility and productivity. Low literacy levels, language barriers, and income are key obstacles to Internet adoption for those in developing countries (OECD, 2004). Citizens in non-OECD member countries account for more than 80% of the world's population, but are only 1/3 of the world's Internet subscribers and 17% of those with broadband access (OECD, 2004). Floridi (2001) argues that members of these cultures are not only marginalized by the digital divide, but that they "live in the shadow of a new digital reality, which allows them no interaction or access, but which profoundly affects their lives" (p. 3).

United Nations research indicates that the OECD nations, such as the United States and Norway, and Asian nations, such as China, are gaining ground with CMC adoption, while the Latin American, African, and South Asian nations, such as Bangladesh and Sri Lanka, appear to be losing ground (United Nations, 2003). This research also indicates that CMC/ICT technologies are more unevenly distributed than older communication technologies such as land-line telephone service. While the newer communication technologies will not fix non-technological problems, they can increase information sharing, knowledge accumulation, and work collaboration through networking. Indeed, the United Nations report states that "developing countries risk being left further behind in terms of income, equality, development, voice and presence on an increasingly digitized world stage" (United Nations, 2003, p. 4).

The Significance of the Divides

Network society involves new forms of social interaction and social organization, including political ones (Castells, 2000). The consequences of network society connection are becoming more significant as information, communication, and networking are increasingly linked to tangible benefits. Channels provide more than nodes or connections to communication networks; they also provide social contexts. Each channel has its own characteristics and capabilities. CMC/ICT systems are not replacing face-to-face interaction but are adding new social structures to it.

As the Internet and CMC become more embedded with economic, social, and political activities, citizens are likely to develop stronger needs to use the networks to maximize their abilities to participate in online opportunities, resources, or social formations. Those who become most skilled and active with ICT/CMC networking will gain more power than those without these skills and activities. This means there may be accelerating gaps in network sophistication. As van Dijk (2002) notes, digital skills are cumulative. Thus, the inequalities resulting from their increasingly embedded nature are cumulative as well. This is also why arguments that imply the gaps will close on their own, such as those of Compaine (2001), are problematic as new gaps emerge in the place of old ones. Holderness (1999) argues that the divides we have been discussing may become self-reinforcing. Those individuals and those nations who accelerate their use of CMC systems build their communication capital at rates that perpetuate how far they stay ahead of others in networking.

It is generally accepted that the increasing organization of societies with the use of CMC/ICT technologies facilitates the importance of information and knowledge for economic growth and a shift of importance from densely-knit bounded groups to computer-supported social networks (United Nations Development Programme, 2004). The emergence of network societies entails social and organizational formations that are constructed in relation to flows of symbolic interaction more than in relation to traditional institutional, governmental, and organizational boundaries (Contractor & Monge, 2003).

Networks are comprised of nodes connected by communication that join together to become influential networks (Castells, 2000). When a node does not connect to other nodes, it may be dropped from the network. Such nodes are then excluded from exercising influence on social organization. Because society is comprised of multiple, interdependent layers, a change in one produces a change in the others. Those who are part of the networks that exert influence on society can work to increase the impact of their influence by stimulating changes in, or reinforcing, existing patterns in the social structures that are beneficial to them.

Those with the most power and resources are the early adopters of new technologies, and their influence shapes the evolution of the technology's place in society (van Dijk, 1999). Thus, social inequalities may be perpetuated as those who use the technologies are increasingly organizing social networks around them. The inability to access or make effective use of the Internet and computers becomes increasingly significant as those with power make their use increasingly prominent in all areas of society. Those who do not have access to new forms of communication technology are increasingly excluded from the organization of society on many levels. Political organization is one such level, and understanding the implications of exclusion from one avenue of access to the political structure is important for understanding some of the social implications of the Divide.

As the digital divide is increasingly manifest through different types of usage, it becomes necessary to understand how this may affect the use of communication technologies in the political arena. Because CMC/ICT systems are used more and more within this arena, an examination of their potential effects on the fundamental principles underlying the political arena is in order. Particularly important is how CMC/ICT systems may affect important aspects of democracy, such as the general will in a population. This requires a discussion of the historical development of the idea of a general will.

Democracy and Communication

Democracy began in ancient Greece at approximately 508 BC with the political designs of the leader Kleisthenes and the earlier reforms of Solon (Dunn, 1992; Hornblower, 1992). Governing by the people (democracy) did not happen by accident, serendipity, or by just chatting about political matters. For Kleisthenes, it appears that democracy offered a way of using popular will against those nobles who opposed him (Meier, 1990).

When Kleisthenes devised Athenian democracy, there were numerous contextual factors that made his efforts possible. These are noted here because they have significance for how systems become more democratic or how democracies arise—both concerns for those who study CMC and political participation. In the emergence of isonomy, or equality under law, the Athenians began to view citizenship and participation in politics as something that unified them against their differences (Meier, 1990). Although those who gained voice in the democracy were still considered inferior to nobles and not every Greek was allowed to vote (e.g., women, slaves, non-Greeks), citizens begin to gain a sense of general will (Meier, 1990). Kleisthenes and his citizens had no formal concept or theory of democracy when they created it. What appears deliberate in their actions, however, is an intention to increase popular participation in politics (Meier, 1990). In other words, interest in politics and participation led to democracy rather than the other way around.

Despite the creation of democracy, and due to their social and political positions, nobles were considered superior in intellect and economics and continued to lead the people in ancient Athens (Meier, 1990). The main political equality that emerged was one in which all citizens were capable of influencing the general will, a concept closely related to community (Meier, 1990). For citizens to mobilize the input into governance they were obtaining, they needed political knowledge, political interest, and political will in relation to important issues (Meier, 1990). They also needed to see that their influence had desired effects. Ancient Greek democracy worked for as it long as it did because the citizens of Athens developed a political identity (Meier, 1990). Meier (1990) observes that "the very fact that they were citizens brought them into a special sphere that they themselves created by their mutual interaction" (p. 72).

The ancient Greek democracies were more participatory than our modern democratic systems (Lloyd, 1992). The kind of direct experience in decision-making debates that the ancient Greek citizens had simply does not exist today in modern demo-cratic systems. Because this fact mistakenly gets transposed into a claim that we could have such democracies today with teledemocracy voting and referenda, it is important to realize that the degree of democracy in a society is not a function of size but rather of philosophy and political will. Embedded in the original formulations of democracy was the assumption that all citizens are equal. This assumption does not fit well with today's presumption that elites should have the task of doing the business of government while citizens need only the task of selecting leaders from time to time. It also flies in the face of arguments which assert that digital divide gaps are socially insignificant.

After the fall of democracy in Greece, the term "democracy" was not used in a widespread positive sense until the late 18th and early 19th centuries. Aristotle's notion of checking democracy with aristocracy and monarchy (polity) continued to overrule notions of democracy as first conceived. Athenian versions of democracy became restricted by constitutional checks against hasty, popular decisions that later proved to be against the best interests of some members of society.

After an extended era of monarchy in much of Europe, some political works emerged that began a sort of reinvigoration of the use of democratic systems to rule. In his *Second Treatise of Government,* John Locke (1996/1762) argued that people are equal and their government is vested with power by those who comprise it. Locke asserted that people can work together for the common good, and that conflicts of interest can be moderated. Locke, importantly, also maintained that government should be impartial, and the constitution should represent the will of the majority.

Jean-Jacques Rousseau, influenced by Locke, also embraced the concepts of citizen equality and a government representative of their will (Noelle-Neumann, 1979). However, Rousseau (1996/1762) conceptualized decision-making by the general will instead of the majority will. In this type of system, citizens would be educated in their obligations and duties as citizens, would engage in debate with other citizens, and would arrive at decisions that best suited all members of society.

Key to Rousseau's (1996/1762) concept of general will is participation in the political institution. Rousseau indicated that those who entered into a social contract should enter into "a part of a larger whole from which this individual receives, in a sense, his life and his being" (p. 482). To do this, members of society must be trained in their "voice of duty" (p. 472) to others, acting upon what is good for the society as a whole rather than what feeds immediate impulses. Social institutions instill in citizens the concept of their existence as a single body with a single will, dedicated to their general well-being, and instruct them in their duties as citizens. So long as they consider themselves as part of one body, Rousseau argued, their decisions will reflect what is good for the society, regardless of their political sophistication. As soon as they no longer see themselves as a unified body, however, private interests begin to take precedence. They cease expressing their opinions to a state they feel does not consider them, and support only what is advantageous to themselves.

Rousseau argued that true equality can be achieved only in societies in which knowledgeable citizens take a sustained interest in the government and are offered adequate opportunities to develop their opinions, which should then be weighed equally by decision-makers. Many political theorists today agree with Rousseau. "Real governments cannot survive without the sustenance and support….of non-governmental people" (Higgs, 1989, p. 6). For democracies to be successful, lasting inequalities created by special interest groups must be prevented, equal opportunities for interaction among groups must be present, and their influence on decision-making should be equal (Shapiro, 1994).

The Role of Computer-Mediated Communication

In order to arrive at Rousseau's general will, deliberation between citizens and among their representatives is crucial. Jankowski and van Selm (2000) argue that, in democratic societies, citizens must have complete access to all information regarding any political issue in order to engage in rational public debate, which is necessary before any political action is taken. Barber (1984) argues that the goal of a democracy is to achieve a common consensus through debate and deliberation. To solicit votes from an electorate that has not deliberated or debated an issue would be "the death of democracy" (Barber, 1984, p. 290). Only in this way, proponents argue, can what is good for society as a whole emerge.

Additionally, systems of representative democracy, such as that found in the United States, depend on a varied group of ambitious citizens to moderate conflicts of interest through a government that checks their influences. When the influence of one interest group becomes too heavily weighed in such a society, the government's responsibility is to open new avenues of influence to its citizens. Deliberation is the key to successful democratic societies so that the citizens may express their opinions to each other and shape the policy of their representatives. This type of large-scale political discourse may have been impractical in large nations such as the United States just a few years ago, but the accelerating adoption of computers and the Internet may provide a practical means of fostering increased levels of political participation in a large democratic system.

Political communication research indicates that CMC has the potential to alter power structures (de Sola Poole, 1983; Tambini, 1999). The Internet appears to provide "more and better information access and exchange" (Hacker & van Dijk, 2000, p. 215). Several researchers (van Dijk, 1996; Bennett & Entman, 2001; Hacker & Steiner, 2001; Stromer-Galley et al., 2001; Anderson, 2003) have established that users of the Internet have increased their political knowledge. Despite these findings, we need more knowledge about the ways in which CMC can be used to generate political will, represent the general will, and increase effective political and democratic deliberation. We also need to know more about how structural inequalities block progress in these areas.

Without the knowledge and ability to evaluate policies and potential leaders, citizens cannot engage in the democratic process in its true sense (Barber, 1984; Yankelovich, 1991). However, as Yankelovich (1991) maintains, information given to citizens in a downward flow means that they possess only that information passed onto them by elites. Receiving information in this type of downward flow pattern does not necessarily empower citizens; rather, it can serve to reinforce existing power structures as citizens maintain the passive role of consumers of information generated by the elite, who maintain control over all information (van Dijk, 1996; Bordewijk & van Kaam, 1986). If high CMC users have more multilateral political communication than low CMC users, the latter are less likely to develop empowering roles for themselves in the polycentric power structures which appear to be part of network societies.

CMC and the Internet offer democratic potential unlike traditional media, yet obstacles to their access continue to be a key obstacle to their implementation for political purposes. Previously marginalized groups (those who do not comprise the influential majority offline) become marginalized online, unable to take advantage of the new information and communication opportunities offered via CMC.

Structural Inequalities

The reality of structural inequalities which produce what we are calling disempowerment is seen in the evidence that (a) CMC and Internet skills are cumulative, and (b) digital divide gaps persist and regenerate with each new communication technology innovation (van Dijk & Hacker, 2000; van Dijk, 2004). Those who use the technologies first can do more with them than those who are only now beginning to use them. A recent OECD (2004) report on the digital divide notes that "those previously characterized as 'haves' as dial-up users would be considered 'have nots' for the emerging broadband divide" (p. 6). Those citizens who could reap the most benefits from the democratic potential of the Internet, those who are already marginalized, are generally those who need them the most, and are those who have the least amount of access and skills (Hacker & Mason, 2003).

In Europe, citizens with few or no skills, as well as the unemployed, comprise the majority of those who use government services, yet are a minority of Internet users (O'Donnell, 2002). Thus, the increased information, communication, and access to these programs afforded by electronic government enterprises in Europe go unused by the majority of those whose need is greatest. We see a similar pattern in the United States, as evident in the statistics cited earlier in this chapter concerning disabled people. The common picture is that those with the greatest needs for CMC are those with the least usage.

There is some support for the mobilization hypothesis (Norris, 2001), which asserts that some traditionally less active groups may be mobilized to engage in political activity by the low communication costs of the Internet. For example, Muhlberger (2002) found that online discussion is employed at a slightly higher rate by those with less education, women, those who do not own a home, and those who are young, all of whom are generally less involved in political activities. Thus, there is evidence that previously uninvolved citizens might take a more active political role if access and usage obstacles did not exist. If left without access, however, those members of uninvolved and marginalized groups will continue to lag behind those of other groups, creating new forms of inequality as the opinion of those who participate in online discussion influences policymakers.

When a new avenue of access becomes available that would facilitate citizens' ability to make informed decisions about policy, to communicate with representatives, and allow for more equal opportunities to influence decision making, it would seem to follow that governments should take measures to enable access to this important platform of social and political communication, serving as a check to ensure equality. This appears to be the reasoning behind the U.S. Telecommunications Act of 1996, which requires the Federal Communications Commission (FCC) and the states "to ensure that affordable, quality, telecommunications services are available to all Americans...and will help to connect eligible schools, libraries, and rural health care providers to the global telecommunications network" (*FCC News*, 1997, para. 1). The Clinton administration took steps toward this type of plan for CMC, indicating that computer use and access should be extended through universal service as telephones were. The digital divide was even suggested to be a civil rights issue since ethnic minorities trailed majorities in usage and access (Hacker

& Mason, 2003; Wilhelm, 2003). The Bush administration, however, indicated that the divide was not really an issue and asserted that the gaps would close on their own (Hacker & Mason, 2003). FCC chairman Michael Powell characterized it as a "Mercedes Benz Divide," implying that access is a luxury rather than a necessity. However, Muhlberger argues that if the Internet enables citizens to exert political influence and obtain political information, then its representativeness is at issue. "Those concerned with the development of a democratic public sphere need to be aware of the representativeness of Internet political activity, … [because] an Internet that overrepresents some political views advantages those views relative to others" (Muhlberger, 2002, p. 2). If we accept that the possibility of increased political influence exists via the Internet, then we must consider that the potential for power imbalances to be created (or exacerbated) also exists when some members of a society may exercise this influence, while others are excluded due to economic, educational, and other social factors. It takes strong political will among leaders to guide both democratization and policies for CMC that facilitate it.

It is important to note that closing digital divide gaps might do more for e-commerce than for democracy in situations where there is no strong political will for democratization. We should also recognize that political will exists at various levels of a political system, including those who govern and those who are governed. When both of these agree, and perhaps only when both agree, that increasing political participation is necessary for democratization, CMC can be useful for democracy. Democratic systems without strong political will of the people or citizens are not likely to benefit from political CMC. If CMC is not politically useful, the gaps in various divides do not raise the ethical issues that they might otherwise. In other words, the more important CMC is for the democratic nature of a system, the more unethical it is to have social exclusion for CMC access, usage, and content.

From Political Theory to Ethics

Hacker and Mason (2003) argue a strong nexus which links issues of political power and issues of morality (ethics). Political policy is often formulated on the basis of factual information and observation, but values serve as the filters through which those facts are used to implement policy. Research is done and facts are generated about social problems, but values inform what is done about them (the policy that is or is not implemented to correct a problem). Ethics considerations are a necessary component of policy making because ethics establish whether or not something is a problem and, if it is, what the best course of action is to remedy it. Political theory sets up the philosophical parameters of what is problematic in political communication.

Those who argue that digital exclusion is not a problem because some groups do not actually need access take an ethical position that says it is morally acceptable to allow some groups to be excluded from the social networking that the Internet enables. Social inequities are legitimized by arguments that some groups do not need access or are not being aversely affected by digital exclusion in the face of documented and potential benefits of connectivity. Additionally, policies implemented to facilitate access are not free of ethical considerations. It may be unethical, for example, to argue that some groups are unable to become digitally connected on their own, without government assistance. This may also further negative stereotypes about some groups among the groups themselves and society in general. The issues of ethnic prejudice in research and commentary concerning gaps in CMC usage need to be taken very seriously since very well-intentioned scholars may contribute to the discursive reserves of others who are not so well-intentioned about matters of ethnicity and technology. When considering facilitation of access, it might also be necessary to consider whether or not such access changes social structure in progressive directions. The important consideration here is that policy formulation should include a consideration of the ethical implications of disregarding the problem or generating solutions.

Globalization increases as economic, political and cultural activities of nations become more interdependent or interconnected. Within one globalization structure, a nation's position can be determined by its pattern of interactions with other nations (Barnett, 2001). This formulates a three-tiered structure of nations and societies such that those with increased interconnectivity and interconnectivity potential represent a core group with other nations representing semi-peripheral and peripheral groupings accordingly (Chase-Dunn & Grimes, 1995). Those nations that are most central in the global network are also those with the highest GDP. Barnett's network analysis of international telecommunications from 1978 to 1996 indicates that the global network has become more centralized and more integrated. Moreover, the study showed that more information is flowing through the core nations (U.S., Canada, Western Europe) rather than being exchanged with nations at more peripheral network positions (Barnett, 2001).

The inability of subpopulations to have access to the global network infrastructures are diminishing their abilities to be as competitive and influential as those populations which do have input and position in the expanding networks of capital, influence, and power. Each developing economy becomes more dependent on CMC/ICT networks for commerce, government, education, and various social services (Montagnier et al., 2002). The most educated citizens may also leave these countries for the economic opportunities offered by more central nations, causing a "brain drain" that further inhibits progress (bridges.org, 2003/2004). Floridi (2001) notes that globalization means that problems are interrelated, none existing in isolation.

The research on the digital divide makes it clear that connectivity remains an unsolved problem for realizing digital democracy. Within the United States, there are pockets of Americans who are living more and more on the periphery of the network society. Hoping that digital democracy can repair the problems of offline democracy is a strong issue for intellectual debate. However, the longer significant groups of people lack meaningful participation in their political system, the more likely that the system will not change for the better and that structural inequalities will take hold.

Hacker (2002a, 2002b, 2004) argues that the issues of digital divide gaps, whether national or global, will not be resolved without political will that is deliberately aimed at increasing citizen participation in digital democracy. Political will stems from political culture and the abilities and willingness of leaders and citizens to make practices match values. Naïve notions about digital democracy can emerge when one does not address political culture and the differences in democratic systems. For example, the political system in the United States contains a form of elitism by which most Americans remain mildly involved in politics and trust their leaders to do most of the actual policy making. Thus, to understand why most American leaders are not encouraging digital democracy past the point of e-government and freedom for citizen discussions, one has to examine American political culture and its history. American political culture began with a strong mistrust of democracy, moved into a 19th century movement toward embracing it, and then into a 20th century gradual containment of how much rights, liberties, and participation would be expanded. Still, the United States has indirect democracy, in which citizens choose leaders to make decisions for them, as do most democratic systems in the world; in contrast, direct democracy involves all citizens in voting for proposals. Today, we usually think of a political system as being democratic if political decisions ultimately must be accounted for to the people of the nation in question (Scruton, 1982).

A global economic infrastructure, as envisioned by Bill Gates and others, is not the same thing as the public spheres for democratic communication envisioned by scholars of political communication. Couldry argues that most developed national governments have focused more on global digital economies than on digital democracies. This focus holds more concern for expanding markets than concern for making sure that citizens are not socially excluded from important spaces of political deliberation (Couldry, 2003). This focus also neglects the need for content that helps disadvantaged people find sources and spaces to improve their social and political positions by helping them with job training, job searches, and other information that is truly useful to them (Couldry, 2003). As Menou (2002) maintains, the focus of many efforts by the private sector to close the divide is to make consumers out of the poor. "What should really be at stake is social change and not the marketing of ICTs" (para. 3).

Light CMC users do different things than heavy users. Heavy users, for example, are less passive in their use of the Internet and are more likely to disseminate information and create content (Couldry, 2003). Like van Dijk, Couldry observes a scale-extension/scale-reduction effect to CMC. He notes that the coffee houses of the 17th and 18th centuries were places where people who were literate would talk about various books and journals (Couldry, 2003). This expanded communication, but also created a gap between the literate and nonliterate. He argues that the same may occur with CMC. As the nonliterate people would stay in the market squares while the literate deliberated in the coffee houses, experienced CMC users may develop exclusive spaces for deliberation that, by their nature, simply are not inviting to inexperienced CMC users. The specific ethics issues that Couldry sheds light on concern presence versus absence, connection versus non-connection, and participation versus hierarchy.

A deliberative design model of political CMC could build upon theories of deliberative democracy from which ethics concerns emerge which say that is wrong to have people non-connected, absent, or socially excluded by hierarchies in political CMC. Deliberative democracy theory says that citizens should have the opportunity to actively participate in decisions made about policies that affect them (Couldry, 2003; Dryzek, 1990). Dryzek's deliberative design principle says that citizens should have spaces for recurrent social interaction about politics where they can communicate only as citizens and not as representatives of any governmental, corporate or hierarchical organization. This concept differs from the Habermasian concept of the ideal speech situation in that it recognizes that much of deliberation about politics will involve emotional interaction and not always appear rational (Couldry, 2003).

CMC can help deliberative democracy in many ways if the ethics issues we have discussed are seriously debated and lead to innovative changes in policies. Nina Eliasoph (1999) interviewed Americans about politics and found that, in general, the interest or lack of interest in politics so often cited in journalistic and academic accounts is oversimplified. She found that Americans do not like to talk about politics in public, but they do in private. For many, the public spaces make political discussion too contentious (Eliasoph, 1999). Ways in which private concerns can be articulated into public spaces can change political communication, especially if it is also learned how various levels of public-space communication can create force and momentum toward societal changes.

Now that we have looked at many issues in regard to history and the development of CMC for political communication, we can postulate several areas of ethics concerns and debate.

Recommendations

Recognize the Dynamic Nature of Online Communication

Jan van Dijk (1999) employs a principle he calls "Scale extension and Scale reduction" (p. 23), a concept which describes oppositional effects from one cause occurring at the same time. In Singapore, for example, one finds a society that extends the communication of its citizens in the economic spheres of Internet usage but contracts their freedoms of political communication on the Net.

Market-based arguments assume that digital inequities go away with continued adoption and diffusion of communication technologies. This ignores the fact that computer-based communication technologies are more interdependent and more cumulative in usages, networking, and required skills than old media which were functionally independent (van Dijk, 2004). Universal-access arguments assume that governments must provide access to everyone because they cannot function in modern society without such access, and the markets are insufficient to provide affordable access. These arguments ignore the fact that some people can prosper without CMC and that market independence does, in fact, help high-technology companies innovate new communication products and services.

While academic debate and controversy over important issues are healthy and necessary, there should not be a tendency to compete with others over who has the best or ultimate definition of the digital divide. It is absurd to say that the divide is only material and simply involves points of access. It is also absurd to say that the divide is only discursive. Language is important and social construction processes are important. However, the divide appears to be both material and discursive. It is multidimensional, and attempts to reduce it to one's favorite paradigm are always subject to refutation. In place of competition for the best paradigm, it is more important to identify why the gaps and their dynamics exist and what can be done to maximize the uses of CMC to facilitate democratization in all nations and for all groups within nations. Research shows that digital divide gaps change with time and do not all move in the same way. Some may move toward closing while others get worse. With successive S-curves, new gaps replace old ones (van Dijk & Hacker, 2003).

Give Voice to Zones of Silence

Where particular groups of people appear to be marginalized in CMC networks and creation of content, there should be efforts to give them voice from a perspective developed here that brings together political theory and communication theory. The United Nations 2004 Human Development Report argues that "unless people who are poor and marginalized—who more often than not are members of religious or ethnic minorities or migrants—can influence political action at local and national levels, they are unlikely to get equitable access to jobs, schools, hospitals, justice, security, and other basic services" (United Nations, 2004).

Researchers have argued that the Internet offers new opportunities to engage in this type of political influence because it offers opportunities to engage in direct, point-to-point argument (Kolb, 1996; Kim, 2003; Fishkin, 1995; Fox & Miller, 1995), opens up new avenues of communication between citizens and their representatives (de Sola Poole, 1983; van Dijk, 1996), increases a citizen's political knowledge (van Dijk, 1996), and provides a vehicle for the type of democratic deliberation (van Dijk, 1996) that can lead to the ability to better evaluate policies and potential leaders (Barber, 1984; Yankelovich, 1991). It is argued here that the Internet is an important platform that can be used for politics, with its role being constrained by the context in which it is implemented.

According to Bennett and Entman (2001) "access to communication is one of the key measures of power and equality in modern democracies" (p. 2). As a form of communication that offers democratic potential unique from previous types of media (Bentivegna, 2002), such as the telephone, access to CMC and the Internet is arguably such a measure. CMC and the Internet offer citizens the opportunity to exercise control over content, offer opinions, exert pressure on the government, and actively participate in its business. Additionally, they offer both citizen to citizen and citizen to official communication opportunities, reduce the role of the media as gatekeepers of information and allow citizens access to previously unavailable (or very difficult to obtain) information. Also unique from previous forms of media, they allow small groups and movements to acquire visibility that would have been unavailable to them in media such as television due to its high cost. Finally, the speed and absence of boundaries offered by the Internet allow for quick mobilization of citizens with similar concerns and unlimited contact and communication between and among them. However, if groups most in need of these access opportunities continue to be excluded, their marginalization may be increased, leading to digital disempowerment.

Note How Inequalities are Related to Political Structuration

An alternative to viewing communication as a revolutionary process is to view it as an incremental process that creates social structures and does so through sustained feedback loops. Structuration processes involving CMC/ICT technology can be closely related to political power to the extent that agents are using CMC to gain more voice, input, and impact (Poole & DeSanctis, 1990; Hacker, 2004). If CMC continues to become more important to such processes, those with low access and usage will be likely to have relatively little influence on hosts of changes in social structures. Political structuration can be facilitated by CMC as users build new forms of political interaction that produce new rules and resources that are used for political interaction. As the changes in rules and resources occur at micro levels of social interaction, their cumulative effects initiate larger changes in the social systems that affect and are affected by the lower levels of social interaction. Through this process of political structuration, citizens are more likely to increase their political efficacy and their roles in democratic systems.

High CMC exclusion does not mean that people have no voice in governance, but rather that they have less than they would if they were able to employ CMC as a key resource in creating or changing social structures related to political issues and causes. The provision of universal access, similarly, does not guarantee radical social restructuring. Menou (2002) argues that the focus of digital divide debate should not be how to bring the technology to the marginalized, but to discover the best ways for those who need the technology to put it to use and improve their social positions. It is important to keep in mind that online inequalities often mirror offline ones, and existing social problems will not be undone by technology. Rather, it is necessary to understand the role of CMC in political structuration and how it may magnify or mitigate inequalities.

Make the Power Gaps Explicit

The impact of the digital divide on different groups within countries may be related to that country's power distance index measure. The power distance index is a measure of acceptance of power discrepancies between and among members of a society. A high score indicates that power discrepancies among groups in society are evident, recognized, and accepted. A low score indicates that power discrepancies are minimized between societal groups. A low power distance score indicates that there is greater equality across societal levels (Hofstede, 2001). Hofstede (2001) argues that a low power distance orientation has the potential to create more stable cultural environments because it reinforces cooperation across power levels (Hofstede, 2001). Within the United States, the relatively low power distance score would suggest that the digital divide is fairly insignificant compared to the global divide, and indeed fairly insignificant all together. However, this is not the case.

This suggests that investigating other discourses aside from the dominant one can lead to a possible explanation of the digital divide as it is manifest in the U.S. While some research points to the U.S. as having low power distance and an egalitarian orientation, other research indicates that ethnic groups, other than the European American majority in the U.S., do not orient to the society as egalitarian. Rather, many members of these ethnic groups indicate that there are societal structures within the U.S. that systematically circumscribe them from full participation in society.

One implication of this hierarchy and higher power distance is a potential increase in the digital divide. One other implication, and one which needs to be avoided if alleviating the digital divide is to ever happen, concerns related actions within society that are linked to ethnic identity assertions. If members of particular ethnic groups are systematically circumscribed from participation in a cultural sphere of communication technology, then lack of participation could become a part of the ethnic identity itself. Thus, when one avows an identity that is not dominant, then that person actively suggests that she or he cannot, and culturally should not, be able to engage in computer mediated communication.

One way to explain how ethnic identity assertion can encompass a lack of CMC participation may be found in the work of Phinney (1993), who has developed a model of minority identity development based on a number of empirical studies (Phinney & Alipuria, 1990; Phinney, 1989). This model describes three stages through which members of minority groups may progress as they come to avow a particular ethnic identity. The first stage is labeled *unexamined ethnic identity*. This stage is characterized by a lack of acknowledgement of the ethnic identity in relation to a majority identity that is different. Indeed, during this stage, ethnic group members will sometimes identify more with the dominant ethnic group than with the minority group of which they are a member, although this is not always the case. What is particularly noteworthy about this stage and comparable to stages from other researchers (e.g., Atkinson, Morten & Sue, 1983; Kim, 1981; Marcia, 1966; Phinney, 1989) is that members will at times recognize their lack of access to a dominant cultural system and yet prefer it. At this stage, members of ethnic groups that are traditionally marginalized within the context of CMC may recognize that they are circumscribed from participation in CMC and its attendant benefits, yet also adopt an attitude that suggests that they must, somehow, deny their ethnic identity in order to fully participate. Thus, CMC as a cultural sphere of activity becomes disassociated from the minority ethnic identity.

The second stage of the model is labeled *ethnic identity search/moratorium*. In this stage there is recognition on the part of some ethnic group members that the values and traditions of the dominant group are not necessarily beneficial to themselves or to their ethnic group. Phinney (1993) notes that there is often a crisis or event that leads members of minority ethnic groups to seek awareness and exploration of their own ethnic group. This stage can often be marked by a sense of anger and frustration with the dominant group. Within the context of CMC, it is necessary, therefore, to disassociate the practice of CMC from a dominant ethnic group. The inherent risk would be that members of the minority group would distance themselves from participation precisely because CMC is associated with a sphere of activity with which they are dissatisfied.

The third and final stage is labeled *ethnic identity achievement*. This stage is characterized by an internalization of one's ethnic identity. Ethnic group members in this stage often report that they are confident in who they are and have a sense of flexibility regarding the practice of ethnic identity. It should be noted that Phinney reports significant movement among the stages between the ages of 16 and 19. For CMC this seems to be vitally important as it corresponds to the same age that American citizens are allowed to engage in the political process through voting behavior. However, Phinney (1993) warns that "For the minority students, ethnicity was rated as equal in importance to religion and considerably more important than political orientation as identity issues" (p. 64). Following from this, the next suggestions become vitally important.

Keep the Ethics Dialogues Open

We have noted that CMC gaps might negatively affect how members of disadvantaged groups self-identify as technology users. A different but related argument is one that says that continuing discussions about ethnic gaps in digital divides could perpetuate a stereotype of ethnic minorities as being technophobic (Young, 2001). Such ethnic gaps have been widely verified since the publication of the first NTIA report on access differentials in the late 1990s. While scholars making the argument about stereotyping do not deny the realities of the gaps themselves, they caution about the research findings being used to further diminish investments in minority communities (Young, 2001). The consequence is the increasing "naturalization" of structural inequality.

It is unethical to think that structural (self-reinforcing) inequalities among various social groups are simply inevitable and normal. The digital divides within nations and across nations both raise strong issues of ethics that individual national and transnational government agencies need to address with more urgency. The result of not doing so is to increase the likelihood that the gaps between high and lower connected citizens of nations and the world will become worse rather than better. Less connection in a networked world quite directly implies disempowerment.

Develop a Deliberation Ethic

Our guiding premise in this chapter has been that policies that minimize the inequalities of access, usage, and participation in digital political communication are more ethical than policies which neglect the democratization of the new communication technologies and networks. We now argue an ethic based on the history of democracy, the democratic potential of CMC, and what we know about structural inequalities.

Democracy began in ancient Greece with a commitment to politics, political equality, and political will that would help people communicate in ways that fostered expression of the general will. Rousseau built on the political theory of the Greeks and other political theorists who expanded the notion of the general will as a central concept to democratic systems. In this line of political theory development, we see that democracy is produced by political will, equality in politics, and a strong commitment to deliberation as a tool of generating and following the general will. Political systems that simultaneously tout democracy yet do not apply these principles create structural inequalities among constituent groups. These inequalities can be compounded if political leaders insist that democratization is facilitated solely by a free market economy. Such an orientation merely justifies the fact that certain groups are continuously marginalized from the best means of political participation.

If CMC/ICT enables democratic deliberation that leads to the development of the general will, the principle of equality in politics is disregarded if some citizens have access and some do not. In light of this background, the digital divide cannot be dismissed as a matter of luxury or insignificance without also accepting the position that it is ethical for some people to have access to democratic systems and for some to be left out or limited in their participation. Rousseau argued that such a situation could very well lead to tyranny. Therefore, the existence of the divide is a strong barrier to democracy, and its continuation and expansion will move in the direction of disempowering the citizens who need more power.

Conclusion

In this chapter, we have attempted to present an argument for an ethic of political communication which says that CMC/ICT systems have democratic potential and can be useful for extending political deliberation that is necessary for democracy. However, the same ethic argues that it is morally wrong to have these systems develop and expand in ways that give more political power to those who are already ahead in how much political influence they have, while not providing more political access to those who tend to lag behind in political power. The key, we argue, is to have political will among leaders, among citizens, and within various social groups such as ethnic groups, to provide CMC access, training, content creation, usage opportunities, and encouragement in order to make digital democracy more open to newly participating citizens and more effective in giving citizens meaningful political deliberation that has actual and viewable effects on political governance.

References

Anderson, D. M. (2003). Cautious optimism about online politics and citizenship. In D. M. Anderson & M. Cornfield (Eds.), *The civic Web: Online politics and democratic values* (pp. 19-34). New York: Rowman & Littlefield.

Atkinson, D., Morten, G., & Sue, D. W. (1983). *Counseling American minorities.* Dubuque, IA: Wm. C. Brown.

Barber, B. (1984). *Strong democracy: Participatory politics for a new age.* Berkeley: University of California Press.

Barnett, G. A. (2001). A longitudinal analysis of the international telecommunication network, 1978-1996. *The American Behavioral Scientist, 44,* 1638-1655.

Bennett, W. L., & Entman, R. (2001). *Mediated politics: Communication in the future of democracy.* New York: Cambridge University Press.

Bentivegna, S. (2003). Politics and new media. In L. A. Lievrouw & S. Livingstone (Eds.), *Handbook of new media* (pp. 50-61). London: Sage.

Bimber, B., & Davis, R. (2005). *Campaigning online.* New York: Oxford University Press.

Bordewijk, J. L., & van Kaam, B. (1986). Towards a new classification of teleinformation services. *Intermedia, 14,* 16-21.

Bridges.org. (2003/2004). *Our perspective on the digital divide.* Retrieved August 7, 2005, from http://www.bridges.org/perspectives/digitaldivide.html

Castells, M. (2000). Toward a sociology of the network society. *Contemporary Sociology, 29,* 693-699.

Castells, M. (2001). *The Internet galaxy: Reflections on the Internet, business, and society.* New York: Oxford University Press.

Chase-Dunn, C., & Grimes, P. (1995). World-systems analysis. *Annual Review of Sociology, 21,* 387-417.

Compaine, B. (2000, June). *Re-examining the digital divide.* Research prepared for Internet and Telecoms Convergence Consortium, MIT. Retrieved August 8, 2005, from http://itel.mit.edu/itel/docs/jun00/digdivide.pdf

Compaine, B. (2001). Information gaps: Myth or reality? In B. Compaine (Ed.), *The digital divide: Facing a crisis or creating a myth?* (pp. 105-119). Cumberland, RI: MIT Press.

Contractor, N., & Monge, P. (2003). *Theories of communication networks.* New York: Oxford.

Couldry, N. (2003). Digital divide or discursive design: On the emerging ethics of information space. *Ethics and Information Technology, 5*, 89-97.

de Sola Poole, I. (1983). *Technologies of freedom.* Cambridge, MA: MIT Press.

Dryzek, J. S. (1990). *Discursive democracy.* New York: Cambridge University Press.

Dunn, J. (ed.). (1992). *Democracy: The unfinished journey.* New York: Oxford University Press.

Eliasoph, N. (1999). *Avoiding politics.* Cambridge, UK: Cambridge University Press.

Federal Communications Commission. (1996, May 7). *Commission implements telecome act's universal service provisions.* Retrieved July 24, 2005, from http://www.fcc.gov/Bureaus/Common_Carrier/News_Releases/1997/nrcc7032.html

Fishkin, J. (1995). *The voice of the people: Public opinion and democracy.* New Haven, CT: Yale University Press.

Floridi, L. (2001). Information ethics: An environmental approach to the digital divide. *Philosophy in the Contemporary World, 9*(1), 1-7.

Fox, C. J., & Miller, H. T. (1995). *Postmodern public administration: Toward discourse.* Thousand Oaks, CA: Sage.

Grant, A. (2002). Retrospective: 10 years of communication technologies. In A. Grant & J. Meadows (Eds.), *Communication technology update* (8th ed., pp. 339-349). Austin, TX: Technology Futures.

Hacker, K. (2002a). Network democracy and the fourth world. *European Journal of Communication Research, 27*, 235-260.

Hacker, K. (2002b, October 9-12). *Network democracy, political will and the fourth world: Theoretical and empirical issues regarding computer-mediated communication (CMC) and democracy.* Keynote address to Euricom Colloquium: Electronic Networks and Democracy, Nijmegen, The Netherlands. Retrieved from http://bascrv.uci.kun.nl/~jankow/Euricom/

Hacker, K. (2004). The potential of computer-mediated communication (CMC) for political structuration. *Javnost/The Public, 11*, 5-26.

Hacker, K., & Mason, S. (2003). Ethics gaps in studies of the digital divide. *Ethics and Information Technology, 5*, 99-115.

Hacker, K., & Steiner, R. (2001). Hurdles of access and benefits of usage for Internet communication. *Communication Research Reports, 18*, 399-407.

Hacker, K., & van Dijk, J. (Eds.). (2000). *Digital democracy: Issues of theory and practice*. London: Sage.

Higgs, R. (1989). *Crisis and leviathan: Critical episodes in the growth of American government*. London: Oxford University Press.

Hofstede, G. (2001). *Culture's consequences: Comparing values, behaviors, institutions, and organizations across nations*. Thousand Oaks, CA: Sage.

Holderness, M. (1998). Who are the world's information poor? In B. Loader (Ed.), *Cyberspace divide* (pp. 35-56). London: Routledge.

Hornblower, S. (1992). Creation and development of democratic institutions in ancient Greece. In J. Dunn (Ed.), *Democracy: The unfinished journey* (pp. 1-16). New York: Oxford University Press.

Horrigan, J. (2004). *55% of adult Internet users have broadband at home or work*. Pew Internet project data memo. Retrieved August 21, 2005, from http://www.pewinternet.org/pdfs/PIP_Broadband04.DataMemo.pdf

Howard, P., Rainie, L., & Jones, S. (2002). Days and nights on the Internet. In B. Wellman & C. Haythornthwaite (Eds.), *The Internet in everyday life* (pp. 45-73). Oxford, UK: Blackwell.

Information Technology Association of America. (2005, June 21). *ITAA diversity study: Numbers of women, minorities in tech too low*. Retrieved August 28, 2005, from http://www.itaa.org/eweb/DynamicPage.aspx?WebCode=PRTemplate&wps_key=0BF6F8EB-20AB-4906-957D-2FFA85EA205B

Institute of Electrical and Electronics Engineers. (2002). *Communications in the 21st century*. Retrieved July 10, 2005, at http://www.ieee.org/organizations/history_center/comsoc/chapter6.html

Jankowski, N., & van Selm (2000). The promise and practice of public debate in cyberspace. In K. Hacker & J. van Dijk (eds.), *Digital democracy: Issues of theory and practice* (pp. 149-165). London: Sage.

Kim, J. (1981). Processes of Asian-American identity development: A study of Japanese American women's perceptions of their struggle to achieve positive identities. *Dissertation Abstracts International, 42*, 04A.

Kim, S. (2003, May). *Opinion climates and deliberative opinion expression in the electronic forum*. Paper submitted to the 2003 conference of the International Communication Association, San Diego, CA.

Klotz, R. (2004). *The politics of the Internet*. Lanham, MD: Rowman & Littlefield.

Kolb, D. (1996). Discourses across links. In C. Ess (Ed.), *Philosophical perspectives on computer-mediated communication* (pp. 15-27). Albany: State University of New York.

Kotamraju, N. (2004). Art vs. code. In P. Howard & S. Jones (Eds.), *Society online* (pp. 189-200). London: Sage.

Lenhart, A., Horrigan, J., & Fallows, D. (2004). *Content creation online*. Pew Internet and American life project. Retrieved July 29, 2005, from http://www.pewinternet.org/pdfs/PIP_Content_Creation_Report.pdf

Levy, S. (2005, July 18). Pulling the plug on local Internet. *Newsweek,* p. 14.

Lloyd, G. E. R. (1992). Democracy, philosophy and science in ancient Greece. In J. Dunn (Ed.), *Democracy: The unfinished journey* (pp. 41-56). New York: Oxford University Press.

Locke, J. (1996). Second treatise of government. In D. Wooten (Ed.), *Modern political thought: Readings from Machiavelli to Nietzsche* (pp. 312-386). Indianapolis, IN: Hackett. (Originally published 1689)

Marcia, J. (1966). Development and validation of ego-identity status. *Journal of Personality and Social Psychology, 3,* 551-558.

McSorley, K. M. (2003). The secular salvation story of the digital divide. *Ethics and Information Technology, 5,* 75-87.

Meadows, J. (2002). Conclusion. In A. Grant & J. Meadows (Eds.), *Communication technology update* (8th ed., pp. 350-352). Austin, TX: Technology Futures.

Meadows, M. S. (2002). *Pause and effect: The art of interactive narrative*. Indianapolis, IN: New Riders.

Meier, C. (1990). *The Greek discovery of politics*. London: Harvard University Press.

Menou, M. J. (2002, October 3-5). *Digital and social equity? Opportunities and threats on the road to empowerment*. Paper prepared for The Digital Divide from an Ethical Viewpoint, International Center for Information Ethics Symposium, Augsburg, Germany. Retrieved from http://www.capurro.de/augsburg2-papers.htm#menou

Montagnier, P., Muller, E., & Vickery, G. (2002, August). *The digital divide: Diffusion and use of ICTs*. Paper presented at the IAOS Conference, London.

Muhlberger, P. (2002, October 9-12). *Political values and attitudes in Internet political discussion: Political transformation or politics as usual?* Paper presented to Euricom Colloquium: Electronic Networks and Democracy, Nijmegen, The Netherlands. Retrieved from http://baserv.uci.kun.nl/~jankow/Euricom/

National Telecommunications and Information Administration. (1995). *Falling through the net: A survey of the "have nots" in rural and urban America*. Retrieved from http://www.ntia.doc.gov/ntiahome/fallingthru.html

National Telecommunications and Information Administration. (1998). *Falling through the net II: New data on the digital divide*. Retrieved August 5, 2005, from http://www.ntia.doc.gov/ntiahome/net2http://www.ntia.doc.gov/ntia-home/fallingthru.html

National Telecommunications and Information Administration. (1999). *Falling through the net: Defining the digital divide*. Retrieved August 5, 2005. from http://www.ntia.doc.gov/ntiahome/fttn99/contents.html

National Telecommunications and Information Administration. (2000). *Falling through the net: Toward digital inclusion*. Retrieved August 5, 2005, from http://www.ntia.doc.gov/ntiahome/fttn00/contents00.html

National Telecommunications and Information Administration. (2004). *A nation online: Entering the broadband age*. Retrieved July 21, 2005, from http://www.ntia.doc.gov/reports/anol/NationOnlineBroadband04.pdf

Noelle-Neumann, E. (1979). Public opinion and the classical tradition: A re-evaluation. *Public Opinion Quarterly, 43*, 143-156.

Norris, P. (2001). *Digital divide: Civic engagement, information poverty, and the Internet worldwide*. Cambridge, UK: Cambridge University Press.

O'Donnell, S. (2002, October 9-12). *Internet use and policy in European Union and implications for e-democracy.* Paper presented to Euricom Colloquium: Electronic Networks and Democracy, Nijmegen, The Netherlands. Available at http://baserv.uci.kun.nl/~jankow/Euricom/

Ono, H., & Zavodny, M. (2003). Gender and the Internet. *Social Science Quarterly, 84*(1), 111.

Organization for Economic Cooperation and Development. (2004). *Regulatory reform as a tool for bridging the digital divide*. Retrieved June 26, 2005, from http://www.oecd.org/topic/0,2686,en_2649_37441_1_1_1_1_37441,00.html

Phinney, J. (1989). Stages of ethnic identity development in minority group adolescents. *Journal of Early Adolescence, 9*, 34-49.

Phinney, J. S. (1993). A three-stage model of ethnic identity development in adolescence. In M. E. Bernal & G. Knight (Eds.), *Ethnic identity: Formation and transmission among Hispanics and other minorities*. Albany: State University of New York Press.

Phinney, J., & Alipuria, L. (1990). Ethnic identity in college students from four ethnic groups. *Journal of Adolescence, 13*, 171-183.

Poole, M. S., & De Sanctis, G. (1990). Understanding the use of group decision support systems: The theory of adaptive structuration. In J. Fulk & C. Steinfield (Eds.), *Organizations and communication technology* (pp. 173-193). Newbury Park, CA: Sage.

Press, L. (1993). *Relcom: An appropriate technology network.* Retrieved August 21, 2002, from ibiblio database, http://www.ibiblio.org/pub/academic/russian-studies/Networks/Relcom/relcom.history

Rousseau, J. J. (1996). On the social contract, or principles of political right. In D. Wooten (ed.), *Modern political thought: Readings from Machiavelli to Nietzsche* (pp. 464-534). Indianapolis, IN: Hackett. (Originally published 1762)

Scruton, R. (1982). *A dictionary of political thought.* New York: Hill & Hwang.

Shapiro, I. (1994). Three ways to be a democrat. *Political Theory, 22,* 124-151.

Stromer-Galley, J., Foot, K., Schneider, S., & Larsen, E. (2001). How citizens used the Internet in election 2000. In S. Coleman (Ed.), *Elections in the age of the Internet: Lessons from the United States* (pp. 21-26). London: Hansard Society.

Talerico, T. (2002, July/August). Has the divide closed in the U.S.? Is it fact or fiction? *HispanicBusiness.* Retrieved August 8, 2004, from http://www.hispanicbusiness.com/news/newsbyid.asp?id=7098&cat=Magazine&more=/magazine/

Tambini, D. (1999). New media and democracy: The civic networking movement. *New Media & Society, 1,* 305-330.

Turner, S. (2005). *Broadband reality check.* Retrieved August 25, 2005, from http://www.freepress.net/docs/broadband_report.pdf

Twist, K. (2001). *A nation online: But where are the Native Americans?* Retrieved August 25, 2005, from http://www.digitaldivide.net/articles/view.php?ArticleID=153

United Nations. (2003). *Information and communication technology indices.* New York: United Nations.

United Nations Development Programme. (2004). *Human Development Report: Cultural Liberty in Today's Diverse World.* New York: United Nations. Available at http://pooh.undp.org/maindiv/hdr_dvpt/reports/global/2004/pdf/hdr04_frontmatter.pdf

United Nations, Economic and Social Commission for Western Asia. (2004). *Foundations of ICT indicators database.* New York: United Nations.

van Dijk, J. (1996). Models of democracy: Behind the design and use of new media in politics. *Javnost/The Public, 3,* 43-56.

van Dijk, J. (1999). *The network society: Social aspects of the new media.* London: Sage.

van Dijk, J. (2000). Widening information gaps and policies of prevention. In K. Hacker & J. van Dijk (Eds.), *Digital democracy: Issues of theory and practice.* London: Sage.

van Dijk, J. (2002). A framework for digital divide research. *The Electronic Journal of Communication, 12*(1 & 2). Retrieved July 31, 2005, from http://www.cios.org/getfile/vandijk_v12n102

van Dijk, J. (2004). *The deepening divide: Inequality in the information society.* London: Sage.

van Dijk, J., & Hacker, K. (2000). Summary. In K. Hacker & J. van Dijk (Eds.), *Digital democracy: Issues of theory and practice.* London: Sage.

van Dijk, J., & Hacker, K. (2003). The digital divide as a complex and dynamic phenomenon. *The Information Society, 19,* 315-326.

Vanston, L., Hodges, R., & Savage, J. (2004). *Forecasts for higher bandwidth broadband services.* Retrieved August 21, 2005, from http://www.tfi.com/pubs/r/r02004_broadband.html

Wellman, B., & Haythornthwaite, C. (2002). The Internet in everyday life: An introduction. In B. Wellman & C. Haythornthwaite (Eds.), *The Internet in everyday life* (pp. 3-41). Oxford, UK: Blackwell.

West, C. (2000). *Techno-human mesh: The growing power of information technologies.* Westport, CT: Quorum Books.

Wilhelm, A.G. (2003). Civic participation and technology inequality: The "killer application" is education. In D. M. Anderson & M. Cornfield (Eds.), *The civic Web: Online politics and democratic values* (pp. 113-128). New York: Rowman & Littlefield.

Yankelovich, D. (1991). *Coming to judgment: Making democracy work in a complex world.* Syracuse, NY: Syracuse University Press.

Young, J. R. (2001). Does "digital divide" rhetoric do more harm than good? *Chronicle of Higher Education, 48.* Available at http://chronicle.com

Endnotes

[1]   We use the American term "computer-mediated communication" as our label for communication done in computer networks. It essentially means the same thing as information and communication technology (ICT).

[2]   We are using the standard capitalized term "Internet" rather than the uncapitalized "internet" because we believe the former is more valid.

[3]   The FCC rate of transmission for defining high-speed transmission also means one-directional versus two-directional (upstream and downstream) transmission.

4   In personal communication e-mail note to one of the authors of this chapter, one of the NTIA report authors justified the omission by stating that there were too few Native Americans surveyed to do appropriate statistical procedures.

5   Which argument is preferred may depend on how one interprets successive S-curves of communication technology adoption. The Compaine view, for example, assumes that adoption increases for everyone on any given S-curve and therefore there is no problem. In contrast, the van Dijk view assumes that the gaps across S-curves are important along with the gaps within any given S-curve.

Chapter VII

Social Justice and Market Metaphysics:
A Critical Discussion of Philosophical Approaches to Digital Divides

Bernd Carsten Stahl
De Montfort University, UK

Abstract

A book on the topic of information technology and social justice would seem to be based on several implicit assumptions. One of these is that there are unequal distributions of technology and access to technology, which can be called "digital divides." Another one is that these digital divides are a problem for justice. A final one is that a philosophical debate of these issues can be beneficial. This chapter aims to question the validity of these assumptions. It asks what philosophy contributes to the debate about digital divides. In order to do so, it briefly reviews the debates concerning justice and digital divides. It then discusses the question whether markets or states are better suited to overcome the unequal distribution of technology. The purpose of these brief restatements of some of the opinions found in the literature is to show that philosophy alone cannot inform us of what we should do. The chapter concludes by suggesting that, in order to address problems of digital divides, we need to go beyond philosophical debate and enter the political space.

Introduction

The world is not just. One striking example of this is the fact that a minority of human beings have access to technology, whereas the majority does not. This, combined with the fact that technology, particularly information technology, can make life easier and provide meaningful activities, strikes many of us as unjust. It is the underlying problem that we try to capture with the term "digital divide." Philosophy has always been interested in ethics and morality. These are linked with justice. It thus stands to reason that philosophy can help us understand and address the problem of justice regarding the digital divide(s). This is, in a nutshell, the reasoning behind the project of creating a book about digital divides from a philosophical point of view. It is a sympathetic thought in that it aims to improve the state of the world or at least lay conceptual foundations for such an improvement. At the same time it is a contentious idea because it rests on the assumption that philosophy can actually provide a useful input to the debate on digital divides whereas it is not clear what would constitute a useful input.

This chapter aims to provide a critical perspective on the possibility of a philosophical contribution to the debate. The fundamental stance of the chapter is a critical one in the tradition of critical social science as informed by a long line of scholars from Marx to the Frankfurt School. This critical tradition has more recently been joined by the ranks of scholars who are often called "postmodern" (Chua, 1986; Orlikowski & Baroudi, 1991; Nord & Jermier, 1992). The commonality of these critical approaches is that they question the basics of research assumptions, that they do not take for granted accepted realities, and that they are deeply reflective. They aim to open discursive closures and to facilitate the creation of new realities by instituting new discourses (Fairclough, 1993; Chouliaraki & Fairclough, 1999).

Applied to the topic of IT and the digital divide this means that, as a critical researcher, one has to ask oneself what the purpose of the proposed research is, how it is framed and expressed, and whose knowledge interests are being served. The tenet of a philosophical discussion of social justice with regard to the digital divide is that philosophers have something to add to the debate, that this knowledge they have is currently missing, and that it will make a relevant difference in some way (Parker, 2003). Presumably in this case the contribution of philosophy is conceptual clarification, something that is often regarded as the task of philosophy (Wittgenstein, 1963). While we can probably grant that philosophy is capable of providing thorough conceptual work, the other two aspects are more difficult to prove. Is the conceptual knowledge philosophers can provide really missing? And if so, do they really have a chance to provide it to those who need it? Indeed, are they even able to identify those who need it? While I am slightly less positive about this second aspect than the first one, I will concede that this is conceivably so, that philosophical investigation may bring clarity to those in need of it. That leaves the final point, namely that all of this will make a difference. This raises the problem of what it means to make a difference. To some extent even the most vacuous activity makes a difference, at least to those who carry it out. But my guess is that the intention of the book is to do more than just lead to a ticked box in the editor's and authors' CVs. If so, then we must ask what the difference is the book intends to make and how we can be sure it actually does make this difference.

In order to demonstrate the problem with the philosophical approach to social justice and the digital divide, I will briefly recount two possible streams of discourse relevant to the topic, namely the discourses of justice and of market metaphysics. The discussion of justice will try to capture some of the aspects of the conceptualisation of justice in philosophy. The main purpose of this discussion will be to demonstrate that there are fundamental conceptual problems that preclude a practical solution of issues regarding digital divides. The very idea of justice, old and venerable as it is, is also unclear and contradictory. Applying it to a newer but similarly problematic concept such as the digital divide produces more problems than it solves. I will demonstrate this by discussing the question who should be responsible for providing access. This is closely linked to the debate between state provision of services versus private provision. The result of this attempt to bring together different streams of arguments will be that a conceptual clarification does not really clarify much, apart from a basic lack of clarity. The chapter concludes with a discussion of possible conclusions that can be drawn from a critical point of view.

Justice

The concept of justice is one of the central ideas of philosophy and has been extensively discussed in the last few millennia. I therefore stand no chance of doing this debate any justice (pun intended). However, the main purpose of this debate on philosophical ideas concerning justice is to show that the very debate is too complex to be able to produce any tangible results. I shall make this point by first looking at some definitions of justice and then looking at the problems they entail.

Definitions of Justice

For the reasons just given, it is not possible to give a comprehensive definition of the term "justice." However, there are some aspects of it that reappear frequently and that have a bearing on problems of the digital divide(s). On a formal level, justice can be seen as a principle of action that treats entities of the same category in the same way (Perelmann, 1967). In a slightly more accessible formulation this means that justice is about getting people their due (Schmidtz, 1998, p. 81). This relates to the first interpretation and can be translated as "treating equals equally, and unequals unequally" (De George, 1999, p. 101). It raises the question who is to be seen as equal with whom and on what grounds. This is where different types of justice come in which are focused on different assumptions about which aspects of humans are of relevance for the definition of justice. I will briefly describe three of these which are to be found in the literature: justice of exchange (*iustitia commutativa*), justice of distribution (*iustitia distributiva*), and legal justice (*iustitia legalis*).

Iustitia Commutativa

Justice of exchange is the basis of interpersonal exchange of goods and values and it is therefore the basis of economic activity. The question is when exchanges are just. There are a number of conditions one can find in the literature: the exchange should be voluntarily agreed upon by the parties affected. This will usually be the case if it is mutually beneficial and if the parties believe it to be just. A key idea of just exchanges is that of reciprocity, which relies on fair and open negotiations and an absence of coercion (De George, 1999). This type of justice is central to classical liberalism and it has been promoted as the main building block of all sorts of justice. It can be used to develop political theory as well as economic practice (Nozick, 1974). The beauty of it is that it is built on the free agreement of consenting individuals and that it is therefore very transparent. If the parties affected agree that something is just, then who should question this agreement? Justice here is defined with regards to individual rights and the central concern is that of liberty (Kohlberg, 1981). However, the exclusive interest in individual freedom can lead to problems, some of which are meant to be addressed by looking at justice from the point of view of the distribution of goods.

IustitiaDistributiva

One problem with a purely procedural and liberal understanding of justice is that it disregards the unequal distribution of goods and privileges, which is also at the heart of the debate about the digital divide. Distributive justice has therefore been established as another important aspect of justice. It is most closely linked with the name of John Rawls who developed his idea of justice as fairness. According to him, a distribution can be understood as just if it conforms to the principles that a community would choose under the veil of ignorance. This means that Rawls's concept is based on a contractualist position that, differing from other forms of contractualism, defines the original position such that the individuals do not know their own position in society. The result of this construct is the difference principle, which Rawls takes to be the representative of fairness and thus of justice. The difference principle holds that all people are entitled to the greatest amount of individual freedom compatible with the same freedom by everybody else. Where there are unequal distributions of wealth, these must be justified by the fact that they are linked to positions that are accessible by everybody and that they must benefit those most who are least advantaged (Rawls, 2001, p. 64).

Rawls's view of justice as being closely linked to questions of distribution has had a strong influence on the debate about justice and it has been so successful and generally accepted that one can talk of a dogma of the justice debate (Höffe, 1996). However, despite the strong influence of distribution on justice, one should see that there is at least one more aspect which is central to our understanding of justice and which is not necessarily covered by exchange or distribution.

Iustitia Legalis

Another integral part of justice is that of legal justice. In English, the words are identical which suggests that there must be a close link. As a brief aside, one should note that this is not the case in every language. In German, for example, one can distinguish between *Gerechtigkeit,* which refers to moral justice (or in the context of this book, maybe social justice), whereas legal justice is better captured by words such as *Justiz* or *Recht*. This raises the interesting point that legal justice and moral (or social) justice are not always identical and that their relationship is not easily defined.

Nevertheless, justice is something that the legal system is concerned with and there is little doubt that the purpose of legal systems reflects the moral underpinnings of the idea of justice. This is an important point at the heart of democratically constituted states (Tocqueville, 1998). Legal justice has to do with equal right of access to legal institutions that will guarantee individuals respect for their rights. It is thus closely linked to the other two definitions of justice, both of which stress the equality of individuals in terms of rights and freedom. It differs from them in that it refers only to procedural rights and makes no material promises. Legal justice also incorporates other thoughts that are not usually present in questions of distributive justice or justice of exchange, such as retribution. Legal justice, particularly criminal justice (as opposed to legal justice based on civil law) aims to punish people for the wrongs they have done. The reason for this may be deterrence, protection, or restitution, but it also often carries an undertone of retribution. This is a concept that will strike many of us as hardly useful when applied to digital divides.

Justice and Ethics

The idea of justice is closely linked to that of ethics. However, trying to introduce another philosophical concept, namely ethics, to the debate, does not necessarily help us clarify matters. The reason for this is that it raises the question what ethics or morality are and how they are to be understood and justified. Nevertheless, one should be aware that justice is one of the central ideas of ethics and has been at least since Plato (Maritain, 1960). For Plato justice was the heart of ethics and consisted of every part of an organism or society doing what it was meant to do. In other ethical systems justice is also central but linked to different ideas. For Aristotle, for example, justice was first and foremost a virtue, which summarises all virtues (Aristotle, 1967). Because of its central standing in different ethical systems, justice has also been called a value, but unfortunately, the manifestation of this value changes despite the fact that it is often given the name "justice" (Kohlberg, 1981).

The central idea of justice that equals should be treated equally is reflected in some newer conceptions of ethics, most notably in those ethical theories that are based on the "other." These ethical theories were developed in 20th century France and result from the influence of phenomenology and existentialism. Here justice is understood as the instantiation of the fundamental intuition that the other, the face in front of me, is equal to me and therefore deserves respect (Levinas, 1988). This recognition of the other which requires us to treat her justly and to avoid violence (Ricoeur, 1995), can then be retranslated into the language of other ethical theories. It can be seen as an expression of universality (Weil, 1960). It can also be translated into the language of duty because the recognition of the other as equal means that there is an obligation to treat her accordingly (Ricoeur, 2001). Similar expressions of the ethics of justice can also be found in other contexts, where justice is seen as "involving people's rights" (Hausman & McPherson, 1996, p. 223) and as a duty towards others. Justice has equally been linked to a different tradition of ethical writing, namely to the idea of human rights (Rawls, 2001).

Problems of Justice

From what has been said so far, some problems of the idea of justice should have become clear. Because of the wide range of possible meanings of justice, it is easy to find meanings that are contradictory. Perelmann (1967, p. 16) enumerates several interpretations of justice that prove this point: justice can be seen to mean that everybody should receive: (1) the same; (2) according to their desert; (3) according to their deeds; (4) according to their needs; (5) according to their rank; and (6) according to what the law attributes them. It is clear that all of these criteria conform to some expectation of justice but they cannot be satisfied simultaneously. The central problem of justice is thus that it has a multitude of not necessarily commensurable meanings, which are subject to change over time. Furthermore, justice (unlike utility) is a highly emotional notion (Mill, 1976). This fact that justice is an emotional concept will be important for the discussion of the role of justice in digital divides and we will return to it later.

Earlier, I have introduced three main aspects of justice, in the hope that these might alleviate the conceptual muddles surrounding justice. Taking a closer look at these, it turns out that they produce complications when analysed in more depth and that they are also not consistent among themselves. The justice of exchange, for example, is usually invoked when an author tries to support capitalist mechanisms of exchange. However, it is often conceded that just exchange would only be just on the basis of ideal assumptions such as a complete knowledge of the individuals involved about their alternatives and a sufficient amount of theoretical and practical freedom by the participants. Furthermore, just exchange is only just if it is based on prior distributions that are themselves just. Since this is a recursive function, it means that all exchanges emanating from a single instance of unjust exchange are consequentially unjust. Applied to real situations, this means that current exchanges cannot be just because it is hard to contend that all prior exchanges which led to them have been just. Furthermore, most proponents of *iustitia commutativa* accept that this cannot capture all aspects of what we mean by justice. Just exchange in a society is only desirable if it facilitates other values such as a free development of the individual (Höffe, 1992).

Even more problematic is the idea of distributive justice. It is the heart of the problem of digital divides because it seems to be obvious to a large part of the world's population that current distributions are not just. However, a closer look shows that it is not clear why this is the case and it is even less clear how it should be changed. Distributive justice is not just a question of owning material goods. There is a "well-being" aspect to distributive justice that relates to question of agency and free development of the individual (Sen, 1987). Another problem is that it is unclear what would constitute a just distribution. A first approximation might be an equal distribution. However, such an equal distribution would not remain equal due to the different interests and abilities of human beings. A related idea might therefore be a distribution according to needs, which would guarantee everybody that their basic needs are met. This seems to be the model of the western social market economies. It raises the problem, however, of what basic needs are and who determines them.

Just distribution also has to deal with the problem that whatever is distributed must first exist. This is where the idea of efficiency enters the picture. A society, in order to be able to distribute anything, must be able to produce goods beyond immediate consumption. Only when there is a surplus can goods be redistributed. The more that is produced, the more that can be distributed. This is linked to the idea of efficiency. An efficient economic system will allow for the production of a sufficient amount of goods that will satisfy everybody's needs (Petersen, 1993). Current conventional wisdom holds that capitalist societies are the ones that have the potential to be most efficient and thereby help their members to achieve the best quality of life. But again, even such simple considerations lead to problems. First, there is the question of the definition of efficiency. While the everyday notion of efficiency may be clear to most of us, it is surprising that there is no corresponding clarity in economics. The most likely contender for a description of efficient states is that of Pareto-optimality. A state is Pareto-optimal if there are no more possible exchanges that would benefit everybody (Sen, 1987). Unfortunately this includes a society where one person owns everything and nobody else owns anything, which would strike most of us as patently unjust.

An added problem is that the different types of justice can be contradictory. The justice of exchange is the basis of successful economic activity and thus of the production of goods to distribute. At the same time it is usually based on unjust distributions. Conversely, a distribution that requires redistributing goods from those who have them to those who need or want them will often not meet the criteria of just exchange. In order to produce justice (through distribution) one will often have to produce injustices (by non-voluntary transfer of goods). On top of this, there is the problem that unequal distributions seem to be a characteristic of capitalist societies, but that these are the societies that produce most goods for distribution. Inequality thus seems to be necessary to create the efficiency that is meant to lead to more equality (Hank, 2000).

All of this is linked to the realisation of legal justice. The law tries to emulate justice but given the problems related to justice, it must make decisions as to which type of justice is promoted (Mansell, Meteyard, & Thomson, 1999). A possible approach to this conundrum of justices is to attempt a more fine-grained discussion than the broad strokes attempted here. The solution may be the definition of different types (or spheres) of justice that call for different approaches (Walzer, 1985). This is an intuition that is shared by several authors, namely that justice translates to equality in some respects (freedom, rights) but not in others (wealth, goods) (Hayek, 1987). At the same time this raises a set of new questions: who defines the spheres and how do we derive the criteria of justice within the spheres?

Justification of Justice

The circularity of this section heading indicates another problem of justice, namely how we can find ways of agreeing what is just. Given the ethical nature of the term, it stands to reason that justice is something that philosophical ethics would be able to define. The circular nature of justice is nicely captured by Wiener (1954, p. 105):

Empirically, the concepts of justice which men have maintained throughout history are as varied as the religions of the world, or the cultures recognized by anthropologists. I doubt if it is possible to justify them by any higher sanction than our moral code itself, which is indeed only another name for our conception of justice.

Justice has to contend with all the problems of philosophical ethics. The fact that there is no generally accepted morality is reflected by the fact that there is no generally agreed concept of justice. Furthermore, there is the problem of acceptance of redistributions that Hayek (1994) points out. It is improbable that we will find a way to distribute wealth in such a way that the people who have to give it up will do so voluntarily for the benefit of someone far removed from their daily lives.

Additionally, there is the theoretical problem of which ethical theory to use to justify justice. We have seen that justice is an important ethical concept that can be incorporated in a number of ethical theories including utilitarianism, deontology, and virtue ethics. However, if all of these see justice as an essential aspect of their theoretical makeup then it stands to reason that philosophers will not easily agree on what justice means and how it can come to be exercised.

Finally, there is the problem that justice has an intuitive character. When hearing a story, reading an article, being confronted with a situation, we often say "this is unjust!". This intuitive character is closely linked with the emotional appeal of justice. This is arguably the main root of justice and effectually overwrites the philosophical discourses about it. Indeed, it has been argued that intuitions of justice are at the heart of even the most elaborate ethical theories concerning justice. Ricœur, analysing Rawls's theory of justice has remarked that the theory of justice as fairness is in fact already hidden in Rawls's description of the original position. If this is true, then theories of justice are essentially circular (Ricœur, 1991). They can at best explain and rationalise our ethical intuitions and render them open to debate. This is an important viewpoint because it will open a solution to the main question of the chapter, namely what the contribution of philosophy can be to the problems of justice and the digital divides.

Justice and (Digital) Divides

The digital divide(s) need to be understood before the background of social distributions that are often viewed as lacking justice. This section will therefore start out with a brief illustration of unjust divides and will then proceed to discuss what this has to do with information and communication technologies (ICT) and therefore with digital divides.

Social Divides

In order to understand the problem of digital divides and why they are perceived to be problematic, one needs to take a look at the problem of distributive justice in other areas. It is common knowledge that the distribution of wealth is highly unequal. Two of the main aspects of this are the different distributions within and between countries. Both are mirrored in some way in the digital divide. A look through the literature reveals a plethora of examples of such uneven distributions that are so extreme that it is relatively simple to see them as unjust. A good example of figures that demonstrate the problem is provided by the UNDP (1998); these figures show that the world's richest 225 people have a combined wealth of over $1 trillion which equals the annual income of the world's poorest 47% or 2.5 billion people. The three richest people have assets that exceed the GDP of the 48 least-developed countries. One explanation why this is perceived as being unjust is that it:

is estimated that the additional cost of achieving and maintaining universal access to basic education for all, basic health care for all, reproductive health care for all women, adequate food for all and safe water and sanitation for all is roughly $40 billion a year. This is less than 4% of the combined wealth of the 225 richest people in the world. (UNDP, 1998, p. 30)

While there is thus an unjust distribution of resources between countries, there are similar problems within countries. Since the United States of American is the wealthiest country in the world and has the largest portion of the richest people, the majority of authors that comment on unequal distribution of wealth take the United States as an example. Another reason why the United States tends to be at the forefront of discussions on distributive justice is that the distribution within its society is highly unequal. The United States is often a trendsetter and one can therefore conclude that more unequal distributions are to come in other parts of the world, notably Europe where distributions are currently more equitable. Also, the difference in wealth between the rich and the poor is growing in the United States (Mishra, 1996; Minc, 1997; Castells, 1997; Schiller, 1999), instead of shrinking as most theories of justice that allow for unequal distribution, notably Rawls, would require. As in the case of international divides, the national divides are often illustrated using striking figures. Schwartz and Gibb (1999), for example state that the personal wealth of Bill Gates (the richest person in the United States) is equal to that of the poorest 40% of the United States population. Another striking example is that of Nike boss Phil Knight, whose 1994 salary of $1,500,000 was such that one of his Chinese employees would have had to work for nine hours a day, six days a week for 15 centuries to earn the same amount (Schwartz & Gibb, 1999, p. 51). Additionally there are problems of distribution of wealth that refer to different types of entities. The important example here is large corporations that often own more assets and have more economic (and arguably political) power than medium-sized states. Velasquez (1998), for example, cites General Motors, at the time the world's largest industrial corporations, which had sales revenues which, at $217 billion, exceeded the government budgets of most states.

Two more ideas are linked to social divides: globalisation and risk. Globalisation as the process of internationalisation of trade supposedly has a large influence on the way goods are distributed within society. The concept of globalisation is increasingly used as an argument defending the status quo and to explain why redistribution by the nation state is not a viable alternative to apparent injustice (Beck, 1998). Globalisation has an obvious impact on the distribution of wealth between states but at the same time it is a driving force concerning the distribution within states. The debate concerning globalisation, its nature and its advantages and disadvantages goes far beyond what this chapter can reflect. It is important to be aware of the concept in the context of social divides and therefore of digital divides. The final term that should be introduced here is risk. Risk as man-made danger has become one of the most important aspects of distribution debates. Distribution is not only about enjoying wealth but also about safety from danger. Where the social divide offers access to wealth and goods to some, depending on nationality or social group, risk seems to concentrate on the other group. Those who have little access to wealth are more exposed to risks, some of which are the result of wealth production. Luhmann (1990) argues that the distribution of risk can replace the distribution of goods as the most important political issue.

Digital Divides

The idea of the digital divide, or digital divides, needs to be seen in the context of the social divides mentioned earlier. Like most concepts, the "digital divide" is hard to define and can be ambiguous (Walsham, 2003). Its essence is that it reflects a concern that the use of ICT can have an influence on divides and the resulting chances to live a fulfilled and autonomous life. The concept of a digital divide has been discussed since approximately the mid 1990s. In a narrow sense, it refers to "significant demographic gaps in computer and Internet access and usage" (Hacker & Mason, 2003, p. 99). During the last decade there has been a large amount of research that tried to establish the reality and relevance of the digital divide. In the United States, for example, the National Telecommunications and Information Administration has collected a large amount of data for a variety of reports, some of which share the title *Falling Through the Net* (www.ntia.doc.gov). Such collection of statistics has been criticised as being one-dimensional and ideologically motivated (Hacker & Mason, 2003). They also structure the possible problem by positing that different levels of access are a problem and by concentrating on the lack of access. This by necessity neglects some aspects such as the possible formation of digital elites (McSorley, 2003). It has furthermore been remarked that there are considerable methodological problems when measuring digital divides. Some authors doubt whether the concentration on the digital divide that we find in some streams of research is actually helpful or whether we should not look at more fundamental issues such as the structure and design of the Internet (Couldry, 2003). Others interpret it as an expression of our collective relationship with technology, which, in turn, reflects underlying metaphysical and religious beliefs, such as the belief in sin, salvation, and redemption (McSorley, 2003).

One can thus state that there is no clear definition of the digital divide (and much less on "digital divides"). It is unclear how they can be described and why they constitute a problem. For the purposes of this chapter I will assume that the reason why many people see digital divides as worrisome is that they can be seen as an expression and also as a possible cause of social divides. The rich find it easier to get access to and use technology such as the Internet. At the same time this difference in access can solidify social differences and deepen the divide between the haves and the have-nots. Digital divide and social divide are therefore often closely related and can be seen as expressions of the same problem (Moss, 2002; Parayil, 2005). And, just as there is more than one social divide, there is more than one digital divide, which explains the use of the plural of the term in this chapter. The two most notable divides are those between countries and within countries. Those countries that are financially well-off find it easier to provide their citizens with access to technology and those social classes that are well-off use technology.

At the same time, the idea of a digital divide is also problematic per se. It signposts an important problem and focuses attention on relevant issues, but it may also lead to a misunderstanding and false evaluation of the problems. One of the major problems is that the term "digital divides" suggests that the problem is a technical one that can be addressed by the provision of technical means of access (Warschauer, 2003). It therefore overlooks that access to technology alone does little about the digital divide since access requires skills and knowledge that go beyond technology (Weckert & Adeney, 1997). The idea that digital divides can be addressed by providing technology is widespread, but it is built on a deterministic view of technology. The assumption that technology will solve the problem is not tenable (Orlikowski & Iacono, 2000; Howcroft, Mitev, & Wilson, 2004).

Another problem of the concept of digital divides is that it implies injustices where none may exist. While digital divides may be expressions or extensions of social divides that disempower and weaken individuals, they may also be voluntarily self-imposed or of no relevance to the autonomous life of the individual. One can conceivably decide not to use ICT for a variety of reasons. This does not necessarily imply social exclusion or a problem of justice, just like the monk's decision to live in poverty does not entail injustice. Similarly, it assumes that there is a coherent and consistent entity called information and that more of this information is better. Again, this is patently not true. A significant part of the information that ICT provides us with is useless and we might be better off without it. Also, the quality of information is not always linked to social status and income. Those who are financially poor, can still live a fulfilled life, whereas some financially and informationally rich people lead impoverished and empty lives (Hongladarom, 2004).

Furthermore, the concept of digital divides can be seen as an expression of cultural imperialism. It assumes that the Western way of viewing and using information is the standard everyone should follow and that those who do not follow it are impoverished. This is particularly visible in cases where ICT is used as a means of economic development of "developing" countries. This is a widespread approach to digital divides, namely to promote the use of ICT in order to support business activities. Apart from a general lack of success of such measures, they can be seen as examples of Western values and culture undermining other ways of life (Walsham, 2001). Digital divides can for all of these reasons easily become self-fulfilling prophecies. Where there used to be no problem, the idea of digital divides may create one that requires a solution, which often creates new problems.

The purpose of this section is not to belittle the problem of digital divides. Rather, it is meant to demonstrate that there is no agreement on what constitutes digital divides and why they are problematic. The main reason for this is that there is no agreement on the definition of the concept of digital divide. In the absence of such an agreement, there is no good reason to hope that one can do objective and useful research. This contradicts plainly the contention of Hacker and Mason (2003) that more ethics is needed in research on digital divides. The problem is not, as they believe, that there is too much ideology hiding the facts. Rather, the facts simply do no not exist outside an ideology, outside a worldview that allows the design of research. There is thus no possibility to do ideology-free research on digital divides.

A Just Approach to Digital Divides?

The purpose of this chapter is to question whether philosophy can make a useful contribution to questions of the digital divide. I am interested in whether philosophers have something to add to the debate, whether the knowledge they have is currently missing, and whether it will make a relevant difference in some way. The current state of the argument is that there is no clear approach to justice and that different understandings of justice are sometimes contradictory. Furthermore, we have found that there are divides within and between countries, which are partly social and often related to ICT. However, there is no clear relationship between ICT and justice. On a very basic level, one could argue that it is unjust that some people have access to ICT whereas others do not and that everybody should have the same chance to use technology. We should realise, however, that this approach is based on an egalitarian ideal of distributive justice which may be difficult to support and which may clash with other ideas of justice. Even if we gave every person on the world the same sort of technical access, there would still be the divide between those who use it for purposes conducive to their wellbeing and those who do not. We would thus have to ensure equal education and knowledge and equal chance of acting upon information.

This describes an ideal communist society. On the one hand, there is the question whether we really want such an egalitarian society or whether we prefer inequalities, which may also work to our advantage, for example, if we do not want to use ICT. On the other hand, the history of communism has shown that it is not trivial to install such an egalitarian society. It requires redistribution of resources, which will clash with the ideal of voluntary exchange of goods as posited by theories of just exchange. It also produces problems of legal justice by presupposing that legal systems will allow such a large redistribution.

It thus stands to reason that equal access to ICT is not to be expected any time soon. A radical development in the direction of equal distribution of technology and access might produce more injustice than justice. However, one can probably safely say that a gradual development in the direction of more generalised access would be a positive event if it did not conflict with other considerations of justice. So, maybe the debate so far can lead us to the conclusion that societies should aim in the direction of more equality of access and that philosophy's contribution may be to support such a conclusion, albeit tentatively. We could thus see this as a starting point for a philosophically motivated development. But how can it be achieved? The next section will discuss one of a number of problems of implementing a more equal distribution by looking at the arguments for state and private sector provision of ICT and infrastructure.

Market vs. State and Market Metaphysics

This section will discuss the problems of implementing the idea that a more equal distribution of ICT would promote justice. It will do so by looking at the arguments which suggest that either state or market should lead this development. The main question in this section is who should be responsible for the creation and maintenance of the infrastructure necessary for more egalitarian access to technology. It will conclude by arguing that this debate is fundamentally a metaphysical one, based on assumptions about the nature of reality that are not subject to observation or rational debate.

The Market as Best Provider of ICT Infrastructure

The question we are interested in here is whether markets or states are better suited to provide citizens with what they need to use ICT for their advantage. This includes questions of the provision of access to the Internet, and also access to hardware, software, and possibly educational facilities required to be able to profit from these offers. The market/state debate is a slightly artificial one because in reality there tends to be a mix between them. We often find partnerships between private companies and governments that provide access or services (Weiser & Molnar, 1996). For the sake of clarity of the argument, this chapter only looks at the extreme positions, namely that exclusively the government or exclusively the mar should provide access. It does not distinguish between the size and scope of such projects, even though there are discernible differences between large-scale infrastructure projects and ad hoc improvements on a local basis (Avgerou, 1991).

The arguments in this debate often mirror some of the questions concerning justice discussed previously. They are therefore worth debating in the context of the question of the relation of justice and digital divides. One of the most important arguments for a market approach to access to ICT is that of cost. The amount of money to be invested in ICT to get it to the point where it is universally accessible is enormous (Castells, 2000). Governments are therefore easily persuaded to give the task to the private sector. Another argument in favour of markets is that they are allegedly better in providing the sort of services that customers require. This is due to the fact that they are more flexible than government bureaucracies (Chapman & Rotenberg, 1995). They are better suited to meet the interests of the customers (McKnight & Botelho, 1997). Then there is the argument that commercial interests have in fact taken over from states as the driving forces of technology and infrastructure development and that policy development is simply too slow to keep up with technical development and new business models (Kahin, 1997).

There are also counter-arguments which emphasise the weaknesses of the market when it comes to the provision of technology. Most of these are directly linked to questions of social justice. One problem is that of diverging interests between state provision and profit-oriented providers. This does not necessarily imply that private companies are overly greedy but their profit motives lead to incompatible interests, often even among themselves. Dewan, Friemer, and Gundepudi (1999), for example, discuss the impact of company size on company interests.

Another problem is that the use of market mechanisms for the provision of access to ICT is in many cases a disguised statement of ideology. Leaving such questions to markets may be a code for economic and political liberalisation (Vedel, 1997), which, in terms of justice, would emphasise just exchange over just distribution. The main obstacle from the point of view of people interested in the digital divide is that there is usually a lack of incentives to close this divide. Those individuals who may lack access to technology are, as we have seen, usually those who also lack economic resources. It is thus difficult to render access provision a profitable enterprise. In the light of this, the question is why market participants should want to do so (Baer, 1997).

The State as Best Provider of ICT Infrastructure

The arguments for and against the state as provider of ICT infrastructure mirror those just enumerated. Nation states have the power to regulate and create ICT infrastructure in their territory. Many of them are large and have more financial power than individual companies. The state can regulate content and form of infrastructure, which is specifically important for the achievement of non-financial aims such as the equity of access (Chapman & Rotenberg, 1995). Furthermore, states tend to be important customers of ICT services and they therefore often have the ability to shape markets according to their needs (Jeong & King, 1997).

From the point of view of economics, one can see the provision of ICT infrastructure and access as a public good with the corresponding problems of public goods (West et al., 1997). Public goods can lead to problems of free riders and incentives have to be set to avoid those problems. At the same time, public goods produce a surplus of benefits over costs and are therefore desirable to have. The typical way to deal with public goods is thus to have collective ownership of them, which means the state should take care of them.

The counter-arguments to state involvement are well-known. States are supposed to be insufficiently flexible and unable to keep up with the changes of business and technology (Currie, 2000). The lack of flexibility of the state leads to inefficiency, waste and to non-optimal distribution of services. Another problem is that of the public good. If it is provided by the state, and if access is made free or cheaper than cost for political purposes such as justice, then there is the problem of overuse and misuse, the problem of the common (Danielson, 1996).

The Metaphysics of the Debate

The previously-mentioned argument of state versus market as best provider of ICT infrastructure and access will be quite familiar to everybody who is interested in political matters in most of the Western world. It is played out over all sorts of issues and certainly not confined to questions of ICT and access. I do not claim to have captured all, or even most, of the important aspects of it. The purpose of this brief argument was to show that there are two convincing sides to the argument that, even in the extreme forms of only state or only market. In the context of this chapter, the question thus is: even if we could agree that more equality of access to ICT is a way to create more justice and bridge the digital divide, how should we go about achieving this goal?

To put this question differently, we could ask whether having states provide infrastructure and access will lead to a more egalitarian, and thus more just, outcome than if markets do so. This is where the market versus state debate gets entangled with questions of justice; both are mixed with metaphysical questions of the nature of (social) reality. Whether markets or states are better suited to cater for needs is a question that is not open to observation or empirical evidence. Depending on one's viewpoint one would see successful experiences of market provision of goods as an example of the strength of markets or of good governance of markets. Failures could equally be interpreted as typical market problems or as a lack of freedom of markets, usually caused by government interference.

This metaphysical view of the world then gets mixed up with questions of justice. For the sake of the argument we have assumed that equal access would be a just approach to digital divides. However, this is not generally recognised. Proponents of markets would argue that prices which individuals are willing to pay for ICT depend on their desire to use these and that therefore an equal provision would not do justice to the different needs of different individuals. An unequal distribution that follows the market logic might therefore be more just than an egalitarian distribution.

If this is true, then we seem to be faced with a serious problem. Not only do we not know what justice would demand from us to address questions of digital divides, but we also do not know how to achieve the aims, even if we were able to agree on. What, then, are we to do?

Conclusion

This chapter set out to provide a critical view of the philosophical debate on justice insofar as it pertains to questions of digital divides. It stated early on that the underlying assumption of this volume was that philosophers have something to add to the debate, that the knowledge they have is currently missing, and that it can make a relevant difference (Parker, 2003). We can now ask whether these assumptions are correct and what the role of the philosophical debate can be in the area of digital divides.

Philosophers are supposed to be good in conceptual work and they, therefore, should be able to help clarify the underlying issues and concepts. The first sections of this chapter on the concept of justice and digital divides were meant to review some of the conceptual work done by philosophers. The main result was that, while philosophy can clarify the different streams of arguments, it cannot provide us with generally accepted definitions. Furthermore, it cannot tell us what exactly the problems are. The most important result that I would draw from the discussion of justice is that it is at heart an emotional notion. Injustice is something that strikes us at first sight. For the more analytically minded philosophers this may not be a very satisfactory explanation. And yet, the emotional appeal of justice seems to reach far and provide some consensus. We may not be able to agree on the meaning of justice, but, to a large extent, we can agree that something is unjust when we see it. The huge social divides discussed earlier are a good example. The reason why many of the statistics on unequal distribution of wealth described earlier are used is presumably that the authors are aware that they will lead to a shared feeling of injustice. If this is so, then all philosophy may have to contribute is an explanation and clarification of the moral intuition concerning justice. This would render moral philosophy a largely circular exercise, but maybe a good circular argument is all that we can hope for (Ricœur, 1991).

That means that the first two aspects of the requirements for useful participation by philosophers in the digital divides debate are partly fulfilled. There is a lack of knowledge concerning the underlying notions and philosophers are able to provide this knowledge. That does not mean that they can clearly and unambiguously define the concepts, but they are able to recount the arguments and show their limits. This leaves the last point: does this make a difference?

The question whether philosophy can and should make a difference is a complex one that cannot be debated in full here. However, given that chapter is intended to be situated in the tradition of critical theory and critical social studies, it can offer a viewpoint on this. Critical theory traditionally aims at the empowerment and emancipation of human beings. There is a good case to be made that ICT has the potential to empower people (and also to disempower them). Digital divides can thus partly be seen as issues for emancipation and for critical theory. The intent of critical theory is to make a difference and not to remain in the purely descriptive tradition of philosophy and social science.

Given the conceptual problems that this chapter has explored, it is not to be expected that philosophical analyses will be able to provide us with a clear view of how we can make a difference and what exactly the aims are. That means that, in order to achieve the critical intention, researchers will have to leave the realm of academia and become politically active. The question remains which actions should be taken and which political aims are to be striven for. Part of the answer will be the justice-related intuitions we (or many of us) share. Extreme inequality in distribution is hard to justify and needs to be addressed. This includes inequalities related to digital divides. How these are to be addressed then becomes a political rather than a philosophical question. The problem of market metaphysics needs to be debated as a matter of finding politically viable solutions, and not as a matter concerning the nature of reality.

But, if the conclusion of this chapter is that philosophers should become politically active, is there any point in continuing philosophical research? I believe that there is a point in continuing and that philosophical and conceptual analysis are useful bases upon which to build political action. Furthermore, conceptual analyses, such as the one regarding the market versus state debate, will allow us to identify ideologies and discursive closures. Only when these are identified can they be changed. Philosophy cannot tell us what to do, lest it become the tyranny of the intellectual. But it can provide us with starting points to make a difference. In this sense, I hope that this chapter, together with the other contributions to this volume, will provide a starting point for a political approach to questions of justice in the digital divides that is well-founded on philosophical debate.

References

Aristotle. (1967). *Die Nikomachische Ethik.* Zürich und München, Switzerland: dtv/Artemis.

Avgerou, C. (1991). Creating an information systems infrastructure for development planning. In *Proceedings of the International Conference on Information Systems 1991* (pp. 251-259).

Baer, W. S. (1997). Will the global information infrastructure need transnational (or any) governance? In B. Kahin & E. J. Wilson (Eds.), *National information infrastructure initiatives vision and policy design* (pp. 532-552). Cambridge, MA: MIT Press.

Beck, U. (1998). *Was ist Globalisierung? Irrtümer des Globalismus-Antworten auf Globalisierung* (5th ed.). Frankfurt a. M., Germany: Suhrkamp.

Castells, M. (1997). *The information age: Economy, society, and culture. Volume II: The power of identity.* Oxford, UK: Blackwell.

Castells, M. (2000). *The information age: Economy, society, and culture. Vol. I: The rise of the network society* (2nd ed.). Oxford, UK: Blackwell.

Chapman, G., & Rotenberg, M. (1995). The national information infrastructure: A public interest opportunity. In D. G. Johnson & H. Nissenbaum (Eds.), *Computers, ethics & social values* (pp. 628-644). Upper Saddle River, NJ: Prentice Hall.

Chouliaraki, L., & Fairclough, N. (1999). *Discourse in late modernity: Rethinking critical discourse analysis.* Edinburgh, Scotland: Edinburgh University Press.

Chua, W-F. (1986). Radical developments in accounting thought. *The Accounting Review, 61*(4), 601-632.

Couldry, N. (2003). Digital divide or discursive design? On the emerging ethics of information space. *Ethics and Information Technology, 5*(2), 89-97.

Currie, W. (2000). *The global information society.* Chichester, UK: John Wiley.

Danielson, P. (1996). Pseudonyms, mailBots, and virtual letterheads: The evolution of computer-mediated ethics. In C. Ess (Ed.), *Philosophical perspectives on computer-mediated communication* (pp. 67-93). Albany: State University of New York Press.

De George, R. T. (1999). *Business ethics* (5th ed.). Upper Saddle River, NJ: Prentice Hall.

Dewan, R., Friemer, M., & Gundepudi, P. (1999). Evolution of Internet infrastructure in the 21st century: The role of private interconnection agreements. In *Proceedings of the International Conference on Information Systems 1999* (pp. 144-154).

Fairclough, N. (1993). Critical discourse analysis and the marketization of public discourse: the universities. *Discourse & Society, 4*(2), 133-168.

Hacker, K. L., & Mason, S. M. (2003). Ethical gaps in studies of the digital divide. *Ethics and Information Technology, 5*(2), 99-115.

Hank, R. (2000). *Das ende der Gleichheit Oder Warum der Kapitalismus Mehr Wettbewerb Braucht.* Frankfurt a. M., Germany: S. Fischer.

Hausman, D. M., & McPherson, M. S. (1996). *Economic analysis and moral philosophy.* Cambridge, UK: Cambridge University Press.

Höffe, O. (1992). Gerechtigkeit als Tausch? Ein Ökonomisches Prinzip für die Ethik. In H. Lenk & M. Maring (Eds.), *Wirtschaft und Ethik* (pp. 119-133). Stuttgart, Germany: Reclam.

Höffe, O. (1996). Soziale Gerechtigkeit als Tausch: Ein Neues Paradigma. In K. Bayertz (Ed.), *Politik und Ethik* (pp. 229-248). Stuttgart, Germany: Reclam.

Hongladarom, S. (2004). Making information transparent as a means to close the global digital divide. *Minds and Machines, 14*(1), 85-99.

Howcroft, D., Mitev, N., & Wilson, M. (2004). What we may learn from the social shaping of technology approach. In J. Mingers & L. Willcocks (Eds.), *Social theory and philosophy for information systems* (pp. 329-371). Chichester, UK: Wiley.

Jeong, K-H., & King, J. L. (1997). Korea's national information infrastructure: Vision and issues. In B. Kahin & E. J. Wilson (Eds.), *National information infrastructure initiatives vision and policy design* (pp. 112-149). Cambridge, MA: MIT Press.

Kahin, B. (1997). The U.S. national information infrastructure initiative: The market, the Web, and the virtual project. In B. Kahin & E. J. Wilson (Eds.), *National information infrastructure initiatives vision and policy design* (pp. 150-189). Cambridge, MA: MIT Press.

Kohlberg, L. (1981). *The philosophy of moral development: Moral stages and the idea of justice.* San Francisco: Harper & Row.

Levinas, E. (1988). *Totalité et infini: Essai sur l'extériorité* (4ᵗʰ ed.). Dordrecht, The Netherlands: Kluwer.

Luhmann, N. (1990). Paradigm lost: *Über die Ethische Reflexion der Moral.* Frankfurt a. M., Germany: Suhrkamp.

Mansell, W., Meteyard, B., & Thomson, A. (1999). *A critical introduction to law* (2ⁿᵈ ed.). London: Cavendish.

Maritain, J. (1960). *La philosophie morale: Examen historique et critique des grands systèmes.* Paris: Gallimard.

McKnight, L., & Botelho, A. (1997). Brazil: Is the world ready for when information highways cross the Amazon? In B. Kahin & E. J. Wilson (Eds.), *National information infrastructure initiatives vision and policy design* (pp. 261-286). Cambridge, MA: MIT Press.

McSorley, K. (2003). The secular salvation story of the digital divide. *Ethics and Information Technology, 5*(2), 75-87.

Mill, J. S. (1976). *Der Utilitarismus.* Stuttgart, Germany: Reclam.

Minc, A.(1997). *La Mondialisation Heureuse.* Paris: Plon Pocket.

Mishra, R. (1996). The welfare of nations. In R. Boyer & D. Drache (Eds.), *States against markets: The limits of globalization.* London: Routledge.

Moss, J. (2002). Power and the digital divide. *Ethics and Information Technology, 4*(2), 159-165.

Nord, W. R., & Jermier, J. M. (1992). Critical social science for managers? Promising and perverse possibilities. In M. Alvesson & H. Willmott (Eds.), *Critical management studies* (pp. 202-222). London: Sage.

Nozick, R. (1974). *Anarchy, state, and utopia.* Basic Books.

Orlikowski, W. J., & Baroudi, J. J. (1991). Studying information technology in organizations: Research approaches and assumptions. *Information Systems Research, 2*(1), 1-28.

Orlikowski, W. J., & Iacono, C. S. (2000). The truth is not out there: An enacted view of the "digital economy." In E. Brynjolfsson & B. Kahin (Eds.), *Understanding the digital economy* (pp. 352-380). Boston: MIT Press.

Parayil, G. (2005). The digital divide and increasing returns: Contradictions of informational capitalism. *The Information Society, 21*(1), 41-51.

Parker, M. (2003). Business, ethics and business ethics: Critical theory and negative dialectics. In M. Alvesson & H. Willmott (Eds.), *Studying management critically* (pp. 197-219). London: Sage.

Perelmann, C. (1967). *Über die Gerechtigkeit.* München, Germany: C.H. Beck.

Petersen, H-G. (1993). *Ökonomie, Ethik und Demokratie: Zu Einer Theorie der Effizienz und Gerechtigkeit Offener Gesellschaften.* Baden, Germany: Nomos.

Rawls, J. (2001). *Justice as fairness: A restatement.* Edited by E. Kelly. Cambridge, MA: Belknap, Harvard.

Ricoeur, P. (1991). John Rawls: De l'autonomie morale à la fiction du contrat social. In P. Ricoeur, *Lectures 1: Autour du politique* (pp. 196-215). Paris: Seuil.

Ricoeur, P. (1995). *Le juste.* Paris: Editions Esprit.

Ricoeur, P. (2001). *Le juste 2.* Paris: Editions Esprit.

Schiller, D. (1999). *Digital capitalism: Networking the global market system.* Cambridge, MA: MIT Press.

Schmidtz, D. (1998). Taking responsibility. In D. Schmidtz & R. Goodin (Eds.), *Social welfare and individual responsibility.* Cambridge, UK: Cambridge University Press.

Schwartz, P., & Gibb, B. (1999). *When good companies do bad things: Responsibility and risk in an age of globalization.* New York: John Wiley.

Sen, A. (1987). *On ethics and economics.* Oxford, UK; New York: Basil Blackwell.

Tocqueville, A. (1998). *De la démocratie en Amérique.* Paris: Gallimard.

United Nations Development Programme (UNDP). (1998). *Human development report 1998.* New York; Oxford, UK: Oxford University Press.

Vedel, T. (1997). Information superhighway policy in France: The end of high tech Colbertism? In B. Kahin & E. J. Wilson (Eds.), *National information infrastructure initiatives vision and policy design* (pp. 307-348). Cambridge, MA: MIT Press.

Velasquez, M. (1998). *Business ethics: Concepts and cases* (4th ed.). Upper Saddle River, NJ: Prentice Hall.

von Hayek, F. A. (1987). Argumente Gegen die Verteilungsgerechtigkeit. In N. Hoerster (Ed.), *Recht und Moral: Texte zur Rechtsphilosophie* (pp. 174-197). Stuttgart, Germany: Reclam.

von Hayek, F. A. (1994). *The road to serfdom* (50th anniversary ed.). Chicago: University of Chicago Press.

Walsham, G. (2001). *Making a world of difference: IT in a global context.* Chichester, UK: Wiley.

Walsham, G. (2003, June 15-17). *Development, global futures and IS research: A polemic.* Presented at IS Perspectives and Challenges in the Context of Globalization, IFIP Working Groups 8.2 and 9.4 Joint Conference, Athens Greece (Research in Progress Papers).

Walzer, M. (1985). *Spheres of justice.* Oxford, UK: Blackwell.

Warschauer, M. (2003). Dissecting the "digital divide": A case study in Egypt. *The Information Society, 19*, 297-304.

Weckert, J., & Adeney, D. (1997). *Computer and information ethics*. Westport, CT: Greenwood Press.

West, J., et al. (1997). Back to the future: Japan's NII plans. In B. Kahin & E. J. Wilson (Eds.), *National information infrastructure initiatives vision and policy design* (pp. 61-111) Cambridge, MA: MIT Press.

Weil, É. (1960). *Philosophie morale* (5th ed.). Paris: Librairie Philosophique J. Vrin.

Weiser, M., & Molnar, K. K. (1996). Advanced telecommunications infrastructure policies: A comparative analysis. In *Proceedings of the American Conference on Information Systems 1996*.

Wiener, N. (1954). *The human use of human beings: Cybernetics and society.* Garden City, NY: Doubleday Anchor Books.

Wittgenstein, L. (1963) *Tractatus Logico-Philosophicus - Logisch-Philosophische Abhandlungen*. Frankfurt a. M., Germany: Suhrkamp.

Chapter VIII

Discourses in Gender and Technology:
Taking a Feminist Gaze

Sheila French
Manchester Metropolitan University, UK

Abstract

The majority of women are not involved in the design, manufacturing or shaping of technology in many Western societies. This is at a time when governments glob-ally see technology as an enabler to economic success. Using feminist scholarship and discourse analysis, this chapter questions why patterns of gender segregation prevail in technology related fields in the United Kingdom. The chapter critically analyses why government policy, and equal opportunities initiatives, have so far largely failed to increase women's participation. Using examples taken from two educational settings, the chapter uses the narratives of individual's experiences of technology, their engagement, or lack of engagement with it, to examine the dominant discourses of the field. It is argued that technology discourses, which shape our understanding and identity with technology, are gendered. It is argued that current policies and initiatives, based on giving women equality of access will continue to make little difference. Until gendered dominant discourses of technology are deconstructed and examined; we will not have the tools to address the current situation of gender segregation.

The Connection between masculinity and technology, reflected in women's under-representation in engineering, and indeed in all scientific and technical institutions, remains strong as we enter a new era of technological change. (Wajcman, 2004)

Introduction

Globally, governments see new technologies as the enabler of economic success in the global knowledge economy.[1] At the same time the United Kingdom, along with many other Western societies, is experiencing a gender divide in relation to the use, development and design of information and communication technologies (ICT). For some time it has been recognized that males dominate the use of technologies in all areas of British society (DFEE, 2001; Hellawell, 2001; Wilkinson, 2001) and that gender segregation in ICT occupations persists (EOC, 2004a). Only a few girls are taking up computing at an advanced level at school, and universities are experiencing a continued lack of interest in applications by women for computing degree programs (Alexander, 2001b; EOC, 2005). In 1996, 19% of computer science students were reported to be female. Today, there has been little improvement; females account for only 20% of computing graduates in Great Britain (EOC, 2005). In the workplace, women hardly feature in the innovation and production of technology and the computing industry is concerned about the lack of women in the sector. British industry continues to experience major skills shortages of technicians and ICT professionals (DFEE, 2001; EOC 2004b). This is contrary to images in the popular press of women—such as Martha Lane Fox, the co-founder of lastminute.com—who are hailed as heroines of the dot.com industry. In reality men dominate e-commerce start-ups, and there is little involvement of women at the investment level of the industry (Hellawell, 2001). There are signs that women are not involved in the new economy and the new technologies, and "that men are firmly in the driving seat" (Wilkinson, 2001). This has not gone undetected, nor has it been ignored. Over a number of years the lack of women's participation in science and technology has been addressed in various United Kingdom government policies and initiatives. However, neither the government nor industry has set specific targets in relation to women entering these male dominated industries (EOC, 2004). Gender segregation still prevails and women are still under-represented in the field of technology.

This chapter begins by looking at the emphasis that the United Kingdom government, along with others around the globe, place on the new technologies in relation to the global knowledge economy. The discussion moves on to look at why the current situation of gender segregation is thought to prevail. I present here a critical analysis of government policy and initiatives based on giving equal opportunities to women, most of which have so far largely failed to increase the participation of women. I then introduce feminist theory and discourse analysis to look at "discourses of technology." Focusing on examples from two educational settings, I use the discussions of individuals' experiences of technology, their process of engagement, or lack of engagement, with the technology. The aim is to demonstrate that issues of gender and technology are by no means simple. I suggest we should not just focus on giving women equal opportunities to access, training and education in technology, we should instead try to identify and understand more clearly how the dominant discourses around technology come to shape our understanding and identity with technology. It is this I suggest that needs deconstructing before we can address patterns of gender segregation.

ICT and the Global Knowledge Economy

Technology and innovation feature highly in future economies, and are seen by governments in the United Kingdom and around the globe to be an essential ingredient to becoming internationally competitive (Brooks & Mackinnon, 2001). Training the population in the use of information and communication technologies (ICTs) is seen as a powerful enabler. The lack of access to ICTs does not only lead to exclusion from the new technologies but also to exclusion from the new knowledge economy (Castells, 2000). Training members of society to be computer literate is regarded as essential to participation in the current and future labor market. In government rhetoric about "education" there is a shift in emphasis from being purely concerned with the education of individuals, to a need to ensure the population has the essential skills that will assist with the nation's wealth creation (Brooks & Mackinnon, 2001; Coffield, 1999). This raises issues about what type of knowledge and skills will be valued by society in the future. It suggests that those with the knowledge and ability to use the new technologies will be favored for their capacity to contribute to the knowledge economy. It suggests that those without the requisite information technology skills will fail to contribute to the economy and, therefore, could be excluded from future prosperity.

UK Government Policy and Initiatives

The UK government has recognised the gender divide and has proposed a number of initiatives to reverse what they refer to as "the challenge of women's participation in ICT" (Alexander, 2001b). The aim is to give women access to information technology (IT) in education, the workplace and their social lives. Strategies are being funded to address socially excluded groups, which often include women, to enable them to acquire what are thought to be essential ICT skills for daily life in future economies (DTI, 2004). The aim is to improve the image of IT in education and work; this, it is suggested, will increase women's participation. Girls will be encouraged to become more enthusiastic about today's technologies, and it is hoped that they will gain confidence to compete with boys in what the government refers to as the male domination of ICT in the classroom. This is aimed at ensuring that all girls along with other socially excluded groups have the necessary ICT skills to work in and meet the skills demands of the new economy. Female role models will be used to improve the image of IT, to encourage young women to take ICT as a subject at school, and to enter careers related to technology. A change in business attitudes will be promoted in the computing sector to encourage flexible working conditions for parents. This approach is well-meaning, but there are a number of problems with it. Already there is evidence that these policies and initiatives are failing to make little difference.

Firstly this approach treats technology as an artifact that has no political or social values attached to it. This is clearly not the case, as social studies of science and technology[2] have provided strong evidence that technology is not gender-neutral (Adam, 1998; Cockburn, 1985; Wajcman, 1991, 2000). In the home, male members of families still have more access to computers than women do (Richardson & French, 2001). Boys are very often given greater priority of access to computers at home by their parents than girls (Habib & Cornford, 2001; Na, 2001). In education it has been argued that there is a maleness surrounding technology, IT and computing subjects (Woodfield, 2000).

Secondly, there is an assumption that women, if the conditions are right, will want to be involved in the field of technology. However, evidence suggests quite the contrary; women may not want to be involved in computing (Clegg, 2001; Na, 2001). While women are quite able to "do computing," for many the image of computing and IT is masculine; it is these gendered notions of what "is" technical which lead to girls becoming reticent about taking up computing and technology (Clegg & Trayhurn, 1999; Clegg, Mayfield, & Trayhurn, 1999). Therefore, suggestions that we can use role models to change the image of ICTs lead us to question where the role models will be found if the majority of women in our society remain uninterested in technology. These initiatives presume that given equality of access and the right workplace conditions, women will begin to participate. It suggests that women and men attach the same perceptions and social values to technology—an assumption I believe to be flawed. This approach is misguided in its treatment of technology. Taking this stance is likely to obscure many of the issues related to our social relationship with technology.

In the following discussion feminist theory and discourse analysis will be employed to help us understand the issues involved. We begin by unraveling the existing social and cultural practices, which have led to the current situation in the United Kingdom and other Western societies.

Taking a Feminist Gaze

Feminism comprises of one but many different theories and perspectives that have some common understandings and some differences. Feminism is complex, so defining it is controversial. Feminists agree that social and political theory has a history of being "written by men, for men and about men" (Theile, 1986), and that issues of women have been largely ignored or trivialised. Feminists critique any practice where there is an "assumption of male superiority and centrality" in which women's subordination is taken as a given (Beasley, 1999). However, they do not necessarily agree about how we might bring about changes to any given situation.

Feminists collectively seek to explain women's oppression and share a belief that women hold an unequal position in society; to use the theories to question the causes for this. The theories do not all suggest the same reasons for oppression or have the same ideals. In their different forms, feminisms collectively "prescribe strategies for women's liberation" (Tong, 1997). The context in which I will use "discourse analysis" is taken from the critical tradition. Critical feminist work is ultimately political in that is seeks to understand the position of those who suffer most from dominance and inequality. Critical feminists are social critics. They outline their point of view, perspective and their aims, as in this chapter. Often they place their own subjectivity in the research rather than attempting to be neutral observers. The aim is to produce knowledge which might make a positive difference for women. In this case the question being asked is what factors or conditions sustain, legitimise and perhaps condone the current state of social inequality and injustice regarding women's participation in technology.

Discourse Analysis

Discourse analysis has evolved from a number of theories about how we should study language and text.[3] The way in which I use it here broadly rests on the work of Michel Foucault (1978, 1981). The concept of "discourse" is taken in a quest to understand the relationship between language, social institutions, subjectivity and power. Discourse, as used in a linguistic context, is taken as a system of representation connected to writing or speech. In Foucault's terms this is not just an analysis of "text" and the spoken word; it is also about how discourses, in his terms, create knowledge or meaning in our social world. Language, in his view, is not necessarily unique to the individual but is shaped by a range of social, political and economic practices. In a way, it places emphasis not only on what one says but also on what one does. Foucault, taking a constructionist theory of meaning and representation, argued that it is "discourse" that gives us meaning, which in turn creates knowledge values or norms in a particular field. There is a range of discourses in society, often overlapping, some of which are more dominant than others. They do not all carry equal weight or power. Foucault argues that the most dominant give meaning to the world and organise social institutions and processes. A dominant discourse in a historical period can then come to be constituted as the norm. Those who hold these beliefs, he argues, have a vested interest in keeping the status quo. This does not mean that individuals cannot contest the discourse, but it may mean that they are perhaps marginalised by what is considered to be the norm in that field. Meaning, therefore, depends on a person's subjectivity. Subjectivity refers to the conscious and unconscious thoughts and emotions of an individual (Weedon, 1997). In these terms, what we say and what we do are shaped by the discourses we inhabit and the norms and values associated with them. Experiences in the home and at school, such as expectations of the way girls and boys should behave as female or male, shape subjectivity. Therefore, if we look at the issues of women's lack of participation in technology in terms of discourse, it is not only about issues relating to "technology," "education," or "careers." It is also about the context and historical moment in which the discourse resides. In this case the context is also to do with the global knowledge economy and our relationship with technology at this time and the meanings such discourses produce.

To illustrate the complexities and put this work in a historical context I want to return briefly to government policy and initiatives to give an example of such discourses. The following demonstrates how knowledge and power are at work in discourses and how they come to make social meaning.

Consider the following statement made by the UK government, "ensure everyone has the requisite skills for the knowledge economy" (DFEE, 2001). As we read this statement we can see it is about giving the population opportunities to contribute in the workplace. However, it is also linked to the "knowledge economy." As an educationalist reading this, I would suggest the education of individuals seems to have shifted from pure interest in an individual's education to securing "economic wealth" for the nation (Brooks & Mackinnon, 2001). Therefore, if we look at the statement in terms of "discourse," we could question if the statement is perhaps located in a discourse of what we might call "future economic wealth," or in what Lucey, Melody and Walkerdine (2003) refer to as the discourse of "social capital." The British government's political position influences the meaning of this statement, as does my interpretation as an educationalist and feminist. As this discourse of "social capital" is constructed further and propagated by the government in policy and in the media, it becomes a dominant discourse in British society and has the power to shape our norms and values around the new economy.

My argument is that these discourses shape our beliefs and what becomes our "knowledge." To understand women's lack of participation, we need to look at norms and values associated with the field of computing and information technology before we can hope to make any difference to women's lack of participation.

Discourses of Technology and Gender

It is important to define the context in which the terms "computing," "IT," and "ICT" are used in this discussion. Computing is a number of disparate and complex practices and technologies where the terms "computing," "IT," and "ICT" are used interchangeably. The term "ICT" is relatively new; my interpretation is that it refers more to the "user end" of the technology. The UK government appears to hold a similar interpretation, as the focus is on giving society the necessary "end user" skills for a future economy. In the following discussion, I will use the term "computing" which includes all of these definitions.

Clegg, Mayfield, and Trayhurn (1999) suggest there is not only one "form," or way, of "doing computing," and that, this being the case, there is likely to be more than one discourse of computing. They have identified two major discourses; what we can term the "hard end" discourse, dependent on formal methods and mathematical models, and the "soft" or "user end" discourse, in which technology assists or supports organisational systems. Therefore, the meaning of the term "technical" can be different, depending on the context, or frame of reference.

These discourses are reflected in the way we organise "computing," for example, in education. A computing department in a UK university might place the emphasis of its computing courses on a "mathematical" model of computing (the hard end), whereas a department in a faculty of humanities or business may place more emphasis on the human and social dimensions and on the real world uses of computers (the user end). In many academic institutions there is a discourse that suggests that "to do" computing requires superior mental powers linked to those of the mathematician or scientist (Edwards, 1990). In academia, the more traditional view of formal mathematical methods can also be strongly associated with math and "technical machismo" (Mahony & Van Toen, 1990, p. 321). In the disciplines of math and science, there is also a long history of a masculine culture (Hughes, 2001). It has been argued that this association of mathematics and science with masculine culture has turned women away from the subjects. This association suggests a gendered discourse of computing in which women may not wish to participate because it conflicts with their gender identity (Clegg & Trayhurn, 1999). Whilst the field of computing is still defined in this way, it may discourage some, but it cannot solely be responsible for the lack of women's participation, as women have increased their participation in other seemingly impenetrable "macho" occupations such as medicine. It is also important to note at this juncture that not "all" females are put off by male-dominated occupations; just as not "all" males favour male-dominated occupations only (Hughes, 2001). However, if we look at our lives through the dominant discourses that help us define our identities, we can see that those discourses discussed so far could maintain the status quo in the field of technology.

Through the following two examples, taken from two different case studies carried out in educational settings, I will demonstrate the pervasiveness of these discourses. Both examples are used here to uncover and illustrate the dominant discourses that operate, or serve to maintain how we perceive computing. Both of the studies used are small and are not, therefore, being used to "claim" anything. They are being used to demonstrate the power of discourse in determining what becomes the knowledge, or norm, and values, and, therefore, maintains the current position. The narratives that follow draw on free association techniques (Hollway & Jefferson, 2000), which means that the interviews were unstructured, allowing the individuals to tell their story. The aim was to take a reflective look at what had informed their experiences in relation to their gender identities and their relationship with technology. Using theories of the "gestalt" (Hollway & Jefferson, 2000), I look to the sum of the "whole," rather than the individual "part"; consequently, the work does not just focus on the subjects' relationship with technology but also on the influence of the other aspects of their lives and experiences. The students may have constructed their accounts to make sense of the world they inhabit through their subjectivity. I add my interpretation, which I acknowledge is influenced by my own subjectivity and experience (Walkerdine, 1997; Hollway & Jefferson, 2000).

For the first example I use excerpts from the narratives of four university students, two males and two females (aged 18-24) who were studying for a degree in information technology at a British university; this study was carried out in 2003.[4]

The Narratives

First we will discuss Simon and Paul. In the following excerpt we can see evidence that for both of them their relationship with technology is embedded in their masculine identities and in several other overlapping discourses around how they played as children and as young adult males. This is not surprising, as there is evidence that the relationship between technology and gender begins in the home where males dominate many of the technologies including computers. When computers first entered the home they were targeted at boys and male hobbyists (Kirkup & Abbott,

1997; Wajcman, 1991). Simon and Paul were not exceptions to this targeting. They had been introduced to computers early in their lives and both of them still played computer games. Simon was proud of what he defined as his "*technical skills*" and how he had recently networked the computers in his home. Simon talked about computers as "*something I'm serious at*" and explained how, through "*trial and error,*" he had learnt to build computers.

For Paul the computer is an "object" of some significance in his life. He described how he was comfortable in an environment where there was a computer turned on and how he would leave it on in his bedroom whilst he was working, listening to music or doing other things—"*You can click on it and it runs itself... I leave it on in the room and just go back to it.*" During the narrative Paul appeared to "confess" to using computers in his leisure time—"*It might sound geeky, but yeah, my friends are geeky ... I sound like I am always playing games and stuff, but it's only when I'm sitting in my room and stuff.*" Paul appeared to know about the popular images of computing and did not seem to want to be associated with them.

Both Paul and Simon claimed expertise in computing; they said they were "con fident," "good at" computing. Like boys in other studies (Beynon, 1993), they claimed expertise in using computers. I suggest that in their narratives they place themselves in what I have described as the "hard" discourse of computing. For both Simon and Paul, using computers allows them to inhabit a discourse in which they are comfortable. This discourse is located, amongst other issues, in how they played as children, and the way they currently socialise with other males. This promotes personal confidence and a sense of ability with technology, which I suggest is worth preserving. Their interest, as they described it, is fundamental to their identity as males and not just an external interest or passing hobby.

As discussed earlier, boys still have more access to home computing than girls, and there is evidence that parents favour boys over girls in issues of access to computers. It is believed that it is this that has led to girls having less experience of computers than boys before they reach school.

Both Asiya and Karima, the other two students in the study, who are female, both located themselves at the "user end" or "soft end" of any computing discourse. They were very explicit about the "usefulness" of computers in the workplace; neither of them used computers in their leisure time. Both of them expressed how their interest in the computer was gained in their experience at school or at work. "*With computers I don't like the hardware, the technical side of it as much. I understand I need to know about it. I find the technical side difficult, it doesn't interest me. I would rather be sitting at a PC designing a database than looking inside a PC*" (Karima).

Their choice, as with the males, was based around feeling they were good at some-thing. Asiya had found she was "*good at using computers*" in her secretarial posi-tion; she had found time in her position as a secretary to "*open program files and discover the PC.*" They used the same sort of terms as Simon and Paul—something they were very "interested in," "good at" —and in Karima's case she had studied IT at her secondary school and was very enthusiastic— "*I absolutely loved it, loved it*" (meaning as a subject at school).

Neither of them continued to play computer games or appeared to see much use for the computer outside their university work or in the workplace. They had both developed an interest in computers in their teens, later than Simon and Paul. Both females identified a "use" for computers, but did not perceive that using computers was part of their social activities. This is very much in contrast to Simon and Paul. Simon linked his interest in what he referred to as "*building computers*" directly to how he played as a boy. We can see in the following how Simon's "interest" in computers is linked to his identity as a child—"*It (computers) are generally like Lego... then it's like slotting everything in... then it's setting it up.*"

This demonstrates how the gendered attitudes of how Simon played as a child and also gendered preferences for toys may have influenced his computer usage. Mead and Piaget have said that children develop a sense of "self" through their play and games (Crossley, 2000). Studies have found that girls and boys play differently and this has implications on the development of their self-identity as girls and boys (Gilligan, 1982). Children's choices of toys are different. Males are associated with mechanical toys and construction toys such as Lego, which encourage technical confidence (Wajcman, 1991). Girls play with toys such as dolls and stuffed animals (Rheingold & Cook, 1975). All four students were introduced to computers through play, though the females lost interest as they matured. We know that most computer games are targeted at young males and it is likely that most computer games that are available are more popular with boys than girls (Griffiths, 1997). Karima explained she had "*grown out of it*" and Asiya stated, "*I don't really play, not in the last few years.*" The females in this study were no longer motivated to use a computer to play games. Thus they rejected the computer as a toy, changing their view of it in adulthood to that of a useful tool. Computing is something both these female students have an interest in, but I suggest it is not strongly linked to their gendered identities.

What I have shown in this small example is that discourses around technology can extend into the home and other parts of our social lives, including in this case our gender identities as young children and young adults. How we play as children and what are acceptable interests for boys and girls in the home contribute to our gendered identities. All four students have been influenced by childhood and teenage experiences of using computers in the home. I have suggested that both of the male students located themselves in the "hard" end of computing, which in their case is intrinsically linked to them as males and bound up in their masculine identities. Both females were very interested in computers but located themselves in what could be described as the "soft end" or "user" discourse in computing. They could clearly see a use for technology in their lives, but the computer has little to do with their gender identity. The males and females in this study inhabit different discourses; we can identify these are open to interpretation and do not have clear borders.

In the next example, I want to demonstrate how these discourses are perpetuated in another area of education and how they can then influence decision-making of young women when it comes to choosing subjects, courses and careers. We know that educational experiences have the power to influence our perceptions of who we are. Research has identified that "education has a mammoth part to play in gendering social worlds, not only through what is taught but also through how it is," and therefore perpetuates a society's norms and values (Evans, 1994, p. 52). There is a great deal of research in the field of gender and education which expands on these issues.[5]

In schools and colleges computing and the skills associated with it are still perceived in gendered terms. There are good reasons for this. Early school computers were usually bought and controlled by male teachers in the math and science subject areas. This perpetuated the "hard" discourse and further marginalised girls as the boys showed more interest. A reluctance of girls to embrace the computer was seen early on as a problem of girls' confidence, rather than rooted within the way technology is perceived (Clegg, 2001). Today there are still only a few women lecturers and teachers in computing and IT at all levels of education in the UK, which may reinforce the idea that it is an area of study most suitable for males. This of course raises the question as to where the government will find their role models.

The following abstracts are taken from a study of 16-18 year old female students studying in two colleges of further education in an inner city area in Manchester, UK. This second study took place in 2004 (French & Saxon, 2006) and was initiated by a number of colleges. They were concerned about the lack of participation of women in their technology courses and the lack of progression of the young women to university and technology industries. The following demonstrates with a few examples how the discourses we have already discussed manifest themselves in this educational setting. Twenty-five female students between the ages of 16 and 18 were interviewed. The narratives demonstrate how the discourses around technology in this study influenced the students' and teachers' perceptions of what is a suitable subject for girls to study.

Even before joining their course these female students encountered a gendered discourse around the information technology courses they were interested in—"*I couldn't believe that people said IT was a lad's (boy's) course... There were a lot of girls being interviewed at the same time as me, but they didn't come on the course*" (Female, 16 years). She was referring to the course tutor's remarks during her interview for the course. In light of the description of the course as a course for boys, it is not surprising that so few young women enrolled.

The girls were asked why they thought girls did not enroll in technology courses. There were many duplications of this type of remark; I include only three examples here.

"I think girls prefer hairdressing and girlie type courses."

"Maybe they think it's a boy's thing."

"A lot of girls think it's too technical and that they wouldn't be able to do it."

We can see a gendered discourse prevails not only through the way the course tutor describes the courses but also around some girls' perceptions of information technology courses. The EOC recently reported (Fuller, Beck, & Unwin, 2005) that there are still strong gendered perceptions of what are suitable careers for "boys" and "girls" in the UK. Girls are still over-represented in childcare fields, while males are over-represented in subjects related to engineering, motor vehicles and construction. This is despite the fact that as early as 1984, Women into Science and Engineering (WISE) (Henwood, 1996) was launched to encourage women to enter these careers. WISE influenced policy and practice as many small and large-scale initiatives were designed to encourage females to join science, engineering and technology courses. Henwood (1998) has criticised the WISE project for taking an equal opportunities approach based on women's choice.

In this study, none of the 16-year-old female students said that they were interested in pursuing a career related to technology. Only the female students whose ages ranged from 17-18 years old stated that they were intending to pursue a career associated with their course and technology. There were only 11 females in the 17-18 year age group, out of a total cohort of 83 students; seven were interviewed; all of them were intending to take up a career in computing. It is unlikely that the choices of the younger students had anything to do with their academic achievement. In the UK girls have shown they have ability in the subject area. In 2001-2002 girls achieved 62% of passes at grade C or above in General Certificate of Education – Advanced level (GCE A level) computer studies, whereas the achievement rate for boys was 56% (EOC, 2003). Despite their success in the subject, young women continue to shun technology subjects at the higher levels. In 2004-2005 around half the number of total students in England who took GCE A level in ICT were female. There were 4,510 females compared to 8,370 males, which is an improvement on 2003-2004. However, the numbers of students taking computer studies are a stark reminder of the gender division in this subject area; a total of 5,336 males, but only 493 females took the GCE A level subject (DFES, 2005). It has been shown that there is a direct correlation between the number of women entering IT or computing degrees at university and those taking the subjects at school and college (Symonds, 2001). In this study, the courses these 17-18 year olds attend are also "feeders" into university degree courses. Whether they can "do" technology is not the issue, they just are not choosing it.

Female tutors and course leaders were in the minority in the two colleges who participated in this study. Several students commented about the male tutors—"*The male programming tutor is a bit strange*" (15 year old). Most of their personal tutors were male, and another student said "*I would rather have a woman to talk to*" (15 year old).

Working with male students presented "problems," or "perceived" problems, some of which had consequences on the course choices as this comment identifies—"*I could have gone straight onto the advanced course, but there were no other girls on the course that year. So I did an extra year on my previous course so that I would have some female company*" (17 year old). This student's perceptions had influenced career choice and academic progression. Young men were the dominant group on the IT courses she had studied. Most of the girls interviewed reported they did not like working with the boys. Other students were initially put off by boys, but got used to working with them. Some, as in that quote, had asked to stay in groups with other girls on the course. Having another female in the class made a difference—"*If I didn't have Julie in the class, I would have felt a bit intimidated*" (16 year old).

One student had noticed that several girls had started the course with her but did not complete the course. It could be that the thought of a class of mostly male students was worse than the actual experience for some of the students. For some it clearly put them off the course; it meant them having to "fit in." Some had compromised their career choices and, in other cases, it led them to leave the course before completion. Therefore the dominant number of males on the courses, and the gendered attitudes of the tutors, influenced their experiences.

From the narratives of the university students and the college students we can identify a dominant gendered discourse in computing which is linked to the use of technology in the home, as well as to education. In the previous examples we can see that this discourse is linked to gendered notions of how we view and experience technology. It is this I would argue, which needs deconstructing. I suggest that gendered perceptions of technology started early in life are further perpetuated as women mature. This discourse is pervasive, as it is not just isolated to the field of computing but extends into many other social spheres.

Clearly, if we want to change the current situation, we need to challenge this gendered discourse around technology. This is not easy because it is so pervasive. However, it is possible. We need to look very closely at our gendered identities and our relationship with technology and how, as parents, educators and government, we perpetuate these images. We need to challenge the current values and norms regarding technologies in our society.

Conclusion

I have shown evidence of a gendered digital divide with regard to technology in British society. I have discussed and criticised government policy. Throughout this discussion, feminism and discourse analysis have been used to unravel the issues and complexities concerning the lack of women's participation in technology. Through the narratives of these two small studies I have identified gendered discourses around computing and technology. These gendered perceptions relate to our identity and our experiences with technology. These two case studies have shown how this discourse manifests itself in the home and is further perpetuated through our education and leads to choices in education and careers. I suggest we need to study this further to enable us to deconstruct this discourse before there is any possibility for change. Gender segregation in ICT is not just an issue of equality; it is also about tackling gendered attitudes and identities in relation to technology. Clearly, it is this we need to address before we can challenge gender segregation and gain women's participation in the future development and use of technology.

Acknowledgments

I would like to thank Diane Saxon, fellow author and research colleague, for her permission to use some of our co-authored work in this chapter. Finally, I would like to thank Helen Richardson for raising my political awareness in our early work together about government policy in relation to gender and technology issues.

References

Adam, A. (1998). *Artificial knowing: Gender and the thinking machine*. London: Routledge.

Alexander, D. (2001a). *Impact of ICT on competitiveness*. Retrieved December 11, 2001, from http://www.dti.gov.uk/ministers/speeches/alexander141101.html

Alexander, D. (2001b). *IT for the common man.* Retrieved November 1, 2005, from http://www.dti.gov.uk/ministers/archived/alexander011101.html

Beasley, C. (1999). *What is feminism? An introduction to feminist theory.* London: Sage.

Beynon, J. (1993). Computers, dominant boys and invisible girls: Or, "Hannagh, it's not a toaster, it's a computer!" In J. Beynon & H. Mackay (Eds.), *Computers into classrooms.* London: Falmer Press (cited in Clegg & Trayhurn (1999)).

Brooks, A., & Mackinnon, A. (2001). Globalisation, academia and change. In A. Brooks & A. Mackinnon (Eds.), *Gender and the restructured university.* Buckingham, UK: SRHE and Open University Press.

Castells, M. (2000). *The rise of the network society.* Oxford, UK: Blackwell

Clegg, S. (2001). Theorising the machine: Gender, education and computing. *Gender and Education, 13*(3), 307-324.

Clegg, S., & Trayhurn, D. (1999). Gender and computing: Not the same old problem. *British Educational Research Journal, 26*(1), 75-89.

Clegg, S., Mayfield, W., & Trayhurn, D. (1999). Disciplinary discourses: A case study of gender in information technology and design courses. *Gender and Education, 11*(1), 43-55.

Cockburn, C. (1985). *Machinery of dominance: Women, men and technical know-how.* London: Pluto Press.

Cockburn, C., & Ormrod, S. (1993). *Gender and technology in the making.* London: Sage.

Coffield, F. (1999). Breaking the consensus: Lifelong learning as social control. *British Educational Research Journal, 25*, 479-499.

Crossley, M. L. (2000). *Introducing narrative psychology: Self, trauma and the construction of meaning.* Buckingham, UK: Open University Press.

Department for Education and Employment. (2001). *Opportunity for all in a world of change* (CM 5052). London: HMSO.

Department for Education & Skills. (2005). GCE/VCE A/AS Examination Results for Young People in England 2004/05 (Provisional). SFR 45/2005, 20th October 2005. Available at http://www.dfes.gov.uk/rsgateway/DB/SFR/s000609/SFR45-2005-2.pdf

Department of Trade and Industry. (2004) *Fairness for all: A new commission for equality and human rights.* London: DTI

Edwards, P. (1990). The army and the microworld: Computers and the politics of gender identity. *Signs, 16*, 172-197 (cited in Clegg & Trayhurn (1999)).

Equal Opportunities Commission (EOC). (2004a). *Occupational segregation, gender gaps and skill gaps* (Working paper series, No.15). Manchester, UK: Equal Opportunities Commission.

EOC. (2004b). *Plugging Britain's skills gap: Challenging gender segregation in training and work.* Manchester, UK: Equal Opportunities Commission.

EOC. (2005). *Facts about women & men in Great Britain.* Manchester, UK: Equal Opportunities Commission.

Evans, T. (1994). *Understanding learners in open and distance education.* London: Kogan Page.

Foucault, M. (1978). *The history of sexuality: An introduction.* Harmondsworth, UK: Penguin.

Foucault, M. (1981). The order of discourse. In R. Young (Ed.), *Untying the text: A poststructuralist reader.* London: Routledge.

French, S. (2003). *Gender equity and the use of information and communication technologies in the knowledge economy: Examining discourses in computing and information technology.* Geneva, Switzerland: World Forum on the Information Society.

French, S., & Saxon, D. (2006). Exploring experiences of females on technology courses in UK colleges. In E. M. Trauth (Ed.), *The encyclopedia of gender and information technology.* Hershey, PA: Idea Group Reference.

Fuller, A., Beck, V., & Unwin, L. (2005). *Employers, young people and gender segregation.* Manchester, UK: Equal Opportunities Commission.

Gilligan, C. (1982). *In a different voice: Psychological theory and women's development.* Boston: Harvard University Press.

Griffiths, M. (1997). Video games and children's behaviour. In T. Charlton & K. David (Eds.), *Elusive links: Television, video games and children's behaviour* (pp. 66-93). Cheltenham, UK: Park.

Habib, L., & Cornford, T. (2001). *Domestication and gender: Computers in the home. Global co-operation in the new millenium.* ECIS 2001 9th European Conference on Information Systems, Bled, Slovenia.

Hellawell, S. (2001). *Beyond access: ICT and social inclusion.* Glasgow, Poland: Fabian Society.

Henwood, F. (1996). WISE choices? Understanding occupational decision-making in a climate of equal opportunities for women in science and technology. *Gender and Education, 8*(2), 199-214.

Henwood, F. (1998). Engineering difference: Discourses on gender, sexuality and work in a college of technology. *Gender and Education, 10*(1), 35-49.

Hollway, W., & Jefferson, T. (2000). *Doing qualitative research differently*. London: Sage.

Hughes, G. (2001). Exploring the availability of student scientist identities with curriculum discourse: An anti-essentialist approach to gender-inclusive science. *Gender and Education, 13*(3), 275-290.

Jorgensen, J. (2002). Engineering selves: Negotiating gender and identity in technical work. *Management Communication Quarterly, 15*(3), 350-380.

Kirkup, G., & Abbott, J. (1997). *The gender gap*. Milton Keynes, UK: Open University.

Luccy, H., Melody, J., & Walkerdine, V. (2003). Uneasy hybrids: Psychosocial aspects of becoming educationally successful for working-class young women. *Gender and Education, 15*(3), 285-299.

Mahony, K., & Van Toen, B. (1990). Mathematical formalism as a means of occupational closure in computing: Why "hard" computing tends to exclude women. *Gender and Education, 2*, 319-331 (cited in Clegg & Trayhurn (1999)).

Na, M. (2001). The home computer in Korea: Gender, technology, and the family. *Feminist Media Studies, 1*(3).

Peters, M. (2001). National education policy constructions of the "knowledge economy": Towards a critique. *Journal of Educational Inquiry, 2*(1). Retrieved November 1, 2005, from http://www.education.unisa.edu.au/JEE/Papers/JEEVol2No1/paper1.pdf

Rheingold, H., & Cook, K. (1975). The contents of boys and girls rooms, as an index of parents' behaviour. *Child Developments, 46*, 459-463.

Richardson, H. J., & French, S. (2001). Education on-line: What's in it for women. In E. Balka & R. Smith (Eds.), *Women, work and computerisation: Charting a course to the future*. Boston: Kluwer.

Symonds, J. (2001). Why IT doesn't appeal to young women. In E. Balka & R. Smith (Eds.), *Women, work and computerisation: Charting a course to the future*. Boston: Kluwer.

Theile, B. (1986). Vanishing acts in social and political thought: Tricks of the trade. In C. Pateman & E. Gross (Eds.), *Feminist challenges: Social and political theory*. Sydney, Australia: Allen & Unwin (cited in Beasley, C. [1999]. *What is feminism?* [p. 4]).

Tong, R. (1997). *Feminist thought: A comprehensive introduction*. London: Routledge.

Wajcman, J. (1991). *Feminism confronts technology*. Cambridge, UK: Polity Press.

Wajcman, J. (1995). Feminist theories of technology. In G. E. M. S. Jasanoff, J. C. Peterson, & T. Pinch (Eds.), *Handbook of science & technology studies*. London: Sage.

Wajcman, J. (2000). Reflections on gender and technology studies: In what state is the art? *Social Studies of Science, 30*(3), 447-64.

Wajcman, J. (2004). *TechnoFeminism*. Cambridge, UK: Polity Pres

Walkerdine, V. (1997). *Daddy's girl: Young girls and popular culture*. London: Macmillan.

Weedon, C. (1997). *Feminist practice & poststructuralist theory* (2nd ed.). Oxford, UK: Blackwell.

Wilkinson, H. (2001). *dot.bombshell: Women, e-quality and the new economy*. London: Industrial Society.

Woodfield, R. (2000). *Women work and computing*. Cambridge, UK: Cambridge University Press.

Endnotes

[1] For a critical discussion of the knowledge economy, see Peters (2001), who argues that the characteristics of the knowledge economy are not necessarily new and that they have been adopted without critical appraisal.

[2] Wajcman (2000) gives a full history and analysis of gender and technology studies.

[3] Potter (2004) offers a guide to the origins and comparison of discourse analysis dependent on discipline.

[4] For a full discussion on this case study, see French (2003).

[5] The *Journal of Gender and Education* (Carfax) is a good source of reports of research in this field.

Chapter IX

Computing Ethics:
Intercultural Comparisons

Darryl Macer
UNESCO Bangkok, Thailand;
Eubios Ethics Institute, Japan and New Zealand; &
United Nations University Institute of Advanced Studies, Japan

Abstract

Computers are a vehicle for the information age, and are central to the dispersal of descriptive accounts of technology, and to interactive discussion between growing communities. Despite the commitment of all countries to free flow of information and access to knowledge sources based upon social justice there are still ethical problems of the digital divide. The attitudes of respondents towards science and computers in both Japan and Thailand is compared between 1993 and a decades later. There is more positive support towards science and technology in general in Thailand than in Japan, but both countries continue to be positive in attitude. There is a clear social mandate in both countries for their government policies promoting the development of information technology and science and technology in general. The perception of benefits and the worries about computers are discussed, as are some emerging issues.

Information Ethics and Global Justice

Ethics is a concept balancing benefits and risks of choices and decisions. Information ethics includes ethical issues in the collection, storage, dissemination and use of information (Manoj & Azariah, 2004). The underlying heritage of ethics can be seen in all cultures, religions and in ancient writings from around the world (Macer, 1994). We cannot, in fact, trace the origin of ethics back to their beginning, as the relationships between human beings within their society, with nature and God are formed at an earlier stage than our history would tell us. There are at least three ways to view ethics (Macer, 1998).

1. **Descriptive ethics:** The way people view life, their moral interactions and responsibilities with others in their life. Information we gather is used to describe many things and there are many ethical issues related to gathering information and storing information.

2. **Prescriptive ethics:** To tell others what is ethically good or bad, or what principles are most important in making such decisions. It may also be to say something or someone has rights and others have duties to them. It is related to policy making and law.

3. **Interactive ethics:** Discussion and debate between people, groups within society and communities, and, clearly, information ethics is central to shaping the types and forms of interactions that are possible.

Computers are a vehicle for the information age and are central to the dispersal of descriptive accounts of technology and to interactive discussion between growing communities. The commitment of all countries to free flow of information and access to knowledge sources based upon social justice is inspired by the UNESCO Constitution, which states that "the wide diffusion of culture and the education of humanity for justice and liberty and peace are indispensable to the dignity of man and constitute a sacred duty which all the nations must fulfil in a spirit of mutual assistance and concern". This widespread concern for information flow is shared in the United Nations system, despite the ethical problems of the so-called digital divide, which has been widely debated (e.g., Loader, 1998; Murelli, 2002; OECD, 2000; UNDP 2001).

The UNESCO World Commission on the Ethics of Science and Technology had a subcommittee issue a report, *The Ethics of the Information Society* (COMEST, 2001), in which they looked at issues like individual freedom and social responsibility, social exclusion and human values in the information society. Inside the digital divide there are gaps between persons in our generation around the world, as well as the gaps between generations. There are expanding differences between persons living in the digital world and those outside of it. There are still one to two billion people in the world who have not made a telephone call, let alone use computers.

In the Rio de Janeiro Declaration on Ethics in Science and Technology from 4 December 2003, at the Third COMEST meeting, we see the recommendation from Ministers of Science that "attention be given to non-proprietary treatment of software, transmissions, and other digital technologies essential to ensuring the linguistic cultural diversity of countries with relatively low representation on the Internet as well as in the use of electronic databases. Thus information society should be used to expand knowledge of, and retention of, cultural diversity (World Commission on Ethics of Science and Technology, 2003).

There is widespread support for increased use of computers among the have-nots, and they also recommended:

that our governments support the increase in use and production of software, seeking autonomy and cost reductions for the countries of the region; That national and regional research groups be established with the objective of studying alternatives for the production of low-cost personal computers, aimed at universalizing usage of such computers, as well as implementing projects for regional cooperation in this field. (World Commission on Ethics of Science and Technology, 2003)

As we may discuss the issues raised by information technology when considering global social justice, we need to know what attitudes people have to information technology after they have been using them for several decades. This chapter makes a comparison between the views of people as measured in surveys conducted on attitudes towards technology in Japan and Thailand in 1993, and follow-up surveys conducted in 2000 (Thailand) and 2003 (Japan). What do ordinary people think about the benefits and risks of computers, in comparison to other areas of science and technology?

Japan has a population of 125 million persons enjoying a relatively high standard of living internationally, being the eighth most populated nation globally. The public in Japan is well educated and is aware of many technologies, perceiving both benefits and risks of most applications, and having a reasonable degree of bioethical maturity (Macer, 1992a). One of the fundamental ethical principles is that of non-maleficence. This principle is behind the commonly accepted principle of safety assessment. There is a need for long-term risk assessment studies of any technology, and we should not just assume information technology is always good.

Thailand has a population of more than 60 million people with an average per capita income of around US$1500 per annum. Most Thai people are aware of and experience the globalization of communication and trading; new sciences and technologies are known to many of them. Thailand is a strongly Buddhist country, with rising living standards and a rapidly developing economy. The vitality of the Buddhist faith does much to bridge social gaps, such as prevail between city and countryside. It is, therefore, of particular interest to see how attitudes to bioethical dilemmas have changed through the 1990s. Recognizing the potential of technology to affect a broad spectrum of industries, the government of Thailand has placed increased emphasis on information technology and biotechnology over the past decade. Today, the opportunities for utilization of these technologies in public and business sectors are expected to grow at the fast pace during the next decade.

Methodology of the Surveys

A range of topics in technology was included in surveys to allow comparisons between examples and with earlier research. Attitudes of respondents towards these applications may reveal their understanding and feeling towards technology. Sampling in 1991, 1993, 2000 and 2003 was done across all prefectures of Japan

Table 1. Selected sample characteristics of surveys

	Japan				Thailand	
	1991	1993	2000	2003	1993	2000
Number	551	352	297	376	689	214
Male	53%	52%	62.2%	52%	48%	28%
Female	47%	48%	37.8%	48%	52%	72%
Rural	-	27%	27.5%	25%	46%	20%
Urban	-	73%	72.5%	75%	54%	80%
Age Mean (year)	39.8%	41.7%	44.5%	46.9%	37.2%	37.2%
Single	29%	29%	25.5%	21%	38%	51%
Married	66%	66%	71.4%	71%	59%	47%
No children	35%	40%	34.8%	30%	22%	34.5%
Education						
High school	37.0%	37.0%	27.3%	-	2%	1%
Two-year college	22.0%	19.0%	14.5%	-	3%	4.8%
Graduate	31.0%	31.0%	40.1%	-	35%	61.2%
Postgraduate	7.0%	10.0%	15.6%	-	59%	29.7%
Religion						
No religion	-	39.0%	55.1%	33%	0.2%	0.9%
Buddhism	-	47.0%	34.1%	55%	99.0%	95.8%
Christian	-	8.0%	2.8%	5%	0.4%	1.9%
How important is religion?						
Very	-	10.0%	6.9%	-	46%	45.5%
Some	-	33.0%	25.3%	-	44%	44.5%
Not too	-	40.0%	39.1%	-	8%	8.1%
Not at all	-	17.0%	28.7%	-	2%	1.9%

Source: Japan 1991 (Macer, 1992); Japan 1993 and Thailand 1993 (Macer, 1994); Japan 2000 (Ng et al., 2000); Thailand 2000 (Kachonpadungkitti & Macer, 2004); Japan 2003 (Inaba & Macer, 2003)

by using random sampling method with the cooperation of many people (Macer, 1992, 1994; Ng et al., 2000; Inaba & Macer, 2003). The sample characteristics are given in Table 1 to allow comparisons with the previous samples.

The International Bioethics Survey was conducted by Macer and Srinives in 1993 in Thailand, using questionnaires translated into Thai language (Macer, 1994; Kachonpadungkitti & Macer, 2004). The 2000 public sample was predominantly urban (80%), and 69% were government workers, 22% company officers, with some other occupations were represented in the sample. There is no significant difference between the 1993 and 2000 surveys in terms of gender and religion. However, there are significantly fewer males than in the 1993 survey, but there are more single people and people with no children. The educational levels were similar, and, as in the 1993 sample, most were university graduates, 25% being postgraduates.

This chapter refers to responses to only a few of the questions included. Several fixed response questions were employed, as well as open questions. The reasons that the respondents gave for their attitudes in the open spaces on the surveys for the open questions were categorized on the basis of the keywords and concepts that were expressed into a total of 30 to 40 types differing between questions, following the methods of Macer (1992, 1994a). Each comment was categorized into up to three concept categories to describe the ideas in the answer.

Attitudes Towards Science and Technology

The general attitude towards science in both Japan and Thailand is that it will provide more good than harm, as shown in Table 2. The attitudes are rather similar in both countries. As shown in Table 3 there is more positive support towards science and technology in general in Thailand than in Japan, but both countries continue to be positive in attitude. There is a clear social mandate in both countries for government policies promoting the development of information technology and science and technology in general.

Table 2. General pessimism about science remains low

Q3. Overall do you think science and technology do more harm than good, more good than harm, or about the same of each?

	Japan			Thailand	
Year	1991	1993	2003	1993	2000
More harm	6%	5%	6%	3%	4%
More good	55%	42%	43%	54%	48%
Same	39%	45%	45%	42%	45%
Don't know	-	8%	7%	1%	3%

Table 3. General attitudes related to technology

a. Science makes an important contribution to the quality of life.					
	Agree Strongly	Agree	Neither	Disagree	Disagree Strongly
Japan 2003	30%	57%	12%	1%	0%
Japan 1993	34%	56%	14%	2%	0.3%
Japan 1991	26%	55%	14%	2%	3%
Thailand 2000	52%	43%	4%	0.5%	1%
Thailand 1993	59%	40%	1%	0.4%	0%
b. Most problems can be solved by applying more and better technology.					
Japan 2003	8%	33%	50%	8%	1%
Japan 1993	12%	34%	33%	17%	4%
Thailand 2000	7%	38%	18%	35%	2%
Thailand 1993	8%	39%	14%	37%	2%

The 2000 sampling in the Thai survey was done in Bangkok, but some respondents come from the rural areas (21%) and were staying in Bangkok to study or work. This being the case, it may be mentioned that some of the responses to the survey may have been shaped or influenced by their upbringing in either rural or urban areas.

Attitudes Towards Computers

In a question asking how much people had heard of several areas of science and technology, we see that the Thai 2000 sample did have a higher self-indicated knowledge of science and technology with the exception of computers compared to Thailand in 1993 (Table 4). We should note that such technology is popularly taught in all schools and in massive industry campaigns for personal computer use in both countries.

Table 5 shows the perception of benefits and the worries about four areas of science and technology. The reasons were examined by analysis of the open comments into categories, and these are presented in Table 6. The attitudes towards in vitro fertilization (IVF) [not shown here] and computers were the same, with some drop in support for biotechnology. Especially, they had a positive view about computers, with around 98% perceiving benefits, similar to respondents in 1993. At the same time, there was a 19% public decline in the proportion that sees benefits from pesticides in 2000.

During the period of the survey in both countries, the results of other questions found that there has been a shift towards television and newspapers as a self-stated information source for people's attitudes. Information technology is central to both

Table 4. Understanding of different technologies (self-evaluation)

Q5. Can you tell me how much you have heard or read about each of these subjects?
N= Not heard of   H= Heard of   E= Could explain it to a friend

		N1993	H1993	E1993	N2003	H2003	E2003
Pesticides	*Japan*	3%	61%	36%	5%	48%	47%
	Thailand	0%	34%	66%	0%	64%	36%
Biotechnology	*Japan*	6%	65%	29%	7%	68%	25%
	Thailand	2%	57%	41%	6%	67%	27%
Genetic Engineering	*Japan*	9%	74%	17%	10%	70%	20%
	Thailand	13%	58%	29%	24%	59%	17%
Computers	*Japan*	4%	61%	35%	7%	47%	47%
	Thailand	0%	57%	43%	0%	51%	49%

Table 5. Perception of the benefits and risks of computers 1993-2003

Q6. Do you personally believe each of these scientific discoveries and developments is a worthwhile area for scientific research? Why?...
Y=Yes   N= No   DK=Don't know

Q7. Do you have any worries about the impact of research or its applications of these scientific discoveries and developments? How much? Why?...
W0=No   W1= few   W2=Some   W3=A lot

	Worthwhile area?			Worried about impact?			
	Yes	No	DK	W0	W1	W2	W3
Computers							
Japan 2003	82%	4%	14%	34%	50%	11%	4%
Japan 1993	85%	3%	12%	57%	34%	7%	2%
Thailand 2000	99%	0%	1%	49%	36%	12%	3%
Thailand 1993	98%	1%	1%	64%	27%	7%	2%
Biotechnology							
Japan 1993	74%	7%	19%	37%	44%	14%	5%
Thailand 2000	75%	3%	22%	35%	32%	27%	6%
Thailand 1993	90%	1%	9%	61%	30%	8%	1%
Genetic Engineering							
Japan 2003	60%	8%	32%	13%	45%	31%	11%
Japan 1993	57%	10%	33%	22%	39%	24%	15%
Japan 1991	76%	7%	17%	19%	29%	21%	20%
Thailand 2000	46%	15%	39%	20%	35%	28%	17%
Thailand 1993	77%	5%	18%	42%	32%	19%	7%
Pesticides							
Japan 2003	75%	10%	15%	15%	42%	29%	14%
Japan 1993	84%	9%	7%	21%	36%	26%	17%
Japan 1991	89%	4%	7%	27%	23%	25%	18%
Thailand 2000	45%	49%	6%	12%	21%	33%	34%
Thailand 1993	63%	33%	4%	14%	19%	37%	30%

sources and provides the basic data as well as user experience, which in turn has an effect on the attitudes people have.

Table 6. Why do you personally believe computers are a worthwhile area for scientific research? (Summary of results by category)

	Japan 1993	Thailand 1993	Thailand 2000
Not stated	47.3%	22.2%	24.4%
Economy	0.9%	0.6%	0.5%
Science	6.9%	13.1%	12.7%
Medicine	-	0.2%	0%
Agriculture/Food	-	0.2%	0%
Energy	-	0.1%	0%
Humanity helped	31.0%	6.7%	0.5%
Increased efficiency	5.1%	51.8%	59.6%
Good for Environment	0%	0.1%	0%
Help if careful	2.4%	2.9%	0.5%
Bad for environment	-	0%	1.4%
Lack of controls	2.4%	0.3%	0%
Dangerous/Health risk	-	0.4%	0%
Play God/Unnatural	0.9%	0.2%	0%
Waste of resources	0%	0.2%	0%
Fear of unknown	0.6%	0.1%	0%
Humanity changed	0.6%	0.8%	0.5%

Table 7. Why do you have any worries about the impact of research or its applications of computers? (Summary of results by category)

	Japan 1993	Thailand 1993	Thailand 2000
Not stated	63.0%	41.4%	49.1%
Don't know	0.9%	1.3%	0.5%
Interfere with nature	0.6%	0.5%	0%
Fear of unknown	2.8%	2.5%	0.9%
Ethical	1.2%	0.8%	10.3%
Humanity changed	6.5%	9.9%	6.1%
Lack of controls	4.7%	1.4%	6.1%
Health risk	0.9%	3.3%	1.4%
Disaster	0.9%	1.3%	0%
Ecology	0%	0.3%	0.9%
Waste	0.3%	0%	1.4%
Misuse	8.1%	5.2%	3.7%
OK if controlled	9.9%	32.1%	19.6%

Public optimism is balanced with growing concern about science and technology. The questionnaire respondents have relatively high levels of support for science and technology in general, especially for computers. Many of them said it improves efficiency and is part of globalization, but there are some people who are concerned about the rapid change of the technology. Some example comments for computers in Thailand included: "It was used within educated persons," or "Cannot catch it, it changed very quickly." It means that computer technology is not for all the people, but it only will help improve the quality of life for rich people. The same was said, and can be said, for other areas of science.

If the general public focuses on the benefits from the development of this technology to industry, rather than to farmers and consumers, then the acceptance of the technology and product will be low among the groups who do not benefit. There is a strong need for effective communication of the perceived risks and benefits among consumers to seek their acceptance. As we can see from the comments, many of the perceived fears about using the new technology were not founded in concrete reasons, but rather in their feelings.

New technology has brought about both job gains and job losses, with gains apparently exceeding the losses. These were discussed in the comments made by some respondents for both positive and negative aspects. Industry and governments have linked their support for biotechnology to hopes that its development could create many new jobs. Some example comments from the surveys include, "Employers have to add capital to use technology and they will not employ more workers so that the ratio of jobless will be high," and "The company would have the philosophy that maximum profit is driving force. Knowing that, the employee has a risk that will effect productivity and investment of the company so that there will be a discrimination problem in employment."

Utilitarian theories of ethics reveal the importance of economic calculations to the principle of justice, where the interests of all members in a society are included in reaching social consensus. One of the central questions for developing countries is whether they have to adopt a modern industrial world-view. Bodley (1999) discussed whether all cultures have to conform to the image of a modern "civilization." In Thailand there are some hill tribes, although they are more exposed to tourism than those in Papua New Guinea. It would be interesting to examine the views of members of those tribes towards some of these issues to see whether they have a more traditional view than the city people of Bangkok.

In order to illustrate the range of comments some sample comments under the different categories for computers in the 1993 surveys from both countries are given next.

Benefits (response: Y = yes; N=no; D = don't know)

Economy
Industrial benefits. Y
We must keep up with world trends. Y

Scientific knowledge
Improved knowledge leads to greater knowledge and therefore greater safety. Y
Marvelous research tool. Y
Models, for example, human brain. Y

Increased efficiency
Makes things easier. Y
Makes work easier and quicker. Y
To make today's society a smoother higher information-oriented society. Y

Humanity
More opportunities for people. Y
Extension of mind/imagination leads to improved quality of life. Y
Can give people more free time. Y

Good for the Environment
"Electronic" filing must save paper (trees). Y

Help if careful
Good for storing information but can take jobs. Y

Playing God/Interfering with Nature/Ethics
I believe in nature's way and man's interference in most of these material things will eventually become the downfall of all mankind. N

Don't need/waste of money
Past the age of being involved. N

Humanity changed

I feel it is at the expense of people's jobs. N

Uneasy - dehumanising, political control. D

Worries (degree of concern N=no; F= a few; S=some; L=a lot)

Interfering with Nature / Playing God

Spiritual knowledge insufficient to cope with the consequences. L

Ethical / Privacy

Information security. S

"Big Brother" syndrome. F

Humanity changed / Bad social effect

More and more unemployment. F

Too much control by computers. F

Dehumanises much work. L

Insufficient control

No control mechanisms. S

Anxiety that humans might become a slave. F

Disaster / Harmful (Both to humans and environment)

Possible undiscovered dangers (e.g., radiation). S

Because harm caused by overuse of computers is happening even today. F

Ecology / Environmental harm

Until inventions, scientists et al. can clean up the dying forests, ozone depletion, nuclear waste proliferation, and other environmental stupidity, we're wasting precious time and resources if we pursue other "interesting" fields. S

Human misuse

Because it could be used for war and as power in politics. F

Can control / Limited use is OK

Some of these areas are not known to me but I understand the need to discover and develop as long as safeguards are maintained by a higher power. N

Humans can control them. N

I don't think it is becoming a thing which is more than a tool. N

According to theories of cultural evolution, adaptation and integration and resistance to change are understandable as, by nature, we gradually specialize to fit the requirements of successful adaptation to a specific environment. In the 21st century it is becoming increasingly difficult to maintain different culture systems because of globalization of media, political treaties and trade. In the point of globalization, cultures have some similarity to civilizations, in that they are all tending to be absorbed into the current global way of thinking. While civilizations may come and go, in the end we expect cultures will continue to follow some traditions, such as Thai or Japanese, even though we may pass through several periods of civilization, as different cultural values dominate the global thinking. We can see periods in history when different ideologies, for example, communism, religious faiths and their associated civilizations have dominated one land, but they may still remain as one "cultural identity" throughout these periods. Civilizations are dynamic; they rise and fall; they divide and merge. Faced with modern science and technology, one wonders whether traditional civilization will be buried soon, as Huntington (1993) wrote, "civilizations disappear and are buried in the sand of time." The rural/urban cultures differ and this difference is a challenge for policy makers in Thailand especially, as in all countries. This research allows us a better picture of how Thai people balance the different impacts of science and technology on human life and on protection of the environment. These are key questions as people grapple with the dilemmas on how to balance economics, progress of technology, improving quality of life and increasing the choices for citizens, and preservation of the environment.

In 1997 telephone surveys (Macer et al., 1997), a question on the perceived impact of seven areas of science and technology was used. Comparisons with the data from the European Commission Eurobarometer 46.1 reveal that there is more optimism about solar energy, new materials and space exploration, in Japan (and New Zealand and Canada), but similar optimism towards computers, information technology, and telecommunications to the European Union (Gaskell et al., 2000) In the same questions in a 2000 survey, the public perceived computers and information technology as the most beneficial examples of science and technology; the third most beneficial was biotechnology, and the least genetic engineering (Ng et al., 2000; Macer & Ng, 2000). Given the past surveys briefly introduced here, the results suggest mixed attitudes towards technology in Japan, which is a healthy sign for the maturity of the society in facing ethical issues of science and technology. Approaches for ethical discussion can involve the public, and these studies show that the public includes people with a diversity of ideas.

Perhaps most distressing for public bioethics was the lack of trust by most persons in any domestic group in Japan. More than half of the respondents to the survey said that they had no trust in government agencies (Inaba & Macer, 2003). This means that, even if information is made available, it may not be trusted. In Japan, 40% said they had no trust in medical doctors or university professors—up from 30% in 1993. The United Nations is the most trusted, so government and industry who want public trust should align themselves closely with the positions of United Nations organizations if they want people to believe them.

What is Novel about Information Ethics in the Age of Computers?

While we can recognize that many more people across the world now have potential access to greater information in the computer age than before, we cannot just assume they have access. The ancient library at Alexandria in Egypt in 400BC no doubt had more books available than any of the readers could have coped with in their lifetime. Thus a person faced with the information available on the Internet may not actually be able to intake more than someone avidly reading in an old-fashioned library.

In Geneva on 12 December 2003, at the World Summit on the Information Society, Yoshio Utsumi, Secretary-General of the International Telecommunication Union cautioned that:

Telephones will not feed the poor, and computers will not replace textbooks. But ICTs can be used effectively as part of the toolbox for addressing global problems. ... The challenges raised—in areas like Internet governance, access, investment, security, the development of applications, intellectual property rights and privacy—require a new commitment to work together if we are to realize the benefits of the information society. (WSIS, 2003)

Sadly, I have noticed that few students today make the time to read through hundreds of traditional books; in fact, they have come to rely on short snippets of information in cyberspace. Thus there may even be a decline in the information content. There are also, of course, concerns about the trustworthiness of information, as many non-peer reviewed sources of information are available on the Internet. Censorship and quality control, however, are not new issues, as we could always find trashy publications. But it is now very cheap to put trash onto the Internet—perhaps it is better for the environment, however, if it stays only in cyperspace.

Ethics involves relationship among people and communication is a tool to facilitate this. There may be few new ethical issues here, apart from people's ability to retain in digital memory what they and others said, or looked like, in the past. Thus the scope of privacy protection can be expanded. There is a struggle for dominance in information technology, as there is for any other field that is linked to economic and/or political power (Fraser, 2000; Garson, 2000; Hamelink, 2000). There are also hackers (Himanen, 2001) who often, I am afraid to say, seem to be involved in a modern forms of criminal activity.

The most challenging area is that of construction of artificial intelligence. Although I am a biocentric philosopher, I also argue that once a being can love others and can balance principles to make moral decisions, it is a moral agent, no matter what it is made of (Macer, 1998). Therefore, if we create an artificial intelligence, or so-called "artificial" moral agent, we have responsibilities to treat he/she/them with respect. This theme has been the subject of numerous movies and books, ranging from *2001 Space Odyssey*, *Terminator*, through to *Matrix* to *I Robot*. Our networks should be open to all moral agents and may even, one day, take on lives of their own! The machines may even become spiritual one day (Kurzweil, 2001). We can ask whether artificial intelligence (AI) should be made. As human agents relinquish more control to, and forms uncritical acceptance of, AIs in an ever-increasing, technology-integrated society, some even contend that moral agency will be inevitably surrendered to AIs in the seamless operation of technology-assisted living.

The word "ethics" is closely related to love. Love is the desire to do good and the need to avoid doing harm. It includes love of others as oneself—the respecting of autonomy. It also includes the idea of justice, loving others and sharing what we have—distributive justice. We can hope that information technology might be used for sustainable development (Mansell & When, 1998). While many have claimed that new technology requires new ethics, when we analyze moral dilemmas we see that people use many familiar principles of ethics and ideas to attempt to deal with moral dilemmas of advanced medicine. While the use or abuse of computing technology seems to be the major ethical question in practice in our world today, and thus not something unique, once the computers become the users who can choose to use or abuse their ability, they become almost as scary as human beings!

One of the most interesting questions before thinking beings is whether we can comprehend the ideas and thoughts of other beings, and, conversely, whether they can also read our minds. In terms of evolution, there could be survival benefit by the capacity to be able to fully understand the thinking of others, both for direct competitive benefit and also for the spirit of altruistic cooperation. Although the human mind appears to be infinitely complex and the diversity of human kind and culture has been considered vast, in 1994 I made a hypothesis that the number of ideas that human beings have is finite (Macer, 1994); and in 2002, I called for a project to map the ideas of the human mind (Macer, 2002a, 2002b; Akashi, 2003). The prospect of mapping all the ideas of human beings raises the possibility that in the future we can transfer all the ideas of people onto computers. There will be challenges for many aspects of our understanding of human beings, though we should be clear, there will always be more questions than answers for humans to attempt to understand ourselves and nature. This is clearly an issue of information ethics in terms of collection, storage and use.

References

Akashi, K. (2003). Mental mapping project kicks off in Japan. *Lancet Neurology*, *2*(4), 206.

Bodley, J. H. (1999). *Victims of progress*. Mayfield.

COMEST (UNESCO Commission on the Ethics of Science and Technology). (2001). *The ethics of the information society*. Retrieved from http://portal. unesco.org/shs/en/file_download.php/3b73bca4a864f199e7b4db9e22f88d26 Meeting+ Info+Society+2001.pdf 104pp

Dawkins, R. (1976). *The selfish gene*. Oxford, UK: Oxford University Press.

Fraser, M. (2000). *Free-for-all: The struggle for dominance on the digital frontier*. New York: Stoddart.

Garson, D. (2000). *Social dimensions of information technology: Issues for the new millennium*. Hershey, PA: Idea Group Inc.

Gaskell, G., et al. (2000). Biotechnology and the European public. *Nature Biotechnology, 18*, 935-8.

Hamelink, C. J. (2000). *Ethics of cyberspace*. London: Sage.

Himanen, P. (2001). *The hacker ethic*. New York: Random House.

Huntington, S. P. (1993). The clash of civilizations. *Foreign Affairs, 72*, 22-49.

Inaba, M., & Macer, D. R. J. (2003). Attitudes to biotechnology in Japan in 2003. *Eubios Journal of Asian and International Bioethics, 13*, 78-89.

Kachonpadungkitti, C., & Macer, D. R. J. (2004). Attitudes to bioethics and biotechnology in Thailand (1993-2000) and impacts on employment. *Eubios Journal of Asian and International Bioethics, 14*, 118-134.

Kurzweil, R. (2001). *The age of spiritual machines: When computers exceed human intelligence*. London: Viking Penguin.

Loader, B. D. (Ed.). (1998). *Cyberspace divide: Equality, agency and policy in the information society*. London: Routledge.

Macer, D. R. J. (1992). *Attitudes to genetic engineering: Japanese and international comparisons*. Christchurch, New Zealand: Eubios Ethics Institute.

Macer, D. R. J. (1994). *Bioethics for the people by the people*. Christchurch, New Zealand: Eubios Ethics Institute.

Macer, D. R. J. (1998). *Bioethics is love of life*. Christchurch, New Zealand: Eubios Ethics Institute.

Macer, D. R. J., Bezar, H., Harman, N., Kamada, H., & Macer, N. (1997). Attitudes to biotechnology in Japan and New Zealand in 1997, with international comparisons. *Eubios Journal of Asian and International Bioethics, 7*, 137-151.

Macer, D., & Ng, M. C. (2000). Changing attitudes to biotechnology in Japan. *Nature Biotechnology, 18*, 945-7.

Macer, D. R. J. (2002a). The next challenge is to map the human mind. *Nature, 420*, 12.

Macer, D. R. J. (2002b). Finite or infinite mind?: A proposal for an integrative mental mapping project. *Eubios Journal of Asian and International Bioethics, 12*, 203-6.

Macer, D. R. J. (Ed.). (2004). *Challenges for bioethics from Asia.* Christchurch, New Zealand: Eubios Ethics Institute.

Manoj, V. R., & Azariah, J. (2004). Status of information ethics and developing countries. In D. R. J. Macer (ed.), *Challenges for bioethics from Asia* (pp. 476-482). Christchurch, New Zealand: Eubios Ethics Institute.

Mansell, R., & When, U. (Eds.). (1998). *Knowledge societies: Information technology for sustainable development*. New York: Oxford University Press.

Murelli, E. (2002). *Breaking the digital divide*. London: Commonwealth Secretariat & SFI.

Ng, M. A. C., Takeda, C., Watanabe, T., & Macer, D. R. J. (2000). Attitudes of the public and scientists to biotechnology in Japan at the start of 2000. *Eubios Journal of Asian and International Bioethics, 10*, 106-13.

OECD. (2000). *Learning to bridge the digital divide*. Paris: OECD publications.

United Nations Development Programme (UNDP). (2001). *Human development report 2001: Making new technologies work for human development*. New York: Oxford University Press.

World Commission on Ethics of Science and Technology. (2003, December). *Proceedings of the Third Session*. Paris: UNESCO.

World Summit on the Information Society (WSIS). (2003). *Declaration and plan of action*. Retrieved from http://www.itu.int/wsis/documents/listing-all-en-s|1.asp

Section III:

Regional and Country Perspectives

Chapter X

500 Million Missing Web Sites:
Amartya Sen's Capabilities Approach and Measures of Technological Deprivation in Developing Countries

William Wresch
University of Wisconsin Oshkosh, USA

Abstract

This chapter examines well-known technological shortages in developing countries in the context of Amartya Sen's capabilities approach. The significant consequences of these shortages include reduced access to necessary professional information, limited production of local cultural information, and the general invisibility of the developing world. The moral situation created by these shortages is reviewed using Sen's analyses. Three practical responses are also examined. By reviewing one vehicle for information transfer—the Web site—the author hopes to highlight the importance of this vehicle and to present reasonably simple responses to current shortcomings.

Amartya Sen's insights have directed much of the world's development efforts during the past two decades. He has greatly influenced the World Bank and the International Monetary Fund and other international bodies. But the one place where his approaches may have the most lasting impact is in the annual reports of the United Nations Development Programme (UNDP). Their *Human Development Report* presents numeric indices for a variety of human conditions, such as life expectancy, adult literacy, school enrollment and gross domestic product per capita. Sen has had two continuing influences on these annual reports. The first was to help summarize a variety of factors into a Human Development Index (HDI). The second was to constantly question what factors should be included in the HDI and in the larger annual report.

Sen's initial influence, the HDI summary, was created even though he is quick to admit that no number could possibly represent all the economic, social, educational, and cultural activity in a nation. Yet the HDI represents a significant improvement over the traditional way of evaluating a country—gross domestic product. In comments published in the 1999 *HDR*, Amartya Sen traces the history of the conflict between the HDI and the GDP numbers and explains how much more useful the HDI is in understanding the real capabilities of a nation. Describing GDP numbers as "overused and oversold", he strongly advocates for the HDI as a means to "broaden substantially the empirical attention that assessment of development processes receives" (Sen, 1999, p. 23). His indices on longevity, education, and income provide a much more comprehensive view of the real lives of people and their opportunities, than does a simple statement of national income.

Sen's second influence has been to never be completely comfortable with the measures of nations. While the HDI broadens our discussion of human development, Sen encourages continuing discussion of what factors should be included—and changed over time. He notes, "many disparate failings and shortcomings need attention. And, furthermore, the world itself is changing even as we look at it and report on it. It is this diverse and dynamic reality on which the enterprise of human development has to concentrate" (Sen, 2000, p. 23). He calls for the creation of and ready discussion of additional means of evaluating the status of people's lives. There is humility in his work that readers must find refreshing. Having designed one of the first truly new measures of the human condition, he has barely presented it when he openly calls for critiques and additions.

The purpose of this chapter is to present an emerging measure of the human condition, and then to describe possible responses—responses at least partially informed by Sen's writings. The emerging measure?—Access to and development of Web sites. This chapter will review Web sites from two perspectives: first, their general use in development efforts, and second, their existence as a cultural phenomenon. The chapter will show that while the development of the World Wide Web has had a mixture of successes and failures in assisting economic development, the Web has been a significant failure as a cultural enabling technology. Yet these current shortcomings need not go unaddressed. Sen has written extensively on global cultural exchanges and has much to suggest as remedies for the current situation.

Global Technology Statistics

First, a quick review of global technology statistics. The *Human Development Report* has been a consistent voice of encouragement in the use of information and communications technologies (ICTs) in development. In the same report that included Sen's comments on the HDI, the 1999 *Human Development Report* also contained a chapter on the impact of technology on human development. Many comments from the chapter are now commonplaces such as "Bringing together computers and communications unleashed an unprecedented explosion of ways to communicate" (*HDR*, 1999, p. 57), and "the Internet is the fastest-growing tool of communication ever" (p. 58). The report then lists the usual hopes for connectivity—distance learning will bring information to poor hospitals, NGOs can supply

Table 1.

Caribbean	Population 2002 (Millions)	GDP per capita PPP US$ (2002)	Telephone mainlines per 1000 people (2002)	Internet users per 1000 people (2002)
Barbados	0.3	15,290	494	111.5
Guyana	0.8	4,260	92	142.2
Jamaica	2.6	3,980	169	228.4
Trinidad and Tobago	1.3	9,430	250	106.0
Africa				
Nigeria	120.9	860	5	3.5
Ghana	20.5	2,130	13	7.8
Kenya	31.5	1,020	10	12.5
Latin America				
Brazil	176.3	7,770	223	82.2
Argentina	38.0	10,880	219	112.0
Chile	15.6	9,820	230	237.5
Venezuela	25.2	5,380	113	50.6
Asian countries				
Philippines	78.6	4,170	42	44.0
Indonesia	217.1	3,230	37	37.7
Malaysia	24.0	9,120	190	319.7
Thailand	62.2	7,010	105	77.6
Vietnam	80.3	2,300	48	18.5
Developed countries				
Canada	31.3	29,480	635	512.8
France	59.8	26,920	569	313.8
Japan	127.5	26,940	538	448.9
U.S.	291.0	35,750	646	551.4

information across borders and make links to supporters, small businesses will find new markets, countries can build businesses around telecommunications jobs, and censorship will become more difficult. Such lists are now familiar to those who work in development and technology.

Given the value they see for ICTs in development, it is no surprise that a count of Internet access rates is now included in each annual report. Unfortunately, these counts show that there is still much ground to be made up if ICTs are to fulfill their potential. For instance, Table 1 displays access rates for a variety of developing nations.

Clearly huge differences in Internet access rates exist between countries. Some developing countries are providing reasonable access rates. But for the poorest of the poor, the countries most in need of online access to medical knowledge, or support for agricultural experts, the picture is not very good. As a group, the least developed countries of the world have an access rate of 2.8 per 1000, which is to say, fewer than three individuals in a thousand can get access to the Internet.

The UNDP is aware of this need. To again cite some of their comments from the 1999 *HDR*, "A U.S. medical library subscribes to around 5,000 journals, but the Nairobi University Medical School Library, long regarded as a flagship centre in east Africa, now receives just 20 journals, compared with 300 a decade ago. In Brazzaville, Congo, the university only has 40 medical books and a dozen journals, all from before 1993" (*HDR*, 1999, p. 59). Clearly, the poorest of the poor have very limited access to local knowledge, and could use all the help they can get in finding remote access to information. But as current figures indicate, ICTs are still in short supply in many countries.

Cultural Imperialism Concerns

Compared to an inability to access fundamental medical information, concerns about cultural imperialism seem trivial. But they are also pervasive. Already in the 1999 *HDR*, its authors were musing about the problem of cultural homogenization. By the 2004 report, two complete chapters are dedicated to culture, primarily to fears that some cultures will be overwhelmed by giant corporations—primarily those in the United States—that produce most of the world's films, and significant portions of its published works. This is a definition of "culture" connected to "intellectual and artistic activity and the works produced by it." Since the definition is connected to work products, those work products can be counted and aggregated by nation.

One function of the United Nations Educational, Scientific, and Cultural Organization (UNESCO) is to count cultural artifacts. Their counts underscore the size of the problem. Table 2 summarizes financial flows in the publishing industry around the

Table 2. Trade in printed materials (UNESCO 2000)

	Imports ($US)	Exports ($US)
Algeria – 1997	$9,717,000	$17,000
Chad – 1995	$994,000	$0
Congo – 1995	$2,435,000	$27,000
Egypt – 1997	$13,358,000	$4,588,000
Ethiopia – 1995	$4,598,000	$0
Kenya – 1996	$12,220,000	$1,888,000
Malawi – 1995	$4,399,000	$12,000
Morocco – 1997	$21,542,000	$860,000
Nigeria – 1991	$31,217,000	$7,000
South Africa – 1996	$133,653,000	$13,406,000
Zimbabwe – 1997	$13,703,000	$1,310,000

world. While the table can be viewed from a purely balance-of-payments perspective, the fact that some countries are overwhelmingly dependent upon other countries for their books and periodicals is really more a question of flow-of-information. Readers in the nations in Table 2 are learning much about the world through the eyes of foreigners. Those foreigners are learning very little about the world through the eyes of African authors.

One can argue that printed materials represent old technology as does the trade in film, which mirrors the flows seen earlier. One hopes that new technology, specifically the Internet, will enable greater diversity in culture as multilingual Web sites reach out to ethnic minorities who may be currently distanced from majority culture. Unfortunately, a quick scan of registered domain names indicates that Web development is as constrained as book development. Table 3 provides counts of Web site domain names in Africa, as well as several other national development indicators.

Current population estimates place the total population of the African continent at more than 800 million, or nearly three times the population of the United States. Yet the entire continent hosts little more than 10 million Web sites, 500 million fewer than the United States.

Amartya Sen is known to many for his calculation that one hundred million women are missing. Given normal birth and health rates, he computed that one hundred million more women should be living than could be found. It is an important insight and led to a careful examination of the treatment of women and girls around the world. Missing Web sites are clearly less important than missing people, but if you compare the Web sites hosted by the United States with its population approaching 300 million, and compare it to the Web sites hosted by an entire continent with approximately three times the population, one finds that more than 500 million Web sites are missing from the sites of African nations. The same comparison could be made for the continents of South America and regions of South and East Asia.

Table 3.

Country	Population (from *CIA Fact Book* 2004 estimates)	Internet code	Income per capita in $US (from 2003 worldbank.org)	Site count (from google. com)	HDI (from undp.org 2002)
Seychelles	80,832	sc	$7,480	67,000	0.853
Libya	5,631,585	ly	$3,036	157,000	0.794
Mauritius	1,220,481	mu	$4,090	172,000	0.785
Tunisia	9,974,722	tn	$2,240	192,000	0.745
Cape Verde	415,294	cv	$1,490	21,100	0.717
Algeria	32,129,324	dz	$1,890	119,000	0.704
Equatorial Guinea	523,051	gq	$930	27	0.703
South Africa	42,718,530	za	$2,780	6,660,000	0.666
Egypt	76,117,421	eg	$1,390	365,000	0.653
Gabon	1,355,246	ga	$3,060	2,490	0.648
Sao Tome and Principe	181,565	st	$320	641,000	0.645
Morocco	32,209,101	ma	$1,320	265,000	0.620
Namibia	1,954,033	na	$1,870	226,000	0.607
Botswana	1,561,973	bw	$3,430	84,900	0.589
Ghana	20,757,032	gh	$320	36,500	0.568
Comoros	766,153	km	$450	245	0.530
Swaziland	1,169,241	sz	$1,350	20,700	0.519
Sudan	39,148,162	sd	$460	2,180	0.505
Cameroon	16,063,678	cm	$640	51,100	0.501
Togo	5,556,812	tg	$310	11,600	0.495
Lesotho	1,865,040	ls	$590	18,000	0.493
Uganda	26,404,543	ug	$240	115,000	0.493
Zimbabwe	12,671,860	zw	$480	153,000	0.491
Kenya	32,021,856	ke	$390	77,500	0.488
Madagascar	17,501,871	mg	$290	91,300	0.469
Nigeria	137,253,133	ng	$320	22,400	0.466
Mauritania	2,998,563	mr	$430	69,100	0.465
Djibouti	466,900	dj	$910	134,000	0.454
Gambia	1,546,848	gm	$310	14,900	0.452
Eritrea	4,447,307	er	$190	1,470	0.439
Senegal	10,852,147	sn	$550	155,000	0.437
Rwanda	7,954,013	rw	$220	27,800	0.431
Guinea	9,246,462	gn	$430	2,680	0.425
Benin	7,250,033	bj	$440	5,350	0.421
Tanzania	36,588,255	tz	$290	94,500	0.407
Cote d'Ivoire	17,327,724	ci	$660	97,700	0.399
Zambia	10,462,436	zm	$380	110,000	0.389
Malawi	11,906,855	mw	$170	33,400	0.388
Angola	10,978,552	ao	$740	20,600	0.381
Chad	9,538,544	td	$250	1,300	0.379
Democratic Rep. of the Congo	58,317,930	cd	$100	151,000	0.365
Central African Rep.	3,742,482	cf	$260	646	0.361
Ethiopia	67,851,281	et	$90	42,300	0.359
Mozambique	18,811,731	mz	$210	98,200	0.354
Guinea-Bissau	1,388,363	gw	$140	48	0.350
Burundi	6,231,221	bi	$100	28,400	0.339
Mali	11,956,788	ml	$290	19,000	0.326
Burkina Faso	13,574,820	bf	$300	81,100	0.302
Niger	11,360,538	ne	$200	53,900	0.292
Sierra Leone	5,883,889	sl	$150	3	0.273
Mayotte FR.	186,026	yt	$9,385	38	
Somalia	8,304,601	so	$765	378	
Rep. of the Congo	2,998,040	cg	$640	1,680	
Liberia	3,390,635	lr	$130	141	
Western Sahara (Morocco)	267,405	eh		57	
Saint Helena	7,415	sh		151,000	
Reunion FR.	766,153	re		29,500	
Totals	**873,856,496**			**10,997,233**	
United States Population	**293,027,571**	us			
		.com		328,000,000	
		.edu		51,500,000	
		.gov		33,400,000	
		.org		109,000,000	
				521,900,000	

Sites that might promote products, describe government actions, link NGOs, or just describe daily life do not exist. The voices of Americans can be heard around the world. Much of the developing world is silent.

Two Cautions about Counts of Web Sites

In fairness, two cautions about these figures need to be explained before moving on. First, many of the "missing" Web sites may exist, but be hosted on United States or other foreign Web servers. I recently conducted a series of interviews with business leaders in Guyana and Trinidad. I discovered that all of them had moved their Web sites to the United States to reduce costs, improve service, and gain additional credibility through the use of a United States domain address. Presumably much of that is happening in other developing countries. It is impossible to know how many Web sites have been moved to remote locations, and the number may be in the millions. On the other hand, it seems incredible that the number would be in the hundreds of millions.

The other caution concerns equating quantity with quality. If the hundreds of millions of missing Web sites are as trivial as most United States Web sites, or as bizarre as the hate-filled, racist, or pornographic sites that occupy substantial portions of any count, one could easily argue that little is lost by their absence. Nevertheless, 500 million is a large number. Even if we assume 99% of Web sites are a waste of perfectly good electrons, we are still left with millions of helpful voices unheard.

What is an appropriate moral response, given this situation? The rest of this chapter will examine this question, looking for answers in the writings of Amartya Sen. Specifically, this chapter will examine definitional concerns with international comparisons, relative importance, capability justice, and inequality responses.

Definitional Concerns with International Comparisons

All the data presented so far, and indeed the very title of this chapter, rest on international comparisons. These comparisons are stark and show obvious shortfalls in the presence of Web sites in many countries. But when presenting a chapter describing Sen's thinking, it would be an egregious oversight to ignore Sen's concerns about international comparisons. As stated earlier, much of his contribution to the development literature has been to seek sophisticated replacements for simple numerical comparisons based on income. But he has expressed additional concerns about the comparisons of nations. He even labels such comparisons as "fantasie," based on the practice of "anthropomorphizing nations, of treating nations as though they are individuals and extrapolating to them on the basis of average per capita income the various ethical arguments that have been developed to apply to individuals" (Sen, 1984, p. 292).

The problem with the presentation of aggregate figures is the absence of distribution figures *within* nations. Whether the resource be money, food, or Internet access, aggregate national numbers tell us very little about how well individuals in a country can actually access these goods. Sen reminds us that "Given the 'power realities' of the prevailing political system in the developing countries, it may indeed be touchingly naïve not to anticipate the failure of asset distribution policies or the appropriation by the rich of a disproportionate share of the benefits of public investment" (Sen, 1984, p. 293). So figures that may tell us that there are, say, 20 telephone lines per 1,000 people, may hide the fact that there are actually 20 telephone lines for the wealthiest 20 families in a nation, and no telephone lines at all for the remaining 980 families.

This is a helpful reminder. National numbers are more easily available, so we tend to use them rather than measures of intra-national access. We should recall that resource distribution is uneven, especially in the poorest nations. On the other hand, some of the numbers we have available are so stark, that it appears there is almost nothing to distribute. If numbers from Google are accurate, and Liberia only hosts 141 Web sites, or Equatorial Guinea really only has 27 Web sites, then distributional issues become less important—there is almost nothing to distribute. Whether these few dozen sites are created by a single family or distributed across the broader population seems inconsequential.

Relative Importance of ICT Shortages

Whatever the availability of Web sites, their presence or absence means little unless such sites have real value. As Sen notes, "in dealing with extreme poverty in developing economies, we may be able to go a fairly long distance in terms of a relatively small number of centrally important functions (and the corresponding basic capabilities, for example, the ability to be well-nourished and well-sheltered, the capability of escaping avoidable morbidity and premature mortality, and so forth" (Sen, 1984, pp. 44-45). No doubt we would all agree that food comes first to someone who is starving. Given the choice between a meal and a Web site, the choice will be an easy one.

But Sen does go on to open the list of additional functionings that might be important. He adds, "In other contexts [beyond extreme poverty], including more general problems of economic development, the list may have to be much longer and more diverse" (Sen, 1984, p. 45). What should be included in that list? Sen never provides a complete list, nor would we expect him to. But his descriptions of his "capabilities model" give us a good sense of direction for any such list. While he has defined his capabilities model many times in his writings, the following citation seems most appropriate for our purposes:

It [capability] represents the various combinations of functionings (beings and doings) that the person can achieve. Capability is, thus, a set of vectors of functionings, reflecting the person's freedom to lead one type of life or another. Just as the so-called 'budget set' in the commodity space represents a person's freedom to buy commodity bundles, the 'capability set' in the functioning space reflects the person's freedom to choose from possible livings. (Sen, 1984, p. 40)

We would no doubt agree that there is much that helps determine a "person's freedom to choose from possible livings." Where do Web sites fit in the mix? How important is information technology in various forms? One can address the question from two directions—importance to the citizen of the developing country looking out at the world, and importance to the citizen of the developed world looking in to the situation of people in developing countries.

Access to Professional Information

For the person living in the developing world, the common approach is to consider their access to professional information. The earlier cited comments by the 1999 *Human Development Report* on access to medical information is typical. In this view, lack of access to medical, or legal, or trade, or agricultural information impedes health or education or economic development. This case for professional need is frequently made and logically reasonable. One's capability to lead a healthy life may well be determined by their physician's ability to access recent medical research.

But the emphasis on such information flows is on access from the developed world. The assumption is that stockpiles of research excellence are available in the "north" and information technology is a simple and relatively cheap way to transfer copies of that information to the needy "south". It can be envisioned as another form of foreign aid, except it requires less of developed countries. Rather than give up food or money, they allow copies of their research to be sent digitally to the needy. And clearly such professional information is useful in developing countries and is gratefully accepted. A number of medical systems have been set up under this model in the past decade, and many would attest to their value.

Since such flows bring information *into* developing countries, they can occur without local Web sites, and so would seem to obviate any concern for Web sites. After all, what might it matter that the entire Central African Republic has just 600 Web sites for its three million people, as long as Web sites are available in the United States and Europe for African doctors to access? It would appear there is no problem, certainly no reduction in capabilities of African people or African physicians, since they can gain information from out of the country.

Unfortunately, the 2001 *Human Development Report* describes significant limitations to what can be learned in the "north." The report points out that researchers in the developed countries spend their time researching diseases that are most common in their own countries. This is not at all surprising, but it does have an impact on information availability. To cite the report's numbers, "In 1995, more than 95,000 therapy-relevant scientific articles were published but only 182—0.2% of the total—addressed tropical diseases. And of 1,223 new drugs marketed worldwide between 1975 and 1996, only 13 were developed to treat tropical diseases—and only 4 were the direct result of pharmaceutical industry research" (*HDR*, 2001, pp. 109-110). The result is that while access to information in the north is valuable, it is incomplete. Physicians looking for information about diseases endemic to developing countries have very limited abilities to find it in the north. The virtual absence of Web sites in the south means they are unlikely to find needed information there either. Physicians may feel that the current situation gives them very little capability to treat patients the way they would like.

Access to Cultural Information

While there may be important shortcomings in the flow of professional information into developing countries, there is another aspect to directional information flow that is drawing increased concern—cultural dominance. The 2004 *Human Development Report* addresses this problem from several angles, but begins with world trade figures that illustrate one aspect of the problem. "World trade in cultural goods—cinema, photography, radio and television, printed matter, literature, music and visual arts—quadrupled, from $95 billion in 1980 to more than $380 billion in 1998. About four-fifths of these flows originate in 13 countries. Hollywood reaches 2.6 billion people around the world, and Bollywood 3.6 billion" (*HDR*, 2004, p. 86). The data from Table 2 detail the startling difference in information flows in books and printed matter. The consequence is that cultural information flows in one direction.

These overwhelming cultural flows are already the subject of significant contention. In early 2005, the President of the European Union, Jean-Claude Juncker, advocated a special EU appropriation to launch a European digital library to counter efforts by the United States company, Google, to digitize millions of books in the libraries of such universities as Harvard and Michigan, the New York Public Library, and the Bodleian Library at Oxford. His proposal came because he says "Europe must not submit in the face of virulent attacks from others" (EU Leader, 2005). It is unclear if Google thought it was launching a "virulent attack" when it committed funds to digitize books and make them freely available on the World Wide Web, but France's National Library president summed up concerns for many in Europe saying, "The real issue is elsewhere. And it is immense. It is confirmation of the risk of a crushing American domination in the definition of how future generations view the world."

The fact that some high-level European leaders would regard free books as "a virulent attack," illustrates how seriously cultural dominance can be viewed. They are not alone. Some in developing countries "fear that their country is being fragmented, their values lost as growing numbers of immigrants bring new customs and international trade and modern communications media invade every corner of the world, displacing local culture" (*HDR*, 2004, p. 85). In this context, the numerical dominance of Web sites in developed countries adds yet another layer of cultural content to the flows in films, books, songs, and other cultural artifacts flowing from the north to the south.

While a large number of policy makers are concerned about these uneven cultural flows, Sen initially seems less bothered. Commenting on the work of a noted Indian filmmaker, he states, "There is much wisdom, I think, in this 'critical openness,' including the prizing of a dynamic, adaptable world over a world that is constantly 'policing' external influences and fearing 'invasion' of ideas from elsewhere" (Sen, 1996, p. 2). He goes on to say, "The growing tendency in contemporary India to champion the need for an indigenous culture that has 'resisted' external influences and borrowings lacks credibility as well as cogency. It has become quite common to cite the foreign origin of an idea or a tradition as an argument against its use" (Sen, 1996, p. 5). This takes him to the misuses of cultural traditions by politicians. Here he asserts:

The resistance to Western hegemony—a perfectly respectable cause in itself—takes the form, under this interpretation, of justifying the suppression of journalistic freedoms and the violations of elementary political and civil rights on the grounds of the alleged unimportance of these freedoms in the hierarchy of what is claimed to be "Asian values". (Sen, 1996, p. 7)

Clearly Sen is not opposed to the introduction of external ideas. He prizes a dynamic world, and is suspicious of those who may attempt to suppress foreign ideas as a pretext for denying local rights. But if he is suspicious of those who would erect barriers to foreign ideas, he is also no advocate of foreign dominance. His reference to resistance to Western hegemony as "a perfectly respectable cause in itself," indicates where he draws the line. Openness to foreign ideas is not synonymous with creating a new cultural homogeneity—this one based on foreign traditions. To Sen, the cultural ideal is a mixture of cultures. He notes "the celebration of these differences—the dizzying contrasts—is far from what can be found in labored generalizations about the unique and fragile purity of "our culture," and in the vigorous pleas to keep "our culture, our modernity," immune from "their culture, their modernity. In our heterogeneity, and in our openness lies our pride, not our disgrace" (Sen, 1996, p. 9).

Sen seems confident that he is seeing "dizzying contrasts" and a celebration of differences in India. Would he find it elsewhere in the world? The UNDP finds "the share of domestic films viewed between 1984 and 2001 declined dramatically in much of Europe" (*HDR*, 2004, pp. 88-89). Other indicators already mentioned in this chapter show how one-sided cultural flows in books can be. A "celebration of differences" requires the existence of multiple cultural products. If the movie industry and book industry are hegemonic in much of the world, what other cultural artifacts can emerge to explain local cultural traditions? Given their low costs of production, one would hope that Web sites might take on this role in at least a few countries. Yet numbers previously cited indicate this has yet to happen, and, if anything, that the hegemony of Web sites may mirror or even exceed the hegemony seen in other media.

The Invisible Developing World

If the information flow is not ideal for residents of developing countries looking out, is it at least adequate for those outsiders looking in? Here the situation may actually be worse, and Sen has much to say about such inadequacies. "One may," Sen says, "with some justice, deny responsibility for inaction about matters the existence of which one does not know. In a small way, even the limited publicity given by OXFAM or UNICEF to human suffering, and to the relatively low cost of removal of some of these sufferings, has the effect of making many people face responsibilities which they would not have otherwise acknowledged. The role of information in the ethics of international income distribution can hardly be over-emphasized" (Sen, 1984, p. 300).

Yet if information about developing countries is important, where is it to be found? Data already presented about traditional publications indicates just how little paper-based information is exported from developing countries. Table 3 demonstrates how little digital information has been made available as well. The story of developing countries is not being told, or at least is not being told by people from within these countries. Web sites to tell that story do not exist, or exist in vanishingly small numbers. Sen notes outside groups such as OXFAM and UNICEF describe the situation in these countries, but it is much harder to find such description originating from within the local communities. There are consequences to that silence. Again to cite Sen, "Informational limitation restricts or distorts consequential judgments, encourages arbitrary agent-relativity, and even provides 'permissive' justification for the make-believe reasoning of 'fantasie' and the unreasoned prejudice of 'evasion' despite the crippling limitation of both these approaches" (Sen, 1984, p. 302). Such an observation seems reasonable on its face. Hearing nothing from large swathes of the planet, it is easy to ignore or misjudge the plight of those communities.

So while simple counts of Web sites might seem unimportant, they indicate three shortcomings in our current information technology utility. First, the lack of local Web postings of professional information leave professionals in developing nations dependent upon "the north" for research information, and there are clearly large holes in the array of data available from that source. Second, the lack of local Web postings indicates yet another medium that could be available to present local cultural information, but is instead dominated by just a few nations. Third, the paucity of Web sites explaining life and living conditions in developing countries leaves these countries dependent upon outsiders to tell their story, if the story is told at all.

Capability Justice

If we assume that current aspects of global information flow are faulty, and that weaknesses in the current system leave individuals and communities at a disadvantage, then we must ask after the current state of justice in global access to information technology resources. Sen begins his description of justice as follows: "In the capability-based assessment of justice, individual claims are not to be assessed in terms of resources or primary goods the persons respectively hold, but by the freedoms they actually enjoy to choose the lives that they have reason to value. It is this actual freedom that is represented by the person's 'capability' to achieve various alternative combinations of functionings" (Sen, 1992, p. 81).

Inherent in this definition are two issues that shape Sen's views of justice. First is choice. If a person has the capacity to read but chooses not to, there is no injustice if we were to find, for instance, that his neighbors read many books a week while he reads none. Simple counts of books read might show substantial variations, but would not automatically indicate deprivations. In Sen's words, "two persons with the same actual capabilities and even the same goals may end up with different outcomes because of differences in strategies or tactics that they respectively follow in using their freedoms" (Sen, 1992, p. 82). So simple counts of outcomes may indicate the result of choice rather than deprivation.

The second issue is the variability of need. Since people are not all the same, giving each the same quantity of a resource may not be justice, and in fact people receiving more of a resource may still be treated unfairly. As he says, "a person may have more income and more nutritional intake, but less freedom to live a well-nourished existence because of higher basal metabolism rate, greater vulnerability to parasitic diseases, larger body size, or simply because of pregnancy" (Sen, 1992, pp. 81-82). Again, we would seem to be cautioned against using simple counts as signs of the presence or absence of justice.

In our general review of information technology access and Web site development, we need to consider whether the lack of Web sites and other forms of information technology in the developing world may be by choice, and whether the presence of demonstrably larger quantities of Web sites in developed countries illustrates not a state of injustice, but a greater need for such resources in the industrialized world. We will examine each question in turn.

ICT Shortages as a Matter of Choice

The question of choice is difficult to resolve. The decision-making processes of billions of the world's people are of course unknowable. Is the lack of Web sites in developing countries an indication of poverty, or, if given sufficient income, would citizens of such countries still not choose to create or use Web sites because of cultural traditions? Might they not have interest in information technologies because they lack the education to use such technologies, or, even when such education is present, may they prefer to communicate by other means?

For answers, we might conduct endless interviews, or track technology sales in the developing world, but neither is likely to give us conclusive evidence of personal choices in these matters. And unfortunately, larger statistical reviews are equally unenlightening. The numbers from Table 3 were analyzed to look for a statistical correlation between the Web site counts, per capita income, and HDI levels of all the countries of Africa. As can be seen in the following table, no statistically valid correlation was found. Neither correlation approaches the required significance level of .05 and even if significant, the correlations indicate that increases in income and HDI might at most account for 3-4% of the increase in Web site presence in a country.

Table 4.

Site Count	Income Per Capita	HDI
Pearson Correlation	.156	.210
Significance	.258	.142

In other words, there is no statistical evidence that Web site development increases in line with income growth in Africa, or that Web site development increases as education and other aspects of the Human Development Index increase.

Without statistical evidence that the creation of Web sites rises with income and/or education, it may indeed be true that even when African people have higher income and higher education, they choose not to develop Web sites—they use their increased financial or educational resources for other matters. But caution would seem warranted before coming to such conclusions. Much more rigorous analysis might indicate that income correlates with Web development—but only after it reaches a particular threshold, or that other infrastructure shortcomings, such as the lack of phone lines, or greater expense for Internet or telephone connectivity, are significant barriers to Web site development no matter what the individual income or educational level. For the moment it seems sufficient to accept that we may not know how choice is interacting with the presence or absence of Web sites in the countries tabulated earlier in this chapter.

ICT Inequality as Justified by Greater Need

What of Sen's second consideration—the possibility that the hundreds of millions of extra Web sites in the United States demonstrate not an injustice, but the greater need of people living in that community? Sen describes relative needs in several ways and specifically addresses the situation of the poor within a richer community. First he notes, "for a richer community, however, the nutritional and other physical requirements (such as clothing and protection from climactic conditions) are typically met, and the needs of communal participation—while absolutely no different in the space of capabilities—will have a much higher demand in the space of commodities and that of resources" (Sen, 1984, p. 336). Much has been said about online communities and their growing presence in the lives of people living in advanced countries. Surely, those with no access to such communities would feel some of the same shame Sen mentions is the fate of people in very poor communities who are unable to participate in community events for lack of proper clothing. As the community changes the way it interacts, community members are driven to change the way they participate.

Sen provides two other examples of potential resource inadequacy in developed countries. There is the example of the child who is unable to receive a full education if she does not have a television, if television ownership is assumed and teaching assignments made accordingly. And there is the example of car ownership in a society where car ownership is common. Once such a state is reached, public transportation services often degrade, so a family without a car becomes less capable in such a society than it might be in a poorer society where car ownership is rare and so public transportation is more widely available. In both cases, he is demonstrating that need can be relative to the community in which one lives.

All his examples demonstrate why it may be more important for individuals in the United States to have Web sites and to have access to other forms of information technology. Once a community communication standard is created, all community members are compelled to participate in the new standard using the new tools. By this standard, the paucity of African Web sites may simply mean that community standards are different there and so no deprivation exists. The current situation is just.

The acceptance of this view, however, requires that community standards not just be modestly different, but be different almost in kind. In the United States, a population of 293 million has created 522 million Web sites, or 1.78 per person. African populations of 862 million have created just under 11 million Web sites, or 0.01 per person. Put another way, American citizens have created 178 times more Web sites than their African peers. It is difficult to think of other resource distributions that are so unbalanced. No American could possibly consume 178 times the food of the average African, or live in homes 178 times as large. For community communication standards to be so divergent is difficult to imagine.

A second possible justification for these discrepancies could be instrumental—the existence of all the millions of extra Web sites has the effect of producing more goods and making more people happier. As Sen puts it, "a person can rightly claim more income not only on the grounds that he has a moral claim to it, but also on the grounds that having more income would have the consequence of serving some other goal, for example, produce more income and make others happier" (Sen, 1984, p. 291). In this argument, somehow the existence of Web sites in the United States improves the income or education or health of citizens in developing countries. As has already been noted, modest support for this position can be found in the medical Web sites available in the north, and the information they provide to physicians in the developing world. The limitations of this position have also already been noted. Other arguments for the instrumental value of United States Web sites have yet to be presented.

So what is the current moral position of these significant technological discrepan-cies? These discrepancies seem impossible to justify either on the basis of greater need in the United States or on the basis of instrumental improvements they can make in the lives of those living in the developing world. This leaves us with the question of an appropriate response.

Inequality Responses

The paucity of technology available to developing countries has been discussed widely for the last decade, and the cultural consequences of these shortcomings have been in discussion for at least as long. A good summation can be found in recent works from the United Nations Development Programme.

The 2001 *Human Development Report*, which focused on technology issues in developing countries, addresses the problem of inadequate technology with a call for global transfers of funds and technologies to developing countries.

Research on and development of technologies for poor people's needs have long been underfunded. Despite the possibilities of technological transformations, this continues to be the case. Without a mechanism for global transfers, there is no dedi-cated source of funding. And voluntary public funding, national and international, has long been inadequate. (HDR, 2001, p. 109)

While this statement puts responsibility for technology development squarely on the shoulders of wealthier nations, the report also comments on the misuse of resources in developing countries, particularly African nations, where the authors note that in 1999 the governments of Sub-Saharan African spent $9 billion on their militaries, monies that could have been available for any number of health, technology, or other development efforts.

The 2004 *Human Development Report* focuses on cultural impacts of globalization. The report presents a series of three recommendations based on four principles:

1.   Defending tradition can hold back human development.
2.   Respecting difference and diversity is essential.
3.   Diversity thrives in a globally interdependent world when people have multiple and complementary identities and belong not only to a local community and a country but also to humanity at large.

4.   Addressing imbalances in economic and political power helps to forestall threats
      to the cultures of poorer and weaker communities (*HDR*, 2004, p. 88).

Response #1: Sheltered Markets

With these principles in mind, the UNDP does not propose any effort to totally
block foreign cultural products, but they do present two approaches to provide some
protection for local traditions. The first possible response is partial protection, with
governments taking positions similar to that of Hungary which requires that 15%
of programs on public channels be of Hungarian origin. With a protected market
guaranteed, the expectation is that local producers will find the resources and talent
to produce enough shows to fill this air time. The drawback is that any protected
industry tends to be less efficient than those facing competition, and so costs may
be higher and quality lower than might otherwise be the case.

Response #2: Government Promotion

The other alternative described by the authors is promotion. Here governments
provide money to such industries as television and movie producers. The primary
example here is France, which provides $400 million each year to its film industry.
The result has been an increase in film production in that country, one of the few to
show an increase in national production.

Variations on these approaches have been tried with newer technologies, with countries putting tariffs on imported technologies in the hope that a local industry will
emerge, or making large purchases of technologies in hopes of building an industry.
One could argue that the Internet resulted from United States government funding
of early network research and development followed by funding of early network
architectures. But it seems more problematic for developing countries to attempt
these strategies, given limited resources, no matter what their military budgets.
So one is drawn back to the strategy promoted in the 2001 *Human Development
Report*—global transfers.

Response #3: Global Transfers

Amartya Sen has written extensively on this topic. To begin with, he has little
sympathy for arguments that maintain status quo. He refers to the "conservative
belief that the population of each country is entitled to what it happens to have currently, and while a change needs justification, the status quo does not. I shall call
this approach that of 'entitlement valid for all substance I own now'— 'evasion'

for short" (Sen, 1984, p. 293). He rapidly dismisses the moral arguments made on behalf of "evasion." He goes on to point out the logical weakness for those arguing that "each government is responsible to its own members is an optimum feasible system for pursuing world welfare…" (Sen, 1984, p. 295). Such arguments ignore too much history.

He does, however, point to two cautions in global transfers. First, he notes that a person with a higher real income in a rich country should not automatically be taken to be more advantaged. As has already been mentioned, people living in a rich country may have more requirements—televisions, cars—than people in poorer countries. He also makes the practical observation that global transfers can only come from taxations placed on peoples in the developed countries. One has to be mindful of the condition of the worst-off taxed individual in the donor country. There are consequences to the capabilities of people in both countries, and these consequences must be minded. But having noted reasonable caution in global transfers, it is clear Sen supports such transfers as morally right. To pretend there is no need for such transfers is "evasion."

This leaves us with the practical question of how to accomplish such transfers, now that we are comfortable that they are morally justified. Here we find much less guidance from Sen and other moral philosophers. We have now moved to the arena of foreign policy instruments, an arena where all appear to be rank amateurs. How is one to transfer resources from one country to another, no matter how morally justified? One treads lightly here, and with great modesty, but we do have the advantage of experience with such transfers. Being mindful that one does not wish to worsen the position of the worst-off taxed individual, one can be careful of huge financial outlays yet still find ways to improve the technological capabilities of those in the developing world. The United States, for instance, currently imposes a small tax on telephones, and uses the money to help support public access technology sites in schools and libraries. An equivalent tax on phones or on movie productions, could create a fund that could support technology development and cultural productions in developing countries. Current attacks on the legitimacy of the United Nations create practical problems for the implementation of any such transfer, but international treaties have worked their way through thicker conundrums than this one. One acknowledges that the political arguments of such a transfer would be more daunting than the moral arguments, but this does not negate the need or the obligation.

Concluding Remarks

Sen sums up economic development very nicely when he says:

The process of economic development can be seen as a process of expanding the capabilities of people. Ultimately, the process of economic development has to be concerned with what people can or cannot do, for example, whether they can live long, escape avoidable morbidity, be well nourished, be able to read and write and communicate, take part in literary and scientific pursuits, and so forth. (Sen, 1984, p. 497)

The figures presented in this chapter make it clear that the capabilities of people in developing nations are severely restricted by lack of access to technologies that would let them gain more professional information, and present more cultural information. The world knows less of these countries as a result, and people in these countries know less about themselves as a result. The 500 million missing Web sites indicate the overwhelming deficiencies to be found. But the rapid advances in information technology and the dramatically lower costs for this technology mean that this discrepancy can be addressed. Relatively modest resource transfers to developing countries could quite quickly advance the capabilities of people to participate in the world medical, cultural, and scientific communities.

References

EU leader backs European digital library to ward off U.S. dominance. (2005, May 3). *Yahoo news.* Available at http://news.yahoo.com

Human development report 1999: Globalization with a human face (HDR). (1999). New York: United Nations Development Programme.

Human development report 2001: Making technology work for human development (HDR). (2001). New York: United Nations Development Programme.

Human development report 2004: Cultural liberty in today's diverse world (HDR). (2004). New York: United Nations Development Programme.

Sen, A. (1984). *Resources, values and development.* Cambridge, MA: Harvard University Press.

Sen, A. (1992). *Inequality reexamined.* Cambridge, MA: Harvard University Press.

Sen, A. (1996). Our culture, their culture: Satyajit Ray and the art of universalism. *The New Republic, 214*(14), 1-9.

Sen, A. (1999). Assessing human development. In *Human Development Report 1999.* New York: United Nations Development Programme.

Sen, A. (2000). A decade of human development. *Journal of Human Development, 1*(1), 17-23.

Chapter XI

Computer Ethics:
Constitutive and
Consequential Morality

A. Raghuramaraju
University of Hyderabad, India

Abstract

This chapter introduces two distinct models of morality, namely, constitutive which is available in traditional moral philosophy and consequential which surrounds the present day computer ethics discourse. It shows how constitutive morality thoroughly rehearses possible problems arising out of new developments or introduction of new products before accepting a moral rule, whereas consequential morality, propelled by liberalism, allows freedom for new products without deliberation and attends to problems only when they arise. The chapter, looking from the point of view of constitutive morality, highlights some of the structural problems associated with computer ethics. In conclusion, it suggests how societies, like India, that are not fully modern, can learn from both of these two models, thereby instituting additional terms to a new discipline like computer ethics.

The Three Fish

A long time ago, there lived three fish in a lake. They were great friends, though each one's nature was quite different. The first fish was very wise. She always thought a lot before she did anything. She did not like to get into any kind of trouble. The second fish was extremely clever. She could make quick decisions, if the situation demanded it. It was easy for her to get out of any kind of trouble. The third fish was fatalistic. She believed in destiny, what had to happen would certainly happen, she believed.

One evening, while the wise fish was swimming about in the lake, she overheard two fishermen pointing towards her and saying, "Look at that big, fat fish. We must come back tomorrow to get her. I am sure there will be more like her in this lake." It was almost sunset and the fishermen were getting ready to leave. The wise fish rushed to her friends and informed them of the fishermen's plans for the next day. Pondering over the issue for a while, the wise fish said, "We should leave this lake at once. Let us swim through the river and find a safe haven." The second fish said aloud, "Why must we leave now? Let the fishermen come here tomorrow. I will certainly make my escape then." The third fish was already resigned to fate, she said, "All my life I have lived in this lake. I cannot leave my home now. What is destined to happen will happen. So, I will stay here."

The wise fish bid farewell to her friends. Alone she swam through the river and found herself a new home in a pond. "Thank God I am safe," she thought to herself. Next morning, the fishermen arrived early. They spread their net and many fish got caught in it, including the two friends who had stayed back in the lake. Quickly, the clever fish thought of a plan to escape. Pretending to be dead, she lay absolutely still in the net. "Let's throw out this dead fish," said one fisherman and flung her back into the lake. "It worked! I am safe!" sighed the fish in relief. The third fish was still entangled in the net. She wriggled and twisted to get free, but to no avail. One fisherman got very irritated, "This fish here is real bothersome, I must put an end to it," so saying the fisherman chopped the third fish. (from Tales from Panchatantra)

Introduction

It is a social fact that the social space occupied by computers within Western developed societies is largely a modern secular social space which is, in turn, a product of series of continuous radical change within these societies. The project of modernity in the West has been largely successful in rejecting and even removing the pre-modern. However, the pre-modern social realities still exist in non-Western societies like India. This variance regarding the social fact, it is argued in this chapter, actively enters into the formation of the discourse of computer ethics in societies like India. In order to argue for this variance, let me make some important historical connections and recall some genealogical trajectories, because what is present today is a result of active negotiations from the past.

This chapter begins by elucidating the basic maxims of the project of modernity within the modern West that clearly rejected and removed the pre-modern Western social realities, presents those sharp differences between moral frameworks of classical Western philosophy, termed here as *constitutive morality*, and modern Western morality, termed as *consequential morality*. In conclusion, this chapter shows how computer ethics in those societies which have not undergone the same historical developments as India, need not imitate the existing computer ethics discourse in the West, but can benefit from both these moral frameworks of the classical and the modern West, thereby adding new dimensions to the existing debates on computer ethics.

Modernity and Computers

The project of rejecting the pre-modern or tradition within the West by modernity is clearly evident in the writings of Rene Descartes, who is considered to be the father of modern philosophy. In his *Discourse on Method* (Descartes, 1985), while declaring his normative framework consisting of cogito, reason and certainty, he embarks on excluding the following:

- Childhood[1] (as it is the domain governed by appetite and teachers rather than reason)

- Language

- History (to him past is like travelling which takes us away from the present)

- Oratory, poetry (poetry is the "gifts of the mind rather than fruits of study" and "moral writings of the ancient pagans")

- "Customs," evolutionary growth of societies (he rejects gradual growth of societies)

- Even classical logic and mathematics are rejected as they are "mixed up with so many other things."

- All these aspects that Descartes excluded evidently form part of the pre-modern Western social reality.

The project of modernity, based as it were on self-justification—such as, the Cartesian "I," or the idea of "man-in-the-state-of-nature", which is hypothetical rather than empirical in Social Contract philosophers[2]—is bereft of justification from neutral grounds. This rejection of the pre-modern past within the West did not remain at the theoretical level but has been put into practice, thus removing the pre-modern. Elucidating the nature of the formation of modern institutions like nation and the transition from the pre-modern to the modern nation-state in the West, Ernest Gellner says that it is a:

general imposition of a high culture on society, where previously low cultures had taken up the lives of majority, and in some cases of the totality, of the population...It is the establishment of an anonymous, impersonal society, with mutually substitutable atomised individuals, held together above all by a shared culture of this kind, in place of a previous complex structure of local groups, sustained by folk cultures reproduced locally and idiosyncratically by the micro-groups themselves. This is what really happens. (Gellner, 1983, p. 57)

This nationalist project—which is derived from the project of modernity, its atomised individual as formulated by Descartes and the Social Contract philosophers—have succeeded in removing the pre-modern social realities. The removal is justified sociologically as a "requirement of industrial society" and its "cultural homogeneity," to which mankind is said to have been irreversibly committed. Gellner, when confronted by the arguments of relativism, evades them by declaring that the "question of concerning just *how* we manage to transcend relativism is interesting and difficult, and certainly will not be solved here." He asserts that:

What is relevant, however, is that we somehow or other do manage to overcome it, that we are not helplessly imprisoned within a set of cultural cocoons and their norms, and that for some very obvious reasons...we may expect fully industrial man to be even less enslaved to his local culture than was his agrarian predecessor. (Gellner, 1983, p. 120)

The epistemological factor consists of self-justification and sociological determinism deeply permeated into its political manifestation on a social plane. The pre-modern within the West has tamely surrendered to it, as a part of sociological determinism, without any critical engagement. That is, it is maintained that pre-modern has to give way to the modern manifestations, be it nation or other subsidiary institutions covering the domains of health, education and other social realms. Moreover, the transformation referred to earlier is not smooth, neither governed by sympathy nor understanding of what is being transformed. As Gellner writes, this transformation of pre-modern to modern nation is not an:

awake[ning]...[of] an old, latent, dominant force...[but] a period of turbulent readjustment, in which either political boundaries, or cultural ones, or both, were being modified, so as to satisfy the new nationalist imperative which now, for the first time, was making itself felt...[and] this period of transition was bound to be violent and conflict ridden. (Gellner, 1983, p. 40)

Through rejection and subsequent removal, the pre-modern in the West has exited, a fact recognised by Anthony Giddens (1984, p. 14) and Susan Bordo (1987, p. 29). This, perhaps, is also the reason why Foucault (1984) suggested the need to conflate pre-modern and post-modern to contrast them from modern. The radical moves that caused this exit need to be kept in mind while understanding the entry of modern realities including computers. Like the formation of nation states, computers are also one of the major institutional tools of modernity. Without this background consisting of the absence of pre-modern communities and the emergence of atomised individual as purely cognitive and bereft of the cultural shades and surrounds of the past, it is not possible to envisage the indomitable role computers play today. It is against this radical and transformative background we have to understand both the emergence of modern machines like computers and analyse ethical problems arising out of, or caused by them, in society. Further, keeping this background in mind is important as this institutes the relation between modern Western societies and computers as necessary. From this it also follows that in those societies that do not have this background this relation need not be necessary but contingent. I shall come to this later. Now let me lay bare the existing terms of computer ethics.

Computer Ethics

Locating the space of computer ethics and the prevailing meanings of the term "computer ethics," Terrell Ward Bynum says:

On the one hand, for example, computer ethics might be understood very narrowly as the efforts of professional philosophers to apply traditional theories like utilitari-

anism, Kantianism, or virtue ethics to issues in computer technology. On the other hand, it is possible to construe computer ethics in a very broad way to include, as well, standards of professional practice, codes of conduct, aspects of computer law, public policy, corporate ethics—even certain topics in the sociology and psychology of computing. (Bynum, 1999, p. 1)

These two meanings of computer ethics given by Bynum, consisting of narrow concern and the broad way, are internal to modern Western society. There is continuity from individualism with freedom and the idea of progress, as expressed by modern thinkers like Kant, to information technology. Incidentally, all the ethical theories referred to earlier by Bynum belong to the modern discourse, including even virtue ethics, which, though it refers to traditional virtues, is nevertheless largely located within the critical space of the modern. Obviously the issues listed under the broad way are not problems faced by traditional or pre-modern morality.

To Bynum's attempt at drawing the boundaries of computer ethics, let me add here that the success of information technology is related to the need generated by modernity that destroyed "the previous complex structure of local groups, sustained by folk cultures," referred to by Gellner. This is a path towards globalization. Globalization, given its immensely extended purview, increases the distance between individuals. A new industry, established as it were in a location which is conducive for its production, generates new jobs. People from different locations are attracted to these new professional jobs and, in the process, they are displaced and migrate away from their home, a consequence outcome of industrialization. As this happens on a large scale, the quantum of social distance amongst individuals is enormously multiplied, thereby creating the need to overcome it. Many earlier communication devices and, now, computers serve the purpose of shrinking spatial and temporal distances. They are particularly useful to individuals, who are outside their community affiliations to relate themselves to distant others of their choice or to form their own chosen communities based on contract and mutual interest. They do not constitute the primary bonds which govern natural communities. So there is a necessary, and even a causal, relation between the project of modernity and computers.

To reinforce the necessary relation between modern society and computers let me here distinguish the nature of communication in a natural pre-modern community from a modern community. The optics of a natural community are analogous to a candle, shedding light on the immediate surroundings but needing to be taken along to see other places. Here it must be stated, lest a kind of irresponsible romanticism creep in, that these candles are vulnerable to natural factors like wind which can blow them out or water which can dampen them. The immediate is the focus of its attention. In contrast, computers are like torches, which makes it possible to search distant spaces, without moving the agent as well as the torch. These are not vulnerable to natural factors. However, they marginalize the immediate which stands as mute or is numbed in its operation. Therefore, when we go to the library or browse the Internet, each of us carries a mental torch and directs it at the books in the library. Even when we see those spaces that are within the vicinities of the candle, we still use torches. A friend in his electrical engineering course asked his students to think about the following situation. What is the volume of communication in a village which has no television, one television for the entire village, or a television in each house? Of course we can add to this a village with a television in each room of every house. Obviously the answer is that there is more communication with the immediate surroundings in a village which has no televisions. However, the village which has more televisions makes it possible to know more about distant places, although this knowledge may be at the cost of interaction with the immediate.[3]

The computer ethics discourse, cutting across the available diversity consisting of utilitarianism, Kantianism or virtue ethics, inhabits this spread which is growing fast. The major sociological studies on computer use in the West assume and take the spread for granted as a sociological requirement. They have not sought to confront them outside their own frameworks. For instance, the recent work on digital divide in American society entitled *Virtual Inequality: Beyond the Digital Divide* (Mossberger, Tolbert, & Stansbury, 2003) discusses the ubiquitous limitation surrounding the existing "digital divide" in American society.[4] This study focuses on how the problem of digital divide in American society is related to the limited understanding of this problem. For instance, the problem is largely construed as the economic problem of "affordability." While agreeing with the fact that this constitutes one of the important problems, this book argues by using extensive empirical data how, along with the economic factor of affordability, "ability" to use technology promotes the digital divide. The authors have classified ability as consisting of skill divide, economic opportunity divide, and democratic divide. While discussions of this kind do provide valuable insights into understanding the spread of computers, they do not, however, provide us with moral insights that might give proper evaluation, rather than mere dismissal, of the use of computers.

Here it is worth recalling Gadamer's reaction to the shrinking of space and time—one of the major tasks of computers—while making a case for the structural necessity and desirability of time lapse between sending a letter and receiving an answer. He says:

The original form of conversation can also be seen in derivative forms in which the correspondence between question and answer is obscured. Letters, for example, are an interesting transitional phenomenon: a kind of written conversation that, as it were, stretches out the movement of talking at cross purposes before seeing each other's point. The art of writing letters consists in not letting what one says become a treatise on the subject, but making it acceptable to the correspondent. But it also consists, on the other hand, in preserving and fulfilling the measure of finality possessed by everything stated in writing. The time lapse between sending a letter and receiving an answer is not just an external factor, but gives to this form of communication its proper nature as a particular form of writing. So we note that the speeding-up of the post has not led to a heightening of this form of communication but, on the contrary, to a decline in the art of letter-writing. (Gadamer, 1975, p. 332)

Referring to the modern attempt to destroy distance, M. K. Gandhi says that:

I wholeheartedly detest this mad desire to destroy distance and time, to increase animal appetites and go to the ends of the earth in search of their satisfaction. (Gandhi, 1927, p. 83)

Taking a clue, as it were, from the previously-mentioned insightful criticisms, let me further contest (though not necessarily debunk) the social space occupied by computers from two other points of view. One is normative and the other sociological. This calls for situating this analysis outside the analysis of the spread of computers, be it virtual unity or divide, referred to earlier, where there is no attempt at critically engaging with the project of modernity, and also outside those attempts, like the one suggested by Bynum, to understand ethical problems arising out of computers from modern ethical perspectives. Both these existing paths take the advent of computers for granted and then seek to provide piecemeal answers. Instead, let me first identify some temporal orderings in the modern ethical theories, especially in Robert Wiener, who is considered the "founding father" of…"computer ethics" (Bynum, 1999, p. 3).

Consequential Morality

Explaining the internal compulsions for restoring communication between machines, Wiener says:

the speed of the airplane made it necessary to give the…machine itself communication functions which had previously been assigned to human beings. Thus the problem of anti-aircraft fire control made familiar the notion of communication addressed to a machine rather than to a person. (Wiener, 1950, p. 176)

This autonomy of machines makes it possible for them to act outside the gaze of persons. Wiener himself warned of the possibility of dangers of this autonomy when he said, "Long before Nagasaki and the public awareness of the atom bomb, it had occurred to me that we were here in the process of another social potentiality of unheard-of importance of good and for evil" (Wiener, 1948, pp. 27-28). In order to circumvent the evil of this new development or device, Wiener suggested the need to have a "society based on human values other than buying and selling. To arrive at this society, we need a good deal of struggle" (Wiener, 1948, pp. 26-27).

I would like to term the model of morality followed by Wiener a consequential model of morality. Computer ethics inhabits this model. Four important designations in Wiener, which loom large in the discourse of computer ethics are:

1.   Introduction of computers as a requirement of war

2.   Possibility of both good and bad emanating from computers

3.   Building up a society with human values

In Wiener, (1) can give rise to (2); to eliminate evil aspects of (2) and retain good aspects of (2), (3) is offered as a solution. That is, a product is first introduced into the society. At the point of introduction it is not put to moral scrutiny. Freedom of thought and pragmatic considerations prevail at this stage. Ethics is called for only consequentially to take care of the evil consequences of the product. This morally unscrutinized product introduction will not be stopped, even if the product is globally detrimental, which is less likely in the case of computers but imminent in the case of nuclear proliferation.

Apart from the details, what is of immense interest in the previous model is the temporal sequence in the argument. To begin with, the implications of bestowing communication functions to the machine is not morally scrutinized, making farce of morality at this stage. It is made to pass through this stage though, indulging in sociological necessity which in this case is the necessity brought out by the "speed of the airplane." So morality is not called into the picture at all at this stage. However, this should not be construed as dispensing with morality, since it is subsequently recalled, of course, in a truncated form. It is recalled to attend to the "social potentiality of unheard-of importance of good and for evil." Morality is recalled here as a tail-ender, as a last segment in this temporal order, to take care of the new moral problems arising out of these developments. Wiener gave an onerous task to the moral realm, in which one has to struggle a good deal to arrive at a society based on human values other than buying and selling. Here a question can be asked about the credentials of those like Weiner who, while making a case for war aeroplanes, have also asked for a value-based society. Apart from this, by recalling morality as a tail-ender, he is presenting a very imbalanced agenda or architecture for computer ethics. What is of interest here is that computer ethics today, across the board, follows exactly this temporal order, be it in discussing piracy, pornography channels, or what have you. This structural imbalance underlies the computer ethics paradigm, whose predicament seems to be like the clever fish. Unless we recognise this structural feature, we will not be able to pose ethical problems arising out of the use of computers, and we will not be able to understand the nature of this new discipline. This imbalance, which is structural in nature, can be better understood by contrasting it with a different model that is available in the morality of non-modern societies, which I call a constitutive model.

Constitutive Morality

In the constitutive model of morality, norms are well rehearsed before they are accepted. This exercise consists of closely identifying the possible future problems that a norm can give rise to. Scrutinize them thoroughly and accept them only if they clear this scrutiny and reject them if they do not. It is in this sense the ethics of this period is primarily normative. In a manner of speaking, norms preceded individual and social activity, à la Aristotle. Let me illustrate this by taking from Plato an example of the constitutive model of morality.

In Plato's dialogue *The Republic*, Cephalus offers the definition of justice "as honesty in word and deed". Socrates rejects this definition of justice by giving the following illustration. An X, when leaving for some other place, entrusted his belongings, which included a knife, to his friend Y, with a promise that the latter would return them to him when he returns. After some time, X returned and claimed his belongings. However, Y was in a dilemma to return them or not, not because he wanted to possess X's belongings but because of X's psychological state. X when returned was mad and, in his madness, was threatening to kill people. In this changed circumstance, if Y returns to X his belongings then he would be making it possible for X to kill someone, or, if he does not return them, then he will not be keeping the promise. Both the positions are feasible and run parallel. Here one possibility is that we can take sides. The choice is posed between the welfare of X and keeping the promise. We might argue that Y should return the belongings as he had promised and not to bother about the consequences. This would be an objectivist position. We might also equally argue that Y, given X's psychological state which surely must be taken into consideration, decides not to return the belongings. This would be the contextualist's position. This is the case of a dead end. The choice between the two positions eventually is arbitrary. The feasibility of both these possibilities leaves Y more confused. Thus, Socrates seems to reject this definition of justice proposed by Cephalus, not so much for its explicit articulation, but for containing a possibility of a dead end, thus giving rise to uncertainty and ambiguity. This also seems to be the reason for Socrates to reject other definitions of justice, such as that of Polemarchus', which is "justice as helping friends and harming enemies." Subsequently, Plato proposes an ideal society to eliminate these aberrations.

This model of morality would anticipate the possibility of pornographic Web sites on the Internet in deliberating about making the Internet open, whereas the consequential framework will only afterwards bring out a law to ban the use of pornography channels, for instance, by children. The classical philosophers reject rules, because they are vulnerable to misuse. This thorough moral scrutiny may reject freedom of thought at the very outset, but it nevertheless circumvents both the possibility of later evil consequences as well, as both informing and inculcating moral individual actions into individuals.[5] This model is nearer to the first fish in opening story.

Another difference between these two models of morality is that the constitutive model presupposes an actual ethical community, be it the Athens of Plato, or that of any other thinker. The models are addressed to these actual communities. This is not withstanding the fact that their morals predominantly talked about universals, which is a vertical movement in contrast to the horizontal one that we see in modern societies. The universals, it must be recognized, are addressed to a broadly defined community. It is also true that they did not explicitly restrict the use of these models to other communities, presupposing a community was crucial to the formation of their ethics. In the classical period ethics presupposed a community and it claimed precedence over human activity. In contrast, the consequential morality is parasitic on the paradigm, which privileges freedom and asserts the primacy of individuals. In the process of its activities, this morality does not only presuppose community; in fact, it also seeks to bulldoze community demarcations.

Here let me deviate a bit and maintain that the globalization of commodity is made possible by globalization of thought. So the process of this demolition and movement towards the global facilitated opening of the faraway spaces, slowly and subtly deflects the attention of the agents of this community from their immediate surroundings. While, for an urbanized modernized individual, computers and Internet access are necessities, their use by those who do not have these backgrounds leads them to live in a virtual way, in which they do not have organic relations with their world and no immediate anchoring in their immediate surroundings.

Having elucidated the structural difference between consequential and constitutive moralities, let me discuss the second point, which is a sociological one. It is a social fact that there exists radical difference in the realm of demography between developed and developing societies. That is, non-modern communities are population-dense societies, where as modern societies which rely on machines in general and computers in particular are less-populated societies, and in the place of slaves they need machines. In other words, there is an internal necessity that relates the phenomena of computers today and machines earlier to modern Western societies.

Machines generally came to occupy, though in an enormously changed scenario, the space left vacant by slavery. Whitehead pointed out that the critique of slavery within the West coincided with, or immediately followed, the advent of machines. This coincidence or necessary relation is reminiscent of Marx's statement that humankind sets itself only to those tasks that it can solve. For the task itself arises when the material conditions for its solution are already formed or are in the process of formation. Slavery has been rejected, but the master's attitude towards the slave has remained unchanged. The old master-slave combination has now metamorphosed into a new man-machine combination.[6]

While computers help in solving problems arising in the service sector like over-employment in developed countries, which face the serious problem of lack of population, in contrast, they further aggravate the problem of unemployment in overpopulated countries like India. That is, while the discipline of computer ethics today may have been at the forefront of ethics in the West, it does not occupy this central position in the order of priority in a society like India. In fact, it might be at the bottom of its priorities. This may be largely due to sociological considerations. That is, unlike the West, which is moving towards massive modernization, which facilitates computers, societies like India contain both modern and pre-modern realities.

Let me elucidate the nature and also the scale of this combination, between the modern and the pre-modern. The following figures might provide a clue to the existing proportion between the modern and the pre-modern in India. Hindustan Lever Ltd "has more than 70% share in the shampoo segment but that translates into just about "8% of hair washes." Ditto with soaps. Two out of every three soaps sold are HLL brands. But only "20% of the people who bathe use soaps" (*India Today*, 2001, p. 69). Further, "barely a tenth of the milk sold in India is packaged" (*India Today*, 2001, p. 71). This data from the encroaching other surely is an important description of the existence of the pre-modern communities.

This important sociological fact ought to be used positively to understand the terms of encroachment from outside, the scale of its success, forces of resistance, and so on. Moreover, if the extension of something like soap is so small, what would be the impact of computers on the Indian society. This recognition of the simultaneous existence of both pre-modern and modern social institutions can facilitate an active negotiation between these contested realms and, similarly, an active interaction between the two models of morality, consequential and constitutive, discussed previously. The modern is largely governed by the former and the pre-modern by the latter. Here it may be noted that, by keeping the distinction between these models, it is also possible to avoid using the morality of one model to solve the problems arising out of the other model.

Conclusion

So, given these differences in the normative as well as sociological realms, societies like India need not replicate the process in the West. India might still follow the West and allow computers to enter into its society. However, unlike in the West, it has the choice of following the insights from the morality of the pre-modern West and ethical discourses within India, both traditional as well as non-traditional, and using these to negotiate some interesting variations. For instance, the thoroughly cautious approach of the constitutive model of morality can be coupled with the freedom facilitated and nurtured by the consequential model. This would thereby iron out the extremities of excessive caution which does not give the elbow-room essential for innovation and would also curb the excessive freedom that can lead to inevitable dead ends. Further, the problem of demography and unemployment can perhaps be more strongly posed in the computer ethics program from India than in the West. Through this engagement, the computer ethics program in India can benefit from both the constitutive model and the consequential model (a facility abundantly available to it), since both the pre-modern and the modern are simultaneously available to India.

References

Bordo, S. (1987). *The Flight to Objectivity: Essays on Cartesianism and Culture*. Albany: State University of New York Press.

Bynum, T. W. (1999). The development of computer ethics as a philosophical field of study. *Australian Journal of Professional and Applied Ethics*, *1*(1), 1-29.

Descartes, R. (1985). Discourse on method. In *The philosophical writings of Descartes* (Vol. 1). Trans. By J. Cottingham, R. Stoothoff & D. Murdoch. Cambridge, UK: Cambridge University Press.

Foucault, M. (1984). What is enlightenment? In P. Rabinow (Ed.), *The Foucault reader*. New York.

Gadamer, H.G. (1975). *Truth and method*. New York: Crossroad Books.

Gandhi, M. K. (1927, March 17). *Young India*.

Gellner, E. (1983). *Nation and nationalism*. Oxford, UK: Basil Blackwell.

Giddens, A. (1982). *Profiles and critiques in social theory*. London: Macmillan.

Mossberger, K., Tolbert, C. J., & Stansbury, M. (2003). *Virtual inequality: Beyond the digital divide*. Washington, DC: Georgetown University Press.

Wiener, N. (1948). *Cybernetics, or, control and communication in the animal and the machine*. Cambridge, MA: Technology Press.

Wiener, N. (1950). *The humane use of human beings: Cybernetics and society*. Cambridge, MA: Riverside Press.

Endnotes

[1]   For instance, Descartes says about childhood, that, "...I reflected that we were all children before being men and had to be governed for some time by our appetites and our teachers, which were often opposed to each other and neither of which, perhaps, always gave us the best advice; hence I thought it virtually impossible that our judgements should be as unclouded and firm as they would have been if we had had the full use of our reason from the moment of our birth, and if we had always been guided by it alone" (Descartes, 1985, p. 117).

[2]   Social contract philosophers clarify that their notion of man-in-the-state-of-nature is not pre-societal, which make it either historical or anthropological but hypothetical.

[3]   I am thankful to Professors Rajiv Sangal and Ganesh P. Bagaria for this example.

[4]   See my April 2005 note of this book (*Political Studies, 3*(2), 246).

[5]   Here I am alluding to Plato only to highlight the problems of modern morality—not to celebrate these classical models as, for instance, MacIntyre does. Moreover, these traditions are not there even if you want to recall them. I have in my 1995 paper entitled "A note on critique and alternative in Alasdair MacIntyre" (*Journal of Indian Council of Philosophical Research, 12*(2), 128-136), pointed out the logical inconsistencies in MacIntyre's recommendation.

[6]   In my 1995 essay entitled "Of thinking machines and centered self" (*AI & Society, 9*, 184-192), I have presented how the logic of AI follows the logic of the project of enlightenment and its human-centredness, hence the problem in maintaining the radical difference between man and machine.

Chapter XII

The Digital Divide in Australia:
Is Rural Australia Losing Out?

Emma Rooksby
Charles Sturt University, Australia

John Weckert
Charles Sturt University, Australia

Richard Lucas
Charles Sturt University, Australia

Abstract

In this chapter, the authors examine the problem of the digital divide in Australia, drawing substantially on a study by carried out for the Australian Capital Territory (ACT) government by the authors. While this study was limited to the ACT region, many of the findings are relevant to rural areas across Australia as well, and also to rural areas of other developed countries. The authors conclude that there is a digital divide problem in Australia, and discuss some initiatives taken to date to address the problem.

Introduction

In the last decade, information and communication technologies have rapidly become integral to most, if not all aspects of society in developed countries. Electronic communication networks within Australia, the developed country considered in this chapter, connect various levels of government, many households, most education institutions, many non-government organizations, and almost all commercial organizations. These networks are used for a wide range of information- and communication-based activities, for both work and leisure purposes. They may either supplement or supplant alternative means of conducting many activities, such as face-to-face, telephonic or printed communication.

The introduction of new information and communication technologies has the potential to bring significant benefits to many members of society, and many have already benefited substantially. Benefits include savings in both time and money for businesses, government, non-government organizations and individuals; new opportunities for education (formal and informal), employment and entertainment; new means of communicating with other people; and new and more comprehensive sources of information than have previously been available.

However, as many studies and reports document, not all members of society have access to these new technologies, or to the benefits they bring. This phenomenon is generally known as the "digital divide." However it is defined, the digital divide marks a gap, more or less clearly delineated, between those people who have a high level of access to certain new information and communication technologies, and those people who have little or no access to those technologies. As new information and communication technologies become increasingly prevalent and integral to life in developed countries such as Australia, those who lack access to them become further disadvantaged, since information and services are provided increasingly, and sometimes even solely, via the new technologies. The following are commonly cited examples of goods and services that are only available (or only cheaply available) by means of the new information and communication technologies:

- Many jobs are only advertised online, or can only be applied for online, and those who apply online may have an advantage of timeliness over those who cannot do so.

- Many commercial services (e.g., airline tickets, banking and financial services) are available only online, or available at a significant discount online.

- Some government information is available only online, is easier to access online, or is cheaper to access online, than by other means.

- Some community consultation services (provided by government, or subcontracted to private providers) are available only online for members of the population (such as inhabitants of rural areas) who cannot attend other consultations.

In this chapter, we will examine the problem of the digital divide in Australia, drawing substantially on a study by carried out for the Australian Capital Territory (ACT) government by the authors (Rooksby, Weckert, & Lucas, 2002). While this study was limited to the ACT region, many of the findings are relevant to rural areas across Australia as well, and also to rural areas of other developed countries.

The Digital Divide Problem

It is worth noting at the outset, that not all believe that there is a digital divide *problem* that warrants government intervention. Optimism was inspired in particular by steady increases in levels of Internet use and access over a number of years. Arrison (2002), for example, argued that evidence shows that there is a dramatic increase in Internet use, and that "if things continue at this rate, it will not be long before virtually everyone who wants to connect can," and that "The DOC report proves that even lower income people can get wired if they see it as a priority." Brady, writing in 2000, agrees that there is no need for government to assist those who lack access to ICTs to acquire such access: "Computers and Web appliances are now relatively cheap, and free Internet access is available in many areas. Even lower income families could find a way to get wired if they viewed it as a high enough priority" (Brady, 2000). But even if they could not be, he does not see a great problem, arguing that the differences are not surprising. They merely reflect differences that already exist between rich and poor, and, in any case, lack of access does not matter much anyway; many other things are more important. Compaine (2001) also argues that there is nothing new, and that the digital divide is just a new label for the old concept of information haves and have-nots.

Leigh and Atkinson (2001), like Arrison, take the view that the digital divide is bridging itself, and that a strong case has not been made for government intervention. They do argue, however, that, given that providing government information online is financially attractive, governments have an interest in forms of intervention that assist citizens to access online information. They suggest that governments:

- Provide matching funds to support private sector community information technology alliances
- Create regional technology access and distribution centres
- Monitor gaps in broadband access

Others, writing about digital divides in countries other than Australia, have suggested that current discussions of digital divides do not reflect "real" moral problems at all, but the strategic interests of individuals and groups concerned to promote technology as a solution to all life's problems. Kevin McSorley, for instance, discussing the British context, argues that discussions of the digital divide:

can be best understood as providing a generative resource through which the various political interests represented in the DOT [Digital Opportunity Task Force] process can normatively reconfigure the conceptual and ethical possibilities it signifies to renew a dominant, singular "secular salvation story" of the global. (McSorley, 2003, p. 75)

On a related note, Kenneth Hacker and Shana Mason argue that current analyses of data pertaining to the digital divide tend not to recognize the ethical dimension of digital divides, and remain too closely linked to the political agendas of the agencies who collect digital divide data (Hacker & Mason, 2003, p. 99).

Despite the chorus of optimistic voices, and a number of more dismissive ones, we argue in this chapter that there is a digital divide problem facing Australians in rural areas of the country, and that, more generally, the diminishing minority of citizens who lack access to new information and communication technologies in an increasingly networked society are likely to face increasing levels of disadvantage as a result. While there is evidence that the proportion of people with access to the Internet is growing in highly developed countries such as Australia and the United States, and that in this sense the divide is narrowing, this does not show that there is no problem now, or that there will not remain one for certain groups. Overwhelmingly the literature supports the conclusion that there is a digital divide problem, and that some kind of government intervention to alleviate it is justified.

What is the Digital Divide?

The digital divide, we saw earlier, marks a gap between those people who have a high level of access to the new information and communication technologies, and those people who have little or no access to those technologies. Given this initial characterization of the digital divide, it is tempting to define it in the following way: "A digital divide exists within a society when some members of that society have access to information and communication technologies and other members of that society lack access to those technologies."

While this is useful as a working definition, it has two related problems. One is that it suggests that the digital divide is a simple matter of some members of a society not owning information and communication technologies, and conceals the need for a more fine-grained analysis. The other problem with this definition that it gives the impression that the way to solve the problem is simply to make networked computers available to everyone. Early responses to the digital divide tended to fall prey to these unfortunate implications, and focused on providing computer hardware to citizens, to the detriment of other important needs, such as providing training in information literacy, the special needs of the disabled, isolated and disadvantaged. A better, more fine-grained way of looking at the problem is in terms of connectivity, a concept that incorporates three different components that are all necessary for citizens to have roughly similar levels of opportunity to benefit from the new information and communication technologies, to the same or to similar degrees.[1]

Connectivity has three main components: *access, ability,* and *affordability.* All come in degrees. For example, skills levels of computer users vary, and so do the hardware and software components of individual computers. Adequate access, ability and affordability can be defined as follows:

- **Adequate access:** A person has adequate access to new information and communication technologies when either she has home Internet access, or she is easily able to reach a public access Internet-linked computer (or other device) that is technically capable of permitting her to perform at least basic Internet-based activities, and she has adequate time to use it.

- **Adequate ability:** A person has adequate Internet ability when she has the skills necessary to perform at least basic Internet-based activities and is at least moderately confident in those skills.

- **Adequate affordability:** Adequate access and adequate ability are available at adequate affordability, when a person can obtain both, without thereby causing herself significant financial disadvantage.

The important point for our purposes is that digital divides exist when some members of a society have a high level of connectivity, while others do not have an adequate level of *at least* one of the three components of connectivity. Adequate skills, and sufficient purchasing power to afford both access and skills training, are just as necessary as adequate access to new information and communication technologies.

One interesting point to be noted about this redefinition of the digital divide in terms of connectivity is the way that it shifts the issue some way away from inequality of access. Instead, connectivity reframes the issue in terms of what is necessary for all citizens to enjoy at least a minimal level of facility with and use of the information and communication technologies that increasingly pervade their lives and that are becoming increasingly essential to effective participation in complex modern societies. The concept of connectivity, rather than focusing on all inequalities in access to and use of ICTs (such as the inequality between those who can afford to play games or trade shares online and those who cannot), focuses on the absolute disadvantages facing those who lack the skills, money and access to participate in the information society. Accordingly, on this account of connectivity, when all members of a society have adequate connectivity, then no digital divide exists in that society.

Of course, there may be reasons also to abhor societies in which wealthier individuals are able to benefit themselves even further, vis-à-vis their fellow citizens, by taking advantage of the opportunities provided by new information and communication technologies. But this seems to us to be a problem of social and economic inequality more broadly, rather specifically a problem of access to information and communication technologies. While we acknowledge that the relationship between inequalities in access to new information and communication technologies and other forms of inequality may also be morally significant, our discussion of the digital divide does not touch on these issues.

So far in this chapter, the notion of connectivity, and the definition of its components, are characterized only broadly; we discuss them in more detail below. But first we turn to an important preliminary question, that of whether there is in fact a rural digital divide in Australia.

The Rural Situation:
Is There a Rural-Urban Digital Divide?

While it is widely agreed that there is a digital divide that requires the attention of policy makers, is there a digital divide between metropolitan and rural areas? It is often suggested that there is. In a recent review of a book by Compaine, Shade (2001) says:

A variety of socio-demographic characteristics were recognized as increasing (or inhibiting) access, including income, education, gender, race, ethnicity, age, linguistic background, and location (rural versus urban).

Here, location is grouped with income, education and so on as a factor in the divide. Adams (2001) makes a similar claim, saying that, "education, *geography* [our emphasis], age, income, ethnic origin and so on, are all important."

But is geography, or location, really a factor in Australia? There is a difference between Internet access in rural and metropolitan areas, although not an enormous one. According to the most recent statistics from the Australian Bureau of Statistics, those for 2002 and 2003, the percentages for household Internet are:

Household Computer and Internet Access

	Computer access (% of households)					Internet access (% of households)				
	1999	2000	2001	2002	2003	1999	2000	2001	2002	2003
In capital cities	51	55	62	65	69	25	36	47	50	56
Outside capital cities	40	48	52	54	61	15	26	34	39	47
All households	47	53	58	61	66	22	32	42	46	53

Source: Australian Bureau of Statistics (2004)

This is only a difference of 9% in levels of household Internet access, but it must be noted that the figures are for access from *home*. In metropolitan areas it is more likely that people will have convenient access to Internet cafes, libraries with Internet facilities, and perhaps schools and other facilities, so the real difference is perhaps greater. Fewer figures are available regarding this disparity. One set of potentially useful figures from the Australian Bureau of Statistics lists levels of general Internet access, at home or otherwise, in and outside capital cities. Here a larger gap of 11% is discernible:

Adults (over 18) Accessing the Internet

	1998	1999	2000	2001	2002
In capital cities	35%	45%	50%	58%	62%
Outside capital cities	25%	33%	40%	47%	51%
Total	31%	41%	46%	54%	58%

Source: Australian Bureau of Statistics (2004)

As the table shows, nearly two thirds of adults in of capital cities access the Internet, compared with just over half the adults who live outside capital cities.

But a further fact that must also be taken into account is that rural areas are not all alike. A resident of a provincial city with a university, for example, is in a rather different position from someone living in an isolated area hundreds of kilometres from any reasonably sized centre of population. Despite there being only a small difference between metropolitan and rural areas in general, there could well be a marked difference between metropolitan and isolated rural areas. The only figures available compare home Internet access on farms with home access in general, in 1999. On those figures, 17.7% of farms had home Internet access, while 25% of homes in general had access. Here again the real difference is probably greater. Few who live on the farms without an Internet connection would have convenient access the Internet in a library or Internet café. It would seem then that there are significant differences between levels of Internet access in urban and rural Australia.

This is further borne out by available figures on broadband access in rural Australia, discussed in a recent report commissioned by the Rural Industries Research and Development Corporation and the Australian Local Government Association (Wondu Business and Technology Services, 2004). The report's executive summary includes the following observations:

There are significant differences in the level of adoption of broadband in agriculture (19% adoption rate in Australia for suppliers of goods and services for agriculture, compared with 82% in the USA). Some of the difference is due to the much larger size of USA agricultural supply firms and that large firms tend to have higher broadband adoption levels, but there are also unexplained issues because Australian suppliers generally have the same access to low-cost ADSL as USA suppliers and a high proportion of them have tertiary education, two factors normally associated with high levels of broadband adoption.

The report notes that, compared with 89% of urban local government councils, only 59% of rural councils use broadband. While many of the under-serviced regions of Australia noted in the report are sparsely populated, there are some sizeable populations, not to mention many small and isolated rural and regional communities that would benefit from greater access to ICTs, located in the areas of poorest service.

It has been argued that, while there is a difference between metropolitan and rural Internet connectivity, this can be accounted for by factors other than region.

Once other factors have been taken into account, region of residence on its own has no significant impact on Internet take-up at home. The observed differences between metropolitan, other urban and rural areas can be fully explained by sociodemographic characteristics of the population, particularly the lower qualification levels and lower incomes of the non-metropolitan population. (Lloyd & Hellwig, 2000, p. 20)

In this vein, Curtin notes that, "Rural and provincial electorates have fewer young, tertiary educated people and high income earners than city electorates, factors which

determine Internet usage" (Curtin, 2001, p. i). Australian Bureau of Statistics figures also illustrate that there is a strong positive correlation between rural Internet
access and larger farm size (an indicator of wealth), providing further support for
the claim that lower levels of income in rural Australia may partly explain lower
levels of Internet access:

Use of Computers and Internet for Business Purposes on Farms
(132 983 farms at June 2003)

Farm size*	Computer use June 2002	Internet use June 2002	Computer use June 2003	Internet use June 2003
All farm sizes	53%	43%	54%	46%
Less than $50 000			38%	30%
$50 000-$149 000			49%	40%
$150 000-$249 000			61%	50%
$250 000-$499 000			72%	62%
$500 000-$999 000			80%	73%
$1 million or more			85%	79%

estimated value of agricultural operations
Source: Australian Bureau of Statistics (2003)

Two other factors mentioned by Curtin that differentiate rural from metropolitan
areas are cost and transmission rate. According to her figures, based on figures from
the Australian of Bureau Statistics, 36.7% of farms spend $101-$250 per annum on
Internet costs while the figure for all homes was $32.6 (these are 1999 figures for
farms and 1998 figures for all homes). For the same years, 23.7% of farms spent
$251-$500 per annum while the figure for all homes was 19%.

In their more recent research, Wondu Business and Technology Services note similar
disparities, and observe that cost is one of the major factors discouraging migration
to broadband services in rural Australia:

*Australia . . . is a land of contrasts with some of the most expensive and also some
of the least expensive broadband in the world. Where there is competition and
higher population density the prices tend to be lower and competitive, though low
broadband speed and download limits tend to limit competitiveness.* (Wondu Business and Technology Services, 2004, p. 9)

Not only is there a cost difference, there is also a difference in connection speeds,
as can be seen in the following table:

Network Coverage and Transmission Rate by Region

	2.4 kilobit per second	9.6 kilobit per second	14.4 kilobit per second	28.8 kilobit per second
Urban and provincial centres	100 %	99 %	95 %	75 %
Rural and remote areas	99 %	90 %	85 %	60 %

Source: Besley (2000, p. 103) reproduced in Curtin (2001, p. 8)

Substantially fewer people in rural and remote regions can access the Internet at the higher speeds necessary for effective Web browsing. The disadvantage of lower connection speeds is directly associated with living in a rural area.

But even where it is other factors, such as lower income or education levels, that limit the take-up of new information and communication technologies in rural Australia, rather than living in a rural area *per se*, this indirect disadvantage is still importantly relevant for considering the rural digital divide. Simply put, this is because, if the lower incomes that discourage Internet access among inhabitants of rural Australia result from the fact that they live in rural areas, then the digital divide in question can still be characterized as rural, rather than simply as economic. The generally lower levels of income in rural Australia have a direct negative impact on rural levels of connectivity. In other words, it seems reasonable to suppose that there are inequalities of access to information and communication technologies and the affordability of those technologies, between rural Australians and their urban counterparts. There is a rural digital divide in Australia.

It is a further question how serious this digital divide is for Australians who live in rural areas. As we have argued in this chapter, access to and familiarity with the new information and communication technologies are becoming increasingly important, if not absolutely necessary, for full participation in the life of the Australian community. Australian governments, at all levels, are committed to continuing to transfer information, functions and transactions online, and to encourage citizens to interact with government online, rather than by other means. As time passes, the social and economic exclusion associated with lack of connectivity can only become greater. This would suggest, then, that the rural digital divide in Australia, where limitations to at least two components of connectivity—access and affordability—appear to be hindering rural uptake of new information and communication technologies is a serious matter. We now turn to a fuller characterization of the three components of connectivity, to flesh out what exactly citizens need to qualify as possessing connectivity.

The Needs of the Disadvantaged

Earlier we gave an account of connectivity in terms of access, ability and affordability. This account provides a way of looking at the main connectivity needs shared by all of the digital divide target groups considered in our study of the digital divide in the ACT (Rooksby, Weckert & Lucas, 2002, p. 4).[2] Many of these are needs that have already been recognized within the "digital divide" literature, and most of them are relevant to the situation of rural Australians, as we illustrate below.

Adequate Access

Adequate access requires that people either own or can easily and conveniently borrow or visit the new information and communication technologies they need to participate at least minimally in social, economic, and government-related aspects of the information society. First, people need *an easily reachable Internet terminal* with a bandwidth speed sufficient to use standard Internet Web pages without substantial delay. The provision of home Internet access points to households based in rural areas would clearly qualify, although it would not be a cheap option for any government to pursue. It could be made more affordable if it were also means-tested, or targeted specifically at those who face additional difficulties in obtaining connectivity (such as people with a disability, people from lower socio-economic groups and seniors).

A nearby public IT access centre that is not overcrowded would reach many people, but not all, but would also be relatively more costly in rural areas than in urban areas. Some people cannot cheaply reach any public IT access centre, either because they do not live near public transport and lack private transport, or because they have disabilities or conditions that mean that they are unable to travel. Home Internet access is essential to provide these people with adequate access. This is particularly important in rural and remote areas, where public transport is often not available at all, and there are no Internet access points available anywhere in the vicinity. A separate strategy to pursue is to ensure that Internet terminals provide adequate bandwidth, with government subsidy of IT infrastructure in rural areas.

Second, members of all groups need *computers that allow them to perform at least a basic range of Internet-related activities*. General needs are for a fairly recent Internet-capable, Internet-linked computer, containing hardware and software that will allow them to perform the range of basic Internet-related activities that a definition of "adequate access" must encompass. These are: word-processing, e-mail, Web browsing and searching, use of newsgroups, discussion groups and chat facilities, downloading information, saving information to a local location or a floppy disk, and printing. Again, special needs will vary widely for this category. Some people need assistive devices and technologies. Others need access to special software, such as accounting, resume-writing and spreadsheet or database software.[3] This again is of particular relevance in areas where connection speeds are low. Access may be suitable for text-based email but not for Web browsing.

Finally, all groups need *adequate information about access*. This is because even where people do have adequate access to new information and communication technologies, and would gladly use that access if they were aware of it, they may still be unaware of the fact that they do have access. Adequate information might be provided through the publication of a small booklet about what exactly is available to them, and how they might get best use out of it, and the distribution of this book to local meeting places in rural towns. This leads us into the issue of adequate ability.

Adequate Ability

Generally, people in all groups need access to appropriate training in appropriate locations (for some people home will be the only option). Appropriate training covers a wide range of training needs. Both very basic and relatively advanced training courses should be available at affordable rates. Additionally, it is important that the provision of courses that provide successful participants with some form of accreditation of certification be prioritized. This is particularly important for people who might use the training they have acquired to seek employment. We list five types of general ability need below.

First, some members of all groups will need *very basic classes with small groups of students*, since their IT skills and confidence are so low that they will need a great deal of individual attention and encouragement to make progress. Second, some members of all groups will need *classes that are operated in accessible locations*. This could include local community groups, local TAFEs (colleges of technical and further education) and primary and high schools (already in practice), and local libraries. In some rural areas of course, there may be no schools or libraries close by, so alternative arrangements would need to be made. One such alternative is the provision of online training suitable for the beginner, such as provided by Victoria's Skills.net. This approach, however, is necessarily unsuitable for the computer-illiterate, and may not suit people from non-English-speaking backgrounds, including Indigenous Australians.

Third, there will be a need for *special services for those who cannot easily reach any existing training venue*. This may involve special transport arrangements for the disabled or frail, or at-home training for people with disabilities, complex needs, or for those in culturally diverse circumstances. Such people may need specifically tailored training, such as training in the use of special software packages. There may also need to be at-home training for some people located in rural areas, including members of remote Indigenous communities.

Fourth, there is a need for *community-wide ability supports*. Many people who ring technical help-lines do so because they are not confident about how to use software packages. These people also need "on-call computer use advice" —an 1800 phone line would be the cheapest option for members of digital divide target groups. Having good, affordable, telephone assistance is even more important in areas where distances are too great for easy travel.

Finally, with regard to people having confidence in their IT skills and abilities, *confidence building strategies* are needed: a system for encouraging the perception that people are capable of using the Internet. Such initiatives could be used to help people see that the Internet satisfies needs that they have, such as saving time and travel, locating information, keeping in touch with family and friends, and so on.

Adequate Affordability

Affordability is an important limitation on the take-up of new information and communication technologies, despite the words to the contrary from some digital divide sceptics. As the data show, rural people have lower incomes than their city counterparts, and face higher setup and recurrent costs for Internet access.

Affordability of new information and communication technologies varies in a range of ways. Of course, poor people find things less affordable than wealthy people, so generic measures of affordability (e.g., average price relative to average income) do not really address affordability for the worst-off. Particularly in societies that are not egalitarian, the worst-off may have much less disposable income than even those on the median income.

First, people with home Internet access need to face only *affordable setup costs* for using that access. Setup costs include connection to the Internet, and the purchase of necessary peripherals such as modems. If setup costs are substantial, this poses both a financial hurdle to worse-off rural households, and a psychological disin- centive. This might come in the form of means-tested subsidies for setup costs. Community organizations providing Internet access to digital divide target groups likewise may need some form of discount on setup costs to be able to afford to provide that access.

Second, people with home Internet access need to face only *affordable recurring costs for computer and Internet use*. Recurring costs include hardware maintenance, troubleshooting for hardware- and software-related difficulties, and ISP charges. These needs could be met, respectively, by a call centre for IT troubleshooting, some subsidy for maintenance costs, and subsidies provided by ISPs under a social service charter (on which further research is required). This, we saw in the previous section, is a particular issue in some rural areas where telephone costs are high. ISP charges continue, as we showed earlier, to be higher in some rural areas than in urban areas, despite years of undertakings from the partly-privatized national telephony company Telstra to increase access and reduce costs for rural Australians.

Third, some people with special needs, primarily people with a disability, will face higher establishment costs for Internet access, and perhaps higher recurring costs as well. The need for access to special equipment and software is set out above; affordability of that equipment is also an important aspect of connectivity for people with a disability. This is especially the case because of existing correlations between disability and low income, which mean that people with a disability are in a worse position than the average citizen to afford computer and Internet technology, let alone complex and expensive assistive devices. This challenge may be particularly severe in rural Australia where services are often more limited than in urban areas.

We should also remember that, while the price of new technologies tends to decrease rapidly and hence to increase affordability of computers and other ICTs, this does not necessarily mean that computers are good value investments. Computers and many other new information and communication technologies depreciate rapidly, become obsolete rapidly, and break down regularly, often requiring expensive repairs and upgrades. While the cost of an average personal computer with a given set of specifications may decline year on year, the specifications required for a personal computer to perform basic functions and to run standard software packages increase; regular upgrades are important to maintain the functionality of home computer systems. Similarly, on the supply side, every year Web sites become more graphics- and animation-intensive, requiring higher-powered computers to access them. These factors, unfortunately, mean that the cost of keeping up with technological change is not negligible.

Motivation

Motivation to use computers and the Internet is rather a different issue from physical access, affordability or ability. It would not appear to be an element in connectivity. We consider it here because lack of interest in new technologies also appears to be a commonly cited reason why people in some digital divide target groups, such as seniors, women and people from a non-English speaking background, may be reluctant to use computers or the Internet. This fact must be taken seriously by any government that is keen to ensure that all citizens have connectivity.

For, whatever is believed about the benefits of full connectivity to *society as a whole* (e.g., lower costs for service delivery, greater integration, more effective communication), it remains a fact, that for many people who are poor, or have low educational qualifications, the perceived benefits of connectivity *to them* are outweighed by the perceived costs *to them*. And some of them are probably right in their perceptions, given the current costs of connectivity. Given the current purchase and maintenance costs of computers, phone-calls, and ISP charges, and the low budget of many people on low incomes, such people are probably better off, in the short term at least, spending their money on clothing, housing, food, health services and other necessities.

To some extent, lack of motivation to use new information and communication technologies may spring directly from lack of affordability. So, we might hope that, if the costs listed earlier were substantially reduced, one of the main barriers to full connectivity would also be substantially reduced. We believe, in line with findings by Lloyd and Hellwig (2000), that, as costs come down, levels of connectivity within Australia will increase. Governments at the federal and state levels are also in a position to test this proposition by putting in place subsidies and grants that will reduce the cost of computer and Internet access for the very poorest and neediest members of society.

But there are other barriers too, such as perceptions that computers and the Internet are "not for me," "not part of my lifestyle or culture," or just plain "boring, a waste of time." People who come from non-English speaking backgrounds, such as Indigenous Australians, may find that the Internet contains little material in their own language, so that even affordable access does not give them as much benefit as it does English speakers. Such views are not necessarily associated with perceptions of low affordability, lack of training, or lack of access, but with perceptions of the functions of new information and communication technologies, and specifically perceptions that these functions will not be useful or beneficial.

Some of these perceptions may well be perfectly accurate. Nevertheless, as we argued previously, new ICTs are increasingly prevalent in all aspects of developed societies, and failure to participate in them is, as time goes on, likely to further disadvantage and isolate the diminishing minority of people who do not have connectivity. This means that, even where there is resistance to adopting new information and communication technologies, this resistance may in some instances be unrealistic, the result of lack of experience of new ICTs, or of an incomplete grasp of the benefits (and costs) that are associated with them. Accordingly, and given that most developed country governments are already firmly committed to a move to e-government, there may be some reason to try to influence motivational structures to encourage those who do not use new ICTs to appreciate their benefits.

Further, publicity campaigns could be introduced to illustrate the uses of computers and the Internet to digital divide target groups. For example, advertisements could show positive images, such as a senior citizen keeping in touch with their family or finding useful information on the Internet, an Indigenous person finding family history or keeping in touch with family members, a young person finding job opportunities, or meeting new friends online, immigrants to Australia reading online newspapers from their country of origin or e-mailing friends at home, a single parent with a sick child paying bills from home rather than leaving the child alone. In fact, campaigns of this sort targeted at older Australians seem to have been in part responsible for the increasing uptake of Internet services by older Australians over the last two or three years. It remains to be seen whether similar changes will occur in rural Australia, where significant affordability and access barriers remain.

A range of other options for encouraging citizens to experiment with new information and communication technologies is also open. One such further option is that of seeding the community with IT users, by use of selective grants of computers and Internet access to the most disadvantaged, for example, by granting computers to schoolchildren from low socio-economic groups, or with an Aboriginal or Torres Strait Islander background, who successfully complete an IT course at school. This is likely to encourage greater connectivity, since interest in the Internet often spreads through personal connections among family and friends. Once one member of a peer group has had experience of the benefits of new information and communication technologies, news of these benefits can spread through peer networks.

Caution is needed with the use of any type of incentive, however. Governments should only employ ethically acceptable incentives, namely incentives that do not at the same time work as *de facto* penalties against those who do not take up the incentives. For example, giving people a discount on service charges if they pay their bills, fines or rates online effectively penalizes those who do not pay online. Similarly, if a project to give needy students a free home PC is not tightly targeted, it will not be equitable; and, whether the project is equitable or not, it runs the risk, if insensitively run, of discouraging those who miss out. Governments should also be mindful of the fact that there may be good reasons behind some citizens' lack of motivation to use new information and communication technologies, such as affordability and ability barriers. In such cases, encouragement to use new information and communication technologies may be ineffective unless complemented by measures to reduce those other barriers.

What is Being Done for Rural Communities?

Various initiatives are in place around Australia that are designed to encourage Internet use in rural areas, in part by providing financial and motivational incentives, and in part by subsidising the provision of (public) Internet access. These are provided by both state and Commonwealth governments. At the Commonwealth level, the document *Australia's Strategic Framework for the Information Economy 2004-2006* (hereafter referred to as the *Strategic Framework*) (Department of Communications, Information Technology and the Arts, 2004a) provides the broad policy framework within which assistance will be delivered over the next year and a half. Taking over from the old *Networking the Nation* initiative of 1997-2004, the new *Strategic Framework* contains one strategy specifically relating to rural Australians, as well as a strategy for increasing broadband coverage nationally. Several of its initiatives are intended to address the recommendations of the Regional Telecommunications Inquiry (also known as the Estens Inquiry) in *Connecting Regional Australia.*[4]

Strategy 1.1 of the *Strategic Framework* is to "develop the networks and capability needed by people living in regional communities, indigenous Australians, older Australians, people with disabilities and others facing economic or social barriers to participation in the information economy" (Department of Communications, Information Technology and the Arts, 2004a, p. 33). Initiatives targeting rural communicates include:

$15.9 million to extend land-based mobile phone services to small population centres and key highways in regional Australia; $4 million to extend a satellite handset subsidy for people in areas of Australia outside terrestrial and mobile phone coverage; $10.1 million funding to provide IT training and support services in areas where commercial training or support services are not accessible; the development of strategies to sustain online access centres for public access, training, and government services, including to indigenous communities.[5]

Under the *Strategic Framework*, the Telecommunications Action Plan for Remote Indigenous Communities (TAPRIC), improves telecommunications services to remote Indigenous communities, and includes language resources for five Indigenous language groups (Department of Communications, Information Technology and the Arts, 2004a, p. 34). This initiative directly addresses the accessibility, affordability and motivational problems faced by remote Indigenous communities in relation to new information and communication technologies.

Strategy 1.3 of the *Strategic Framework*, which contains the main financial commitment made to rural communities, is to "promote investment in broadband infrastructure, content, capabilities and networks in regional areas and key industry sectors" (Department of Communications, Information Technology and the Arts, 2004a, p. 36), and thus addresses the rural digital divide. Initiatives funded as part of this strategy include $50 million "for a National Communications Fund to support the roll-out of large-scale infrastructure and high-speed telecommunications networks to deliver education and health services to users in regional and rural Australia" (Department of Communications, Information Technology and the Arts, 2004a, p. 36). Additionally, some of the "elements of TAPRIC, such as the Online Access Centre Business Study and Internet Access Program, provide enhanced access to remote areas" (Department of Communications, Information Technology and the Arts 2004a, p. 36). Some of the initiatives in the *Strategic Framework*, such as "the development of strategies to sustain online access centres for public access, training and government services" and the provision of specific assistance to people with disabilities (Department of Communications, Information Technology and the Arts 2004a, p. 33), remain unfunded.

In addition to broadband initiatives funded under the *Strategic Framework*, funding at the Commonwealth level has been provided through the National Broadband Strategy (Department of Communications, Information Technology and the Arts, 2004b), announced in the 2004 federal budget. This provides for a total of $142.8 million over four years, from 2003-2004 to 2006-2007. The action plan for this Strategy is "to improve the prices and increase the availability of broadband services in regional, rural and remote Australia, with a particular focus on consumers, SMEs [small and medium enterprises] and the health and education sectors." Funding initiatives include the $107.8 million Higher Bandwidth Incentive Scheme (HiBIS) to ensure the wider availability of broadband services by providing subsidies to service providers to offer broadband to regional, rural and remote areas at prices comparable to those available in metropolitan Australia. HiBIS is also intended to encourage greater competition among service providers (Department of Communications, Information Technology and the Arts, 2004b). Commonwealth initiatives on broadband initiatives are also informed by another government-funded report, *Broadband Adoption by Agriculture and Local Government Councils* (Wondu Business and Technology Services, 2004).

At the state level, a number of initiatives have been set up in recent years. Many of these complement the strategic efforts of the commonwealth government, as state-based initiatives tend to focus on issues other than broadband coverage. In New South Wales, for example, the CTC@NSW programme is a major NSW/Commonwealth Government initiative to establish community technology centres (CTCs) throughout regional NSW. The funded CTCs provide a wide range of services, programs and facilities designed to support the social economic, cultural and educational life of people in small rural NSW towns. CTCs are located throughout NSW targeting areas that need them most, small communities with less than 3000 people (CTC@ NSW, 2002). The Victorian Government's Connecting Communities strategy operates throughout Victoria's library branches through the Libraries Online program. The access@schools program provides the wider community with access to Internet equipped workstations in schools, including schools in rural and remote areas. The Skills.net program provides free or affordable Internet training and access to those Victorians who would not otherwise have such access. In particular, Skills.net is assisting technologically disadvantaged communities, including those in rural and remote Victoria (*Multimedia Victoria—Connecting Communities*, 2001). At present, debate continues about how best to maintain the viability of online access centres, which were well funded in the initial stage, but have an uncertain future (see, for example, Department of Communications, Information Technology and the Arts 2003a, p. 1).

Both commonwealth and state governments accept that there is a rural digital divide problem in Australia, and that they have some responsibility to assist in alleviating the divide. The range and type of initiatives discussed earlier suggests that governments are aware of the access, affordability and ability dimensions of connectivity, and that work is being put, in particular, into addressing access and ability constraints to higher connectivity in rural areas of Australia. Less work appears to be happening in relation to the ability dimension, and it would appear that the "recurring costs" component of some initiatives, particularly online access centres, may need additional attention. The motivational issues we discussed as being one aspect of affordability appear to be less well addressed by the current range of initiatives.

One particularly contentious issue that overshadows discussion of rural telecommunications in rural Australia is the fate of Telstra, the partially government-owned telecommunications giant that provides the backbone of telecommunications infrastructure in Australia. Telstra currently subsidizes the cost of services to regional Australia, although, even with subsidization, telecommunications costs are higher in rural areas than in metropolitan areas. Under the Howard government, Telstra has been partially privatized, and there is a standing intention to move to full privatization of Telstra in the future. This intention is strongly resisted by rural lobby groups and by some members of the National Party, which is presently part of the governing coalition. It is widely agreed that a privatized Telstra would be unlikely to provide comparable levels of service and affordability to rural Australia in the future, so that privatization is likely to exacerbate the rural digital divide in Australia.

The federal government has made an undertaking not to privatize Telstra fully until standards of telecommunications service to rural Australia attain benchmarks set out in the Regional Telecommunications Inquiry, and the strategies set out in the *Strategic Framework* are intended to ensure that those benchmarks are obtained. Yet there is persistent disagreement about whether they have indeed been attained, or are likely to be. The government is confident that they have been attained, or will be shortly, while advocates for rural communities, such as the National Farmers Federation claim that action taken to date is insufficient and that rural communities are still short of equality with metropolitan areas (NFF in call on phones, 2005). Hence, the generally positive picture regarding government initiatives to bridge the rural digital divide should be accepted with reservations. If the full sale of Telstra goes ahead, it is unlikely that the government will have anything like its current capacity to intervene in the provision of telecommunications services in rural Australia, and the rural digital divide might only widen.

Conclusion

In this chapter we have tried to show what the digital divide is, and what the typical needs are of those on the wrong side, whether in rural areas or not. While there is no consensus that geography in itself matters, we raised some considerations that suggest that it might. Additionally, research by Curtin has showed that cost and connectivity speeds disadvantage more rural than non-rural people, and this is a function of living away from large population centres. So in our view, geography does matter! We also indicated that geography may be causally connected to some of the other factors that put rural citizens on the wrong side of the digital divide, such as low income and low educational attainment. Finally, by considering a few initiatives, it was noted that various governments are aware of the problems rural Australians face in gaining connectivity and are trying to overcome them. In a developed country like Australia, the Internet is quickly becoming indispensable, whether for work, social life or interacting with private and government organizations. Hence it is quickly becoming essential that all members of Australian society, including those located in rural areas of Australia, have the wherewithal to use the Internet.

References

Adams, A. R. (2001). Introduction: Beyond numbers and demographics: "Experience-near" explorations of the digital divide. *Computers and Society, 31*(3), 5-8.

Arrison, S. (2002, March 13). What digital divide? *Tech News—CNET News.Com.* Retrieved from http://news.com.com/2010-1078-858537.html

Australian Bureau of Statistics. (2003). *Use of information technology on farms, Australia* (8150.0). Canberra, Australia: A.C.T.

Australian Bureau of Statistics. (2004). *Household use of information technology, Australia, 2002 and 2003* (8146.0). Canberra, Australia: A.C.T.

Besley, T. (2000). *Connecting Australia.* Report of the Telecommunications Service Inquiry. Retrieved from http://www.telinquiry.gov.au/

Brady, M. (2000, August 4). The digital divide myth. *E-Commerce Times.* Retrieved from http://www.ecommercetimes.com/perl/story/3953.html

Compaine, B. M. (2001). *The digital divide: Facing a crisis or creating a myth?* Cambridge, MA: MIT Press.

CTC@NSW. (2002). Web site available at http://www.ctcnsw.gov.au

Curtin, J. (2001). *A digital divide in rural and regional Australia?* Department of the Parliamentary Library, Information and Research Services (Current Issues Brief No. 1 2001-02). Retrieved from http://www.aph.gov.au/library/pubs/CIB/2001-02/02cib01.htm

Department of Communications, Information Technology and the Arts. (2003a). *Maintaining the viability of online access centres in regional, rural and remote Australia.* Retrieved from http://www.dcita.gov.au/__data/assets/word_doc/7789/Maintaining_Viability_of_Online_Access_Centres_Regional_Rural_Remote_Australia_-_Discussion_Paper.doc

Department of Communications, Information Technology and the Arts. (2003b). *The government's response to the regional telecommunications inquiry.* Retrieved from http://www.dcita.gov.au/tel/regional,_rural_and_remote_communications/telecommunication_inquiry_-_government_response/the_governments_response_to_the_recommendations_of_the_regional_telecommunications_inquiry

Department of Communications, Information Technology and the Arts. (2004a). *Australia's strategic framework for the information economy 2004-2006.* Retrieved from http://www.dcita.gov.au/__data/assets/pdf_file/20457/New_SFIE_July_2004_final.pdf

Department of Communications, Information Technology and the Arts. (2004b). *Australian national broadband strategy.* Retrieved from http://www.dcita.gov.au/ie/publications/2004/march/australian_national_broadband_strategy

Hacker, K. L., & Mason, S. M. (2003). Ethical gaps in studies of the digital divide. *Ethics and Information Technology, 5*(2), 99-115.

Leigh, A., & Atkinson, R. D. (2001, June). *Clear thinking on the digital divide.* Progressive Policy Institute (PPI) Policy Report. Retrieved from http://www.dlc.org/documents/digital_divide.pdf

Lloyd, R., & Hellwig, O. (2000). *Barriers to the take-up of new technology* (NATSEM Discussion Paper No. 53). Retrieved from http://www.natsem.canberra.edu.au/publications/papers/dps/dp53/dp53.pdf

McSorley, K. (2003). The secular salvation story of the digital divide. *Ethics and Information Technology, 5*(2), 75-87.

Mossberger, K., Tolbert, C. J., & Stansbury, M. (2003). *Virtual inequality: Beyond the digital divide.* Washington DC: Georgetown University Press.

Multimedia Victoria – Connecting Communities. (2001). Retrieved from http://www.mmv.vic.gov.au/uploads/downloads/Resource_Centre/ConnectingCommunities1.pdf

National Office for the Information Economy. (2000). *National office for the information economy.* Retrieved from http://www.noie.gov.au/projects/access/community/digitaldivide/Ddaccesscentres.doc

NFF in call on phones. (2005, April 20). *The Weekly Times*. Retrieved from http://global.factiva.com/

Regional Telecommunications Inquiry. (2002). *Regional telecommunications inquiry (Estens Report)*. Retrieved from http://www.telinquiry.gov.au/rti-report.html

Rooksby, E., Weckert, J., & Lucas, R. (2002). *Bridging the digital divide: A study into connectivity issues for disadvantaged people*. Report prepared for ACT Information Management, Australian Capital Territory (unpublished).

Shade, L. (2001). Review of *The digital divide: Facing a crisis or creating a myth*, B. M. Compaine, Cambridge, MA: MIT Press. *Computers and Society, 31*(2), 42-43.

Warschauer, M. (2002). Reconceptualizing the digital divide. *First Monday, 7*(7). Retrieved from http://www.firstmonday.dk/issues/issue7_7/warschauer/

Wondu Business and Technology Services. (2004). *Broadband adoption by agriculture and local government councils—Australia and the U.S.A.* Retrieved from http://www.rirdc.gov.au/reports/HCC/04-127.pdf

Endnotes

[1] Some recent work on the digital divide has suggested that the concept itself is misleading and should be replaced by other conceptual frameworks, such as the concept of technology for digital inclusion (Warschauer, 2002). Our discussion of connectivity in this chapter (particularly our use of a standard of "adequacy" rather than of "equality" in levels of connectivity) can be considered as part of a move away from the most simplistic, binary understanding of digital divides, towards an inclusion-based conceptual framework.

[2] Our study also included six major target groups: seniors, people with a disability, people of Aboriginal or Torres Strait Islander descent, women, people from a non-English-speaking background (NESB), and members of a low socio-economic group.

[3] Many need Web sites and other content designed for low literacy levels, poor vision, or the use of computers with non-optimal hardware and software. This involves the use of universal design for Web sites.

[4] In its response to the Regional Telecommunications Inquiry, the Commonwealth Government accepted all 39 of its recommendations (Department of Communications, Information Technology and the Arts, 2003b).

[5] This last initiative is intended to complement the earlier Rural Transaction Centres Program. This program is designed for communities with populations under 3000, to help them establish centres that "provide access to basic transaction services, such as banking, post, phone, fax, the Internet, Centrelink Services and Medicare Easyclaim" (National Office for the Information Economy, 2000).

Chapter XIII

The Digital Divide within the Digital Community in Saudi Arabia

Yeslam Al-Saggaf
Charles Sturt University, Australia

Abstract

This chapter looks at the effects of the widening of the gap between the "haves" and "have-nots," in terms of the digital divide, in Saudi Arabia. It focuses on the divide among members of the Saudi society who already have access to the Internet and synthesises results from four studies about the Internet in Saudi Arabia conducted between 2000 and 2005. It discusses the factors that could be blamed for the digital divide in the country and some of the groups of people who have access to the Internet but are still among the "have-nots."

Introduction

While researchers in Western nations are becoming increasingly concerned about the effects of the widening of the gap between the so called "haves" and "have-nots" in their countries and across the globe, researchers in the Arab world, particularly in Saudi Arabia, have not yet started looking at the situation in their countries. This chapter takes a step in the direction of addressing the gap concerning the digital divide in Saudi Arabia. For the purposes of this chapter, the discussion of the digital divide will focus mainly on the divide among members of the Saudi society who already have access to the Internet. The situation will be described here by synthesising results from four studies about the Internet in Saudi Arabia conducted by this author between 2000 and 2005 (Al-Saggaf, 2004; Al-Saggaf & Weckert, 2005, 2005; Al-Saggaf, Weckert, & Williamson, 2002). After briefly discussing the digital divide in the literature, a discussion of the studies from which the results were obtained will be presented. Next, a discussion about the Internet in Saudi Arabia and the factors that could be blamed for the digital divide in the country will be offered. Finally, the chapter will talk about some of the groups of people who have access to the Internet yet still stand among the "have-nots."

The Digital Divide in the Literature

A quick look at the literature revealed that there are many definitions of the digital divide. Perhaps one of the most popular, and most often cited, definitions of the digital divide is that it refers to disparities in Internet access to, and usage of, information and communication technologies between rich countries and poor countries. Another popular definition is that it refers to the difference in access to, and usage of, information and communications technologies between people within the same country (Norris, 2001). For this chapter the latter definition will be used as it suits the situation of the digital divide in Saudi Arabia better than any other definition, because it looks at differences in access to, and usage of, the Internet among people within the same country who already have access to it.

The literature also revealed that most of the definitions attached to the "digital divide" vary in the way they ground the term—that is, identify its social, political or geographical context. This suggests that the "digital divide" issue is context-dependent. Indeed, there are many accounts of the digital divide, and each of them considers the issue from a specific context that is different to any other. Perhaps this is a good thing, because according to the literature, the term means different things to different people. Thus, if the term is not grounded in a particular context, it may leave wide open doors that could lead to misconceptions about the issue.

Hongladarom (2004) recognises the importance of context in understanding the notion of the digital divide. In his philosophical account about the digital divide he discusses the issue from a number of perspectives, including social, educational and non-western cultural philosophy. Recognising the role cultural context plays in shedding light on the digital divide, he makes the point that not everyone considers access to information technology a "good thing". Consequently, thinking about the digital divide as a social inequality may not be relevant in the case of some people who, for example, come from different cultural backgrounds. Confronted with this he raises the question "how non-western philosophies, such as the Buddhist or Chinese, can shed light on the digital divide problem?" (Hongladarom, 2004, p. 88).

Interestingly, Kitiyadisai (2004) offers an answer to Hongladarom's last question regarding providing a Buddhist perspective on the digital divide. Kitiyadisai notes that, while Western values encourage people to conquer the frontiers, Buddhist values emphasise spiritual development and living in moderation and harmony. Arguing from the view that different cultural contexts are very important when debating the digital divide, she notes that different groups of people encounter different types of problems depending on their social context. Thus, while teachers, researchers and students may be seriously at a disadvantage if the digital divide is not bridged, to groups of people suffering from malnutrition, disease and poverty, the digital divide is not relevant to their suffering. Towards the end of her article, Kitiyadisai suggests that Thai public policy makers should bridge the digital divide in the country from within a Buddhist perspective.

While Hongladarom is perhaps right in saying that not everyone considers access to information technology a "good thing," there is an underlying assumption that inequalities in access to technologies such as the Internet are a very serious and need immediate attention from everyone, particularly from governments. It is true that inequalities in access to a technology such as the Internet, for example, may deny people or groups of people, such as women, the elderly and the disabled, the opportunity to acquire knowledge, participate in the economy and in the civil and political society (Moss, 2005). However, this assumption fails to see the significance of the digital divide in these people's lives as compared to their other needs and pursuits in life, for example, for some, just staying alive.

There is also another underlying assumption regarding inequalities in access, in particular, to the Internet. Many assume that the problem of the digital divide will end when people are given access to the Internet. It is true that access to the Internet is an essential step towards alleviating the problem, but this assumption fails to take into account other factors, such as knowledge of how to use the Internet, which could be as important as the access to the technology. For example, the undereducated, despite the availability of access, may not still be able to use the technology to obtain the information that one could use to enhance his/her plan for life (Hongladarom, 2004). In the case of Saudi Arabia, for example, access to the Internet is one of the problems that is causing the digital divide among the people within the country; another is knowledge of how to best use the Internet. The biggest problem, however (as discussed next), lies in other factors such as culture. In the face of this, the situation of the digital divide should not then be looked at only from the perspective of access to communication technologies, but also from the perspective of other significant factors such as usage of communication technologies and/or culture.

So what can be done to bridge the digital divide? Although there are numerous studies that offer solutions to the problem (Hongladarom, 2004), there is, unfortunately, little agreement in the literature on what should be done about it (Fallis, 2004). Fallis regards the digital divide as inequalities in access to information technology, which, according to him, have implications for people's ability to acquire knowledge. He argues that the solution to the digital divide lies in identifying polices that address the problem. He also argues that in order to decide on an appropriate digital divide policy, we need to know exactly what our goal is with respect to the distribution of knowledge. Building on ideas from the theory of justice and social epistemology, he proposes that, rather than distributing knowledge "equally" among the members of society, knowledge should be distributed "equitably" or "fairly." According to him, while distributing knowledge "equally" would completely eliminate the digital divide, doing so may not necessarily benefit the less fortunate. To demonstrate his point, Fallis uses the example of the need to have more than one level of service in trains. He says that meeting this need means that the service can be provided to more people, as some may not be able to afford some of the levels of service. Thus, a digital divide policy that aims for a distribution of knowledge where the information "have-nots" have as much knowledge as possible is the most acceptable.

The Research

Philosophical Underpinnings

As mentioned earlier, the situation of the digital divide in Saudi Arabia is described here by synthesising results obtained from four studies about the Internet in Saudi Arabia conducted by this author between 2000 and 2005. The purpose of these studies was to understand, from the social, cultural and political contexts, how online forums are being used in Saudi Arabia and how they are affecting people. The studies were interpretive and naturalistic, and the method used in the collection of data followed a constructivist paradigm (Berger & Luckmann, 1967). Understanding the perspectives and meanings that people construct about their situations is what this paradigm is all about. Social construct theory provided the philosophical framework that guided the research method used in these studies and the way the results were grounded. Social constructivists take the effect of the social environment, culture and religion seriously when they look at how people form their perspective about their world. Social constructivists also point out that people co-create meaning when they interact with each other and that language and religion and other factors influence the creation of their meaning (Berger & Luckmann, 1967). In Saudi Arabia, religion and culture strongly influence the way people conduct themselves in relation to others. Thus, social construct theory seems suitable to use as a framework for studying online forums in Saudi Arabia.

From Philosophy to Method

Ethnography, one of the methods favoured by constructivists, was chosen for the mentioned studies. The method allows multiple realities and alternative interpretations of the results to be presented (Fetterman, 1989), which is a feature that is in line with the goal of constructivism. Ethnography also is very similar to participant-observation. For example, Saule (2000, p. 160) describes ethnographers as "studying people in their everyday contexts" and Minichiello et al. (1990, p. 18) describe participant-observation as "studying people by participating in social interactions with them in order to observe and understand them." Modern ethnography or participant-observation uses a range of techniques such as interviewing, focus groups, observation and questionnaires (Bow, 2000, p. 249).

Data were collected for these studies using a number of techniques. These were: silent observation of five online forums; a participant role taken by the author in an online forum similar to the observed ones; online semi-structured interviews with forum participants; face-to-face semi-structured interviews with key informants; and thematic content analysis of two online forums.

In one study, silent observation was conducted over a period of one year, and in another, over a period of a year and half. For the whole of that time, observational field notes were recorded daily in a journal. The process of observation was divided into two stages. In the first stage of observation, which was a little unstructured, the researcher entered the settings with a broad view, which entailed looking at all the discussion topics posted in one day. In the second stage, the researcher focused his attention on events, activities, patterns, and behaviours that were salient in the observed forums. On the other hand, the researcher gained enormously from being a participant in an online forum similar to the ones observed. In this forum, the researcher was able to interact with forum members, immersing himself in different situations and engaging in different activities that enabled him to gain insights and to understand, in depth, the experiences and perceptions of the online forum members. This, in turn, enabled him to report his perceptions about his own online experience.

The online interviews and face-to-face semi-structured interviews with key informants were conducted in Arabic and followed a semi-structured format with open-ended questions. Potential interviewees in the case of both types of interviewing were selected from the online forum, a social Web-based forum used predominantly by Saudi nationals, which had been silently observed for a year in the first study (Al-Saggaf et al., 2002). Participants in the community were not advised that their conversations were being observed, because the community in which they operated was a densely-populated public space where it is assumed that anyone with a computer, Internet connection can watch the ongoing conversations. This was consistent with the standards for ethical research as set by Eysenbach and Till's (2001) and Ess and AoIR Ethics Working Committee (2002). The participants in the first type of interviewing were interviewed online using the MSN Messenger. Participants in both types of interviewing were interviewed after a sheet seeking their informed consent was forwarded to them. The online interviews and the transcribed face-to-face interviews were later translated into English and the data were then analysed.

Finally, the researcher used thematic content analysis of two online forums for two separate studies. Doing thematic content analysis offered the researcher numeric values that allowed reflective inferences about the themes contained in the forum topics to be made. Conducting content analysis in this way allowed the themes and patterns of the online forums studied to emerge from the text.

Data Analysis

Data obtained from all the earlier-mentioned techniques, except for the thematic content analysis, were analysed as they were collected. Field notes and interview transcripts were entered daily into NVIVO, a Software package for managing qualitative data. Next, themes that revolved around a specific concept were located and coded as nodes after the field notes and interview transcripts had been thoroughly read through. These nodes became like buckets because they held all the information that related to a specific theme. Finally, all themes were again divided into groups or categories so that a broader sense of the results could be gained.

The thematic content analysis was carried out using a software program developed by the author using Microsoft Access. The unit of analysis was each individual topic. The basis for coding was the occurrence of selected themes within each topic. The broader nature and the context and purpose of each topic posted were taken into consideration during the process of analysis. It should be noted that findings obtained through these techniques were triangulated to assist in establishing the trustworthiness of the results that transpired from these studies (Lincoln & Guba, 1987; Maxwell, 1996; Bow, 2000).

Background

Saudi Arabia

Saudi Arabia is one of the conservative Arabian Gulf states. Its population is mainly Arab and is estimated to be 22.6 million, including 6 million foreigners (Al-Watan, 2005). The country is the custodian of the two holy cities of Mecca and Medina, where Islam emerged and was spread by the Prophet Mohamed (s.a.w.[1]), and where the religion's holy book, the Qur'an, was revealed and documented. Saudi Arabia is considered to be one of the richest countries in the world in its reserves of oil, because underneath its surface lies 25% of the world's total reserves of petroleum (CIA, 2005). These religious and economic factors have earned Saudi Arabia a strong position in the Arab world and have allowed it to play a leading role in the politics of the region.

Internet Service in Saudi Arabia

On 15 December 1998 the public in Saudi Arabia officially experienced the Internet in the country (Internet Services Unit, 2005) for the first time. Before that the Internet was offered by King Abdul Aziz City for Science and Technology (KACST). In 2003, the service was handed over to the Communication and Information Technology Commission (Internet Services Unit, 2005). Until now the vast majority of people in Saudi Arabia access the Internet through dial-up telephone lines and modems and, because of this, accessing the network is really slow and frustrating.

In the face of this, it may be safe to assume that the slow speed of access to the Internet has discouraged many people in the country from using the Internet service. The results of a recent survey conducted by the Internet Services Unit (ISU) and completed by 537 Saudi Internet users strengthened this assumption. In addition to its coverage of some of the important points regarding the Internet service in Saudi Arabia, the ISU survey provided some interesting socio-demographic figures. The ISU survey questions were published on the ISU Web site on 2 May 2002 and the data were gathered on 24 December 2003. When asked if there were things in the Internet service that they wanted to see improved, 80% of the Internet users who completed the survey said they wanted the speed of access to be improved.

In relation to the use of the Internet service, 60% of those who completed the survey indicated that they access the Internet in the night. This could be because demand on Internet access lessens at night and it is consequently faster. Or it could be due to the fact that people in that society prefer to access the Internet at night. During the night the temperature is low and people have generally finished their work or study. The majority of users access the network from the two big cities in Saudi

Arabia—Riyadh and Jeddah—with the people in the Riyadh accessing the service a bit more than those in Jeddah. Interestingly, these two cities are where the only two ISUs are located. The two ISUs are the only nodes through which all Internet users in Saudi Arabia get their Internet access. Given that this access is through dial-up telephone lines and modems, it is possible that access to the Internet from outside these two cities is even slower, and in some places unavailable. When King Abdul Aziz University, one of only six universities in the country, forced female prospective students to submit their applications through the University's Web site, hundreds of females from remote areas in the country lost their chance to apply (Okaz, 2005).

Meanwhile, since its inception, Internet service in Saudi Arabia has improved drastically. The number of domain names under the ".sa" domain name space registered by SaudiNIC, the domain registering authority in the country, has reached 7067, of which 5599 are ".com" (Internet Services Unit, 2005). At the moment, there are 23 Internet service providers (ISPs), instead of only a very few not long ago, and this increase has brought competition to the Internet access provision market. While the Internet in Saudi Arabia is linked with international lines that can support 950 Mbps of Internet content coming to the country, at the request of the country's ISPs, only 400 Mbps are actually used (Internet Services Unit, 2005). This means that the lines that connect Saudi Arabia to the Internet outside Saudi Arabia are in good shape; the problem lies in the lines that connect the people to the Internet inside the country, because access to the Internet is still through dial-up telephone lines and modems.

While there are no confirmed figures in relation to the total number of Internet users in the country, they are estimated at two million (Al-Watan, 2004). Many of these users spend their time on the Internet sending e-mails, getting political or scientific information, visiting entertainment Web sites, chatting with their peers and friends, or finding "romance" (Al-Farim, 2001). In addition, results from a recent survey indicated that, of the 322 participants who took part in this survey, 50% use the Internet to read or post messages to Web-based forums (JeddahNews.net, 2005). The messages that are read or posted to these online forums vary in their nature and purpose and may relate to social relationships, women's issues, medical information or political events, to name a few.

Web-based forums in Saudi Arabia have become increasingly popular in recent years, particularly after the September 11th attacks on the United States and the wars against Afghanistan and Iraq. The number of people who operate in these forums is in the order of hundreds of thousands (Al Arabiya, 2004). Again, while there are no confirmed figures about the number of forums in Saudi Arabia, when the phrase "Saudi Arabian forums" was entered (in Arabic) in the Google search engine, 358,000 hits were returned.

This shows that forums in Saudi Arabia are receiving unprecedented attention. A topic like "the War on Iraq," for example, in Al-Saha Al-Syiasia, a political online forum which is by far the most widely spread forum in Saudi Arabia, was read more than half a million times. Perhaps it is because freedom of expression in Saudi Arabia is limited and content disseminated from traditional media is censored that these forums have become so popular. It is also possible that, because of their decentralised nature and their many-to-many communication, these forums have become effective in enabling people to express their views, exchange ideas, discuss their public affairs, analyse political events, and reach others.

Internet Users in Saudi Arabia

The findings of the four studies conducted by the author show that there were many types of frequent Internet users in Saudi Arabia. In terms of the socio-economic background of participants, there were medical doctors, businessmen, university lecturers, senior government officials, government servants, prominent intellectuals and journalists. These findings appear to be consistent with the findings in the literature (for example, Wheeler, 2002), that the typical Internet user elsewhere is often middle-aged, educated and well-off.

The findings are also in line with the results of the ISU survey discussed previously. The majority of participants who took part in this survey were men (95%). Furthermore, 55% of the participants were single and 44% were married. While 45% aged were between 26-35 years, about 40% were between 16-25 years. In terms of education, it seems the majority of participants had some form of education. Some 54% had university level education, 13% had diplomas, and 17% had undergone high school education. Most of the participants were either high-income earners (28% earn between 5000 to 10000 Saudi Riyals a month) or middle-class earners (19% earn between 2000 and 5000 Saudi Riyals a month), and only 27% of the participants, who indicated that they were students, had no income, supported by their parents or by small allowances from their universities. Participants also mentioned that Internet access cost them about 700 Saudi Riyals a month, which is about 14% of a monthly salary of 5000 Saudi Riyals.

In terms of the ideological backgrounds and the religious or political currents that the Internet users supported, they were perceived by others as either dissidents, or Islamic fundamentalists, or Mujahideen,[2] or pro-government, or secularists, or modernists. Apparently events like the 1991 Gulf War, the acceptance of the United States' Army to liberate Kuwait, the US$65 billion bill paid by Saudi Arabia as its share of the cost of the war (Stern, 2002), the decline of the Saudi economy as a result, the September 11 attacks on the United States, and the wars against Afghanistan and Iraq, have all contributed in some way or another to the sudden emergence of dissidents, modernists and terrorists in the country.

Factors Contributing to the Digital Divide in the Country

Internet Censorship

In addition to the slow speed of access to the Internet, discussed earlier, there are a number of factors that could be blamed for the divide within the digital community in Saudi Arabia. One of the major ones is the strict censorship of the Internet content by the government, which makes the Internet less interesting and less useful to many. Material that contains pornographic, anti-Islamic, or criticism of Saudi Arabia, the Royal Family, or other Gulf states is blocked. In fact, Internet access for the whole country is controlled through a single node, which makes the government the ultimate arbiter of what can be viewed online.

Saudi Arabia filters all Web traffic that flows to the country by implementing country-level proxy servers. These proxy servers contain massive databases of banned sites (Whitaker, 2001). This is achieved by first caching approved Web sites in very large storage systems. This allows the most popular Web sites to be accessed quickly without the system having to check their suitability each time. Second, when Web sites that are not stored in the cache are requested, they are passed to the second stage of the system, which has the ability to ban millions of Web sites that are deemed unsuitable (Whitaker, 2001). This means that what Internet users in Saudi Arabia see is not the original page on a server outside the country, but a copy on the computer servers in Riyadh and Jeddah.

Filtering the Internet in this way not only stops pornographic, anti-Islamic or anti-government sites from arriving to users' computer screens, but also stops other sites, for example, medical information sites. For instance, any Web site that contains the word "breast" is banned. It is believed that many users, including, in this case, students studying medicine or anatomy, are deprived from accessing this kind of material because of this filtering and, as a result, deprived from accessing the knowledge contained within these sites. This has earned Saudi Arabia a reputation for being among those countries that repress freedom of expression. A report by Reporters Without Borders has described Saudi Arabia and 19 other countries as real "enemies of the Internet." Of the 45 nations the report identified as imposing some form of filtering or another, these 20 countries, according to the report, are the worst because they make all Internet users access the network through a single, state-run node. Other countries among these 20 are China, Cuba, Iran and North Korea (Reporters Without Borders, 2001).

Culture

Another major factor that could be blamed for the digital divide in the country is the culture of the society itself. Saudi society is largely conservative and religious. Islam greatly influences how people in that society behave and live their lives. One of the features that characterise Saudi culture is the requirement that people do not engage in conversations that touch on sex, slander, or obscenity. It is inappropriate for a person to utter filthy language in the presence of others. From an early age, individuals are warned against uttering obscene references, so that when they grow up, they are not accustomed to such utterance. Uttering only decent language is not only highly praised by the society members, but is also believed to be a cause for reward from Allah. Uttering obscene references is considered as *ayb* (shameful) and can make people feel embarrassed.

While the relationship of the earlier discussion with the digital divide may not appear to be obvious or direct, the author would argue that these matters have played a significant role in discouraging people from accessing information that could be beneficial, educational, or even informative. It is possible that people fear that some of the material they are about to view may contain obscenity. Although, in this case, neither access to the Internet nor knowledge of how to obtain information online are issues, the cultural barrier prevents many people from benefiting fully from their access to the Internet. One would think that because many people access the Internet from Internet cafes or from their private bedrooms, privacy is not an issue for them. If people surf the Net from the privacy of their bedrooms, they can view what they want; no one is going to find out what they watched and they are spared any embarrassment they might experience if someone looked over their shoulder in an Internet cafe. But safety from embarrassment does not eliminate the fear of Allah, whom they believe is watching them at all times. Thus accessing material that might be of an obscene nature means committing a sin, so many people would still feel discouraged from doing that.

Another cultural feature related to the digital divide is power distance (Hofstede, 1997) or hierarchy among people. Hierarchy in family structure is mainly a result of tribal traditions. In real life, and particularly during the social events and family gatherings, elders or high- status individuals often dominate discussions. Younger individuals, to show respect for the senior members of their tribe, do not normally speak out. This makes it difficult for them to voice their opinions. In online forums, it was observed that this practice was carried over to the online world. Although the anonymity inherent in the medium helped some people hide their age, gender, wealth and race, thus weakening the effect of hierarchy, for others were not much helped by the anonymity. Members with high status and artistic writers enjoyed most of the attention online while many others were left unnoticed. It is possible that this practice discouraged many from participating in online forums. If they feel they do not fit or are not being appreciated in comparison to the well known, they might ask why should we stay?

Finally, fear of being caught for uttering derogatory remarks against an individual or a government authority put a lot of pressure on freedom of expression. As mentioned before, because freedom of expression in general in Saudi Arabia, and indeed in many other Arab countries, is somewhat limited, people are less capable of speaking their minds in real life. To overcome this problem, people turned to online forums because they found in them a venue where they could express themselves and present their ideas and views to others in a way not previously possible. While this, to a great extent, is the case with the online forums, it was observed, however, that there were many people who feared being caught by the Saudi authorities. A number of members in one of the forums observed reported that their friends had been captured by the Saudi Secret Services. Incidents like these will no doubt have an effect on the minds of those who treat the forums as "an opening" or a "gateway" where they could "breathe" by voicing their opinions freely.

Saudis with Internet Access but still Among the "Have-Nots"

Women

The fact that 95% of those who took part in the survey discussed previously were men does not really mean that only 5% of Saudi Internet users are women. Cuneo (2002) reports that the gender gap in Internet use is greater in Saudi Arabia than in other countries, with only 22% Internet users being women—considerably less that the 56% of world Internet users. But even 22% is not an accurate representation of the presence of women on the Internet in Saudi Arabia. Al-Zaharni (2002), for example, put the figure of women who use the Internet in Saudi Arabia at 45%. BBC News (2005) was more optimistic and raised that figure to two-thirds of the total Internet users.

Unfortunately, the four studies conducted by the author did not produce any figures in relation to the presence of women online. However, the findings of these studies showed that women were actually well-represented online, particularly in social online forums and forums related to women's issues. The results of these studies indicate that they learned a great deal from their participation online and overcame many of the restrictions on their movements offline. While the interaction with others, particularly members of the opposite sex, made them less inhibited about males and more aware of the diverse nature of their personalities, the ability to express themselves raised their self-confidence and self-esteem. Listening to multiple views and opinions online and sharing life experiences made them become flexible in their thinking and expression. On the other hand, the features inherent in the technology, particularly its addictive nature and the anonymity, have caused them to become less shy and negligent of their family and friends' commitments, which are very much against the teachings of their culture.

In political online forums (POFs) such as Al-Saha Al-Syiasia, which was observed for a long time, very few female participants were noted. The vast majority of topics and discussions were dominated by men. The belief that politics are mainly for men to talk about is one obvious reason for the notable absence of women in POFs. Another possible reason could be that discussing politics sometimes involves confrontation and upfront argument which are not compatible with the traditions of Saudi women (Al-Saggaf & Weckert, 2004).

A related cultural issue is the separation of genders, which is seen in many aspects of women's public and social life in Saudi Arabia. The separation between genders is observed in schools, banks, public transportation and the workplace. The separation, which does not permit women to mix with unrelated men or have casual conversations with them, is an Islamic rule (AlMunajjed, 1997; Ember & Ember, 1998; Wheeler, 2000). In the social online forums observed, there was no requirement for genders to be separate. Men and women engaged with each other on almost all the topics posted and even developed genuine online relationships. However, it is quite possible that many other women refrained from interacting with men online out of fear that to do so might undermine cultural values. Women who are very conservative or attached to their culture and religion may not find it easy to join the online discussions and benefit from the experience. For this reason they may be considered disenfranchised.

A final point is the cultural demand on women to be shy and modest, attributes that men are also highly encouraged to uphold, although shyness is stressed more in women than in men. The prophet Mohamed (s.a.w.) was heard to say that, "Modesty is a branch of Faith. He, who has no modesty, has no Faith," and also, "Verily, every religion has a nature and the nature of Islam is modesty." Darussalam (2000, p. 272) highlights this by saying, "Modesty is the feeling of rejection for every disgraceful matter … it is a deterrent from committing sinful deeds". Arab virgins are expected to be shy, reserved, and modest. Arabs use the proverb "more shy than a virgin in her private rooms" to describe someone who is very shy. For women being shy means that they should not stare at someone of the opposite gender, should not be too outgoing and should not utter obscenities. For Arabs shyness should be considered a good thing because it puts pressure on people to behave themselves. In other words, Arabs see shyness as a value that should be adopted because it regulates behaviour. This sounds good, but it is possible that many women chose not to take part in discussions within online forums (particularly those topics that revolve around sensitive issues such as sex or involve communicating with men) because they are trying to meet the requirement of being shy and modest. This attitude may again make the reserved women stand among the "have-nots."

Dissidents

Dissidents and their proponents are another group of people who could be considered disenfranchised. The government blocks all their Web content from coming into the country. No matter how often Dr. Saad Al-Fagih, Saudi Arabia's most renowned dissident (McLaughlin, 2003), changed the Web address of his Web site, the Saudi government would always quickly update their ban records blocking Saudi access to his Web site. Of course a large number of Saudis can still access his Web site as can be seen from the messages they post to the forum that he makes available to them.

Dr Al-Fagih is the director of the Movement for Islamic Reform in Arabia (MIRA). The movement, which for a long time operated from London, officially began its operations in 1996. Initially the movement aimed at educating the public about what they believed to be "prevalent malpractices of the government." In the early days of its operations, the movement communicated with the public through letters sent to them by fax. In recent years, it has communicated with them through a high-tech Web site (http://www.islahi.net/) and a state-of-the-art Web-based forum. MIRA has decided that it is not enough just to inform the public about their rights but that they should start to get them to demand these rights. In 2003 (BBC Arabic, 2003) and 2004, when the author was in Saudi Arabia, MIRA managed to get people to protest in the streets of some of the main cities to demand political, economic and social reforms. People in Saudi Arabia, where demonstrations for any reason are banned, have never in their lives seen protests before. To see people marching in the streets, protesting against the government handling of the country is indeed a big change.

The government is not without support in fighting Al-Fagih and other dissidents, such as Dr. Mohammed Al-Masari. Many Saudi forum members from all walks of life are critical of them and their actions. The results of one of the studies showed that dissidents are hardly allowed to contribute to political forums and are heavily criticised on a regular basis in these forums. In Al-Saha Al-Siyasia forum, for example, 2.6% of the total content during one month was dedicated for the criticism of dissidents. Qualitatively speaking some of the criticisms were very harsh and dissidents had no supporters at all, unlike in the case of the modernists (see the following text), who at least found 1.2% of topics posted during the same month supportive of dissidents.

Modernists

Modernists are another group of people who find it extremely difficult to join or contribute to discussions in any forum other than their own—Dar Al-Nadwa and Tuaa. The reason for this is that most discussion forums, particularly those of a political nature, such as Al-Saha Al-Siyasia and Al-Husn[3] Al-Siyasi, are dominated by Islamic fundamentalists. Because they fear a change to their approach to their lives and their religion, Islamic fundamentalists do not tolerate modernists. Again in Al-Saha Al-Siyasia forum, approximately 7.12% of the total forum content during the month of September 2004 was derogatory and belittling of modernists.

Modernists, for the purpose of this chapter, are those who adopt a moderate tone in terms of their perceptions of Islam and how it ought to be practised. They generally embrace a version of Islam that is less strict in nature and accommodating of others' beliefs. Modernists are not like dissidents who oppose the Royal Family and demand political, economic and social reforms. Modernists aim, through what they write or say, to influence people's thinking and persuade them into accepting modernism or secularism as a way of life. They try to express their ideas through the topics they post in their own forums and through the articles they write in the local newspapers and through their appearances in the local media.

Shiaa and Sufi Muslims

Finally, the exclusion from all Saudi forums except perhaps their very own, experienced by Shiaa[4] and Sufi Muslims, should be mentioned here. Because most discussion forums are dominated by Sunni Islamic fundamentalists, who do not also tolerate Shiaa or the Sufis, the former do not allow the latter to participate in their forums and do not allow anyone to provide links to their sites. Sunni Islamic fundamentalists also criticise Shiaa and Sufi Muslims on the former's forums on a regular basis.

One study by the author found that about 3.73% of all topics posted to one of the forums during the month of September 2004 criticised Shiaa Muslims. The figure could be considered a little high, if one takes into account the fact that members in that forum are not allowed to say things that may make Shiaa Muslims, whose numbers in the Saudi society are small anyway, look good in the eyes of others. It is possible that the Saudi government and the rest of the Gulf States are sceptical about the Shiaa Muslims.[5] Perhaps the war which Iraq waged against Iran from 1980-1988, financed by the Gulf States, serves as evidence of this scepticism.

In Al-Saha Al-Siyasia forum, for example, it was observed that there were members whose job was just to post topics that condemn Shiaa Muslims or belittle them in the eyes of others. Some of the topics posted, for example, provided links to movies and images that are controversial according to Islamic fundamentalists. Others discussed the problems with Shiaa ideology and philosophy, while others showed pictures of their self-torture in memory of the 4th Imam (Ali) and their attacks against the Sunni Muslims.

Since the September 11th attacks on United States, the "Wahhabi" proponents are on the defensive. One of the reasons for this, in addition to the explicit and severe American criticism of the "Wahhabi" doctrine (Butt, 2005), is the support the Shiaa and Sufi doctrines received from the United States and Europe. The reason the Sufi way, which some say is similar in a few aspects to the Shiaa approach, is favoured is that the approach itself encourages giving up the material world and dedicating oneself to the worship of Allah. This implies that Sufi Muslims generally leave politics and Jihad aside and concentrate only on the worship of Allah, which is what the United States and Europe want.

Discussion and Conclusion

This chapter has presented a discussion about the digital divide in Saudi Arabia, based on four research studies conducted between 2000 and 2005. The results of the studies indicated that the digital divide in Saudi Arabia is not a problem stemming from lack of access to the Internet or lack of knowledge about how to use it to obtain information (although this is the case for many people). It is a problem mainly because of the strict censorship of the Internet and the conservative nature of the Saudi culture. It was found that these factors cause groups of people in the country (and outside it) such as women, dissidents, modernists and Shiaa, who do have access to the Internet, to stand among the "have-nots." That is, the censorship that the government is practising and the demands placed on these people by their culture to behave in certain ways have limited their ability to either access certain information on the Internet or use it to communicate their message to the other groups, resulting in their social exclusion. This is not to say, however, that the digital divide in Saudi Arabia is not also a problem for the poor and uneducated, or for people who can afford the Internet but do not know how to use it. It may be the case, as mentioned earlier, that it is a problem for them, even if bridging its gap is not among their most immediate needs, but because the research did not look into these groups, their situation has not been described here.

Nor did the research investigate the implications of exclusion from access to the Internet of the groups whose exclusion was discussed earlier. However, given the author's experience and familiarity with Saudi society, some speculation about how this exclusion might affect these groups in the long run can be made. In the case of women, their lack of access to the Internet and their exclusion from the online public sphere will make it difficult for them to improve their lives. The decision on whether or not to grant women the right to drive cars, for example, has been put on hold by the government after 118 Saudi scholars (all males) and 500 women (14 of which are female academics) wrote a letter to King Abdullah Bin Abdul Aziz asking him to reject the proposal to allow women this. It could be argued that unless women themselves collectively say more loudly in online forums that they want to drive, nothing will happen.

In the case of other groups such as Shiaa, their exclusion from Saudi online forums will result in an absence of a dialogue between them and Sunni Muslims in the country, which will result in a lack of understanding for each other. Not allowing them to co-exist will mean that each group will continue to have misguided ideas about the Islamic way that the other group follows and each group will continue to hold the view that there is only one way to practise Islam and that that way is theirs. In the case of modernists, their attempts to make people in the country enter into a dialogue that could make them become open-minded in their views and accepting of others will not have a great effect. They will continue to be alienated and criticised and their motives questioned, while, on the other hand, the beliefs of the majority will continue to remain beyond doubt. In the case of dissidents, their endeavour for reform may not be successful either. Dr. Al-Fagih recently suffered a major setback when the United States decided to list his movement as a terrorist organization. He must also have lost some credibility when what he has been saying for years never happened—that as soon as King Fahad dies, Prince Abdullah and Prince Sultan in their battle for the throne will lead the country into civil war. These problems, combined with people silencing him in online forums, will make his mission to introduce reform in the country a lot tougher or even sabotage it entirely.

To conclude, it appears that the findings in relation to the groups whose exclusion was discussed earlier are relevant to the dialogue about the importance of culture when looking at the digital divide. Certainly in a country like Australia, for example, a factor like culture cannot be imagined to stand in the way of Internet users. This reiterates the importance of the point mentioned in the literature and outlined earlier about the digital divide being context dependent.

Acknowledgments

The author would like to thank Professor John Weckert and Dr. Emma Rooksby for reviewing this manuscript and offering a number of insightful comments and suggestions. The author would also like to thank the Centre for Applied Philosophy and Public Ethics for providing some funding to release him from some of his teaching duties during the writing of this chapter.

References

Al Arabiya. (2004). *The owner of Al-Saha is in the "cage of accusation."* Retrieved August 11, 2004, from http://www.alarabiya.net/

Al-Farim, K. F. (2001). *The Internet and its audience in Riyadh.* (Master of Mass Communication dissertation). Saudi Arabia: King Saud University.

AlMunajjed, M. (1997). *Women in Saudi Arabia today.* London: Macmillan.

Al-Saggaf, Y. (2004). The effect of online community on offline community in Saudi Arabia. *Electronic Journal of Information Systems in Developing Countries, 16*(2), 1-16.

Al-Saggaf, Y., & Weckert, J. (2005). Political online communities (POCs) in Saudi Arabia. In S. Marshall, W. Taylor, & X. Yu (Eds.), *Encyclopedia of developing regional communities with ICT.* Hershey, PA: Idea Group Reference.

Al-Saggaf, Y., & Weckert, J. (2004). Keeping the public in Saudi Arabia informed: The role of virtual communities. In P. Rushbrook & G. Whiteford (Eds.), *Proceedings of the 2004 conference: Continuing professional education conference 2004 (CPE 04)* (pp. 1-8). Wagga Wagga, Australia: Charles Sturt University.

Al-Saggaf, Y., Weckert, J., & Williamson, K. (2002, November 13-15). What do individuals in Saudi Arabia say about their participation in online communities? In *Proceedings of the IADIS International Conference WWW/Internet,* Lisbon, Portugal.

Al-Watan. (2005). *The main features of the population in Saudi Arabia.* Retrieved February 25, 2005, from http://www.alwatan.com.sa

Al-Watan. (2004). *To improve services for subscribers and promote research.* Retrieved April 15, 2004, from http://www.alwatan.com.sa

Al-Zahrani, S. (2002). *45% of the Internet users in Saudi Arabia are women.* Retrieved January 7, 2002, from http://www.alwatan.com.sa

Baker, C. (2000). Culture shock: Saudi Arabia. *The Internet Society.* Retrieved June 30, 2000, from http://www.suite101.com/article.cfm/5785/4021

BBC Arabic. (2003). *Arrests in Riyadh after demonstrations demanding reform.* Retrieved April 1, 2005. from http://news.bbc.co.uk/hi/arabic/middle_east_news/newsid_3192000/3192170.stm

BBC News. (2005). *Country profile.* Retrieved March 30, 2005, from http://www.bbc.co.uk/go/pr/fr/-/1/hi/woorld/middle_east/country_profiles/791936.stm

Berger, P. L., & Luckmann, T. (1967). *The social construction of reality: A treatise in the sociology of knowledge.* New York: Anchor Press.

Bow, A. (2000). Ethnographic techniques. In K. Williamson (Ed.), *Research methods for students and professionals: Information management and systems* (pp. 247-262). Wagga Wagga, Australia: Centre for Information Studies, Charles Sturt University.

Butt, G. (2005). *Saudi Arabia: Political overview.* Retrieved April 1, 2005, from http://news.bbc.co.uk/1/hi/world/middle_east/3784879.stm

CIA. (2005). *World fact book.* Retrieved July 6, 2005, from http://www.cia.gov/cia/publications/factbook/geos/sa.htm

Cuneo, C. (2002). Globalized and localized digital divides along the information highway: A fragile synthesis across bridges, ramps, cloverleaves, and ladders. *The 33rd Annual Sorokin Lecture.* Retrieved July 6, 2005, from http://socserv2.mcmaster.ca/sociology/Digital-Divide-Sorokin-4.pdf

Darussalam. (2000). *Selected Friday sermons.* Riyadh, Saudi Arabia: Darussalam.

Ember, C. R., & Ember, M. (1988). *Anthropology.* Upper Saddle River, NJ: Prentice Hall.

Ess, C., & AoIR Ethics Working Committee. (2002). *Ethical decision-making and Internet research: Recommendations from the AoIR ethics committee.* Retrieved April 3, 2003, from http://www.aoir.org/reports/ethics.pdf

Eysenbach, G., & Till, J. E. (2001). Ethical issues in qualitative research on Internet communities. *British Medical Journal, 323*(7321), 1103-1105.

Fallis, D. (2004). Social epistemology and the digital divide. In J. Weckert & Y. Al-Saggaf (Eds.), *Conferences in research and practice in information technology* (Vol. 37, pp. 79-84). Sydney, Australia: Australian Computer Society. Available at http://www.crpit.com/confpapers/CRPITV37Fallis.pdf

Fetterman, D. M. (1989). *Ethnography: Step by step.* Thousand Oaks, CA: Sage.

Hofstede, G. (1997). *Cultures and organizations: Software of the mind.* New York: McGraw-Hill.

Hongladarom, S. (2004). Exploring the philosophical terrain of the digital divide. In J. Weckert & Y. Al-Saggaf (Eds.), *Conferences in research and practice in information technology* (Vol. 37, pp. 85-89). Sydney, Australia: Australian Computer Society.

Internet Services Unit. (2005). *Users' survey.* Retrieved July 6, 2005, from http://www.isu.net.sa/surveys-&-statistics/new-user-survey-results.htm

JeddahNews.net. (2005). *Where do you spend most of your time over the Internet?* Retrieved July 6, 2005, from http://www.jeddahnews.net/modules.php?name=Surveys&op=results&pollID=6&mode=&order=&thold=

Kitiyadisai, K. (2004). Bridging the digital divide from a Buddhist perspective with implications for public policy. In J. Weckert & Y. Al-Saggaf (Eds.), *Confer-*

ences in research and practice in information technology (Vol. 37, pp. 91-95). Sydney, Australia: Australian Computer Society.

Lincoln, Y. S., & Guba, E. G. (1987). *Effective evaluation.* San Francisco: Jossey-Bass.

Maxwell, J. A. (1996). *Qualitative research design: An interactive approach.* Thousand Oaks, CA: Sage.

McLaughlin, S. (2003). The use of the Internet for political action by non-state dissident actors in the Middle East. *First Monday, 8*(11). Retrieved July 6, 2005, from http://firstmonday.org/issues/issue8_11/mclaughlin/index.html

Minichiello, V., Aroni, R., Timwell, E., & Alexander, L. (1990). *In-depth interviewing: Researching people.* Melbourne, Australia: Longman Cheshire.

Moss, J. (2005). Fixing the digital divide: Sustaining or undermining local values? Asia Pacific Computing and Philosophy Conference, 7-9 January 2005, Novotel Hotel, Bangkok, Thailand.

Norris, P. (2001). *Digital divide?: Civic engagement, information poverty, and the Internet worldwide.* Cambridge, UK: Cambridge University Press.

Okaz. (2005). *25 thousand students applied to its colleges: Electronic registration destroys the hopes of the female applicants to King Abdul Aziz University.* Retrieved July 17, 2005, from http://www.okaz.com.sa

Reporters Without Borders. (2001). *The enemies of the Internet.* Retrieved July 6, 2005, from http://www.rsf.org/rsf/uk/

Saule, S. (2000). Ethnography. In K. Williamson (Ed.), *Research methods for students and professionals: Information management and systems* (pp. 159-176). Wagga Wagga, Australia: Centre for Information Studies, Charles Sturt University.

Stern, M. (2002). *Threat of U.S. action against Iraq further tests key anti-terror ally.* Retrieved March 28, 2005, from http://www.signonsandiego.com/news/nation/terror/dispatches/20021222-9999_saudimain.html Wheeler, D. (2002). Islam, community and the Internet: New possibilities in the digital age. *Journal of Education, Community and Values, 3.* Retrieved April 23, 2003, from http://bcis.pacificu.edu/journal/2002/03/islam.php

Wheeler, D. (2000). New media, globalization and Kuwaiti national identity. *Middle East Journal, 54*(3), 432.

Whitaker, B. (2001, February 26). Losing the Saudi cyberwar. *The Guardian.*

Williamson, K. (2000). *Research methods for students and professionals: Information management and systems.* Wagga Wagga, Australia: Centre for Information Studies, Charles Sturt University.

Endnotes

[1]   Similar to saying "peace be upon him."

[2]   Mujahideen are, in the context of this chapter, those who consider their militant acts a form of Jihad. The government sees them as terrorists.

[3]   Al-Husn means a fortress.

[4]   "A branch of Islam deriving authority from the prophet's cousin and son-in-law, Ali, and his appointed successors, the Imams' (*Penguin English Dictionary*, 2003, p. 1288).

[5]   The author is a Sunni Muslim, not a Shiaa.

About the Authors

Emma Rooksby is a research fellow at the Centre for Applied Philosophy and Public Ethics, Charles Sturt University, Australia. She has worked in the field of computer ethics since 1996, and has published numerous articles and a book in the field. Recent publications include *E-mail and Ethics* (Routledge, 2002) and "Understanding Condemnation: A Plea for Appropriate Judgement", with Peta Bowden, in Pedro Tabensky (Ed.) *Judging and Understanding: Essays on Free Will, Justice, Forgiveness and Love*, Ashgate, 2006 (forthcoming).

John Weckert is a professor of information technology in the School of Information Studies and is professorial fellow at the Centre for Applied Philosophy and Public Ethics, Charles Sturt University, Australia. He is founding editor-in-chief of the Springer journal *Nanoethics. Ethics for Technologies that Converge at the Nanoscale*. He has published widely on the ethics of information technology and more recently has begun research in the new area of the ethics of nanotechnology.

*   *   *   *   *

Yeslam Al-Saggaf is a lecturer in the School of Information Studies and Associate Course Coordinator for the Master of Information Technology at Charles Sturt University, Australia. He holds a bachelor's degree in engineering, with honors in computer and information engineering, from Malaysia, and a Master of Information Technology and PhD from Charles Sturt University, Australia. Dr Al-Saggaf's research interests lie in the areas of online communities (both social and political) and the social impact of ICT on society. He has published in those areas in a number of international refereed journals and has presented at a number of international conferences.

Charles Ess is a professor of philosophy and religion and distinguished professor of interdisciplinary studies, Drury University (Springfield, Missouri, USA), and professor II in the Programme for Applied Ethics, Norwegian University of Science and Technology (Trondheim). Dr. Ess has received awards for teaching excellence and scholarship, and published in comparative (East-West) philosophy, applied ethics, discourse ethics, history of philosophy, feminist Biblical studies, and computer-mediated communication. With Fay Sudweeks, Dr. Ess co-chairs the biennial conferences "Cultural Attitudes towards Technology and Communication", and has been visiting professor at IT-University, Copenhagen (2003), and a Fulbright senior scholar, University of Trier (2004).

Don Fallis is an associate professor of information resources and an adjunct associate professor of philosophy at the University of Arizona, USA. The main focus of his research is social epistemology and its applications to information science. His articles have appeared in such journals as the *Journal of Philosophy*, *Library Quarterly*, the *American Mathematical Monthly*, the *British Journal for the Philosophy of Science*, *Philosophical Studies*, and the *Journal of the American Society for Information Science and Technology*. He has edited an issue of *Social Epistemology* on "Social Epistemology and Information Science" and has also written a chapter on this topic for the *Annual Review of Information Science and Technology*.

Sheila French is a senior lecturer in the Department of Information and Communications at Manchester Metropolitan University, Manchester, UK. She teaches subjects related to information systems for the department's postgraduate and undergraduate programmes. Her main research interest focuses on issues relating to gender, technology and identity. Other research interests include the management of information systems and e-learning.

Kenneth L. Hacker (PhD, University of Oregon) is professor of communication studies at New Mexico State University, USA. He co-edited the book (with Jan van Dijk) *Digital Democracy: Issues of Theory and Practice* (Sage, 2000) and is currently planning a second book on issues of computer-mediated communication and political participation.

Sirkku Kristiina Hellsten is a reader in development ethics and the director of the Centre for the Study of Global Ethics. Before coming to Birmingham, Dr. Hellsten spent four years as coordinator for the Philosophy Programme and the head of the Philosophy Unit at the Department of Political Science, University of Dar es Salaam, Tanzania. While in Tanzania, she also conducted research as a senior research fellow and a leading team member in an international development ethics project funded by the Academy of Finland. Dr. Hellsten holds the title of Docent of Social and Moral Philosophy at the University of Helsinki and has published widely in the field of social justice, global ethics and human rights.

Kenneth Einar Himma is an associate professor of philosophy at Seattle Pacific University, USA. He is the author of more than 100 articles, essays and book reviews on issues in information ethics, philosophy of law, applied ethics, and philosophy of religion. He formerly taught at the University of Washington, with appointments in the philosophy department, information school, law school, and comparative religion department. He is on the editorial boards of *INSEIT Annual Journal* and *International Review of Information Ethics*.

Soraj Hongladarom is an associate professor of philosophy at Chulalongkorn University in Bangkok, Thailand. He has published books and articles on such diverse issues as bioethics, computer ethics, and the roles that science and technology play in the culture of developing countries. His concern is mainly on how science and technology can be integrated into the life-world of people in so-called third world countries, and what kind of ethical considerations can be obtained from such relation. His work has been published widely, in such titles as *Eubios: Journal of Asian and International Bioethics*; *The Information Society, AI & Society*; *Philosophy in the Contemporary World*; and *Social Epistemology*.

Richard Lucas has been an IT professional for 28 years, with experience in both the public and private sectors. For the past 15 years, he has been teaching about IT generally, and ethics in particular, in the tertiary sector. Richard also researches in the areas of IT ethics and philosophy of sport. Exemplifying a wide range of interests, he has degrees in mathematics, adult education, IT, and philosophy, as well as gaining senior coach qualifications in the field of distance running.

Darryl Macer is a regional adviser on social and human sciences in Asia and the Pacific, UNESCO Bangkok, Thailand, and an affiliated professor in bioethics at United Nations University Institute of Advanced Studies. He is also the director of the Eubios Ethics Institute in Japan, New Zealand and Thailand. He has taught bioethics at the University of Tsukuba in Japan since 1990. He is a member of the International Union of Biological Sciences (IUBS) Bioethics Committee, HUGO Ethics Committee, Board Member of International Association of Bioethics, and

Secretary of Asian Bioethics Association. He is editor of *Eubios Journal of Asian and International Bioethics* and has written and edited 19 books in English, seven in Japanese, and more than 160 academic papers.

Shana M. Mason (MA, New Mexico State University) is a communication studies instructor at the Dona Ana Branch of New Mexico State University, USA. Her work has appeared in *IT & Society* and *Ethics and Information Technology*. Her research interests include computer-mediated communication and political participation.

Eric L. Morgan (PhD, University of Massachusetts) is an assistant professor of communication studies at New Mexico State University, USA. His research interests include cultural, intercultural, and international communication.

A. Raghuramaraju has a PhD from Indian Institute of Technology, Kanpur, taught at Goa University, has been a fellow at the Indian Institute of Advanced Study, Shimla. He presently teaches philosophy at the University of Hyderabad, India. He is a visiting faculty at International Institute of Information Technology, Hyderabad. His essays are published in *Economic and Political Weekly, Social Scientist, JICPR, Indian Philosophical Quarterly, AI & Society, Seminar*, and various edited volumes, which includes "West", in *The Future of Knowledge and Culture*, eds. Vinay Lal and Ashis Nandy, Viking, New Delhi, 2005. His book entitled, *Debates in Indian Philosophy: Classical, Colonial and Contemporary* is forthcoming from Oxford University Press, New Delhi.

Bernd Carsten Stahl is a senior lecturer in the Faculty of Computer Sciences and Engineering and a research associate at the Centre for Computing and Social Responsibility of De Montfort University, Leicester, UK. He is interested in philosophical issues arising from the intersections of business, technology, and information. He is the editor-in-chief of the *International Journal of Technology and Human Interaction*.

William Wresch is a professor of management information systems at the University of Wisconsin, Oshkosh, Wisconsin, USA. Dr. Wresch was named a Fulbright scholar and taught computer science at the University of Namibia in southern Africa. His book about the impact of the Internet on that region of the world, *Disconnected: Haves and Have Nots in the Information Age*, was published by Rutgers University Press in 1996. Since that time, he has prepared a number of articles on the economic development implications of information technology.

Index